J. ALDEN WEIR
An American Impressionist

The American Art Journal/University of Delaware Press Books

Editorial Committee

John I. H. Baur, General Editor
Wayne Craven
Lawrence A. Fleischman
E. P. Richardson
Thomas Yoseloff

Photograph of J. Alden Weir, about 1915, Peter A. Juley and Son Collection. National Museum of American Art, Smithsonian Institution, Washington, D.C.

J. ALDEN WEIR

An American Impressionist

Doreen Bolger Burke

An American Art Journal Book
Newark: University of Delaware Press
New York, London, and Toronto: Cornwall Books

© 1983 by Doreen Bolger Burke

Associated University Presses
and Cornwall Books
440 Forsgate Drive
Cranbury, NJ 08512

Cornwall Books
25 Sicilian Avenue
London WC1A 2QH, England

Cornwall Books
2133 Royal Windsor Drive
Unit 1
Mississauga, Ontario
Canada L5J 1K5

Library of Congress Cataloging in Publication Data

Burke, Doreen Bolger, 1949–
    J. Alden Weir.

    (An American art journal book)
    Bibliography: p.
    "J. Alden Weir bibliography": p.
    Includes index.
    1. Weir, Julian Alden, 1852–1919.   2. Artists—United States—Biography.   I. Weir, Julian Alden, 1852–1919.
II. Title.   III. Series.
N6537.W355B87   1983   760′.092′4 [B]   83-47901
ISBN 0-87413-220-7 (Delaware—cloth)
ISBN 0-87413-263-0 (pb.)
ISBN 0-8453-4779-9 (Cornwall)

Printed in the United States of America

For Cora

Contents

Foreword

THE ENCOURAGEMENT, APPRECIATION, AND STUDY OF AMERICAN ART HAS BEEN A serious concern of The Metropolitan Museum of Art since its establishment in 1870. Important American painters, sculptors, and architects were among the founding Trustees, and their interest in American art has been reflected from the start through acquisitions (mostly by gift and bequest), exhibitions, and publications. By 1915, the Museum's forty-fifth year, when J. Alden Weir was appointed to the Museum's Board of Trustees, it had already assembled an extraordinary collection of American paintings and sculpture and had received substantial funds for its purchases of American art, especially the endowments of George A. Hearn and Amelia B. Lazarus. During those early years the Museum had presented a number of important monographic and memorial exhibitions of American artists, among them the work of John F. Kensett, William T. Richards, Sanford R. Gifford, Frederic E. Church, James Abbott McNeill Whistler, and Winslow Homer. In 1909 the Museum mounted the exceptionally influential Hudson-Fulton Exhibition, a bench-mark pronouncement of the Metropolitan Museum's interest in American decorative arts, architecture, and painting, which led directly to the establishment of The American Wing, in 1924, by Mr. and Mrs. Robert W. de Forest.

In the years after Weir's becoming a trustee, the Metropolitan was especially active in presenting important American art exhibitions and publications. William Merritt Chase, Thomas Eakins, Albert Pinkham Ryder, and George Fuller were given exhibitions at the Museum between 1917 and 1924, the year that the J. Alden Weir memorial exhibition occurred. In the more than fifty years since, the Metropolitan has displayed major exhibitions of paintings by George Bellows, John Singer Sargent, Samuel F. B. Morse, John La Farge, William Sidney Mount, Winslow Homer, and Mary Cassatt, among other artists.

The opening of the new American Wing in 1980, with its generous exhibition spaces, presents a new potential at the Metropolitan Museum for the display and study of American art in all its aspects. A full schedule of American exhibitions is under way, and most of these exhibitions are to be accompanied by substantial publications, such as Doreen Burke's catalogue now in your hands.

The Weir exhibition, the first major re-examination of his artistic career since 1924, is an appropriate and worthy undertaking that both continues a distinguished scholarly tradition and points the way for future projects.

We are deeply grateful to those who, corporately and individually, have made the Weir exhibition possible through generous financial support. Principal underwriting for the exhibition has been provided by the Atlantic Richfield Foundation. Additional support facilitating Dr. Burke's scholarly researches came from Cora Weir Burlingham, one of J. Alden Weir's daughters. The William Cullen Bryant Fellows of The American Wing contributed substantial funds toward catalogue costs, the first such effort by the Bryant Fellows.

John K. Howat
Lawrence A. Fleischman Chairman
of The Departments of
American Art

Acknowledgments

THIS BOOK, AND THE EXHIBITION IT ACCOMPANIES, WOULD NOT HAVE BEEN POSSIBLE without the constant cooperation and support of J. Alden Weir's family. Each of the artist's three daughters made a contribution to preserving his memory and reputation: the late Dorothy Weir Young compiled information on his paintings, transcribed his letters, and wrote his biography; the late Caroline Weir Ely studied her father's etchings and reissued some of them in small editions; and Cora Weir Burlingham has encouraged the current project since our first meeting in 1975, establishing a fund to support my ongoing work on a catalogue raisonné of Weir's paintings, watercolors, pastels, and drawings. Charles Burlingham, Jr., William B. Carlin, and especially Ann Ely Smith and Caroline P. Ely have continued their family's tradition by their unflagging cooperation with my research. The Reverend DeWolf Perry, the grandson of John Ferguson Weir, has been equally helpful in my study of J. Alden Weir's close relationship with his brother. The wealth of information that the Weir family has preserved and collected, and their recollections about the artist, his work, and his contemporaries have made him and his era come alive for me.

I am grateful to the institutions and individuals whose generosity have enabled me to bring this project to a successful conclusion. The exhibition at its three stops—The Metropolitan Museum of Art, the Los Angeles County Museum of Art, and The Denver Art Museum—has been sponsored by a generous grant from the Atlantic Richfield Foundation; I am particularly grateful to Eugene R. Wilson, Executive Director, and Anna Arrington, Program Officer of the Foundation, for their assistance. The book has been supported by a grant from the William Cullen Bryant Fellows of The American Wing at The Metropolitan Museum of Art. Two travel grants from the museum enabled me to visit collections and archives here and abroad during the course of my research.

I must also acknowledge the many institutions and collectors all over the country who have shown me works by Weir, provided information on their histories, and permitted them to be recorded for the forthcoming catalogue raisonné. Special mention should be made of the staff members at several institutions that possess significant collections of works by Weir and by other members of his family: at the National Academy of Design, New York, John Dobkin, Abigail Gerdts, and Barbara Krulik; at The Phillips Collection, Washington, D.C., Martha Carey; at the Yale University Art Gallery, Helen Cooper; at the West Point Museums, United States Military Academy, Michael Moss; and at the Brigham Young University Fine Arts Collection, Sharon Heelis, Richard Hilligass, Lynda Redd, and Brian

Bates. Among the many art dealers and auctioneers who helped me locate works are Jeffrey Brown; Jay Cantor and Betty Krulik of Christie, Manson & Woods; O. Kelley Anderson, Jerald D. Fessenden, R. Frederick Woolworth, and Warren Adelson of Coe Kerr Gallery; Thomas Colville; Peter H. Davidson; Nancy C. Little of the library staff of M. Knoedler & Co.; Roy Davis and Cecily Langdale of Davis and Langdale; Ed Goldfield of Goldfield Galleries, Los Angeles; Stuart P. Feld and M. P. Naud of Hirschl & Adler Galleries; Lawrence A. Fleischman and Cynthia Seibels of Kennedy Galleries; the late Harold Milch; Russell E. Burke III of Phillips Son and Neale; Max Schweitzer; Donald D. Webster of C. G. Sloan & Co.; Peter B. Rathbone, Grete Meilman, and Ann Wiegert of Sotheby Parke Bernet; Ira Spanierman; and Robert C. Vose, Jr., at Vose Galleries of Boston.

I consulted many libraries and archives in the course of my research, among them the Archives of American Art, the Inventory of American Paintings, the Peter A. Juley and Son Collection, and the Library of the National Museum of American Art and the National Portrait Gallery, all part of the Smithsonian Institution, Washington, D.C.; the Frick Art Reference Library, New York; The New-York Historical Society; the New York Public Library; and, of course, the library of The Metropolitan Museum of Art. I am particularly indebted to those institutions that made important collections of Weir manuscripts available to me. At the Harold B. Lee Library at Brigham Young University, Provo, Utah, Dennis Rowley guided me through the Weir Family Papers that the university acquired with the estate of the artist's son-in-law the sculptor Mahonri M. Young. The John Ferguson Weir Papers at the Sterling Memorial Library at Yale University, the gift of the Reverend DeWolf Perry and his mother, Edith Weir Perry, were crucial to the study of the artist's early career. Helpful too were the Charles Erskine Scott Wood Papers at the Henry E. Huntington Library and Art Gallery in San Marino, California. I am grateful to the Frick Art Reference Library, New York, for permitting me to quote from the diaries of Theodore Robinson.

Several colleagues have been helpful in providing information about their special areas of knowledge: Jennifer Bienenstock on the Society of American Artists, William H. Gerdts on still-life painting, George Gurney on Olin Levi Warner, Ronald G. Pisano on William Merritt Chase, H. Barbara Weinberg on the French training of American artists, and Gabriel P. Weisberg on P. A. J. Dagnan-Bouveret and the art dealer S. Bing. I am grateful to the friends and colleagues—Drs. Gerdts, Weinberg, and Weisberg—who kindly read sections of the book in manuscript form and made valuable suggestions for its improvement.

The staff of The Metropolitan Museum of Art has, as always, been helpful in the completion of this project. I thank Richard Dougherty, Vice President for Public Affairs, and Emily Rafferty, Manager of Development, who raised the funds that made this show a reality; Katherine Baetjer, European Paintings; Julia Meech-Pekarik, Far Eastern Art, and Joan Mirviss, a volunteer in that department; William H. Walker and his capable staff in the Thomas J. Watson Library, particularly Maureen Cassidy-Geiger, who obtained material for me on interlibrary loan; the Departments of Paintings and Paper Conservation, particularly Dianne Dwyer and Marjorie Shelley, who have undertaken the conservation of a number of the works in the show; Lynda Sylling, Operations, and Wendy Chittenden, Finance, who prepared budgets and made financial arrangements for the show; Linden Havemeyer Wise, Assistant Secretary and Counsel; and John Buchanan, Registrar, Herbert Moscowitz, Associate Registrar, and Laura Grimes, Assistant Registrar, who made arrangements for its packing and shipping. I am of course grateful to my colleagues in the Department of American Paintings and Sculpture, particularly to John K. Howat, Lawrence A. Fleischman Chairman of The Departments of American Art, who first involved me in this project eight years ago, and Kristine Schassler and especially Sheila S. Newbery, who have assisted me in the preparation of this manuscript and in the many details connected with the exhibition. Several volunteers—Laurene Banks, Barbara Buff, Martha Deese, Jo-Nelle Long, Elisabeth Quackenbush, Miriam Stern, and Rebecca Tennen—and interns Christine Bergman, Lauretta Dimmock, Anne Hickok, Ellen Herrgesell, and Caroline Mortimer have all been willing research assistants.

Michael Quick and Myrna Smoot at the Los Angeles County Museum of Art, and Thomas Maytham, Mary Ann Igna, David Curry, and Molly Singer at The Denver Art Museum have been most helpful in making arrangements for the exhibition at their institutions. I would like to thank in particular Julian Ganz, Jr., President of the Board of Trustees of the Los Angeles County Museum of Art, for his vital support of the exhibition.

I am especially grateful to the lenders to the exhibition, both public and private, who have enabled me to assemble so many of Weir's finest works; without their cooperation, this endeavor would have been impossible.

I deeply appreciate the encouragement that this book has received from those individuals who have organized the American Art Journal Press—Lawrence A. Fleischman, for his usual enthusiasm for the serious study of American art; John I. H. Baur, General Editor, for inviting me to contribute a book to this series; and Thomas Yoseloff of the Associated University Presses for the generosity of his patience during the completion of my manuscript.

Mary-Alice Rogers has edited this book skillfully, endowing it with whatever elegance it possesses. I am enormously grateful for her professional involvement and personal support throughout the project.

Finally, I thank my husband, Russell E. Burke III, for his many valuable insights and his constant support of my work.

Introduction

J. ALDEN WEIR IS RIGHTFULLY DESCRIBED AS AN AMERICAN IMPRESSIONIST, BUT EVEN at the height of his impressionist period—which occupied the years from about 1890 to his death in 1919, roughly the second half of his life as a painter—his style, working procedure, and aesthetic philosophy differed significantly from those of the French artists who founded the movement. Weir's impressionist style was molded by the experience of his younger years: a thorough academic training at the École des Beaux-Arts, in Paris; his esteem for his mentor, Jean-Léon Gérôme, and his friendship with the naturalist Jules Bastien-Lepage; his faithful study of the old masters; and his interest in the early paintings of Édouard Manet. Weir's conversion to Impressionism was not so much a rejection of his previous work as a natural progression from it.

During Weir's life, styles in French art—academic, realist, and, eventually, impressionist—determined his own artistic direction. He responded in the 1880s and 1890s to each of these influences in succession, developing swiftly and with facility from one to another. At certain points, especially while he was in Paris and immediately after his return to New York, his progress was almost simultaneous with that of his European contemporaries. Again, during the mid-1890s, the variations in his painting style that reflected his reaction to Japanese art paralleled some of the innovations of the European Post-Impressionists. These periods were nevertheless isolated ones in a career that usually lagged some ten or twenty years behind the work of the French artists who were its inspiration, and by 1900 the pace of Weir's development had so slowed that he was no longer able to absorb new ideas or to respond to any but conventional forces. To him the harsh realism of Robert Henri and his followers and the abstraction practiced during the 1910s by American counterparts of European Fauvists, Cubists, and Futurists were anathema, and he reverted to an idealized world represented in his late work by charming rural landscapes and portrayals of elegant, contemplative women. Weir, who during the late 1870s had been a leader among the progressive artists then transforming American art, retreated from the challenges of the rising generation of modernists and, for the remainder of his active life as an artist, painted pictures that were beautiful but prosaic.

Weir's career spanned half a century. When he began to paint, around 1866, American art was still dominated by men who had reached their maturity at mid-century. Landscape subjects were being depicted by such second-generation members of the Hudson River School as John F. Kensett and Sanford R. Gifford. American artists trained in Düsseldorf in the 1850s—including Albert Bierstadt, Worthington Whittredge, and Eastman Johnson, whose work would have been well known to Weir—were continuing to set the standards for both landscape and genre painters. A few precocious artists like John La Farge, William Morris Hunt, and George Inness had already studied or traveled in France, but they made little impression on Weir until he too had acquired a thorough grounding abroad.

Weir's art education was initiated at his home in West Point, New York, where his father, Robert, was drawing instructor at the United States Military Academy. Under his father's tutelage he began to study the old masters, acquiring an admiration for the Italian Renaissance and Dutch seventeenth-century painters that would endure well into his maturity. He made copies after the old masters and, probably, after his father's paintings. In those early years, most of his original works were portraits, but he also did landscape views of the Hudson River and at least one interior scene, *Carrie in the Studio at West Point* (1868, fig. 1.12), which in style and subject matter emulated the work of his elder half brother John Ferguson Weir, who made a specialty of such genre pictures. While Julian pursued in his art a course very different from those of his father and brother, he always maintained his regard for them; they shaped his personality as well as his artistic attitudes. When he continued his studies in New York, it was at the National Academy of Design, where both Robert and John had already been elected full members. There his primary training consisted of drawing, both from casts after antique statues and from living models.

After Weir's arrival in Paris, in 1873, he enrolled almost immediately in the École des Beaux-Arts studio of Jean-Léon Gérôme. The following year, having passed a competitive examination, he became a matriculant in the École, his curriculum then including a drawing class taught by Adolphe Yvon. The four years Weir spent at the École turned him into an accomplished figure painter, giving him a thorough training far exceeding that of many of his American contemporaries, relatively few of whom had then studied in Paris. While he was not the first American student to enroll at the École, he was one of the earliest to participate fully in its rigorous program. He placed successfully in several *concours*, or competitions, and he won a second-class medal, the highest year-end award presented in Gérôme's studio in 1875—a real achievement for any student, a greater one for an American. Weir's progress at the École is documented not only in the school's voluminous archives but also in letters he wrote to his parents and to his brother John narrating in detail his experiences and impressions, his studies and friendships, his disappointments and successes. Only a few of Weir's student works have survived—a painted *académie* showing a male nude, drawings of antique statues and living models, and some pictures he painted independently in his rooms or in the French countryside. Sparse as this material may seem, it constitutes perhaps the most complete record of any major American artist's studies at the École, and from it the important role Gérôme played in Weir's development can be deduced.

Remembered today as an arch-academician, Jean-Léon Gérôme was also a sympathetic and effective teacher who instilled into Weir a knowledge of drawing that was to be the foundation of his work and an academic discipline that he was never to abandon. Gérôme's emphasis on the observation and reproduction of nature caused Weir to strive for greater realism in his art; his enthusiasm for the old masters, particularly Frans Hals and Rembrandt, encouraged Weir's studies of the great artists of the past. Although Weir never chose the historical or orientalist subjects that preoccupied Gérôme, he did follow his master's working method, which encompassed thorough research into settings and costumes and the executing of elaborate preliminary drawings to create carefully composed pictures. Weir did consider leaving his mentor to study with other masters—in 1875, Charles-Émile-Auguste Durand (called Carolus-Duran), and in 1876, Raimundo de Madrazo y Garreta—but in the end, he remained with Gérôme. None of the other Paris teachers with whom he briefly studied— Charles Jalabert and Gustave Boulanger, who were substitute teachers at the École; Amédée

1. J. Alden Weir, *Children Burying a Bird,* 1878, oil on canvas, 18 1/8 x 22 1/8 in., signed at lower left: J. Alden Weir (Mr. and Mrs. Henry C. White).

2. J. Alden Weir *The Orange Ribbon (The White Cravat)*, 1890, oil on canvas, 33 1/2 x 24 in., signed and dated at upper left: J. Alden Weir—90 (private collection).

3. J. Alden Weir, *Portrait of a Child*, 1887, oil on canvas, 49 1/8 x 36 in., signed and dated at lower left: *J. Alden Weir—1887* (private collection).

4. J. Alden Weir, *Self-Portrait,* 1886, oil on canvas, 21 x 17 1/4 in., signed and dated at upper right: *J. Alden Weir/1886* (New York, The National Academy of Design).

5. J. Alden Weir, *Flora (Carrie Mansfield Weir)*, 1882, oil on canvas, 44 x 34 in., signed and dated at upper left: J/Alden/Weir/———/1882 (Provo, Utah, Brigham Young University).

6. J. Alden Weir, *Anna with a Greyhound,* about 1882, oil on wood, 49 x 37 1/2 in., unsigned (private collection).

7. J. Alden Weir, *Against the Window,* 1884, oil on canvas, 36 1/8 x 29 1/2 in., signed at lower right: J. Alden Weir '84 (private collection).

8. J. Alden Weir, *The Christmas Tree,* 1890, oil on canvas, 36 3/4 x 25 1/2 in., signed at upper left: J. Alden Weir (private collection).

Faure and Aimé Millet, who instructed Weir in sculpture at the Petite Ecole; and Jacquesson de la Chevreuse, who taught a private class—had anything approaching Gérôme's influence on him.

Weir, while abroad, copied the work of the old masters in oil and made sketchlike notations of them in pencil and watercolor. After his return to New York, he drew on his exhaustive study repeatedly, incorporating old-master styles, compositions, and subject matter into his work. While he remained committed to the art of the past until about 1890, his idols changed over the years. Soon after his arrival in Paris, and again after his trip to Holland in 1874/75, he particularly admired Hals and Rembrandt; he also prized the works of Sir Anthony Van Dyck and Diego Velázquez, whose work he saw in Paris and on visits to England and Spain. Near the end of his four years abroad, however, under the influence of Bastien-Lepage, he studied the Italian primitives as well as the seventeenth-century realists. Later, when other types of art—Japanese prints, for example—attracted his interest, he assimilated them just as he had the old masters.

Weir's circle in Paris included many Americans, among them Edgar Melville Ward, James Carroll Beckwith, John Singer Sargent, and John Ward Stimson, but by the second spring of his stay he had begun to develop friendships with European artists, mainly those of French origin. He roomed with the Finnish painter Albert Edelfelt in the winter of 1874/75, and during that academic year he joined the group of artists gathering around Bastien-Lepage, among whom he counted as close friends Bastien himself, Pascal-Adolphe-Jean Dagnan-Bouveret, Gustave Courtois, and Joseph Wencker, all leading students at the École. Weir's association with Bastien, who during his short life informed almost every aspect of Weir's work, placed him near the hub of an emerging art movement, the naturalism that during the late 1870s and early 1880s sought a compromise between established academic standards and the experiments of Impressionism.

When Weir returned to New York in 1877, he was to emerge as a leader among the younger artists who were coming home from studies in Munich and Paris. This is the period for which we have the least documentary evidence of Weir's activities: newspaper and periodical articles on his art and activities were still relatively rare, and little of his correspondence of the time survives. From what remains of it we know that he maintained close ties with his European colleagues through letters and through his frequent trips abroad. He was a founding member of the Society of American Artists, a group of progressive painters and sculptors who formed their own exhibition organization in 1877 after a number of disagreements with the conservative members of the National Academy of Design. At the Society's annual exhibitions Weir displayed some of his important works, among them, *In the Park* (about 1879, see fig. 3.4), an outdoor scene of modern life among city-dwellers. Weir's early figure paintings were not often so radical; the many portraits he did of his friends and family members, usually three-quarter-length works, represented the sitters in dignified, formal poses. The revival of interest in flower painting led in America by John La Farge inspired him to do a series of ambitious still lifes depicting flowers and decorative objects in crowded, complicated compositions. These he exhibited often until the mid-1880s.

Weir found a niche for himself in New York during those early years, joining many of the clubs and associations established by the younger artists—the Tile Club and the Society of Painters in Pastel, to name but two. He taught at the Cooper Union and at the Art Students League, and also conducted private classes. In 1883, he married Anna Dwight Baker; their honeymoon trip seems to have been his last visit to Europe until 1889. The Weirs spent their time in New York and in Connecticut, where the artist worked at the Branchville farm he had acquired in 1882 and at his wife's family home in Windham.

During the mid-1880s Weir found fresh inspiration in the paintings of Édouard Manet, whom he had met in Paris in 1881. His portraits became more informal; he favored a smaller scale, usually bust-length; and he set more intimate poses for his models. The peasant subjects of his youth were supplanted by domestic genre scenes featuring his wife and their daughter Caroline, in which the light—sunlight streaming in from open windows or lamp-light glowing in darkened interiors—demonstrates his growing interest in French realist and impressionist painting. His palette lightened considerably and his paintings became less highly finished. His figure style was still somewhat academic: figures were well drawn and firmly modeled, particularly their faces and hands. He took greater liberties in his still lifes, which, like his portraits, became smaller in scale, more intimate in conception, and less formal in composition. Now often casual arrangements of just a few flowers and decorative objects, they resembled the still lifes of Manet and other French artists who admired the work of Jean-Baptiste-Siméon Chardin, the great eighteenth-century master. At the end of the decade Weir was painting more landscapes, his interest stimulated by the French Barbizon painters whose work he had seen in Paris, by the French Impressionists whose paintings and pastels were exhibited in New York in 1886, and by his friend John H. Twachtman, who was already an established landscapist.

Weir had begun by then to achieve a certain reputation. He was elected an associate member of the National Academy of Design in 1885 and an Academician the following year. In 1888, his painting *Idle Hours* (1888, fig. 3.39), which had won an award in the Prize Fund Exhibition, entered the collection of The Metropolitan Museum of Art. In 1889, Weir was awarded a silver medal at the Paris Universal Exposition. That same year, in New York, an exhibition and sale of paintings, watercolors, and pastels by both Weir and Twachtman brought a large group of Weir's works before the public for the first time, but his growing academic recognition and popular success did not deter him from continuing to expand the horizons of his work, which was gradually evolving into the realm of the French Impressionists.

During the 1880s and 1890s Weir began an extensive exploration of the possibilities inherent in pastel and watercolor, with results, particularly in his pastels, that do not appear in his oils until some time later. Occasionally he did ambitious exhibition pieces, but more often he experimented with a smaller format and less predictable techniques. He turned to brighter colors, often white, sometimes applied so freely that the works seem rough and unfinished. From about 1887 to 1893 he also made prints, mainly etchings and drypoints, which in their informal composition, fragmentary appearance, and use of broken lines to suggest light and air captured effects that were to become characteristic of his greatest oil paintings. Weir may in fact have reached his mature painting style through his work in the secondary mediums.

While aspects of Impressionism would continue to inspire Weir's art until the end of his career, it was during the 1890s that he first assimilated the French style and formulated his own original response to it. His actual exposure to the style was limited; since he traveled abroad infrequently after 1883, his knowledge of it was derived mainly in America, from examples in exhibitions and from the works of his friends, Twachtman and Theodore Robinson among them. Because Weir turned to Impressionism long after academic standards had shaped his approach to art and about twenty years after Impressionism had been introduced in France—that is, when its first practitioners were already modifying its principles—his mature work in that style contains elements of Post-Impressionism superimposed on the enduring elements of his early training.

Weir's rapid acceptance of Impressionism is seen in his paintings of the early 1890s. In the beginning, he simply used its obvious features—lighter colors and broken brushwork—in informal compositions, resembling his earlier landscapes, sometimes incorporated with cropping or asymmetry to create a spontaneous effect. Some of his most unconventional pictures were done during the summer of 1891, when he began two dozen landscapes and outdoor studies of figures. Many of that summer's figure paintings, among them *Family Group* (1891, fig. 5.9) and *The Wicker Chair* (1891, fig. 5.10), were never completed, but even in their unfinished state their bolder compositions, more brilliant colors, and flattened three-dimensional forms proclaim Weir's new, venturesome outlook. Work on these paintings was interrupted early in 1892 by the death of Weir's young wife, their model. Losing Anna precipitated a crisis in the artist's career: he generated but few easel paintings during the next year, devoting much of his creative energy instead to a mural for the 1893 World's Columbian Exposition in Chicago.

Weir's personal life regained some tranquillity in October 1893, when he married Ella Baker, Anna's sister. He returned to his work with renewed vigor and a new source of inspiration—Japanese art, which he seems just to have discovered. By the following year he was an enthusiastic collector of Japanese prints, and, under their influence, he created paintings that were more consciously designed than his earlier work had been, showing strong patterns, delicate pale colors, and definite contours, sometimes drawn in darker colors. Departing from strict representation in his landscapes—for example, *The Red Bridge* (about 1895, color plate 24)—Weir employed several compositional devices that defied the conventional treatment of space: raising the horizon line so that the view receded up rather than back; enlarging some elements such as tree trunks or branches or the side of a barn and pressing them close to the picture plane. He undertook a series of large figure paintings, often arranging the life-size figures in a vertical format in the foreground. Some of them, such as *In the Dooryard* (probably 1894/95, color plate 28), are set outdoors in the sunshine; others, such as *Baby Cora* (1894, color plate 25), are indoor figures surrounded by carefully selected accessories. In spite of the enduring academicism of his figure style, these are impressionist paintings in which he took a great step forward. Several of them go beyond Impressionism; in certain respects, mainly in their decorative use of color and line, they resemble works by some of the French Post-Impressionists.

This progress was of brief duration, however, for by the end of the decade Weir's work had begun to retreat from his innovative and somewhat controversial style. In figure paintings like *The Donkey Ride* (1899/1900, color plate 31), he continued to paint out-of-doors, but the tenets of his training were reasserting themselves with new force. His figures were more fully modeled and more realistically portrayed; pattern remained an important feature of his style but was less boldly represented; and a heightened sentimentality governed his choice and treatment of subjects. Around the same time a new idealism appeared in his work: his favorite models, long the members of his family, were replaced by less recognizable ones. His figure paintings gradually become more generalized in treatment; his models, almost always attractive but seemingly more mature women, display a sameness of appearance and attitude. They are contemplative, but the reasons for their contemplation are not so easily ascertainable and appear less serious than those that had absorbed the earlier models. In some works, his earlier decorative power and academic strength are retained, but in many of the later ones, especially those painted after 1910, the figures appear languid, almost bored.

Parallel trends can be traced in Weir's landscape subjects. In works of the late 1890s, *The Factory Village* (1897, color plate 30), for one, he achieved a delicate balance between representing the character of an individual site and creating a powerful visual image, but he soon began to return to artistic sources that had inspired him in his earlier days. From about 1894 to 1897 he painted snowscapes that recall those his friend Twachtman had done in the late 1880s. Some of the scenes of rural life on and around his Branchville farm—for instance, *Noonday Rest* (1897, fig. 5.33)—resemble Barbizon prototypes in their choice of subject. Stylistically, they show a renewed academicism; once again broken brushwork and lighter colors are set down over firmly drawn, conventional compositions. Weir remained more committed to Impressionism in his landscape paintings, which by 1902 began to lose the structured quality characteristic of his mid-1890s work in that genre. He was now using more consistently broken brushwork to soften contours, his palette assuming the silvery green and blue cast that is associated with his late years. His landscapes lose their particularity; to identify their sites becomes difficult, if not impossible. Many of them are simply gentle views of nature that evoke pleasant memories. In others, *Pan and the Wolf* (1907, fig. 6.13), for instance, he likely intended to convey some meaning, however vague it may be. Around

1905, nocturnal scenes, even views of the city at night, appear regularly in his work. In a few landscapes done between 1908 and 1910—for example, *Building a Dam, Shetucket* (1908, fig. 6.20)—the decorative structure of his earlier style is restored.

Weir did not merely turn to Impressionism, absorb its characteristic features, and continue to paint in a consistent style. Instead, his work underwent several phases neither progressively modern in their inspiration nor clearly defined in their chronology. His development was erratic: many times he moved forward, then back, until the direction of his art became clear to him. As William H. Gerdts, in his book on American Impressionism, has so aptly summarized Weir's oeuvre and his contemporaries' reaction to it: "Critical tributes to Weir abounded immediately after his death, though many writers appeared puzzled by a lack of consistency, unsure whether to judge his art as inconsistent or inventively varied."[1]

Weir's ambivalence toward Impressionism and his eventual retreat from modernism were partly the result of his success. His participation in the shows of The Ten American Painters established him as a leading exponent of Impressionism. By the late 1890s, when his work became less innovative in style and more lyrical in subject, he was achieving greater critical and commercial success. He was honored with awards and retrospectives; esteemed by his fellow artists, he was elected president of the National Academy of Design in 1915. Unfortunately, his acclaim in the early years of the twentieth century overshadowed the magnitude of his artistic contribution in the previous decade when Impressionism had still been a young and vital style in America. Articles published soon after Weir's death in 1919 were written by Royal Cortissoz, Frank Jewett Mather, and Duncan Phillips, who, reactionary in their views, all praised the modified impressionist style he had assumed after 1900.[2] Weir was honored by the Century Association's publication of an appreciative monograph in 1921, and by a large memorial exhibition at The Metropolitan Museum of Art three years later. His prints gained an especially wide audience during the 1920s. Interest in his work (and that of most of the American Impressionists) diminished during the next three decades, though a notable exception to this neglect was his inclusion, along with Twachtman, Mary Cassatt, and F. Childe Hassam, in the exhibition *Leaders of American Impressionism* organized by John I. H. Baur at The Brooklyn Museum in 1937. By 1952, though the American Academy of Arts and Letters commemorated the centennial of Weir's birth with an exhibition, his achievements had been all but forgotten. Only the diligence of one of his daughters saved Weir's reputation from the oblivion that claimed so many of his contemporaries. Dorothy Weir Young, who had prepared a preliminary checklist of her father's works for the Century Association's 1921 publication, continued to compile information on their locations and histories, producing a multivolume manuscript record of notes and photographs that is still maintained by members of the Weir family. The perspicacious Mrs. Young borrowed and collected letters and other documents relating to Weir's life, and transcribed and annotated their contents. Divided between members of the Weir family and Brigham Young University, which purchased the estate of her husband, the well-known sculptor Mahonri M. Young, her material remains the principal source of information on the artist. Mrs. Young's biography of her father, based on a lifetime of faithful research, was published posthumously in 1960, and to this day is the most thorough and informative book on any of the American Impressionists. In recent years Weir's work has been featured in books and articles and in exhibitions on American Impressionism, most notably that held in Seattle in 1980 at the Henry Art Gallery at the University of Washington.

J. Alden Weir: An American Impressionist builds on the solid foundation of Mrs. Young's work on her father's life and career, which it will complement by focusing on Weir's artistic achievements. In addition, it will seek to accord him his rightful place in the context of one of the richest and most exciting eras of American art.

J. ALDEN WEIR
An American Impressionist

1.1 John F. Weir, An Artist's Studio, 1864, oil on canvas, 25½ × 30½ in., signed and dated at lower left: J. F. Weir. / January 1864 (Jo Ann & Julian Ganz, Jr.).

1.2 Detail of 1.1.

1

Studies in West Point and New York

JULIAN ALDEN WEIR BEGAN HIS ARTISTIC CAREER UNDER FAVORABLE CIRCUMSTANCES: he was born, in 1852, into a family that produced several American artists. His father, Robert Walter Weir (1803–1889),[1] was a leading painter of portraits, landscapes, and genre and historical pictures. Between 1834 and 1876 he was drawing instructor at the United States Military Academy at West Point, New York, where he was Julian's first teacher. Another son, John Ferguson Weir (1841–1926),[2] Julian's half brother and his senior by eleven years, also studied with Robert. During the late 1860s, when Julian was beginning his first artistic endeavors, John, who had already achieved a reputation of his own, greatly influenced his younger brother's development.

Robert's studio at West Point must have been the setting for his sons' first art instruction. *An Artist's Studio* (1864, fig. 1.1), a painting of John's, depicts his father at work just before the time when Julian started his studies. The studio is crowded with Robert's paintings, among them *Taking the Veil* (1863, New Haven, Yale University Art Gallery), shown on his easel (fig. 1.2); *Santa Claus, or Saint Nicholas* (original version, 1837; this version, before 1864, present location unknown), which hangs on the wall to the right; and *Evening of the Crucifixion* (by 1864, present location unknown), which is propped up on the cabinet.[3] The room is crowded with the assorted studio accoutrements that also appear in other paintings by the two younger Weirs—unframed canvases turned against the wall, casts after European sculpture, a marble bust of Washington Allston by Shobal Vail Clevenger, and a cabinet for filing prints and art books. It was a place of lasting meaning for John, who remembered being "brought up in an artist's studio, surrounded at all times with what was actively related to the professional practice, with the opportunity for giving such familiarity with the art of the past as the excellent collections of the home inspired."[4] It was equally important to Julian. He was an art student in Paris when his father retired in 1876, but the occasion prompted a dream in which he returned to visit the studio before it was dismantled. As he wrote to his parents: "I went to sleep last night thinking of the old place and took a walk all over, visiting the places where I had so often trod in the days dearest to me in my imagination. I hauled down father's portfolios last night, climbed to the top of the old cabinet and got down dressed in his armor and covered with dust. I rummaged in the two corners where the mannequins are, found several old familiar relics and lots of good canvas, [and] ground paint in the table in front of

23

the large pane of glass. . . . It seemed to me today as if I had really been with you all for I retraced those good old days with so much pleasure."[5]

Robert probably started his sons' education with the study of the old masters, for he had amassed an enormous collection of prints and books, many of which he acquired during a sojourn in Italy in the late 1820s. He likely instructed the boys to make copies after exemplary works of art that were represented in his collection. Such copying was standard practice in mid-nineteenth-century America, where many art students gained their first experience with paint in this manner.[6] Robert had begun his own artistic career by copying a portrait and, later, while he was studying in Italy, he made watercolor copies after the Italian Renaissance painters.[7] The latter were usually highly finished works; one of them (about 1826, fig. 1.3), after Justice, a figure from the fresco *Pope Urban I* attributed to Giulio Romano,[8] demonstrates the care Robert took with his copies: outlines are drawn in pencil and the color added with delicate hatching strokes that resemble a miniaturist's technique. The precise paint application is particularly noticeable in the hair of Justice, in the folds of her drapery, and in the variegated colors of the marble plinth that supports her. Robert later regretted having lavished so much time and effort on these copies. "I think too much time was consumed in making them, when sketches of the compositions of one color merely, without entering into the minutiae of tints, would have answered all the purposes as well, and perhaps better," he commented to the art critic William Dunlap.[9] (Julian must have remembered his father's opinion when he himself was studying the old masters in Europe—few of his old-master copies are highly finished, and many are simply rapid pencil sketches with summary color notes, just enough for reference.) Robert also maintained that those who chose the old masters as their model rather than nature "thus copy nature at two or three removes . . .[which] would, in a short time, reduce art to the lowest degradation and servility."[10] It was for their truth to nature that Robert particularly admired the Dutch old masters, who in "their simple imitations speak with the voice of nature, and teach us how to represent her."[11]

Although their copies were presumably an important part of both John's and Julian's training, relatively few of them are known today. From lists John made of his early work we can reconstruct more or less what he did during his art-student years.[12] His "first oil painting" was a fourteen-by-nine-inch copy of *The Five Senses: Seeing*, followed in the same series by two more, *Hearing* and *Feeling* (present locations unknown).[13] These were almost certainly copied from engravings or other reproductions belonging to his father. John also made copies after Robert's own works. He mentioned two in one of those early lists: his copies (present location unknown) after *Evening of the Crucifixion* (by 1864) and *Marmion and De Wilton* (by 1831, present locations unknown).[14] It seems likely that Julian followed a similar course. Among his many copies is one after an unidentified Flemish painting (about 1867, fig. 1.4) that he made at the age of fourteen, during his West Point years, which suggests that he may have begun to paint at an even earlier age than had his elder brother. Somewhat small in scale, the crudely painted picture reveals Julian struggling to master his medium. The awkwardly posed figures are shown against a dark, flat background, their faces and the textures and folds of their costumes represented in a linear manner; there is little three-dimensionality.

Robert's method of instruction undoubtedly emphasized the importance of color. This was the one area in which he was critical of Italian Renaissance painting. "With much skill in drawing, among the Italian artists, there is a great deal that retards their progress as painters; they continue too long with the port crayon, and lose their eye for color; and when they take their palette in hand, and with the living model before them, they find it too much to embody both color and drawing at once," he commented to William Dunlap.[15] He thus would have insisted on his sons' developing their skill as colorists. (Shortly after his arrival in Paris in 1873, Julian was to express his appreciation for his father's "great judgment in making me use my colors so much.")[16]

Much of Julian's early career was devoted to portraiture. His letters mention a painting of his father, which may be the unsigned one (Provo, Utah, Brigham Young University) that remained in his possession at the time of his death. It is closely related to the self-portrait

1.3 Robert W. Weir, copy after the figure of Justice in the fresco Pope Urban I, *attributed to Giulio Romano (about 1524, Rome, Vatican Palace, Sala di Costantino), about 1826, watercolor on paper, 10½ × 6 in., unsigned (West Point Museum Collections, United States Military Academy).*

1.4 J. Alden Weir, copy after an unknown Flemish master, about 1867, oil on canvas, 9¹/₁₆ × 7 in., inscribed on reverse: Age 14 yr / J. A. Weir / 1867 (private collection).

(New York, The New-York Historical Society) that Robert had done early in the 1860s; Julian may well have worked from that head in his painting of Robert.[17] A number of Julian's early portraits remain at Brigham Young University, but their deteriorated state makes his development during this early period difficult to judge. They include two bust-length portraits of unidentified male sitters, one of which seems to have been an attempt to convey a strong emotion, possibly grief; a bust-length portrait of the Weirs' gardener, Zwinge; a three-quarter-length portrait of a seated huntsman holding a gun; and a self-portrait. All were probably painted before 1870.[18] They are dark in palette and show little variation in color. Julian painted them thinly, using glazes, a technique he later rejected in favor of more opaque pigments and a direct paint application. An improvement can be seen in his military portraits of the early 1870s. One of these, *Henry C. Weir* (about 1870, fig. 1.5), depicts one of his other brothers, and shows how strongly Julian's work depended on his father's example. Henry, who had served in the army during the Civil War, assumes a pose identical to that of General Winfield Scott in Robert's portrait of him (late 1850s, fig. 1.6), complete to the hand inserted in the jacket. Here Julian has followed the format most often used by his father: a bust-length portrait of a sitter who is posed against a flat, neutral backdrop and at a slightly oblique angle in relation to the picture plane. Julian's paint application, however, is labored, especially in the face, and he seems to have had some difficulty suggesting the three-dimensionality of his model's torso.

During their West Point years, both John and Julian did landscape views of the Hudson River which they sold to the cadets, tourists, and local residents. No fewer than fifteen of these appear in one of John's painting lists, each sold at a price ranging from five to twenty

1.5 J. Alden Weir, Henry C. Weir, *about 1870, oil on canvas mounted on maso-nite, 29½ × 25½ in., inscribed at upper left: Bvc. Colonel Henry Cary Weir/U.S.——uls / 1861–1865 (present location unknown).*

dollars. John's *View of the Highlands of the Hudson* (1862, fig. 1.7), which fetched a more substantial price, two hundred and fifty dollars, is larger than those early potboilers, but it gives some idea of their appearance.[19] In it, the darkened foreground with its blasted tree and grazing cattle leads us into a panoramic view, suffused in glowing light, of the Hudson River and its surrounding mountains. Although the conventional composition was undoubtedly based on similar efforts by his father, a comparison of this landscape with one by Robert will show the differences in their painting styles. The elder Weir's *View of the Hudson River* (1864, fig. 1.8) was painted two years after John's landscape, but its style and composition repeat a formula that he had developed by the 1830s.[20] It is somewhat idealized; the treatment of the foliage is generalized and the arrangement of the figures is contrived. In his landscape, John demonstrates a closer observation and a more exacting painting technique, particularly in the detailed rendering of the blasted tree and the tall birch beside it. He was clearly influenced by the Hudson River School painters, many of whom visited his father at West Point and depicted the view there. In 1858, John was only seventeen years old, but he made frequent trips to New York City, where he would have had additional opportunities to study the work of these artists. In November 1859, for example, he saw Frederic Church's *Heart of the Andes* (1859, New York, The Metropolitan Museum of Art), which he later described as showing "what paint can do toward rendering what Humbolt vainly endeavoured to describe."[21]

1.6 Robert W. Weir, General Winfield Scott, *late 1850s, oil on canvas, 33¾ × 26⅞ in., unsigned (New York, The Metropolitan Museum of Art, Gift of the heirs of William B. Isham, 1910).*

Julian would have been exposed to some of these same influences. Although none of his early Hudson River views are known today, they undoubtedly resembled those by other members of his family. His letters record one that he did for a local hotel owner in order to finance a sketching trip with the painter Julian Scott (1846–1901). This he described as "another one of those plagued views of 'Up the River,'" so he apparently painted a great number of them.[22]

The United States Military Academy, the setting of Julian's youth, helped to shape his personal and professional habits. John described the sense of discipline and duty that characterized West Point: "There was a certain tone or distinction of its own in the life at West Point, as I recall it, something not due to military efficiency, nor to anything technical in army-life, but to its fine morale, or spirit; to the high estimate placed upon duties and obligations of whatever kind, public or private."[23] It was just this sense of duty that impelled John to write in one of his sketchbooks: "Must paint daily at least six hours / from 9 till 12½ and from 2 o'ck till 5 / and draw & design some every evening / from this time forth / *Nil Desparandum.*"[24] Julian pursued his art studies with equal fervor: while he was in Paris, for example, he worked all day and all evening, diligently avoiding social calls and other time-consuming student pastimes.

*1.7 **John F. Weir**, View of the Highlands of the Hudson, 1862, oil on canvas, 20 × 34 in., signed and dated at lower right: **J. F. Weir**/1862 (New York, **The New-York Historical Society, The Robert L. Stuart Collection**, on permanent loan from the New York Public Library).*

*1.8 **Robert W. Weir**, View of the Hudson River, 1864, oil on canvas, 32⅛ × 48 in., signed at lower left: Robt. W. Weir/1864 (West Point Museum Collections, United States Military Academy).*

It is possible that young Julian attended some of the classes his father presented to the cadets at West Point (1836, fig. 1.9). Only the bare outline of Robert's curriculum has been recorded. The course was intended to teach the cadets how to draw the maps then needed for reconnaissance purposes or military strategy, but judging from the drawings they produced over the years (West Point Museum Collections, United States Military Academy), some of Robert's pupils exceeded the army's requirements and created creditable works of art. The course began with the study of topography and its various symbols—to indicate mountainous terrain or wild, uncultivated areas, for instance. Later, the students did freehand work, first making outline drawings of the human figure in three different positions and then copying engravings by such artists as John Flaxman (1755–1826), the English draftsman and sculptor. The cadets' study of landscape mainly involved drawing from "models in the flat," although Robert also encouraged them to draw from nature by giving them exercises in aerial perspective, the effects of light, and the use of color.[25] Elementary as this instruction may seem, it was the general type of work that art students of the period pursued prior to antique and life drawing. Familiarity with even a simple form of draftsmanship would have been helpful to a young artist. John and Julian and the many cadets trained under Robert Walter Weir's direction also had access to a large collection of study prints, some of which, an engraving after Raphael (1830, fig. 1.10) among them, still remain in the collection of the United States Military Academy.

Though Julian's art eventually developed in a direction totally different from his father's, he retained a deep admiration for him. Even after Julian had left for Paris, his father continued to advise him on his courses in school and on his study of old-master techniques in the art galleries; he encouraged him to persevere in his work in color and his experiments in modeling clay, and offered him criticisms on his paintings.[26] Robert Weir remained a demanding taskmaster to the end of his life, and both Julian and John appreciated how much of their knowledge had come from him. When John became an associate member of the Na-

1.9 Robert W. Weir, Cadet at Drawing Board, *1836, ink on paper, 5¼ × 3¾ in., signed at lower left: R. W. Weir/1836 (West Point Museum Collections, United States Military Academy).*

1.10 André Joseph Mecou, La Belle Jardinière, *1830, after a figure in Raphael Santi,* Virgin and Infant with Young Saint John, *called* La Belle Jardinière, *1507 (Paris, Musée du Louvre), engraving, 20 × 13¾ in. (West Point Museum Collections, United States Military Academy).*

tional Academy of Design, in 1864, he asked his father to paint the required portrait (New York, National Academy of Design). Twenty-one years later, when Julian too became an associate, he submitted a self-portrait that included in its background a portrait he had done of his father in 1878, [27] an acknowledgment of the debt he owed him as his first mentor. Robert Weir is literally looking over his son's shoulder—a quiet but constant influence on Julian's life and career. [28]

Julian's development was profoundly influenced also by John's art, taste for the art of the past, and philosophy. The bond between the two brothers, always close, continually strengthened. During his youth at West Point and in New York, Julian admired his brother and emulated his style. Their relationship altered while Julian was studying abroad, but after a brief alienation, the two returned to what would be a lifelong friendship and artistic comradeship.

Between 1862, when he settled in New York, and 1868, when he visited Europe, John created several paintings that earned him a significant reputation at the early age of twenty-seven. In 1864 he exhibited *An Artist's Studio* (1864, fig. 1.1) at the National Academy of Design in New York, whereupon he was elected an associate member. Two years later, when he showed *The Gun Foundry* (1866, Cold Spring, New York, Putnam County Historical Society), he was made a full member. The industrial scene and *Forging the Shaft* (1867, destroyed; replica, 1877, fig. 1.11) were exceptional not only in their large scale but also in their use of complex groupings of many figures. John's abilities were recognized by the art community almost at once. As he wrote in an undated letter to his childhood sweetheart and

1.11 John F. Weir, Forging the Shaft, *1877, replica of a destroyed 1867 painting, 52¹/₁₆ × 73¹/₄ in., signed at lower right: John F. Weir (New York, The Metropolitan Museum of Art, Gift of Lyman G. Bloomingdale, 1901).*

future wife, Mary French, "I am *beginning* to discern the first sparks of *Reputation*."[29] In 1867, Henry T. Tuckerman praised him in his important *Book of the Artists*, asserting of *The Gun Foundry*, "We know of no picture which so deftly elaborates our industrial economy as this clever and effective picture of the West Point Foundry."[30] The same year, John exhibited the work at the Universal Exposition in Paris. That was undoubtedly the high point of his career. His success must have been a source of inspiration to Julian, an aspiring artist who was experimenting with his first oil paintings around the same time.

John's influence on his brother's stylistic development can be seen in Julian's painting *Carrie in the Studio at West Point* (about 1868, fig. 1.12), his earliest known original picture. Here Julian depicts his sister in a setting—Robert's studio at West Point—and a quiet domestic scene not unlike those John showed in *Sunny Moments* (1864, fig. 1.13). He has obviously borrowed many features from the earlier work. Carrie is posed frontally rather than in profile like John's model, but otherwise Julian has followed John's example to the point of imitation. John balanced and unified his composition with the poses of the seated woman and the child below her on the floor and with the gazes between them. This device is repeated in Julian's picture, where Carrie, interrupted in her reading, looks down at a dog which is looking expectantly up at her. The easel in the left foreground of John's picture has been replaced by a chair and some drapery; positioned diagonally, it is meant to lead us into the picture space and direct our attention to the subject. Like his brother, Julian has chosen side-lighting (presumably from a window to the right), which creates strong patterns of light and shade on the carpet, but he has selected a different vantage point: his expands our view of the room and places the figures in the middle distance rather than in the foreground. He has also represented a far more crowded interior; no area of the studio wall is left empty. John has demonstrated more selectivity—for example, the wall behind the seated woman is stripped to its unadorned, cracked surface so that the pattern of light and shade cast by the window receives greater dramatic emphasis. Julian's composition is thus far less cohesive than John's. His inexperience is also reflected in his modification of certain elements requiring a superior knowledge of perspective—the doors of the cabinet that swing open in John's picture and the easel that is placed in the foreground, close to the picture plane, in order to create a trompe l'oeil effect. A close examination of *Carrie in the Studio at West Point* reveals that Julian had some technical difficulties as well. Carrie's figure has undergone some changes during the course of his work (she may well have been originally posed in profile, like the woman in John's painting). Julian has borrowed John's dark, warm palette and his rich paint application, but he does not yet have John's command of the medium. Whatever its faults, the painting remains a remarkable achievement for a boy of fifteen or sixteen.

John had an equally strong effect on the development of Julian's aesthetic ideas. John believed that painting was an intellectual art, one that required great education and knowledge. "An artist is necessarily as much of a Poet as any writer of poems," he wrote to Mary French. "A Poet expresses his ideas and sentiment in verse and a painter with colour and form. One uses the language of lines and colour. . . . There is no profession which requires more general knowledge than painting. It is as absurd to talk of anyone with an inferior brain or limited education being a great Artist as it is to talk of a fool becoming a great orator."[31] John sought to endow his works with meaning. *The Gun Foundry* and *Forging the Shaft* make a statement about America's industrial destiny; the former, painted during the Civil War, may also allude to the industrial superiority that enabled the North to win the conflict. Even John's seemingly simple genre scenes may contain a hidden message. His painting *Sunny Moments* (1864, fig. 1.13) may be a comment not only on the sunlight reflected on the studio wall but also on the happiness of the woman and child who exist in contentment far from the war which was then raging.[32] "I want to paint *ideas*—something to address the mind or the imagination and am beginning to abhor this senseless stuff called 'the picturesque,'" John explained to his sister Louisa in an 1869 letter.[33] In the same letter he condemned the school of Dutch genre painting "with its low-lived pictures, of the lowest sentiment and lost meaning, forever painting brass pails, cabbages, and old kettles, and dirty Dutchmen like tubs and putting all their art in broomsticks and backgrounds." He favored art with intellectual or spiritual meaning, and for this reason he particularly admired Italian painting, a legacy he passed on to Julian, who, after a period of great enthusiasm for the Dutch and Flemish seventeenth-century painters, developed a similar appreciation of Italian Renaissance art.

Julian certainly would have seen his brother at work on several of his major paintings. *An Artist's Studio* (1864, fig. 1.1) was finished at West Point, and John made studies for his industrial scenes at the West Point Foundry at nearby Cold Spring. Julian also visited John in New York, but when he did or how often is not known. In an account book that John kept

1.12 J. Alden Weir, Carrie in the Studio at West Point, *about 1868, oil on canvas, 23¼ × 20¼ in., unsigned (private collection).*

1.13 John F. Weir, Sunny Moments, *1864, oil on wood, 15¼ × 12¼ in., signed and dated at lower right: J. F. Weir. 1864 (New Haven, Connecticut, Yale University Art Gallery, Gift of Mr. and Mrs. Russell C. Graef, 1953).*

between 1858 and 1871 he records only one visit from Julian, late in November 1864, when he took his twelve-year-old brother to the theater and, presumably, to some art exhibitions.[34] Julian is said to have visited John in New York during the winter of 1867/68,[35] but it seems unlikely that his visits were extended or frequent, for at this time Julian was just fifteen years old and John had only recently married Mary French. In the following winter, as John later reminisced, he turned over his New York studio (1860s, fig. 1.14) to Julian.[36] (That would have been while he visited Europe, from December 1868 to August 1869.) Julian would have used it until 1872, since John continued to maintain it even after accepting a teaching post at Yale in the autumn of 1869;[37] Julian probably worked in it while he was a student at the National Academy of Design during the early 1870s. John's studio would have conveyed a rich artistic spirit to the young artist, for many of John's pictures would have been there in varied states of completion. There were also the countless objects that John had collected over the years, among them photographs or plaster casts of Erastus Dow Palmer's *Morning* and *Evening;* a photograph of Palmer's *White Captive;* an ambrotype of one of Rosa Bonheur's pictures; prints purchased from Goupil's, a French art gallery and publisher of prints that had opened a branch in New York; and a collection of photographs of antique and modern

*1.14 A photograph of John Ferguson Weir's studio, late 1860s (New Haven, Connec-
ticut, Sterling Memorial Library, Yale University, John Ferguson Weir Papers).*

sculpture and old-master paintings.[38] Further, the studio was situated in the famous Tenth
Street Studio Building, where Julian would have had an opportunity to meet many of the
artists in his elder brother's circle, among them Sanford R. Gifford (1823–1880) and Jervis
McEntee (1828–1891). Some of them even offered the young painter advice on his work.
Julian took two of his portrait heads to John Beaufain Irving, Jr. (1825–1877), and William
Page (1811–1885) for criticism. "They seemed to like the color very much but not the drawing
so much," he reported to John.[39] It also seems likely that Julian visited John at New Haven
after John assumed his post at Yale, and it was possibly on one of those occasions that Julian
began the copybook he kept in 1869 and 1870. In this he wrote out quotations from books that
discussed the methods of great artists of the past, including Peter Paul Rubens and Sir Joshua
Reynolds.[40]

    John encouraged his younger brother to study in Paris at the École des Beaux-Arts, and
helped him secure the means to do so. John's own trip to Europe had heightened his appreciation of French painting. "I think modern French Art incomparably finer than *any* modern art
I saw in England," he commented in his diary after a visit to the Luxembourg Gallery in
Paris. (He condemned English art as "maimed & wooden. colorless.") On January 4, 1869, he
visited the École and "was very much gratified . . . with the fine fragments of Sculpture and
the casts—as well as with the various halls and rooms." John was certainly the one who made
the financial arrangements for Julian's Paris schooling with Mrs. Bradford Alden, Julian's
patroness and the widow of one of his baptismal sponsors, explaining that he had written a

letter to Julian "to impress upon him his responsibility in the matter . . . I believe he will do his utmost to prove himself worthy of your liberality on his behalf."[41]

Soon after his arrival in Paris, Julian began to urge his brother to come to Europe for another visit and to exhibit one of his works (usually suggesting *Forging the Shaft*) at the annual Salon. "In the Salon there is no work resembling yours, your subject and style of work is different and I feel convinced that your picture will hold a good place," he wrote. "Keep the idea before your eyes and work for it, it will do wonders for you." John never did go during Julian's student years, but he followed his work and travels with great interest. "Your travels remind me of a young Sir Joshua," he wrote to Julian wistfully. "I seemed to be with you over every foot of the road." He warned his brother that he must take advantage of his student years, because "This is just the very brightest period of your life and you will in the future always look back to it as such. . . . The sun will never again cast so few shadows as it does now, and it will never seem quite so full of mystery and light."[42]

John, seemingly discouraged by the demands that his teaching and administrative duties made on his time, urged Julian to remain abroad as long as possible. "Perfect yourself in your art—return already great," he counseled. "Make your reputation over there, for it's a hard and *vague* thing to make here—if made over there it is more enduring and profitable." From abroad, Julian assisted John in developing the academic program for the Yale School of the Fine Arts. He provided information on the course of study at the École des Beaux-Arts and sent John sample studies by its students. In spite of their great mutual affection, the two brothers encountered some problems in their relationship as Julian became more experienced and more independent. The young art student began to question his elder brother's artistic judgment. Having seen photographs of one of John's portraits and of his painting *The Confessional* (present location unknown), Julian criticized the absence of "individual and solid flesh work" in the former and the lack of "fullness" in the latter. The remedy for these problems, suggested Julian, would be a year at the École des Beaux-Arts, where John "would get just what he wants so much to know, solidity." He chided John for his enthusiasm about the native American school of painting. "Now, old John, with regard to buying Giffords and such, if you could trust me to invest in some of the pictures of the young and strong men I think you would do much more for your school," he wrote to his brother in 1875. When John cautioned Julian about losing his "individuality" in favor of "an adopted manner" learned abroad, Julian bristled and replied, "One cannot lose his originality unless one is a very weak mortal and then it would be the best thing for him."[43] Their dialogue underscores the widening philosophical gulf between John's native-trained contemporaries and Julian's cosmopolitan generation.

In 1875 and 1876 there were times when the brothers quarreled openly. John became annoyed with Julian, who in his opinion was not trying hard enough to secure some casts which he had asked him to order for Yale. Julian, in turn, was angered by John's inability to understand how many difficulties he faced in accomplishing this task. Around the same time, Julian wanted to submit one of his works to the Centennial Exhibition in Philadelphia, but John advised against it. Later, when John was the only member of the family represented at this important exhibition, Julian imagined that John had discouraged his and his father's participation so that he would "be the only one of the name, as it would otherwise take some of his glory away."[44] These minor disagreements soon passed, and the two brothers remained close for the remainder of their lives, their friendship ultimately bridging the differences in their training and their art. In 1881 they finally made their European sojourn together, painting primarily in Holland. John, less familiar with the latest European developments than Julian, was influenced by him in the development of his later style. It was likely Julian who sparked John's interest in floral still-life painting, a major interest with both brothers during the 1880s. By the turn of the century Julian had overcome John's initial negative reaction to Impressionism, and John began work on some landscapes (private collection) whose informal compositions and impressionist style show his younger brother's influence.

The National Academy of Design

After Julian's years at West Point, he continued his studies in New York at the National Academy of Design during the winters of 1870/71 and 1871/72, a decisive time in that institution's history. In January of 1870, the Council of the Academy had voted to hire its first full-time teacher, Lemuel Wilmarth (1835–1918).[45] Prior to his appointment, instruction at the Academy had been somewhat haphazard, with different Academicians teaching for brief periods in rotation. Wilmarth's appointment demonstrates the Academy's interest in enabling a student to establish a closer, more constant relationship with a master. For Weir, of course, such a relationship would have been less crucial, since he had already worked in the studios of his father and his brother. The actual program of instruction at the Academy during his enrollment remains unrecorded. The previous year, when a special committee had first proposed expanding the Academy's educational program in order to make it " 'a higher school of instruction' in the two arts of Sculpture and Painting," its intention was to make a wide range of classes available to the students. These were to include an elementary class (probably basic drawing, mainly after two-dimensional images such as engravings); an antique class, where students drew after plaster casts; a life class; a painting class, "to include study from the living Model, both nude and draped, and from still life"; anatomy; perspective; and landscape painting. To be added to the classes were art lectures, public exhibitions, an "annual concourse," or competition, and awards of merit—all features taken from the French academic system.[46] The proposal was accepted by the Academy's Council, but there is no way to ascertain how much of it was put into practice. Certainly the painting class was not officially noted in the Council's Minutes until 1873.[47] During Weir's studies at the Academy, the student registers were simply divided into two "schools," or classes—antique and life.

Weir was first admitted to the antique class on November 7, 1870, and worked there until his promotion to the life class on March 20, 1871. He was readmitted to the antique class on October 9, 1871, and does not seem to have moved on to the life class during his second year at the Academy.[48] One of his drawings after a plaster cast, a careful study of a bust of a woman (Provo, Utah, Brigham Young University), is hesitant and overworked; it could well have been done at this early date. Among the 147 students studying the antique in 1870/71 were several aspiring artists who would later play roles in Weir's career. George de Forest Brush, Henry Plumb, Walter Blackman, and Arthur Daintry all were to become students of Weir's Paris mentor, Jean-Léon Gérôme; Abbott H. Thayer, Francis Lathrop, and Helena de Kay all were later to join and support the Society of American Artists; and Albert Pinkham Ryder was to become one of Weir's closest friends.[49] In 1871/72, the antique class numbered 175 students; among them were two who would join Weir in Gérôme's atelier—John W. Love and Frederick Gortelmeyer.[50] Wilmarth is listed as the instructor for the antique class for the two years of Weir's enrollment, but during the second year, Raymond Dabb was his assistant.[51]

When Weir was promoted to the life school, in 1871, he joined a much smaller group—seventeen students—who were also receiving instruction from Wilmarth.[52] The male and female students met in separate classes, on weekdays from eight o'clock in the morning until nine-thirty in the evening, and on Saturdays from eight in the morning until two o'clock in the afternoon.[53] One of Weir's academy drawings, *Male Nude* (1871, fig. 1.15), dated October 29, 1871, shows the model in a modest pose, his back turned to the viewer. The post and vantage point also eliminate such difficulties as the portrayal of the model's face or any suggestion of movement: he is clearly stationary and likely to remain so. Weir has drawn the outline of the figure with great care. Some alterations are evident, mostly in the figure's elbow which rests on a pedestal beside him. The modeling is somewhat generalized; the overall drawing does not reflect close observation of a particular person.

1.15 J. Alden Weir, Male Nude, *black and white chalk on blue paper, 23 × 15 in. (sight), inscribed at lower left:* Julian A. Weir/[torn] School/October 29th 71 *(Provo, Utah, Brigham Young University).*

In addition to his studies in drawing, Weir attended lectures. He mentions hearing one on perspective on December 16, 1871,[54] which would have been presented for the Academy's students and members by James Renwick Brevoort (1832–1918), a landscape painter who had begun his career as an architect. Brevoort's background as an architectural draftsman would have made him an authority on this subject.[55]

During the 1871/72 academic year, Benjamin Waterhouse Hawkins (1807–1889), an English sculptor, author, and naturalist who had come to the United States in 1868, offered a series of five lectures on "a comparative view of the human and animal frames."[56] The text of his lectures probably resembled that of his *Comparative Anatomy as Applied to the Purposes of the Artist* (1883), which assumed a certain familiarity with anatomy on the part of the reader and was intended to acquaint the art student with the similarities and differences between the

1.16 Benjamin Waterhouse Hawkins, Plate VII. Human Figures and Bears, *reproduced in his* Comparative Anatomy as Applied to the Purposes of the Artist *(London, 1883), p. 49.*

human body and the animal. In plates (for example, fig. 1.16) Hawkins shows animals and clothed men; he also silhouettes their skeletons in identical poses. His mode of teaching anatomy thus seems to have involved some theorizing (however poorly conceived), as well as the study of the skeleton, of which the students made a scale drawing.[57]

William Rimmer (1816–1879), then America's leading anatomy teacher, also spoke at the Academy while Weir was a student there. Some notion of his lectures can be gleaned from his "Observations on Art and Life," included in Truman H. Bartlett's 1881 monograph, and from Rimmer's own *Elements of Design* (1864) and *Art Anatomy* (1884, fig. 1.17).[58] For this instructor, the study of anatomy was at once scientific, intellectual, and aesthetic. He taught his students to represent not just the human body but its movement and expression as well. His attitude toward the body, particularly to the male nude, was reverential. He permitted his students to work from the living model only after they had mastered the basic principles of anatomy from diagrams, charts, and casts. Although Weir probably attended his lectures while a student at the National Academy, there is no record of his response to this eccentric instructor.

During the 1871/72 academic year, the Academy's president, William Page, offered a series of five lectures in which he discussed "imitative art."[59] While no text of these lectures is known, their contents can be surmised from several articles Page wrote on similar topics.[60] For Page, imitation in art involved studying and reproducing the effects of nature, the route he believed the old masters had followed to achieve their renowned presentations of the human condition. Page's philosophy was not unlike that of Julian's father, who years earlier had expressed similar sentiments to William Dunlap.

Julian enrolled for only two academic years at the National Academy of Design. He probably would have returned for additional studies if ill health had not forced him to make a trip to Minnesota during the winter of 1872/73. Weir's studies at the Academy were never-

1.17 William Rimmer, Expression Non-Personal, *reproduced in his* Art Anatomy *(Boston, 1884), plate 26.*

theless essential to his development as an artist. During his two years there he learned much about drawing from casts and from life; he was also introduced to the essentials of perspective and anatomy. Further, his experiences at the Academy took him from the family surroundings at West Point and placed him in a broader and more competitive context: his studies in New York prepared him for the rigors of the four years he was to spend at the École des Beaux-Arts in Paris. When Julian left for Europe in September 1873, it was with the confidence that he had already taken advantage of the finest training offered in his native land.

2

The Training of an Academic Artist

THE EXPERIENCE J. ALDEN WEIR GAINED AS A STUDENT IN FRANCE FROM THE AUTUMN of 1873 until the autumn of 1877 shaped his entire career. Much of his time was spent in the art schools of Paris, mainly in the École des Beaux-Arts but also at the École Gratuite de Dessin, or the Petite École, as it was known, and at independent ateliers then gaining in popularity. Weir also visited private and public collections to study works by contemporary artists as well as those of the old masters, some of the latter when he was stopping in London on his way to and from Paris. He also took side trips to Belgium and Holland and to Spain while he was living in Paris and going to school. During the summers he worked in small French villages, painting peasant subjects and landscapes. As his technical ability and self-confidence grew, he submitted works to the Paris Salon, an exhibition he attended each year with great interest and enthusiasm. He gradually developed friendships, first with American students and later with such European artists as Émile and Jules Bastien-Lepage, Joseph Wencker, Gustave-Claude-Étienne Courtois, Pascal-Adolphe-Jean Dagnan-Bouveret, and Albert Edelfelt. These artists drew Weir into an international circle of naturalists whose style of painting offered a compromise between the academic and the avant-garde. As a result, Weir returned to America with the knowledge, technical ability, and assurance he needed to establish himself in the vanguard of a generation that was to transform the American art scene during the late 1870s. In order to understand fully the original style that Weir developed as he matured during the 1880s and 1890s, his formative years in Paris must be examined in some detail.

Paris Teachers

When Weir arrived in Paris, he had reached no firm conclusion about his choice of teachers, although many possibilities were open to an art student in the French capital of that era. Several private ateliers conducted by such instructors as Léon-Joseph-Florentin Bonnat, Charles-Émile-Auguste Durand (called Carolus-Duran), and Louis-Marie-François Jacquesson de la Chevreuse were already attracting many American students. The École des Beaux-Arts, however, was unquestionably the preeminent educational institution for artists in Paris, and it is hardly surprising that Weir selected it as the primary source of his education. In 1863, the École had expanded and enriched its curriculum. Classes in perspective, anatomy, and history had been combined with practical instruction; distinguished writers such as Hippolyte Taine lectured on the history of art and aesthetics; and the students in each discipline—painting, sculpture, architecture, and engraving—could work in a studio under one master's regular direction.[1] For most of Weir's four years in Paris he worked at the École

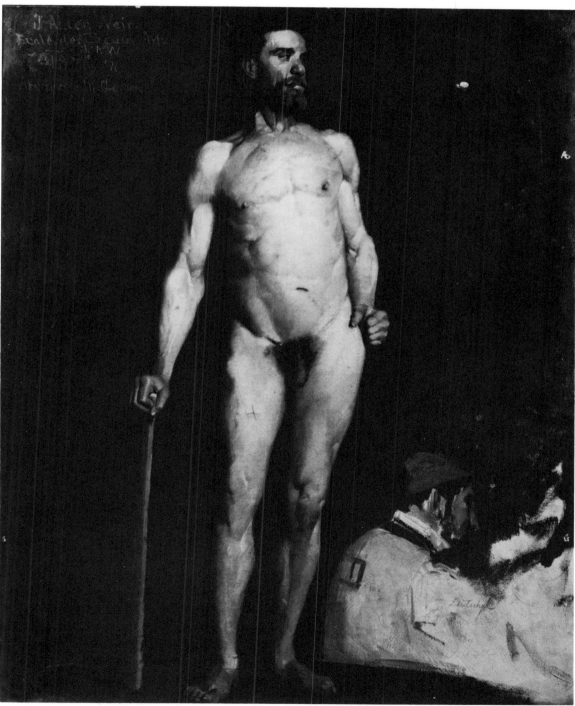

2.1 J. Alden Weir, Study of a Male Nude Leaning on a Staff, *1876, oil on canvas, 25½ × 31½ in., signed, dated, and inscribed at upper left: J. Alden Weir/Ecole des Beaux-Arts/1876/Atelier de M. Gerome, JAW/'76; at lower right:* Deutschul/by/J.A.W. *(New Haven, Connecticut, Yale University Art Gallery, Gift of Julian Alden Weir, 1914).*

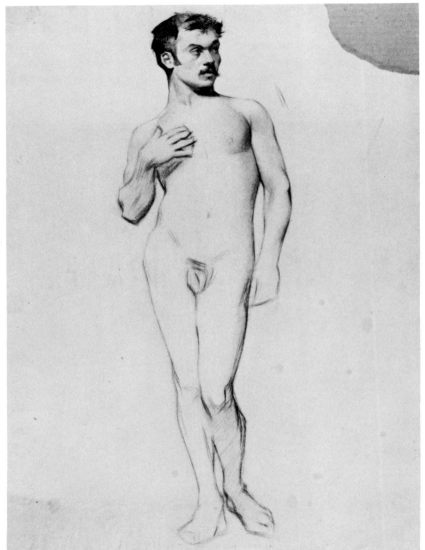

2.2 J. Alden Weir, Standing Male Nude, *probably 1873–77, charcoal on paper,*
24¼ × 18½ in., unsigned (Provo, Utah, Brigham Young University).

in the studio of Jean-Léon Gérôme, between the beginning of October and the end of July,
six days a week, from Monday to Saturday, from seven or eight o'clock in the morning until
about four o'clock in the afternoon. He normally spent his mornings drawing and painting
from life (figs. 2.1–2.3) and his afternoons drawing from casts after antique statues (figs. 2.4–
2.5).[2] These studies were intended to prepare him for the *concours des places*, held each year in
March and October, a series of examinations that all students had to pass before being
officially matriculated into the École. The *concours* included tests in anatomy and perspective,
as well as in drawing from casts (fig. 2.6) and from the nude. Students were required to pass
these examinations in order to gain admittance to the evening drawing class conducted by
Adolphe Yvon (1817–1893) and to participate fully in the various competitions held at the
École. (Although only French students were eligible for the Prix de Rome, the most sought-
after award, other *concours* were open to students of all nationalities.) The *concours des places* not
only gained a student admission to the École, it also assessed his standing among his class-
mates. Entrance achieved did not guarantee continued matriculation; students were required
to take each semiannual examination in order to stay on. Weir must have taken the *concours* for

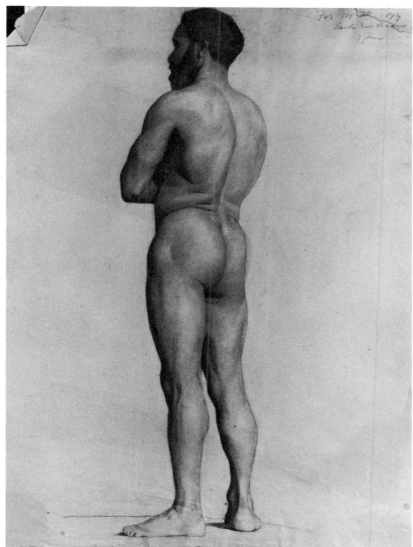

2.3 J. Alden Weir, Standing Male Nude, Viewed from the Rear, *1874, charcoal on paper, 24 × 18¾ in., inscribed at upper right:* Fev. 14ᵐᵉ 1874/École des Beaux Arts/3 jours *(Provo, Utah, Brigham Young University).*

the first time in March 1874, but he did not pass it until the following October, when out of one hundred sixty-two students, he placed thirty-first. (It was common for students to prepare as long as a year before passing the *concours.*) It cannot be determined in exactly which subsequent *concours* he competed; only the successful students are listed in the *jugements des concours,* not those who tried and failed or those who did not try at all. Weir placed fifty-eighth in the *concours* judged on August 24, 1875, and sixteenth on March 20, 1877. In the year-end competition judged on July 23, 1875, he was awarded a second-class medal for his work in Gérôme's studio during the 1874/75 academic year.[3] No first-class medal was given, so Weir's award made him the most outstanding student in the studio that year—an accomplishment for any student, but a formidable achievement for an American. When in January 1875 Weir's friend Edgar Melville Ward had received a third-class medal from the École, for drawing, *The American Register* had hailed him as "the only American to whom a medal has ever been awarded at this school:"[4]

The program of instruction at the École des Beaux-Arts during that period shaped the prevalent style and subject matter of painting, and made an entire generation, including

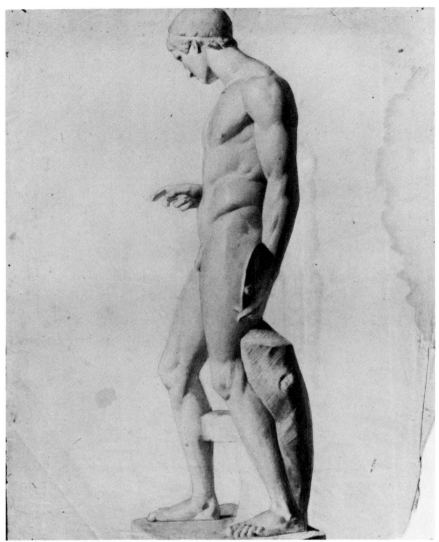

2.4 J. Alden Weir, Copy after Standing Discobolos *(Rome, Vatican Museums), probably 1875, charcoal on paper, 23¹³/₁₆ × 18³/₈ in., inscribed on reverse:* Alden-Weir/Éleve de M. Gérôme *and* 3/Weir/e. de M. Gérôme *(Provo, Utah, Brigham Young University).*

Weir, masters in the art of painting figures. Study of the nude at the École gave Weir and his fellow students a new technical command and the confidence to make the figure the principal subject of their paintings. The classroom exercise of the *académie* (drawing or painting of the nude) as it was executed at the École des Beaux-Arts was a major factor in the development of this new approach. Students drew and painted male and female nudes, some full-length, other *demi-figure*, working from different models each week.[5] While in many *académies* the backgrounds are merely suggested, in others the students seem to be striving for a pleasing composition: Weir, in his only known *académie*, *Study of a Male Nude Leaning on a Staff* (1876, fig. 2.1), has conveyed the model's function to the artists who study him by adding a second figure, a painter, in the lower right. The *académies* inevitably have compositional features in common; they focus on the figure, which is almost always shown in a scale large in relation to the size of the canvas. Weir's *Study of a Male Nude Leaning on a Staff* demonstrates this point. As in most student life drawings, the figure fills the available space; its head and feet touch the vertical limits of the canvas. Despite the similarities of subject matter and composition, these

2.5 *J. Alden Weir,* Copy after Jason *(Paris, Musée du Louvre), probably 1875, charcoal on paper, 24⁵/₁₆ × 18¹¹/₁₆ in., inscribed on reverse: 26/Alden Weir/e. M. Gérôme and Alden-Weir/eleve de M. Gérôme (Provo, Utah, Brigham Young University).*

exercises differed in style from one student to another. While Weir's *académie* is broadly painted, with little transition between the extremes of light and dark, one (1875, fig. 2.7) by his friend Pascal-Adolphe-Jean Dagnan-Bouveret (1852–1929), a student of Alexandre Cabanel's, is more highly finished, more evenly lit, and more smoothly modeled. Weir must have appreciated the subtle variations among these studies; he collected a number of *académies* done by his schoolmates and sent them back to his brother John for use in his classes at Yale.

As a member of Gérôme's studio and later as a matriculant, Weir must have been familiar with the students' assignments in all the programs, and would have seen how the various problems were solved. Many of the exercises would have prepared Weir to compose a serious figure painting. For the *concours Caylus*, for example, students painted a *tête d'expression*—a head whose aspect and expression conveyed a designated attitude or emotion. The students were expected to work quickly and to complete their task in three sessions of six hours each.[6] The exercise was the continuation of a long-standing academic process stretch-

2.6 J. Alden Weir, Drawing after a cast of an architectural ornament, *1873–
77, charcoal on paper, 23³⁄₄ × 18³⁄₄ in., inscribed on reverse at upper left:* 27/Weir;
and at upper right: Weir (Eleve de M. Gerome) *(Provo, Utah, Brigham Young
University).*

ing back to Charles Lebrun's treatise, *Méthode pour apprendre à dessiner les passions* (Paris and
Amsterdam, 1698), which illustrated standard formulas for artists to use in depicting expressions. While Weir was a student at the École, some of the subjects assigned for the examination were *La Fermeté* (firmness or steadfastness), *Le Sourire* (smile), *La Réflexion* (reflection or
thought), and *La Prière* (prayer).[7] Although none of Weir's academic studies can be identified
as the product of one of these assignments, his *Head of an Old Man* (1873–77, fig. 2.8) shows
that Weir had absorbed the academic principles behind the *tête d'expression*. In this oil sketch
Weir exaggerates the facial expression of his model, who gazes purposefully off to the side,
his mouth closed and his jaw set. He could be a personification of *La Fermeté*. In Weir's late
career, when he made a specialty of paintings of contemplative women, this part of his
training would have assumed an even greater importance.

At the École, students were also given compositional assignments, sometimes as a part of
the formal program—perhaps the *Concours trimestriel de composition sur esquisse* or the competition for the Prix de Rome—at other times, as an informal exercise. For the *Concours trimestriel
de composition sur esquisse* (compositional sketch), Adolphe Yvon assigned the subject, providing
a detailed commentary. The subjects were drawn almost exclusively from the Bible—the

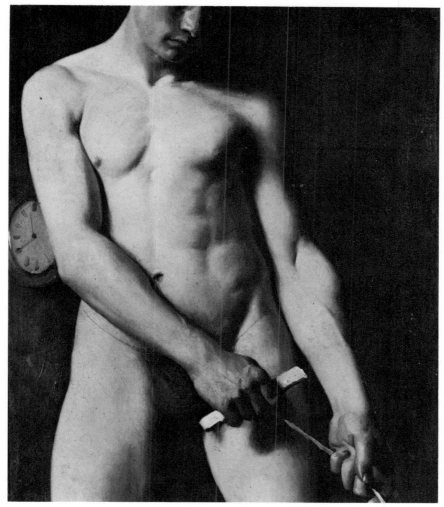

2.7 Pascal-Adolphe-Jean Dagnan-Bouveret, Nude, *1875, oil on canvas, 16 × 13 in., signed and dated at upper right: P. A. J. Dagnan—/1875 (New Haven, Connecticut, Yale University Art Gallery, Gift of Julian Alden Weir).*

resurrection of Lazarus; the burial of Sarah, wife of Abraham; Jesus crowned with thorns—or from classical history and mythology: Hecuba and her children; the death of Caesonia, wife of Caligula; the death of Hippolyte; Achilles at the home of the children of Lycomedes.[8] These were themes that had often inspired contemporary French painters. On January 11, 1875, for example, Yvon selected as the assignment "The Assassination of Caesar," which the École students could not fail to associate with Jean-Léon Gérôme's *Death of Caesar* (1867, fig. 2.9).[9] Yvon set forth the subject:

> Drawing their swords, the conspirators surround him on all sides. Like a wild animal cornered by hunters, he struggles against the blows they rain on him.
> But when even Brutus stabs him to the vitals, Caesar covers his head with his toga and surrenders himself to the conspirators' steel.
> By chance, or by design on their part, he was shoved to the base of Pompey's statue, which became bathed in his blood.[10]

Several of Weir's surviving small oil sketches of classical subjects may have been executed during this period. Among them are *Diana and Acteon* (probably 1873–77, New York, Hirschl & Adler Galleries) and *Nocturnal Scene with Male Figure* (probably 1873–77, fig. 2.10).

2.8 J. Alden Weir, Head of an Old Man, *1873–77, oil on canvas, 13 × 10½ in., unsigned (Provo, Utah, Brigham Young University).*

2.9 Jean-Léon Gérôme, The Death of Caesar, *1867, oil on canvas, 33¹¹/₁₆ × 57 ³/₁₆ in., signed and dated at lower left (Baltimore, The Walters Art Gallery).*

2.10 J. Alden Weir, Nocturnal Scene with Male Figure, *probably 1873–77, oil on wood, 14⅛ × 10 in., unsigned (Provo, Utah, Brigham Young University).*

Weir had the choice of three masters under whom to pursue his actual studio training at the École des Beaux-Arts. The studios in which painting students worked were then headed by Alexandre Cabanel, Isidore-Alexandre-Augustin Pils (later replaced by Karl-Ernest-Rodolphe-Heinrich-Salem [known as Henri] Lehmann), and Jean-Léon Gérôme. Prior to his departure from New York Weir had been attracted to Cabanel, whose work was well known in the United States.[11] He did not decide on the issue, however, until after he got to Paris. "The first thing I shall do now is to go about and look at the different masters and see what kind of students they have, and get with the one that I think I can learn most with," he wrote to his mother a few days after his arrival. Within three weeks, he had selected Jean-Léon Gérôme, a prominent academic French painter, as his instructor, and had enrolled in his studio.[12]

Weir's selection of Gérôme was a logical outgrowth of his previous experience and training. Gérôme's work was widely collected and appreciated in America. Lemuel Wilmarth, Weir's teacher at the National Academy of Design, had studied with Gérôme in the late 1860s and would very likely have discussed his Parisian experience with his students. Soon after Wilmarth became the Academy's first full-time instructor, in 1870, the Academy's council authorized the purchase of plates from a book on drawing that had been compiled by Gérôme's student Charles Bargue, written with the master's advice and illustrated with his drawings. At least one plate from this publication (fig. 2.11) is still in the Academy's collection.[13] George de Forest Brush, Henry Plumb, Walter Blackman, John W. Love, Frederick Gortelmeyer, and a number of other students who had begun their instruction at the Academy with Wilmarth continued their training with Gérôme when they went to Paris.[14] Wyatt Eaton, a student whom Weir had known in New York and whose opinion would have held some weight with him, had enrolled in Gérôme's studio almost exactly a year earlier. Weir's decision must also have been influenced by Gérôme's reputation as the most sympathetic to American students of all the French masters, but he mentioned only one reason for his choice and this was an aesthetic one: Gérôme's emphasis on draftsmanship. As Weir explained in a letter to his father, "[compared to Cabanel's students,] Gérôme's students are more on drawing."[15] This particular feature of Gérôme's teaching program was to remain a preoccupation of Weir's over the next four years.

Jean-Léon Gérôme (1824–1904),[16] who had himself been a student of Hippolyte (known as Paul) Delaroche and Charles Gleyre, taught at the École des Beaux-Arts for forty years. During the 1870s, when Weir was his student, he enjoyed tremendous popularity and success. He was specializing at that time in genre scenes, which were usually set in an exotic locale—most often North Africa or the Middle East—or in a historic era such as the classical period or the seventeenth century. Gérôme was an exacting realist whose detailed paintings reflect the thorough research and careful preparation that went into their creation. Gérôme's effect on Weir's development is not easy to assess, for it is difficult to isolate his influence from that of the overall program of the school in which he taught or that of the various artists to whom Weir was exposed during his four years in Paris. Although Gérôme was Weir's principal teacher, he was not his only one, even at the École. Further, while the École's three painting ateliers worked separately, they were in close physical proximity. Many École courses were attended by members of all the ateliers, a process through which Weir must have become familiar with the philosophies and teaching methods of Gérôme's colleagues Cabanel, Pils, and, later, Lehmann. Since many of Weir's friends studied with artists who conducted independent ateliers—mainly Carolus-Duran—he would have known the styles and philosophies of other teachers then active in Paris. A factual assessment of Gérôme's influence on Weir is also complicated by the lack of visual evidence. Much of the work Weir did in Gérôme's studio has been lost; indeed, many of Weir's most important Paris paintings, discussed in his diaries and letters, remain unlocated. Although Gérôme's art is fairly well known, he never compiled a cohesive account of his teaching practices or aesthetic opinions. Most of his random comments on these subjects either date from the final years of his career or are contained in memoirs written by his students long after their years of study with him.[17] During the time he spent in Gérôme's studio Weir mentioned him often in his letters to his parents and to his brother John. These letters and two somewhat vague written statements published by Weir much later give some idea of the nature of his continually evolving relationship with Gérôme.[18]

At first Weir was pleased with just simple encouragement from his master. Shortly before his formal enrollment in the studio (he had not yet registered, but was attending classes), he commented: "I keep so busy that I have no time to get blue and the criticism of Mr. Gérôme has encouraged me."[19] Later, as Weir became more aware of the inadequacies of his own work, he looked for more concrete advice from Gérôme, who was winning his increasing respect. As Weir's artistic abilities developed, Gérôme clearly became more interested in his student; in 1876 he presented Weir with a plaster cast of the portrait head that Jean-Baptiste Carpeaux had done of him.[20] This gift Weir immortalized in a drawing (about 1876, fig. 2.12) of the bust crowned with laurel leaves. (Shortly before leaving Paris for New York, Weir gave his master "a piece of sculptured marble" that he had found in Spain. Gérôme, he said, later "came up to me and thanked me very heartily and said he was sorry to

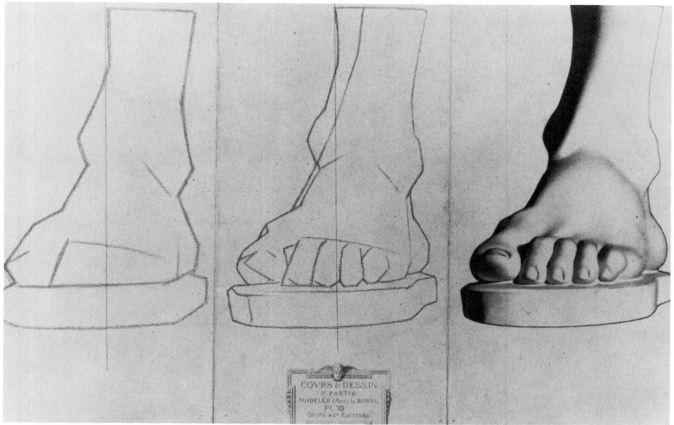

2.11 Jean-Léon Gérôme, plate 10, reproduced in Charles Bargue, Cours de Dessin par C.B., avec le concours de J.-L. Gérôme, *3 vols. (Paris: Goupil, 1868–70), 1,* Modèles après la bosse *(New York, National Academy of Design).*

2.12 J. Alden Weir, Jean-Baptiste Carpeaux's Bust of Jean-Léon Gérôme Crowned with a Laurel Wreath, about 1876, pen and ink on paper, 11⅞ × 9⅝ in., unsigned (Caroline P. Ely and Ann Ely Smith).

hear I was going to leave him. . . . I owe much to Gérôme which I can never repay and, had I the means, would have made him a regal gift.")[21]

Gérôme visited his class at the École only twice a week, usually on Wednesday and Saturday mornings, but his advice, however brief, was tremendously important to his students. Gérôme's involvement with them extended far beyond the classroom: in Weir's case, he not only reviewed his student assignments but also criticized paintings that Weir had executed independently in his rooms or during the summer months. When Weir was preparing works to submit to the Salon jury, he relied on Gérôme's suggestions. Weir's reactions to contemporary art and to the old masters were undoubtedly colored by Gérôme's opinions. Gérôme also advised Weir on trips he took to Holland and Belgium in 1874/75 and to Spain in 1876. Gérôme facilitated acceptance of his students' works when he served as a member of the jury for the Salon, and he promoted his French students as candidates for the Prix de Rome. He even became involved in their personal lives: it was he who interceded with Weir's father to allow Weir to make his trip to Spain and, on meeting Weir's patroness, Mrs. Bradford Alden, he praised her protegé highly. The breadth and depth of his relationship with Weir is astounding, especially when one considers the number of students who depended on Gérôme for similar advice and support.

The character and intensity of Weir's relationship with Gérôme must be considered in two different phases—first, the initial force that Gérôme exerted during the time Weir spent at the École and, second, his enduring influence on Weir's artistic development and philosophy. (Traces of that influence can be found even in Weir's late paintings, but it is most evident in his student work and that of his early years in New York, which continued to reflect an academic style.) Gérôme's shaping of the early stages of Weir's career can be seen in several major areas: in the young artist's concern with draftsmanship; in the changes in his palette, which lightened, yet generally remained gray and tonal; in his compositions, which were derived from those of his master; in his working method, which involved elaborate preparatory works prior to his executing the finished painting; and, most important, in his growing awareness of nature—whether the figure for its own sake or a specific landscape—as the basis of art.

Judging from Weir's letters home, he found Gérôme's method of instructing his students

2.13 Jean-Léon Gérôme, Pollice Verso, *1874, oil on canvas, 39½ × 58⅝ in., signed at lower right: J. L. Gérôme (Arizona, Phoenix Art Museum).*

2.14 *J. Alden Weir,* Interior—House in Brittany, *1875, oil on canvas, 29¾ × 32⅝ in., signed, dated, and inscribed at lower left:*
J. Alden Weir/Paris 1875 *(private collection).*

to draw from the figure impressive. For those familiar with the highly finished details of
Gérôme's pictures the manner by which he taught his students may seem out of character.
Gérôme appears to have emphasized the extreme contrasts of light and shade on three-
dimensional forms and the general movement of the figure rather than detail and high finish.
In describing Gérôme's drawing instruction, Weir noted that he made "his pupils practice
first in blocking in and drawing in outlines with merely the [principal] shade, striving entirely
for the action of the figure." The enthusiastic pupil continued: "He believes in leading the
student on slowly, not allowing him to finish up highly until he knows how to draw the figure
in well. Then by degrees he pushes one on in modeling and wants him to model and carry his

figures as far as he possibly can, but not to attempt this until he becomes acquainted with the figure and knows what he is about."[22] In adding three-dimensional modeling to the figure, Gérôme required beginning students to put in only the principal darks, leaving out the more subtle shading until the students were more advanced.[23]

The drawing technique taught by Gérôme can be seen as perpetuating the academic tradition that had shaped him during his own student years. Jean-Auguste-Dominique Ingres, that paragon of academic achievement in nineteenth-century France, had offered his students almost identical advice. Cautioning them to concentrate on line and mass when they began to work from life, Ingres noted: "The model's movement should be dashed off in a few lines and there should be no detail in the light and dark patches, or if there is, it should be subordinated to the two essential masses of light and dark."[24] The concern for capturing the totality of a subject, however, took a new direction after the reforms at the École in 1863, when its teaching practices were influenced by some of the more advanced instructors outside the institution. These men were encouraging their pupils to use simplified and abbreviated drawing methods in order to capture the ensemble in a more spontaneous and original way. This change of approach altered the drawing style practiced by École students: figure drawings became less fully finished.[25] Gérôme, who began to teach at the École after the reforms, must have been affected by these ideas.

A group of Weir's life drawings, most done in charcoal and some bearing dated inscriptions, are in the collection of Brigham Young University. His *Standing Male Nude* (probably 1873–77, fig. 2.2)[26] might have been drawn in Gérôme's studio; it certainly shows the effect of the working procedure set forth in Gérôme's illustrations for the *Cours de Dessin*. In plate 10 of the first volume (fig. 2.11), three drawings of a foot, shown in successive stages of completion, demonstrate his method. He first draws a plumb line, and around it summary lines that suggest the foot's contours; he next adds lines to indicate the strongest areas of light and dark value; and, finally, he finishes the drawing with more subtle areas of modeling. Weir drew *Standing Male Nude* in the same way. The position of the figure has been suggested by a series of three gently curved lines down the middle of the model's torso. The outlines of the figure

2.15 J. Alden Weir, Harvesters in Brittany, *1874, oil on canvas, 15 × 25½ in., unsigned (private collection).*

2.16 Photograph of Weir's party in Spain, 1876 (Caroline P. Ely and Ann Ely Smith).

have been blocked in with relatively short repeated strokes that create angular outlines, particularly in the less finished areas of the feet and the left hand. Parallel hatching lines begin the shading of the right forearm and the left leg from knee to ankle, but only the head and chest are fully modeled, and even here it is the overall effect that has been the artist's goal. The balance between the ideal and the real, however, has shifted; working in typical late-nineteenth-century fashion, Weir has depicted a person rather than an idealized or improved figure. The languid sensuality and specific facial features—the prominent cheekbone and nose and the arched eyebrow—mark this as a portrait of a closely observed individual.

Gérôme's own interpretation of the academic tradition, his commitment to an individual form of realism in particular, created a lasting impression on his followers. He himself studied the elements of his picture with almost archaeological thoroughness, and apparently urged his students "to study nature assiduously."[27] He would never have confused such a preliminary study with the finished work of art, which would transcend and improve upon its individual component parts. The duality in Gérôme's attitude toward nature has been explained:

> As a good academician, Gérôme could talk of imitating Nature accurately and at the same time ask for "structure, delicacy of modeling and purity of form" as a correction to pure, uncritical Realism. . . . Academicians have always walked the tightrope between imitation of nature and of the ideal, leaning one way or the other at various times. This was because they could very easily be foggy about whether they were talking about *nature* around us, or *la belle Nature* as revealed by thought and study.[28]

2.17 J. Alden Weir, Landscape at Toledo, *1876, oil on canvas, 7 × 8⅞ in., inscribed at lower left:* [illeg.] de Toledo (*private collection*).

There is no question that Weir absorbed Gérôme's point of view. Throughout his student years and later in his career, Weir always composed his pictures conscientiously, often working from preliminary sketches and then improving these studies and manipulating their elements to create carefully arranged and balanced paintings. As he observed during that first summer in France, "There is considerable difference between making a study and composing a picture."[29]

In a letter to his father, Weir expressed his admiration for the exacting character of his master's approach, particularly with reference to his *Pollice Verso* (1874, fig. 2.13). "To show how serious he is in his work; while he was at work on his gladiator picture the only suit of brass armor of the time was in Rome; he went down there, got permission to have it cast, came back here and had one made exactly after it, which cost him over three thousand dollars," he wrote. Gérôme's thoroughness informed a picture from its conception to its completion. When developing a major painting, he began with a study of the general composition. He then made studies of the individual figures, accessories, and settings that the picture would include. Weir's adherence to his master's method of working and to his advice to use nature as his model can be demonstrated by the two major pictures he worked on in Brittany during the summer of 1874, after only one year of study under Gérôme. In executing these paintings, *Interior—House in Brittany* (1875, fig. 2.14) and *Harvesters in Brittany* (1874, present location unknown), Weir chose native subjects, models that were as exotic and picturesque to the young American as Gérôme's Arab subjects were to him. The novice painter then worked toward his finished pictures through a process of careful research, observation, and preliminary studies. In order to get an authentic setting for *Interior—House in Brittany*, for example, he rented working space in the home of one of his models. He hired a woman to pose all day spinning, and he made studies, only one of which seems to have survived, to use for completing the picture back in Paris. On September 21, 1874, Weir wrote: "I have just been in my studio to make a sketch of the head of the old woman in the study of the spinning wheel picture; this is a little less than half the size that I have painted it." In Portrieux, Weir began *Harvesters in Brittany* (1874, present location unknown), an outdoor scene of Breton peasants threshing grain, and he continued work on it after he left. Following Gérôme's exacting method, he purchased his models' costumes so that he could take them with him and continue work on the picture uninterruptedly. After deciding on the subject, Weir first made studies for the principal group of eight figures, for the individual threshers, and for the landscape setting. The character of these studies is suggested by the only one now known (1874, fig. 2.15). It would have been painted outdoors on an overcast, gray day—the only sort of weather for creating the effect he wanted in his finished picture. When he began working on the final canvas, which was three feet by four in size, he carried it to the actual site of the buildings he had selected for the setting, and he painted there. A deep concern for fidelity to nature was thus firmly rooted in Weir's working procedure from the first summer he spent in France, and Gérôme's training must have been the major factor in developing his attitude.[30]

The work that most closely resembles that of Gérôme was done during the trip Weir took to Spain during the summer of 1876. Weir and his friend and fellow student the Italian Filadelfo Simi (1849–1923) made the trip on Gérôme's recommendation, and may have been joined on it by Gérôme's nephew Maxim Lafine. When Weir first mentioned the trip to his parents, he asserted that it would be made so that he could study the old masters, particularly Velázquez. He soon dropped this pretense and explained in a letter to his father that the trip had another purpose entirely, one which was dictated by his master. "Gerome said to S[imi] and myself . . . that we must not travel about too much, nor lose time in copying, that nature must be our aim and that we must make careful serious studies, observing the character of the people and their habits, and at the Alhambra we must collect material for future work," he wrote. He also described their preparations for the trip. He and Simi left Paris well armed for their study of Spanish life and culture. They took a camera, with which, Weir reported, they intended to make "photographies of the things we sketch, for the drawing, so that our time will not be taken up with the little work."[31] This method would not only have given them an accurate record of what they had seen but would also have allowed them to measure their realism in painting against the realism of the photograph. One of the few surviving photographs taken on this trip (1876, fig. 2.16) shows Weir's companions gathered around a table outdoors. It captures the details of the setting, the figures and their costumes, and the accessory elements with remarkable clarity. In subject and composition the scene recalls Gérôme's genre paintings of the Bashi-Bazouks, Turkish troops of the Ottoman Empire. In addition to taking photographs, Weir and Simi made oil sketches on small strips of canvas that they carried with them. A number of Weir's show sun-drenched Moorish architecture and landscape views that were clearly done in emulation of Gérôme's style. One of them, *Landscape at Toledo* (1876, fig. 2.17), is remarkably like the small oil sketches (Musée de Vesoul) that Gérôme painted on his trip to Egypt, Palestine, and Syria in 1868.[32] Like Gérôme's sketches, Weir's *Landscape at Toledo* is thinly painted. The preliminary pencil lines remain visible, and the canvas is sometimes left bare. In some areas, Weir has taken a pointed instrument, probably the wooden end of his paint brush, and incised lines in the pigment while it was still damp. Although crisply painted, with strong contrasts of light and dark, the sketch lacks detail. The artist has concentrated instead on the play of brilliant light falling on stone and sand and stucco walls. The shadows in the crevices of the rocks, which vary greatly in color and intensity, demonstrate particularly the degree to which the artist was studying natural effects. Throughout the trip, Weir felt Gérôme's presence strongly. As he wrote to his parents: "I think I can rightly say that I have never before worked with such energy and . . . made so much progress. I find the sayings of Gérôme true, which before I did not understand, and am therefore encouraged to work harder than ever. The tricks in the art which I acquired when beginning I find have prevented me from taking a hold rightly at once, but now that I am learning to see nature simply and to place the tone as near as possible at the first start, studying each brush mark, and abhoring nothing that I see, but [seeking] that all should hold its place in the grand mass—that a sharp line must be rendered sharp, and that a stone must be painted different from mud—in fact, each object has its own values."[33]

Weir made at least one major figure study, *Moorish Figure* (1876, fig. 2.18), while in Spain. It too was painted in Gérôme's style and by Gérôme's method. In September 1876

2.19 Jean-Léon Gérôme, Greek Slave, *1870, oil on canvas, 21¼ × 14½ in., unsigned (Gift of George A. Goddard, courtesy, Museum of Fine Arts, Boston).*

2.18 J. Alden Weir, Moorish Figure, *1876, pencil and oil on canvas, 18¾ × 11 in., signed with a monogram at upper left:* JAW *(Provo, Utah, Brigham Young University).*

Weir and Simi hired a gypsy model who had once posed for the Spanish artist Mariano Fortuny y Carbo. "We got permission from the proprietor, and posed him on top of the house, which is terraced as in these hot countries," Weir told his parents in a letter. "We had him from six till nine in [the] hot sun. His picturesque costume and fine head in full sunlight gave us a chance to search for that brilliancy of color which made Fortuny in that respect stronger than Gerome."[34] The subject—a Moorish figure armed, exotically costumed, and posed against a shallow, elaborately patterned backdrop—recalls figures in many of Gérôme's paintings. As a comparison between *Moorish Figure* and one of Gérôme's unfinished paintings, *Greek Slave* (1870, fig. 2.19), shows, Weir has used the same technique employed by his master in his oil paintings. Like Gérôme, Weir has brought his figure to a higher degree of completion than its setting. In both pictures, simple lines indicate areas that were to be finished later. The background is most resolved around the contour of the figure, with much of the setting merely suggested by the light touches of somewhat thin pigment.

Toward the end of his visit to Spain, Weir declared that his admiration for his master had grown. "I have appreciated him more this summer . . . than ever before," he wrote to his parents. In the same letter he laid out his plans for the remainder of his stay abroad. He would return to Paris and Gérôme; the following May, he would set out for Spain again. On this second trip, he said, he would "hope to paint my first serious picture" before visiting Italy and returning home. If Weir's European sojourn had ended as proposed, this "first serious picture," like the sketches he executed in 1876, would have shown the strong imprint of his master Gérôme.[35]

At the Water Trough (1876/77, fig. 2.20), the only major painting known to have resulted from Weir's Spanish trip, was probably painted almost entirely in Paris from studies. Only one study for the picture survives, an oil sketch (1876, Provo, Utah, Brigham Young University) that shows the setting without the figures and under slightly different lighting conditions. Weir hired models in Paris in order to complete the picture. "I have an Italian model coming, who poses in my little Spanish picture and am advancing it as fast as I could hope to," he wrote on February 8, 1877.[36] He certainly followed Gérôme's precepts in executing the painting, which is based on observation and on careful studies made in an exotic locale. Its composition uses several devices favored by the master. The figures are posed in a balanced pyramid on a shallow foreground stage and in front of a wall that not only limits spatial recession but also reflects brilliant light. In spite of the differences of subject matter, *At the Water Trough* could be compared to Gérôme's *Idylle* (1852, fig. 2.21). While Weir has reproduced his master's composition, he has attired his figures (in Gérôme's painting the figures of Daphnis and Chloe) in peasant costume and has replaced the graceful fawn with an awkwardly drawn child. In his painting Weir has abandoned the tight, linear quality that characterized so many of his Spanish sketches for a looser, more richly painted approach.

Although Weir mentions Gérôme's paintings often in his letters, their subject matter seems to have had little or no effect on his own works, aside from those he did in Spain. Subtle reminders of Gérôme's compositions nevertheless appear continuously in his early work. For example, the placement of the two figures in *Interior—House in Brittany* (1875, fig. 2.14) may have been inspired by Gérôme's composition for *Bashi-Bazouk Singing* (1859, fig. 2.22), where Gérôme places a single, self-absorbed, brightly lit figure in the right foreground of the picture. Figures to the left are cast into shadow and relegated to the middle distance; the wall behind them limits spatial recession. Weir follows a similar formula in *Interior— House in Brittany*. At the right, on a shallow foreground stage, a solitary woman spins; a male figure sits behind her on the left. As in Gérôme's composition, the foreground figure is well lit, while the figure in the middle distance is obscured by darkness. That Weir borrowed Gérôme's compositions rather than his painting style and that he chose as his models paintings Gérôme had sold and exhibited twenty years earlier suggest that he was familiar with the 1850s pictures through the innumerable reproductions of Gérôme's paintings made during the period.

2.21 *Jean-Léon Gérôme*, Idylle, *1852, oil on canvas, 83½ × 61½ in., signed and dated (Tarbes, Musée Massey).*

2.20 *J. Alden Weir*, At the Water Trough, *1876/77, oil on canvas, 17 × 14 in., signed at lower right: J. Alden Weir (Washington, D.C., National Museum of American Art, Smithsonian Institution).*

The other instructors with whom Weir studied in Paris had far less effect, either immediate or enduring, on Weir's development than had Gérôme. It is almost impossible to identify any contribution from Gustave-Clarence-Rodolphe Boulanger (1824–1888),[37] a substitute instructor with whom Weir worked at the École during Gérôme's absences and at his independent studio in April and May 1874.[38] Both Boulanger and Gérôme had studied under Paul Delaroche, and they chose similar orientalist subjects and worked in similar styles. Little is known about Boulanger's teaching methods, but it is logical to assume that he simply reinforced Gérôme's training and philosophy. Charles-François Jalabert (1819–1901), another substitute teacher at the École during Weir's attendance, was also a student of Paul Delaroche's. Lack of concrete information about this artist makes conclusions about his effect on Weir difficult to draw. He does not seem to have been an orientalist like Gérôme and Boulanger, although it is likely that he espoused similar artistic principles. Boulanger and Jalabert may actually have been appointed as substitute teachers precisely because of the artistic values they held in common with Gérôme.

The influence of Louis-Marie-François Jacquesson de la Chevreuse (1840–1903) was also minimal. Weir seems to have entered Jacquesson's studio simply as a stopgap when he was suspended from Gérôme's studio for two months, following a fight late in November or early in December 1873. (He had apparently violated the informal rules of the studio governing the

2.22 *Jean-Léon Gérôme,* Bashi-Bazouk Singing, *1859, oil on canvas, 18³/₁₆ × 26 in., signed at lower right (Baltimore, The Walters Art Gallery).*

"nouveau," or newly arrived student, by wearing a hat. He was attacked and he retaliated, causing a scuffle.)[39] His joining Jacquesson's studio was a temporary solution, and one undoubtedly chosen so as to avoid having to acquaint his father with the details of his suspension. Weir offered his family a number of explanations for the precipitous change in his educational plans. He claimed that the antique room at the École was "too cold and damp"; that the hours at Jacquesson's were more convenient than those at the École; and that Jacquesson spent five days in the studio offering criticisms compared to Gérôme's two.[40]

Jacquesson had been a successful student at the École during the late 1850s and early 1860s; he was reportedly a student of Ingres, of one of the Flandrins, and, perhaps, of Gérôme.[41] Jacquesson's studio was small, rarely exceeding twelve pupils. This intimate group included many Americans during the 1870s, among them John Ward Stimson, Robert Brandegee, Charles and Montague Flagg, Dwight William Tryon, William Bailey Faxon, William A. Coffin, Samuel Isham, and Paul Wayland Bartlett, several of whom are shown in a class photograph (fig. 2.23). Weir seems to have been directd to Jacquesson's studio by Stimson, whom he met in Paris. John Henry Niemeyer, who served with John Weir on the faculty at the Yale School of Fine Arts, had also been a student of Jacquesson's, and that may have further influenced the younger Weir's choice.[42] Even before leaving for Europe, Weir would undoubtedly have been familiar with Jacquesson's copy (present location unknown) of Thomas Couture's *Romans of the Decadence* (1847, Paris, Musée du Louvre), which Niemeyer owned and had lent to an 1873 exhibition at Yale. (Years later Weir contributed to a subscription to purchase the copy for Yale.)[43]

2.23 Photograph of the studio of Jacquesson de la Chevreuse, about 1877, showing the teacher with his students, including the Americans Robert B. Brandegee, Montague Flagg, and William B. Faxon (Collection of Robert Brandegee).

According to Jacquesson's more enthusiastic students, this French master seems to have offered regular, thorough criticisms, with particular attention to the needs of the individual student. In his studio, however, because drawing from the antique was emphasized, the students had a live model only one week a month. This was, of course, a reversal of the situation at the École, where the students worked from the model for three out of every four weeks. Jacquesson's method of life drawing can be seen by comparing Weir's *Standing Male Nude* (probably 1873–77, fig. 2.2), done in the style recommended by Gérôme, with Weir's *Nude Boy with a Pole* (1874, fig. 2.24), done in Jacquesson's studio. The pose of the latter model is far stiffer, a rigidity accentuated by Weir's drawing style. Outline was an essential part of Jacquesson's technique of drawing, and here the figure is surrounded by a continuous, firm pencil line that offers a marked contrast to the looser, overlapping lines defining the contour of the figure in the first drawing. Either the student or his master has corrected the outline of the model's torso, repeating the line along its right side. This drawing is also more highly finished than the other: Weir has represented the individual digits on the model's hands and feet; the ribs protrude in the torso; and the bones and muscles of the legs have been more fully realized. The actual technique of the two drawings differs markedly. While both are executed in charcoal, the drawing done in Jacquesson's studio makes greater use of the stump, a coiled piece of paper or parchment that the artist used to rub the charcoal and create shadowed areas.[44]

Weir's comments illuminate the philosophy behind Jacquesson's drawing method. As the young artist wrote to his brother John: "Jacquesson puts one in front of a cast and if one seeks the shape and action as I have been used to do with many lines, he wants to know 'what the use of so many lines is' and says the model has but one outline and that one must not attempt to draw it until he has studied each line and knows where to place it, drawing it in very carefully and studying each line, and after it is drawn in to begin, and now that you have studied the silhouette of its shape, go to work and study the silhouette of its form and carry it as far as it is possible to carry it."[45] This emphasis on contour and shape must have seemed retardataire to Weir, who had been studying the movement and form of casts and figures under Gérôme's direction; why Gérôme's influence was the enduring one on this aspect of Weir's work is easily understandable.

Jacquesson's was not the only independent studio that Weir considered during that first winter in Paris. While he was suspended from Gérôme's class Weir began to think seriously

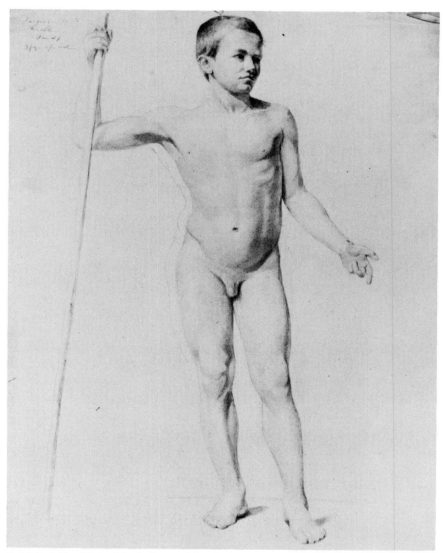

2.24 J. Alden Weir, Nude Boy with a Pole, *1874, charcoal on paper, 24 × 18⅝, inscribed at upper left:* Jacquessin de la/Ches[?]allin/Jan 29/3 figure apres [illeg.] *(Provo, Utah, Brigham Young University).*

of leaving Gérôme and enrolling in Carolus-Duran's studio.[46] Although a highly successful portraitist and the recipient of several medals, Carolus-Duran (1837–1917) was somewhat outside the French academic establishment. In works of his such as *Sleeping Man* (1861, Lille, Musée des Beaux-Arts), the informal subject, the rather unconventional composition, and the broad paint application ally him to progressive artists typified by Gustave Courbet and Édouard Manet, whom he had met after his arrival in Paris from Lille in 1855. In his teaching, Carolus-Duran was noted as a colorist and a proponent of painting rather than of drawing. He urged his students to take Velázquez as their model. Weir learned of Carolus-Duran's teaching methods from his several friends, among them James Carroll Beckwith (1852–1917) and, later, John Singer Sargent (1856–1925), both of whom studied with him. Certain aspects of his approach, particularly his emphasis on color, would have appealed to Weir, whose instructors Gérôme and Jacquesson de la Chevreuse stressed drawing almost to the exclusion of all else. "Carolus Duran, who is the greatest portrait painter of France of the present day, teaches his pupils still in a different way," he wrote to John. "He puts them in front of the living model with the brushes in their hands to represent the model as well as possible, making them draw and paint both at the same time."[47] In spite of his enthusiasm for Carolus-Duran's work, Weir hesitated to study with him because he believed that he needed additional training in drawing before he would be ready to work so extensively in color. When Weir attended an exhibition of the artist's portraits at the end of the year, his comments were far less positive. "I was very much disappointed with them, there were but two or three that I liked; they seemed brutal and vulgar," he wrote to his mother.[48] By the end of his first year of study with Gérôme he had become so committed to the academic ideals of his teacher that even the work of a moderate realist like Carolus-Duran was no longer acceptable.

In the spring of 1875, Weir again spoke of leaving Gérôme's studio, this time to study with Raimundo de Madrazo y Garreta (1841–1920),[49] who was then organizing a small class of twelve pupils. "Madrazo will be able to devote more attention than Gérôme, there will be more room, and I expect a better class of men," Weir wrote to his father shortly after William H. Stewart, an expatriate American art collector, had proposed the idea to him.[50] However, he soon had misgivings about this idea and, for some of the same reasons he had ultimately decided not to study with Carolus-Duran, he elected to remain with Gérôme. "I have thought a good deal of the idea that I entertained of leaving Gérôme, and now I only think of leaving during the time that he is away," he told his mother. "The last two times that he has been to the school he has seemed to speak so encouragingly, and advises me to be severe with my drawing. Knowing that this is my great weakness, I feel that maybe it would be a bad idea to go with one who would give me more freedom."[51] There is no record of Weir's having attended Madrazo's class, although he certainly maintained his friendship with Stewart and with his son Julius L. Stewart (1855–1919), who had studied with Madrazo and with the Spanish artist Edouardo Zamacois y Zabala (1842–1871) as well as with Gérôme. Weir may even have painted with Julius in his studio. The Stewarts' admiration for the modern Spanish school may have provided further impetus to Weir's desire to visit Spain, and may have been the reason for the brighter colors and bolder brushwork in some of his late 1870s paintings.

Weir also studied at the École Gratuite de Dessin, better known as the Petite École, during the winters of 1873/74 and 1874/75. The school, founded in the eighteenth century to train young workers in drawing and mathematics, had developed in the 1800s a program for teaching ornamental design. Its students could study anatomy, drawing (both from casts and from life), and the history of ornament. While the Petite École was ostensibly for the education of ornamental sculptors, it also served as a training ground for painters and sculptors who intended to move on to the more ambitious program at the École des Beaux-Arts but who lacked the artistic skills necessary to gain admission.[52] The working conditions at the school were as cramped and chaotic as at any of the Parisian studios. As Augustus Saint-Gaudens, who had studied there in 1867, about six years before Weir, wrote: "We worked in a stuffy, overcrowded, absolutely unventilated theater, with two rows of students, perhaps twenty-five in each row, seated in a semi-circle before the model who stood against the wall. Behind those who drew were about fifteen sculptors."[53]

A large contingent of Americans, among them some artists whom Weir knew well, enrolled in the Petite École around the same time. The largest group came from Jacquesson's studio, where Weir was then working. There were also George de Forest Brush and Douglas Volk, Gérôme's pupils, as well as pupils of Carolus-Duran's—James Carroll Beckwith and Will H. Low.[54] Any one of these students (or one of Weir's European friends, perhaps Alfred Berthoud, a Swiss artist also enrolled in the Petite École) could have interested Weir in the school. The reasons behind his enrollment, however, are evident. He began work at the Petite École during the period when he was suspended from Gérôme's studio. His attendance would have given him another concrete affiliation; moreover, it would have expanded his opportunities for working from life. This was particularly important, since Jacquesson, in whose studio he was spending his daytime hours, all but neglected life drawing. Then, too, the curriculum of the Petite École was particularly well-suited for the development of the basic artistic skills of drawing, anatomy, and perspective—skills Weir needed in order to pass the *concours* required for matriculation into the École des Beaux-Arts, unquestionably the goal toward which he was working.

How regularly Weir attended the Petite École or in which classes he was a student is not known, although in his letters he mentions studying with Amédée Faure (1801–1878), who in the École's records is designated as "Professeur de Dessins," and with Aimé Millet (1819–1891), "Professeur de Sculpture."[55] Millet was at the height of his success during the 1870s, when he was at work on a large sculpture group for the Paris Opera House. Not much has been recorded about his teaching theories. Some idea of his philosophy and values can nevertheless be gleaned from the comments he made during meetings of the *Conseil des Professeurs*. Millet described drawing from the antique as "our geometry," and regretted that whenever a model from the antique rather than a living model was assigned, there were "many fewer students in attendance."[56] He also advocated requiring beginning students to do copies from antique models. In spite of his enthusiasm for the antique, Millet recommended spending one of the five days allocated to it by studying instead plant shapes, which he considered particularly important for those students who planned to work in the decorative arts.[57]

Of all the courses offered by the Petite École, sculpture seems to have interested Weir the most. Even so, when describing his work in this medium he admitted that it was not really sculpture but "rather modelling in clay," which suggests that he considered his work a mere student exercise. He gave more details in a letter to his father: "I have for the past two weeks been at work on the head, first modelling the skull, then putting the muscles on. I am not making very rapid headway but I feel that what I do is the thing most necessary, the learning to draw correctly and knowingly." None of Weir's sculpture seems to have survived.[58]

There may have been another practical reason—an astute one—behind Weir's enrollment in the Petite École. His interest in studying sculpture and even the decorative arts coincided with an important development at the École des Beaux-Arts, where, since its reform in 1863, an interest in the synthesis of all the arts had been growing. In 1873, the year Weir arrived in Paris, the École had instituted the *cours supérieur d'art décoratif*, in which advanced students of architecture, painting, and sculpture were assigned comprehensive architectural projects that required their working together.[59] Weir would have had an opportunity to take part in such projects at the Petite École. In addition to drawing and modeling, he may have participated in the *concours* that tested students in decorative assignments. Among the *concours* assignments during Weir's time was one for a panel above a door in a natural-history museum requiring in its design a crocodile in reeds at the water's edge.[60] Irrelevant as such tasks might seem for an artist whose primary activity remained easel painting, they provided training that Weir could call on in later years when he occasionally undertook a decorative project.

Friends and Travels

In his first winter in Paris, Weir associated almost exclusively with fellow-American students, with whom he visited the Louvre, took Sunday walks in the Bois de Boulogne, and dined in small cafés. Among Gérôme's students, Edgar Ward, Wyatt Eaton, and George de Forest Brush seem to have been his most frequent companions. He also saw a good deal of his colleagues from Jacquesson's studio, especially John Stimson and Robert Brandegee, as well as three of Carolus-Duran's pupils—Robert Hinckley, Will Low, and J. Carroll Beckwith. That Weir sought companionship from his compatriots was only natural. It was a difficult year for him: he was still not fluent in French; he had been suspended from Gérôme's studio for two months; and he had been exposed to the rigors and disappointments of the competitive *concours* for the first time.

He had arrived in Paris with a number of letters of introduction, few of which he presented, for, as he explained to his father, "I have no time to call on the people I already know."[61] He approached his time abroad with the utmost seriousness, making social calls only about once every two weeks, and rarely attending the opera or the theater, two favorite

2.25 *J. Alden Weir,* Portrait of a Young Man, *probably 1873–77, oil on canvas, 35⅝ × 29⅛ in., unsigned (Provo, Utah, Brigham Young University).*

pastimes for art students in the French capital.[62] Outside of his fellow students, the only people he saw regularly were Mrs. Robert Anderson (the widow of the hero of Fort Sumnter) and her children, who frequently invited him for Sunday dinner.

Although Weir concentrated his efforts on classroom work during his first academic year, he was anxious to begin painting in earnest. Almost immediately he began to work independently on a few portraits of his friends and fellow art students, among them a Mr. Mason (possibly Henri Mason, an American student of Gérôme's) and Walter Blackman, both in November 1873; Mr. Bass, an amateur artist, in January 1874; Robert Hinckley, in February 1874; Mrs. Bass, and Arthur Douglas Peppercorn, an English art student, in March 1874.[63] These portraits, like many studio exercises, seem to have been lost, but *Portrait of a Young Man* (probably 1873–77, fig. 2.25) gives some indication of what these student works must have been like. Realistic and unpretentious and showing little concern for elaborate costume or setting, the portrait captures the sitter in a relaxed pose. It has not even been brought to completion; the sitter's hands are barely sketched in. Weir took some of these portraits to his mentor Gérôme for criticism. Gérôme's reaction to his portrait of Mr. Bass was not entirely negative: "Although he did annihilate it, he seemed pleased, and asked me to show it to him again, after I had some more sittings."[64] Weir's portrait of Mrs. Bass elicited a *"Ce n'est pas mal de tout, de tout!"*[65]

During the school year Weir had begun to make sketching excursions around Paris, visiting Saint-Cloud and Sèvres, Melun and Barbizon. By June he had decided to spend the summer months in Brittany working on a major composition for submission to the Salon. At

2.26 *Robert Wylie,* A Fortune Teller of Brittany, *about 1872, oil on canvas, 33⅞ × 47¾ in., signed at lower left:* R. WYLIE *(Washington, D.C., The Corcoran Gallery of Art, Museum Purchase).*

first he planned to visit Portrieux, a fishing village where Edgar Ward, Carroll Beckwith, and Douglas Volk were to join him. Weir arrived in Portrieux at the end of July, but he stayed only about ten days before leaving with Ward for Pont Aven. There they remained until the end of September working on peasant paintings and landscapes. For Weir and his fellow students, the most important artist then working in Pont Aven was Robert Wylie, an Anglo-American who had already established himself as a painter of Breton subjects.[66] *A Fortune Teller of Brittany* (about 1872, fig. 2.26) is typical of his work. Supposedly recorded from everyday life, this is a carefully staged scene of elaborately costumed peasants crowded in a dark interior, and each pose and gesture is calculated to enhance the drama of the picture. Wylie's dark palette, rich paint application, and tendency to spotlight figures against a dark ground all affected Weir's painting style in *Interior—House in Brittany* (1875, fig. 2.14), which Wylie saw in progress on August 30, 1874, Weir's twenty-first birthday. "He spoke very well of it and gave me considerable encouragement on my work," Weir wrote to his father. "He invited me to go to his studio and showed me all his work."[67] On this and on other visits to Wylie's studio Weir saw a great many of his pictures, among them his scenes from Breton history. Wylie was exacting in his study of costumes and accessories, and must have strengthened Weir's appreciation of the academic method he had developed under Gérôme's tutelage.

2.27 J. Alden Weir, Portrait of W. T. Norman, *about 1873–77, oil on canvas, 20⅛ × 16 in., unsigned (private collection).*

Weir made great progress in his studies during the winter of 1874/75, his second in Paris. He also worked extensively in his own rooms, mainly on two portraits for exhibition in the Salon the following spring. These he submitted under the name Julien Alden-Weir, because the jury reviewed the entries in alphabetical order and he believed that he stood a better chance for acceptance if his work was considered early in the deliberations.[68] His *Portrait de M. N.*, possibly *Portrait of W. T. Norman* (about 1873–77, fig. 2.27), was accepted. "It has given me a good name, being more difficult to get accepted this year with a portrait as two of the best portrait painters were on the Jury, Cabanel and Carolus Duran," he wrote to his mother.[69] Weir became increasingly anxious about the portrait after it was hung; he actually claimed that he "was almost ashamed to be seen varnishing it."[70] He was later pleased to discover that the portrait had been moved from its original place to a room which contained a portrait by Jules Bastien-Lepage, whose work Weir considered "the strongest" in the exhibition.[71]

Weir's horizons began to expand. He took his first long trip away from Paris from December 1874 to January 1875, when he visited Holland and Belgium. In Paris, he began to make many new friends among the international group of artists working there. During the winter of 1874/75 he shared his rooms at 5 rue du Pont de Lodi with Albert Edelfelt, a Finnish artist who had arrived in Paris the previous spring, and who recorded the appearance of their rooms in a watercolor sketch (1874/75, fig. 2.28).[72] Like Weir, Edelfelt was enrolled in Gérôme's atelier. They both became friendly with several of the more accomplished students at the École des Beaux-Arts, among them Bastien-Lepage, Pascal-Adolphe-Jean Dagnan-Bouveret, Gustave Courtois, and Joseph Wencker, who were all in the process of developing a powerful naturalism during that time.[73] Much of their philosophy and style had

2.28 Albert Edelfelt, Edelfelt and Weir in their studio, *sepia watercolor on paper, 11.8 × 18.5 cm., inscribed at top:* Rue du Pont de Lodi 5, au sixième/à 10 heures du soir; *and at lower right:* Les deux bonshommes que violà/Ils sont <u>Weir</u> et <u>moi</u>. *(Helsinki, The Art Museum of the Ateneum).*

been inspired by the instruction they received at the École des Beaux-Arts. Their working method stressed extremely diligent study before the execution of a painting and careful technical work during it; they made many studies before beginning, some of which were photographs for recording details with unwavering accuracy. They painted in a hard, precise style strongly influenced by the study of the old masters, especially the Flemish painters and those of the Italian Renaissance. As they began their mature careers in the late 1870s, they chose as their subjects scenes from rural French life, and they ennobled the peasants they depicted by endowing them with expressions that they believed conveyed religious sentiment or psychological mood. Most of their pictures were set outdoors in bright, generalized light, but unlike their impressionist contemporaries, who dissolved forms in light, these artists used it to articulate details and to emphasize three-dimensionality. This sort of painting was to occupy an enviable place in the French art of the 1870s and 1880s. Its heightened realism and humble subject matter made it attractive to younger, more progressive artists, while its exacting technique and moralizing sentiment satisfied conservative academic standards.

Bastien-Lepage was the undisputed leader of the group.[74] The circumstances of Weir's first meeting with Bastien are not documented, but the two were probably introduced by a mutual friend, possibly Joseph Wencker. Bastien studied with a different master, Alexandre Cabanel, at the École des Beaux-Arts, and was a far more advanced student, having been enrolled in the École since 1869. Weir's interest in Bastien is easily explained. In 1875 the French artist was the most outstanding student in Cabanel's studio; he had exhibited several acclaimed pictures at the Salon, *La Communiante* (1875, Tournai, Musée des Beaux-Arts) just previously; and he was a finalist in the competition for the annual Prix de Rome at the École. Weir's rapid acceptance into Bastien's group is more unusual. Weir, who had exhibited few works in Paris, must have won the respect of the French students on the strength of his school exercises and by the independent work he had done in Paris and Pont Aven. That spring Weir spent a significant amount of time as one of the artists in Bastien's circle. His letters from this period often mention having had dinner with the other students in a café, almost certainly Mademoiselle Anna's, in the rue Benoit, where Bâstien's Salon painting *La Chanson du Printemps* (about 1874, Verdun, Musée de la Principerie) was then hanging.[75] By the spring of 1875 the relationship between Weir and Bastien had ripened into friendship, and they remained close friends until Bastien's untimely death in 1884. Weir, the only American who seems to have been an intimate member of Bastien's circle, was among the artists who consoled him when he lost the Prix de Rome competition in July 1875. The following September Weir went with Dagnan-Bouveret, Courtois, Edelfelt, Wencker, an art student named Maysat, and the engraver Charles Baude on a visit to Bastien's home at Damvillers, a small village near Verdun in northeastern France.[77]

When the École closed for the summer at the end of July 1875, Weir decided not to return to Pont Aven, and went instead to Cernay-la-Ville, a village in Ile-de-France, southwest of Paris. Several factors influenced his decision not to return to Pont Aven. Of Brittany he wrote: "Everybody is going down there to paint Breton subjects this year, and I know I will learn more and be more serious if I remain with the Frenchmen."[78] Weir wanted to avoid the more social aspects of life at Pont Aven and to devote himself exclusively to his art. He also preferred the companionship of French painters to that of the Americans who were then flocking to Pont Aven. Cernay-la-Ville was a less popular artists' colony, although Weir mentions meeting several French artists, among them François-Louis Français (1814–1897) and Léon-Germaine Pelouse (1838–1891), who were there at the same time. The previous summer Weir had made studies for several pictures, only one of which, *Interior—House in Brittany* (1875, fig. 2.14), seems to have ben completed, but in the summer of 1875 he resolved to make only "three, large enough to keep me at work all the time, and by working in that way I think I search more after that [which I] formerly neglected, viz: to try and finish the studies as far as possible."[79] In his letters home Weir mentions the three paintings he began while in Cernay-la-Ville: "a landscape, portrait figure, and a small study of a girl sitting in a chair."[80] *Study of a Woman in a Brown Dress* (about 1875–76, fig. 2.29), may be the third of

2.29 J. Alden Weir, Study of a Woman in a Brown Dress, *about 1875–76, oil on canvas, 25½ × 18 in., unsigned (New Haven, Connecticut, Yale University Gallery, Gift of Julian Alden Weir).*

these. Weir's thinner, tighter paint application, his lighter, more tonal palette, and the contemplative mood of his subject show how strongly his work had been influenced by Bastien's. *Jeune femme* (1875, fig. 2.30), a small head of a child, was probably executed around the same time. In spite of its diminutive scale, this is probably the work Weir exhibited at the Salon of 1876 as *Tête de jeune fille, étude.* The most ambitious painting he undertook that summer was *The Oldest Inhabitant* (1875/76, fig. 2.31), a full-length portrait of an elderly woman in peasant costume that he had begun by September 10.[81] Weir's focus is clearly on the humble but dignified figure who stands on a shallow foreground stage with few accessory elements to distract the viewer's attention. Weir is obviously less concerned with costume and setting than he had been the previous year. The woman's well-lit face is framed by the white cap and apron she wears. Her frail physical condition—her right elbow rests weakly on the cabinet beside her and her left hand grasps her cane for support—is belied by her determined gaze. Weir's paint application is thick and bold; broad strokes of color have been applied side

2.30 J. Alden Weir, Jeune femme, *1875, oil on wood, 14 × 10⅜ in., inscribed in upper right: J./Alden/Weir/75, and——mi* AW[?]——/Autumn/1875/Weir J—— *(private collection).*

by side to create a lively paint surface. Weir did not complete *The Oldest Inhabitant* during his visit to Cernay-la-Ville, but returned to the village in November and during the following summer in order to finish it for the year-end exhibition at the École. The painting bears an inscription "carved" into the cabinet beside the woman. A curious blend of schoolboy French and English, truth and fiction, it reads: "July 4th 1876/La Plus Vielle de Cernay/ne le 4 Juin/1794." Weir probably wished to endow the painting with a significance beyond that of his subject's advanced age. The "July 4th 1876" does not refer to the date of the subject's death or the completion of the painting, for the model was still posing for Weir on July 5 and the painting was not finished until later in 1876. The only part of the inscription written in English, "July 4th 1876," may well be a reference to the American Centennial then being celebrated with a major exposition in Philadelphia.

In the autumn of 1875, after two years abroad, Weir began to make plans for the remainder of his time in Europe. He wanted to go home for a visit during the summer of 1876, and mentioned several reasons—to see his family and to spend some time with his fiancée, May Goodrich. (They had become informally engaged after meeting on his trip to

2.31 J. Alden Weir, The Oldest Inhabitant, *1875/76, oil on canvas, 66 × 32 in., signed and dated at upper left: J. A. Weir 1876, and inscribed at lower left (on chest): July 4ᵗʰ 1876/La plus Vielle de Cernay/né le 4 Juin/1794 (Youngstown, Ohio, Butler Institute of American Art).*

Minnesota during the winter of 1872/73.) He also planned to paint a portrait of his father and to see the Centennial Exhibition in Philadelphia. He proposed the visit as a prelude to returning to Europe for at least four more years.[82] Once back in Europe, he planned to travel to Italy to continue his study of the old masters. "I am wild to get to the land of art . . . to see the greatest of the great," he wrote to his mother.[83] After winning his medal at the École in July 1875 his resolve to remain abroad had deepened. He wrote candidly to his brother John: "I fear I will never return to America to live. When I do return it will be a visit if I am forced to stay even for ten years, but when I have amassed enough material in the way of knowledge and become possessor of such costumes and draperies as will enable me to paint the class of subject that has always been my dream, I will then hope to return to follow your example, but the gulf between this time and that is dark and the happy time may never arrive."[84] His parents opposed the idea of his just visiting and then returning to France, perhaps because they believed that once he came home Mrs. Alden would be unwilling to continue to finance his art education.

Weir was still attending the École des Beaux-Arts during the winter of 1875/76, but much of his energy was focused on his independent work. He concentrated on the paintings that he intended to submit to major exhibitions. In November, he began a full-length portrait of Miss Eba Anderson (present location unknown), which was ultimately accepted for the Salon of 1876.[85] Before beginning the actual painting he hired models to pose for the study of a nude that would serve as the basis for his model's figure. He then spent three weeks developing a preliminary drawing for the composition. As late as February 7 he had not yet begun to paint the actual portrait, and even then he devoted the first month of work to the background and draperies. It was not until March 7, about two weeks before he had to submit the portrait to the Salon jury, that he began to paint Miss Anderson's face and arms. In order to finance the models and materials needed for this painting, Weir accepted a commission to paint the portrait of an American child, Victor Thorn (1875/76, fig. 2.32).[86] The surviving preliminary works for it are further evidence of the care Weir took in the preparation of his paintings. A charcoal drawing of Victor's head (1875/76, fig. 2.33) is highly finished and fully modeled. A small watercolor sketch (1875/76, fig. 2.34) establishes the overall composition to be used in the eventual portrait.

In the early summer of 1876 Weir again visited Cernay-la-Ville, and after the École closed he made his trip to Spain with Filadelfo Simi. Returning to Paris, he settled in for what would be his last year at the École des Beaux-Arts. Only one major work can be dated to this period, At the Water Trough (1876/77, fig. 2.20). Although not totally satisfied with it—he considered "the composition . . . very ordinary in figures"—he sent it to the National Academy of Design in New York.[87] Anticipating his arrival in the United States and the necessity of developing his reputation there, Weir exhibited five works at the Academy in the spring of 1877: At the Water Trough; Washerwomen of Brittany (1874, present location unknown); Peasant Girl of Brittany, perhaps Study of a Woman in a Brown Dress (about 1875–76, fig. 2.29); Study of an Old Peasant, most likely The Oldest Inhabitant (1875/76, fig. 2.31); and an unidentified portrait. At first, Weir decided not to prepare a painting for the Paris Salon of 1877, preferring instead to "get several pictures ready for the Academy,"[88] but by March he was nevertheless at work on a portrait for the Salon. The work was either never submitted or was rejected, as it does not appear in the catalogue of that year's exhibition.[89] During that last winter, he associated even more closely with Bastien-Lepage and his circle and, under their influence, became a more exacting naturalist. These artists also encouraged his ever-growing interest in Italian Renaissance art; Weir reported that he was spending his evenings "in the Library, where I drink in the lives of the old Florentine masters, as well as the painters of the north."[90] He also worked outside Paris, again in Barbizon, where he painted the background for one of his pictures.[91] During the last months of his European sojourn, he was exposed to two artistic influences that would later have tremendous influence on his career. In April, he attended the third of the Impressionists' group exhibitions, which he described as "worse than the Chamber of Horrors."[92] In London, where he stopped to visit family and friends on

2.32 J. Alden Weir, Victor Thorn, *1875/76, oil (present location unknown)*.

2.33 J. Alden Weir, Victor Thorn, *1875/76, charcoal on paper, 19³/₈ × 12³/₄ in., unsigned (Provo, Utah, Brigham Young University)*.

2.34 J. Alden Weir, Victor Thorn, *1875/76, chalk and watercolor on paper, 3¹/₈ × 2¹/₄ in., unsigned (Provo, Utah, Brigham Young University)*.

his way home, he went to call on James Abbott McNeill Whistler, a former student of his father's who had already established himself as that city's leading avant-garde artist with his important series of nocturnes and figure paintings. Like any loyal student of the École des Beaux-Arts, Weir dismissed a portrait that Whistler showed him as "not positively bad but what one would take for a good ébauche or first painting."[93] Whistler was unwise enough to express his regret that Weir had studied with Gérôme, whereupon the young artist "'boo booed' in his face."[94] Weir was soon to revise his youthful opinions of Whistler and the Impressionists.

The Old Masters

During Weir's formative years in Paris, he made a careful, deliberate study of the old masters, which is recorded in his letters and diaries and in the copies he made after works by artists he admired. Later, when he returned to New York and began to work on original paintings, his emulation of the old masters exerted a lasting influence on the development of his painting style, his choice of subject matter, and his compositions. Typical nineteenth-century academic methods required a student's systematic copying of the old masters so that their positive qualities would be absorbed by him and reflected in his own work. When the work was completed, of course, its imitative features were obvious to the educated viewer, who admired rather than disparaged these reminders of the art of the past. While he was in Paris, Weir's taste for the old masters changed direction, perhaps, but continued to grow. During his youth, working under the influence of his father, he had developed an admiration for his father's muses, the Italian artists of the Renaissance and the Dutch and Flemish little masters of the seventeenth century. In Europe, his taste turned toward the painters then admired by members of the French realist movement—Rembrandt and Hals, principally, but also Rubens and Van Dyck and Velázquez. Late in his student years, Weir's admiration for Italian art was renewed, largely through his exposure to the lectures and writings of Hippolyte Taine, then professor of aesthetics and the history of art at the École,[95] and through his association with Bastien-Lepage. Weir's artistic enthusiasms were often to be influenced by his contemporaries; for him, as for most of the artists of his generation, the art of the present and the art of the past were inextricably linked.

At the École, Weir would have been expected to familiarize himself with the history of art not only by reading and by attending lectures such as Taine's but, more important, by actually studying and copying paintings, at the Louvre, for the most part, but in the galleries and museums of Paris and other European capitals too. Albert Boime, in his history of French academic method, distinguishes between two basic types of copies—academic and sketch. The academic copy was strictly imitative. Usually executed in oils after careful study, it was a literal reproduction of an existing work of art, the sort of work that the state commissioned for provincial institutions or for the Musée des Copies in Paris, a shrine to this aspect of the academic program.[96] Later in the century, when the original sketch in a variety of mediums was accorded greater emphasis in the academic curriculum, it acted as a counterbalance to the academic copy—a creative and generative work of art as opposed to an imitative and highly finished reproduction. The sketch eventually influenced the actual style and purpose of copies. When originality and spontaneity in painting techniques became the norm, copies were far less carefully realized. Instead of an attempt to duplicate a work of art in its finished state, they emulated the unfinished appearance of the sketch—the preliminary, or generative, phase. This was the aspect of the working process which late-nineteenth-century artists found most inspiring.[97]

The technique of Weir's oil copies varied widely; some are highly finished, others are extremely sketchlike. He seems to have altered his method of copying according to the choice of model: his copies after Hals and Rembrandt seem to be somewhat more hasty than are his copies after the Italian masters, whose original paintings showed a higher degree of finish than did those of the more painterly Dutch and Spanish artists.

Weir's copies were not limited to oils. He often made watercolor copies, some carefully studied, most just rapid pencil sketches with washes of color added. He may have colored the sketches after leaving a museum or gallery, for in some, preliminary notations about color are still visible: in his copy (1874/75, fig. 2.35) after *Portrait of a Young Girl* (Antwerp, Koninklijk muzeum van schoone kunsten), then attributed to Van Dyck, the penciled "blue" on the dress and "grey" on the sky can still be seen. His pencil sketch (1874/75, fig. 2.36) of Hals's *Marriage Portrait of Isaac Abrahamsz Massa and Beatrix van der Laen* (Amsterdam, Rijksmuseum)[98] illustrates his recording procedures. The basic poses of the figures are captured with little or no attention to details—the faces of the couple are simply blank ovals. Dark areas are suggested by strong, parallel diagonal hatching. The colors of the paintings seem to

2.35 J. Alden Weir, copy after Portrait of a Young Girl *(Antwerp, Koninklijk muzeum van schoone kunsten), once attributed to Sir Anthony Van Dyck, now believed to be by Erasmus Quellin and Jan Fijt, 1874/75, pencil and watercolor on paper, 3⁷/₁₆ × 2³/₈ in., unsigned (Caroline P. Ely and Ann Ely Smith).*

2.36 J. Alden Weir, copy after Frans Hals, Marriage Portrait of Isaac Abrahamsz Massa and Beatrix van der Laen *(Amsterdam, Rijksmuseum), 1874/75, pencil on paper, 4 × 5⅜ in., unsigned (Caroline P. Ely and Ann Ely Smith).*

have been noted last, in the most general terms: on the jacket and on the woman's skirt, "black"; on the foliage, "green"; and on the cloudy sky, "lighter." The generality seems to suggest that Weir planned to use the pencil sketches as visual notes on the compositions rather than as approximations of the style and colors of the paintings themselves.

Weir became enthusiastic about Frans Hals's work first. He would have had few opportunities to study Hals before going to Europe—the only painting he could have been familiar with was *Malle Babbe* (New York, The Metropolitan Museum of Art), which the museum acquired in 1871.[99] Weir's early ignorance of that artist is understandable, since his work was not "rediscovered" until the 1860s, but events in Paris just before Weir's arrival served to bring him to his attention. Thoré-Bürger's landmark articles on Hals appeared in 1868; the first genuine work by Hals, the *Gipsy Girl*,[100] was acquired by the Louvre in 1869; and W. Unger's lavish portfolio of etchings after Hals was published in 1873.[101] Weir saw Hals's paintings in Paris in an 1874 exhibition held at the Palais du Corps Législatif, after which he commented that he had taken "great pleasure in looking at all [Hals's] works."[102] Around this time he began to plan a trip to Holland and Belgium to study works by members of the Dutch and Flemish schools, especially those by Hals. This was not a chance decision; he was likely inspired by Gérôme, who himself had gone there just previously for the same reason. Although Hals's influence on Gérôme has been questioned by at least one scholar, there is no doubt that he was interested in the works of this master and that he encouraged his students to study them.[103] Gérôme certainly would have been attracted to Hals's subtle, tonal palette with its limited contrasts in value and hue.

Weir discussed his proposed trip with Gérôme at a student banquet shortly before the 1874 Christmas vacation. After dinner, when the teacher had retired to a reception room with his students for coffee and cigars, Weir approached him. "I told him that I was thinking of making a tour in Holland to see the works of Frans Hals," he wrote to his brother John. "He said he went there last summer for that express purpose and gave me some valuable information in regard to finding his best works."[104] When Weir returned to Paris, he brought his copies after Hals to Gérôme, who examined them and pronounced "that they were good."[105]

Weir traveled by himself in Belgium and Holland for nine days during the Christmas vacation, and was exposed to the largest possible number of Hals's paintings. The young artist visited museums and collections in Rotterdam, Haarlem, The Hague, Antwerp, Breda, and Amsterdam. He made a special effort to visit private collections of Dutch art, most of them amassed in the nineteenth century. There were two famous ones in Amsterdam—the Six collection, and the collection that Adriaen van der Hoop had bequeathed to the city in 1847. Weir also saw the Johan Steengracht van Oostcapelle collection in The Hague and, in Rotterdam, the remains of Frans J. O. Boymans's collection, which had been partly destroyed by fire in 1864.[106] Weir's enthusiasm for Hals became boundless. As he wrote to John shortly after his trip, "As genius of the first order, Frans Hals takes the palm."[107]

While Weir's letters and copies after Hals document his interest in that master, it is hard to know which qualities of Hals's style Weir admired most. Certainly he was fascinated by the originality of Hals's figural compositions. Most of his copies after Hals are simply small pencil sketches that record the placement of the figure within the picture frame. Echoes of these compositions and emulations of Hals's bravura brushwork appear regularly in Weir's early portraits and figure paintings. How much Weir actually knew about Hals and his working method is not clear, but he probably shared some of the common contemporary ideas about this artist. Many writers, including Thoré-Bürger, had commented on Hals's ability to complete works quickly. Whereas earlier writers had perceived this facility and its resultant lack of finish as faults, Thoré-Bürger presented them as achievements. In his oil copies of Hals's pictures, Weir seems to have affected the master's virtuosity, particularly in a copy which he made in the Koninklijk muzeum van schoone kunsten in Antwerp. He relates how he entered the gallery and introduced himself to a French artist who was making a copy: "Soon we became friends, and he told me that if I wished I could make use of his palette and colors, but said it would be impossible to do anything in so short a while; he had been at work at it for two weeks and had not finished the head, etc. However I accepted his kind offer and went out, bought a canvas and returned at about one o'clock. The guardian cleared the way for me and I lost no time. He returned in about a half hour and found me at work with the color. There were some six or seven people standing around me, and when the gentleman came up the guardian said to him in a confidential manner, 'He knows the road.' I finished the sketch at three."[108]

The sketchlike, unfinished appearance of Weir's oil copies after Hals confirms his attempt to emulate his idol's panache. Weir's copy (1874/75, fig. 2.37) after Hals's *Officers and Sergeants of the St. Hadrian Civic Guard Company* (about 1633, Haarlem, Frans Hals Museum)[109] is a good example: the animated group of figures is just blocked in, and only the most general suggestion of light and shadow is given. Facial features are but summarily represented, and details of setting and costume have been totally eliminated. Here, more than in any of Weir's copies, we are aware of his brushwork—he has applied the thick, creamy pigment in bold, strong strokes.

Another Dutch painter Weir greatly admired was Rembrandt, who even in the nineteenth century was accorded a special place in the history of Dutch art. His work was seen as representative of his nationality, yet exceeding that of his fellow countrymen. Rembrandt was praised for the diversity of his subject matter (unlike most of his contemporaries, he did not specialize in one genre) and for the worthiness of his subjects, particularly the poor, whom he depicted with great compassion.[110] As a youth, Weir must have been familiar

2.37 J. Alden Weir, copy after Frans Hals, Officers and Sergeants of the St. Hadrian Civic Guard Company, about 1633 (Haarlem, Frans Hals Museum), 1874/75, oil on canvas, 17³⁄₄ × 25¹⁄₄ in., unsigned (Charles Burlingham, Jr.).

with Hippolyte Taine's *Philosophy of Art in the Netherlands*. The translation was published in New York in 1871; he would have known John Durand, the book's translator; and his brother John had written a review of the book. Noting that Taine viewed Rembrandt as "the accepted type of art of this people," John Weir quoted the author's comments on Rembrandt's ability to represent objects by means of "the spot *(tache),*" and on his use of colors, which were "infinitely complex [because] every visual sensation is the product of its elements coupled with its surroundings." To Rembrandt, according to Taine, the principal feature of a picture is "the ever present, tremulous, colored atmosphere into which the figures are plunged like fishes in the sea."[111] Weir had probably begun his study of Rembrandt's work in his father's studio, where there were books about him, examples of his prints, innumerable reproductions of his work, and even a copy of one of his pictures.[112] Some paintings attributed to Rembrandt or copied from his pictures were also on view at The New-York Historical Society.[113] Nevertheless, it was in Europe that the young artist first had an opportunity to study a large number of original works by the Dutch master.

Weir commented favorably on the many Rembrandt portraits and figure paintings that he saw in London on his way to France, but the first picture to elicit an excited response from him was in Paris—*The Slaughtered Ox* (1655, Paris, Musée du Louvre), which had been acquired in 1857. "Lately France has bought a picture by Rembrandt which represents merely a piece of beef," he wrote to his patroness, Mrs. Bradford Alden. "This picture to me is one of the wonders there, it shows [itself] to have been painted by the hand of such a genius that it would be impossible to copy it. . . . When seen close by it is a puzzle, but viewed at a distance of about ten feet it looks like reality itself under the most picturesque light."[114] Rembrandt's paintings may have been the source of the soft, suggestive lighting of Weir's later still-life paintings, but *The Slaughtered Ox* had an immediate effect on him. Within a couple of months he had painted his own still life of raw meat—a leg of mutton (1874, present location unknown). In spite of his attempt to make the choice of his subject seem original, it was undoubtedly inspired by Rembrandt's. "As I passed the butcher on the way from the École I saw a fine leg, so I went in and hired it for two francs an afternoon," he related in a letter to his mother.[115] In 1874, the same year in which Weir undertook this still life, Rembrandt's picture inspired similar responses in François Bonvin and Antoine Vollon, both of whom painted pictures which feature raw, hanging meat.[116] The selection of such a realistic, almost brutal subject placed Weir outside the academic norm and allied him to the French realists, who were interested in themes that expressed the actual events of daily life. It is perhaps significant that Weir showed his still life of meat first to several students of Carolus-Duran, one of the more liberal Paris art instructors. Only after learning that these students "seemed to like it very much" did Weir bring the still life to his own mentor, Gérôme, for a critique.[117]

Gérôme may actually have nurtured Weir's interest in Rembrandt. While it is all but impossible to demonstrate Rembrandt's stylistic influence on Gérôme, he unquestionably admired the Dutch master. When asked to name his ideal painter, Gérôme responded: "A man, notable by his love of nature, his naïveté, his sincerity, that's Rembrandt, who because of these two masterful qualities is at the same time a great painter and a great poet. If he had some plastic sense, he would be absolutely without fault. As a master painter, he would be my ideal."[118] Gérôme also paid homage to Rembrandt in a painting (present location unknown) that showed the Dutch master working on an etching, which suggests that he particularly admired Rembrandt's work in that medium. Weir certainly shared Gérôme's enthusiasm; he collected etchings by Rembrandt that later exerted a telling effect on his own etching efforts.

With Rembrandt, as with others of the old masters, it is difficult to identify the specific aesthetic qualities that Weir admired most. His letters suggest that he was somewhat critical of Rembrandt's best-known paintings, for example, *The Company of Captain Frans Banning Cocq and Lieutenant Willem van Ruytenburch*, known as *The Night Watch* (1642, Amsterdam, Rijksmuseum). He noted in his catalogue that he was "very much disappointed in this celebrated work, not to be compared to Frans Hals's works at Haarlem." He was ambivalent about *The Anatomy Lesson of Dr. Nicholaes Tulp* (1632, The Hague, Mauritshuis). While remarking that it did not please him as much as some of the Rembrandt paintings he had seen in Amsterdam, he praised it as "a great work." His observations on the picture are revealing; he found that "everything was finished very highly and painted in a smooth and offensive manner, neat and clean without the atmosphere that one finds generally in his work, still the character and color of his heads as well as the cadence is admirably managed, and each a close study of nature." Weir's comment and his evaluation of *The Slaughtered Ox* demonstrate his admiration for Rembrandt's evocative use of light and his ability to envelop the figure in an "atmosphere" that unified it with its setting.[119]

Weir's reactions to other Rembrandt pictures, as well as his choice of works to copy, show that he preferred certain types of subject. In general, he liked Rembrandt's less elaborate group portraits. Of *The syndics: the sampling officials (wardens) of the draper's guild* (1661/62, Amsterdam, Rijksmuseum) he wrote: "The best picture I have ever seen of his; in it is all one could wish for; it is exceedingly rich and simple."[120] The subject matter of this painting—successful, middle-class merchants—must have appealed to Weir, for he does not seem to have been as attracted to Rembrandt's portraits of humbler, less affluent subjects. He chose more prosperous models for his pencil sketches after Rembrandt; for example, he made a drawing (1874/75, Caroline P. Ely and Ann Ely Smith) after Rembrandt's *Jan Six* (1654, Amsterdam, The Six Foundation). Weir's pencil sketch (1874/75, fig. 2.38) of Rembrandt's *Portrait of a Couple as Figures from the Old Testament*, known as *The Jewish Bride* (Amsterdam,

2.38 *J. Alden Weir, copy after Rembrandt,* Portrait of a Couple as Figures from the Old Testament, *known as* The Jewish Bride *(Amsterdam, Rijksmuseum), 1874/75, pencil on paper, 3¹³/₁₆ × 5¹³/₁₆ in., unsigned (Caroline P. Ely and Ann Ely Smith).*

Rijksmuseum), is a record of this intimate picture's composition, specifically of the tender gestures which join the famous couple. He finished his pencil sketch (1874/75, fig. 2.39) of Rembrandt's *Portrait of the Artist* (The Hague, Mauritshuis) in watercolor. The portrait, with its austere setting and dramatic light effects, shows the forceful character of the man who gazes directly out at us. Like most of his artistic contemporaries, Weir was clearly fascinated by Rembrandt as a personality.

Weir responded to the Flemish school far more equivocally than he did to the Dutch. The two Flemish painters who interested him most were Anthony Van Dyck and Peter Paul Rubens, both of whose work he would have known from his father's studio.[121] His reaction to Van Dyck was instantly laudatory. In England, he had seen Van Dyck's *Duke of Alba* (Warwick Castle), which left him "awe struck." Of this portrait he wrote to John: "I had been taking notes of the ones I saw, but when I stood in front of this I did nothing but look and if ever I have a chance to go to England again, I will make it a point to go there."[122] Although he made some pencil and watercolor copies after Van Dyck's portraits and religious works on his trip to Holland and Belgium, he rarely commented on Van Dyck thereafter. He had far more to say about Peter Paul Rubens. While at first he admired Rubens's color, he criticized his subjects, which he found "incomprehensible."[123] To the young artist, the Flemish master's works were "coarse" and displayed "a lack of feeling."[124] It is interesting that the one painting by Rubens that Weir is known to have copied (probably 1877 or 1881, fig. 2.40) is *"Le Chapeau de Paille"* (about 1622–25, London, National Gallery), a sensitive half-length portrait of Rubens's future sister-in-law Susanna Fourment Lunden, a work that seems somewhat restrained when compared with Rubens's more exuberant treatment of his religious and mythological subjects.[125] Weir's disappointment in Rubens was tempered somewhat during his trip to the Low Countries, where he saw some of the finest examples of Rubens's paintings. Of *Christ on the Cross* ("*Le Coup de Lance*") (Antwerp, Koninklijk muzeum van schoone kunsten), he wrote: "This for action is one of the strongest pictures I have ever seen. . . . All composes well and is strongly and really masterly painted."[126] Rubens's *Adoration of the Magi* (Antwerp, Koninklijk muzeum van schoone kunsten) he praised as "the finest Rubens I have ever seen; it is nature in a happy effect, well drawn and more seriously studied than his works generally are."[127] For Weir, however, Rubens was an example of "the first sign of the decadence of art"; he lacked "purity" and "sincerity," not only in the choice and treatment of his subjects but also in his contempt for the academic principles of drawing and design.[128] Had he developed these qualities, Weir believed, Rubens "might have ranked with some of the Italian masters."[129]

Weir's opinion of Velázquez,[130] one of the most popular old masters during the 1870s and 1880s, changed considerably during his years abroad. "From what I have seen of the Spanish painter, Velázquez, I admire, so that I look forward to the time when I can study him," he wrote to Mrs. Alden shortly after his arrival in Paris.[131] He equated the Spanish painter with his great idol Frans Hals, stating that these were the two artists whose work he

2.39 J. Alden Weir, copy after Rembrandt, Portrait of the Artist *(The Hague, Mauritshuis), 1874/75, pencil and watercolor on paper, 4⅝ × 3⅝ in., unsigned (Caroline P. Ely and Ann Ely Smith).*

2.40 J. Alden Weir, copy after Peter Paul Rubens, "Le Chapeau de Paille," about 1622–25 (London, National Gallery), 1877 or 1881, oil on canvas, 11 × 6¼ in., unsigned (Charles Burlingham, Jr.).

most wanted to study, since "these men's works are full of character and value of color, which constitutes good work."[132] In his first flush of enthusiasm over Velázquez, Weir actually described him as "Frans Hals in a little more refined state."[133] He made his trip to Spain in the summer of 1876 at least in part to study Velázquez's paintings. Although he was impressed by Velázquez's *Bacchus*, known as *The topers*, or *Los borrachos* (1628/29, Madrid, Prado),[134] Weir was not pleased by the other Velázquez works he saw in Spain. "Strange as it may seem to you, for the first time in my life I was disappointed in Velazquez. I had expected too much!" he wrote to his parents. "In his color and pose of a figure he is maybe the greatest, but his drawing there showed his uncertainty, and which now I regard as the greatest thing in the art, and which I feel is my weakest point."[135] A second visit to Madrid before he left Spain restored Velázquez as "the leader of the Spanish art" in his estimation.[136] Nevertheless, Weir's criticism of Velázquez's supposed lack of draftsmanship is meaningful. Drawing held an even more important place in Weir's estimation when he became interested in the painters of the Italian Renaissance again, and by the end of his European sojourn these masters typified to him all the best artistic qualities. And drawing was to remain the standard by which he judged both the art of the past and the present.

Weir's admiration of the Italians had been kindled by his father, who had studied in Italy and who revered Italian art, especially the works of Raphael and Titian.[137] After Weir's initial enthusiasm for the Dutch and Spanish masters, his interest in the Italians was gradually renewed. His attendance at Hippolyte Taine's lectures at the École des Beaux-Arts, his friendship with Bastien-Lepage and Filadelfo Simi, and the general enthusiasm for Italian art among his contemporaries accounted for this shift in attention. Taine considered the Italian Renaissance—specifically, the last quarter of the fifteenth century and about the first third of the sixteenth—a "glorious epoch." To him the artists working at that time, who included Leonardo, Raphael, and Titian, created a perfect art. That which had preceded it was "incomplete" (such artists as Giovanni Bellini were "dry, stiff and colorless") and that which came after it was "degenerate." Artists of a later epoch—for example, the Carracci—were mere "exaggerating disciples or defective restorers." According to Taine, "this perfect art" found its worthy subject in the human body, "the ideal human body, akin to the Greek type, so well proportioned and balanced in all its parts . . . that the whole forms a harmony." Landscape, inanimate objects, and reminders of everyday life received far less emphasis. Further, "as art becomes more perfect," more and more "literal exactness and positive resemblance" were to be avoided.[138]

Weir certainly shared Taine's admiration for Raphael and Titian. As he wrote to his mother, "Raphael has that in his work which I most need to study, the form, purity of drawing, and his grand composition. Even in a single figure by him he carries his composition to the full height, and the more I study the more I see that this is the only road, and the more I see that this is the only road, and the more I feel my weakness."[139] Weir's 1876 copy (private collection) of Raphael's *Cardinal* (about 1510, Madrid, Prado) demonstrates his concern for these artistic qualities. His brushwork is tightly controlled, with pigment applied in small, thin strokes; there is a crisp linearity usually absent in Weir's painting style. Here he was clearly emulating Raphael's draftsmanship in order to master its positive qualities. Weir found the same standard of draftsmanship in Titian's work. As he wrote to John, "Of the pictures I have seen here of Titian and the other great masters, their color takes third or fourth place."[140]

While Taine's lectures stimulated Weir's interest in Italian art, they did not always determine the direction that interest would take. In the spring of 1877, near the end of his European sojourn, he developed an enthusiasm for the Italian primitives, whom Taine had described merely as an imperfect prelude to the greater accomplishments of the late fifteenth and early sixteenth centuries. "I have been searching for something in my painting that before I detested," he wrote to his parents. "I make often trips to the Louvre to study the early Italian masters. . . . I find that which I greatly admire and which makes me regret much not having seen Italy."[141] In a portrait he was submitting for the Salon of 1877, he said, he was "working up under the influence of the primitives and the inspiration of Bellini. There is an excellent example of his (of two brothers) in the Louvre, done in a manner that shows more his love of his art, than the work of today, when one tries to astonish people with boldness."[142] Weir's copy of *The Doge Leonardo Loredan* by Giovanni Bellini (about 1501, London, National Gallery) displays the psychological tone and aesthetic qualities—lighter, more subtle colors, strong but delicate draftsmanship, and a general, clarifying light—that would be present in the best of Weir's early paintings.

Weir reached his decision to return to the United States only after it became apparent that he would not be able to make a visit home during the summer of 1876 and then return to Europe for additional study. Having acquiesced to his parents' wishes on this issue, he told them that he wanted to remain abroad for an even longer period of time. When his parents continued to press for his return, he strongly opposed their request. "Let this idea if possible drop. It would be a great loss if I should have to spend the next winter away from the schools. The more I study the more I see the necessity," he wrote to his mother.[143] As time went on, however, he no longer emphasized his school work. As he admitted, "I have felt less interest lately in my school work—that is to say I worked without the determinedness which I would like to."[144] He eventually decided to make the winter of 1876/77 his last at the École, and expressed his desire to visit Munich, whose students had achieved some reputation in Paris.[145] He also hoped to submit a major painting for the Paris Universal Exposition scheduled for 1878.[146] In the end, it was only his father's advanced age that convinced him that it was time to return home. "I feel it my duty . . . to return, to be if possible a comfort to Father in his old years. Nothing seems to me more sad than old age," he wrote to John.[147] He had not abandoned his hope of returning to Europe, however, with or without Mrs. Alden's support. "I will return abroad here again when I have some means of my own, if the time ever comes, to continue where I have left off."[148]

When Weir left Europe at the end of September 1877, he had already achieved far more than had most of his artistic contemporaries back home. He had studied for four years at the best art school in Europe, under one of the most esteemed living teachers. He had mastered figure painting, which would be his principal genre during the following decade. He had exhibited work in the Paris Salon, the most celebrated annual exhibition in the world. He was on intimate terms with several artists, among them Bastien-Lepage, who would rise to the forefront of French art during the late 1870s and early 1880s. Perhaps most important, he had developed a cosmopolitan point of view: he was committed to creating paintings that would be seen and appreciated by an international audience. In spite of his superior training and his achievements at the École and at the Salon, Weir still faced his return with some trepidation. "I am neither tadpole nor frog, which is a dangerous moment. To grow fast and learn to float, it must have the right soil and atmosphere as well as good instruction. This may strike you as a queer simile but a poor artist is less to be envied," he wrote to his parents.[149] No longer a student and not yet an established artist, Weir was about to return to New York and begin his serious career.

3

Early Years in New York
1877–1890

THE FIRST YEARS IN NEW YORK AFTER J. ALDEN WEIR'S RETURN FROM EUROPE SAW HIM emerging as a leader of the generation of American artists then coming home from Munich and Paris. He concentrated on ambitious figure paintings, but also did many portraits, occasionally commissioned, mostly of family members and friends. The international spirit of his work was reinforced by his repeated trips to Europe during which he kept up his friendship with Bastien and other Paris friends with whom he had continued to correspond. He began to specialize in large-scale still-life paintings obviously intended as major exhibition pieces; these combined rich, often antique objects with floral arrangements.

Several events during the early 1880s signaled a new era in his life and, subsequently, in his art. In 1882, he acquired a farm in Branchville, Connecticut; the following year, he married Anna Dwight Baker, whom he had met in New York. (His engagement to May Goodrich had been broken some years previously.) On their honeymoon, they went to Europe, a trip that would be Weir's last visit there until the end of the decade. From 1883 to 1889 the Weirs divided their time between New York and Connecticut, in Branchville and in Windham, where Anna's family had a farm. In those years, Weir began to develop a more individual style and more personal subject matter, producing several domestic genre scenes in which he depicted his wife and their first daughter, Caroline, who was known as Caro. Many of these are paintings and watercolors executed in an academic style, but some show the growing influence of such French realists as Jean-Désiré-Gustave Courbet (1819–1877) and Édouard Manet (1832–1883), whose work Weir may have been introduced to by Bastien-Lepage and his friends. Traces of realism can also be seen in Weir's still-life paintings of the time, which were smaller in scale, more intimate, and less finished. Landscape, while still a relatively minor part of his oeuvre, became more frequent. There too he responded to developments in French art, most notably to the style and subject matter of the Barbizon artists. Weir began to work more often in watercolor and pastel, secondary mediums in which his experiments resulted in radical innovations that were not to appear in his oil paintings until the 1890s. He also began a series of etchings, a technique that occupied his attention intermittently for a short period.

The year 1889 was a turning point in Weir's career. In February, Weir and John H. Twachtman (1853–1902), who had been friends since the late 1870s, held an exhibition and sale of their paintings and pastels that brought a group of Weir's works before the public. In the spring, Robert Weir, his father and first teacher, died. That summer the Weirs spent abroad, visiting first England and then France, where they attended the Paris Universal Exposition. When they returned to New York in the autumn, Weir's outlook was transformed: landscape became his major interest; his palette lightened noticeably; and many of his pictures assumed a sketchlike, unfinished appearance. He was on the threshold of the impressionist style that would characterize his work during the next decade, one of the first Americans to embrace the movement and one of the few who developed in an original manner under its influence.

When Weir arrived back in New York in October 1877, he found a city much more responsive to art and artists than the one he had left four years earlier. There had been an unprecedented growth in America of art schools, exhibitions, and organizations, partly stemming from the Centennial Exhibition held in Philadelphia in 1876, but unquestionably given its real thrust by the artists then returning from their studies abroad. These young men, who owed their inspiration to their European mentors and contemporaries, demanded a new level of technical accomplishment; they expected their fellow American artists to draw and paint with the facility they had admired in their European colleagues. Their subject matter was often European in origin, having little to do with American themes. They favored figure painting, a natural outcome of the emphasis on the study of the nude in their training. Their work took a new direction; figures were now embodiments of moods, sentiments, and feelings, rather than mere characters in anecdotal scenes. They made comparable changes in other genres: the grandiose panoramas of the Hudson River School gave way to a more intimate, interpretative mode of landscape painting, and the bountiful fruit and vegetable still lifes popular at mid-century were replaced by imaginative arrangements of flowers and decorative objects. Not unexpectedly, these aesthetic changes caused some conflict between the established artists and those of the rising generation, a rift that manifested itself most dramatically at the National Academy of Design. There, ongoing controversy over the acceptability of their work and the allotment of space at the annual exhibition moved some of the younger, more progressive artists to form in 1877 their own exhibition organization, the American Art Association, soon to be renamed the Society of American Artists.

While a student in Paris, Weir had often submitted paintings to the exhibitions held in New York at the National Academy, mainly to establish his artistic reputation at home. His first Academy exhibition piece, *Interior—House in Brittany* (1875, fig. 2.14), was shown in 1875. Two years later, when a relatively liberal Academy jury selected and hung more works by the younger painters, he was represented by five paintings, including *At the Water Trough* (1876/77, fig. 2.20) and *The Oldest Inhabitant* (1875/76, fig. 2.31). The display of these paintings may have served to introduce Weir to progressive painters working in America. Writing from New York, his painter friend Wyatt Eaton had assured him, "Your things in the Academy have attracted a good deal of attention & most favorable. You will find yourself less unknown in this country than when you left—& I believe that things will go easily with you."[1]

Eaton, a founding member of the Society of American Artists, may have been instrumental in electing Weir to that group on October 22, 1877, within a couple of weeks after his return from Paris.[2] When the Society (numbering twenty-four members) held its first exhibition, in 1878, Weir contributed seven paintings, mostly portraits and studies for portraits. For the next decade he was a regular contributor to the Society's shows, which were held annually except for a one-year hiatus in 1885. Weir was most active in the Society of American Artists during its early years: he was on the hanging committee in 1879, and served as secretary in 1880, vice-president in 1881, and president in 1882. One of several artists who furthered the international spirit that characterized the Society's early shows through the ties they maintained with American expatriates and European painters, it was Weir who wrote to

Mary Cassatt (1844–1926) to invite her to contribute to the Society's first exhibition. Her response reveals her support of the independent course taken by Weir and his friends. "Your exhibition interests me very much. I wish I could have sent something, I am afraid it is too late now . . . I always have a hope that at some future time I shall see New York the artists ground, I think you will create an American school."[3] In 1881, Weir was responsible for securing the loan of Bastien's *Joan of Arc* (1879, New York, The Metropolitan Museum of Art) from its owner, the collector Erwin Davis, who was later honored by the Society at a reception in Weir's studio.[4]

In spite of his involvement with the Society during the late 1870s and early 1880s, Weir continued to show his work at the Academy's exhibitions, although the paintings he displayed there differ stylistically from his contributions to the Society's shows. Those exhibited at the Academy are more tightly painted, with particular attention given to the anatomy of figures and to the surfaces and textures of fabrics and accessory elements. Their finished treatment contrasts with the heavy impasto and fluid paint application of his contemporaneous Society paintings, which sometimes resemble works by his Munich-trained friends Frank Duveneck (1848–1919) and William Merritt Chase (1849–1916).

The differences in choice and treatment of subject matter are most evident in the figure paintings that Weir contributed in that period to each organization's exhibition. In 1878, for example, he exhibited his *Robert W. Weir* (1878, fig. 3.1) at the National Academy while

3.1 J. Alden Weir, Robert W. Weir, *1878, oil on canvas, 46 × 36 in., signed at upper right: J. Alden Weir (private collection).*

3.2 J. Alden Weir, Study for Robert Walter Weir, *1878, oil on wood, 10¼ × 7⅞ in., unsigned (New Haven, Connecticut, Thomas Colville, Inc.).*

showing the study (1878, fig. 3.2) for it at the Society. Although the latter work was titled *Study for a Portrait*, thus acknowledging its nature as a preliminary exercise rather than a finished exhibition piece, Weir felt free to exhibit it at the Society's first show, for that exhibition organization seems actually to have encouraged its members to submit studies and sketchlike paintings—that is, works of unfinished appearance.[5] The differences between the genre paintings Weir exhibited with both groups are equally pronounced. Those he displayed at the Academy were almost exclusively peasant subjects in which he used poses, costumes, and accessory elements to convey an anecdotal meaning, often of sentimental overtone. Two examples are *Children Burying a Bird* (1878; color plate 1), which depicts three idealized peasant youngsters weeping over their dead pet, and *The Mother* (1884, fig. 3.3), which shows a young woman contemplating her sleeping infant. Weir's exhibition pieces at the Society were more daring. *In the Park* (about 1879, see fig. 3.4), shown in 1879, represented a group of urban types—a man reading a newspaper, a blind beggar, a poor flower seller, a fashionable woman, and two homely urchins—gathered in New York's Union Square, all arranged in a crowded frieze close to the picture plane. In the 1880 Society show Weir exhibited his most important religious painting, *The Good Samaritan* (1880, fig. 3.5), in which the wounded traveler lies prostrate in the foreground, a bold placement of the partly draped figure that heightens its effect. Weir's treatment of these subjects was outside the limits of the Academy's current aesthetic standards; it is even possible that his exhibition of such works at the Society delayed his election to the Academy.

Weir gradually became involved in the New York art scene. He joined the Tile Club, which was founded in 1877 by artists, architects, musicians, writers, and art enthusiasts who met regularly to decorate tiles. Each member was known by an amusing, appropriate pseudonym. Included in the group were Francis D. Millet (1846–1912), Arthur Quartley (1839–1886), Stanford White (1853–1906), and Augustus Saint-Gaudens (1848–1907) ("The Bulgar," "The Marine," "The Builder," and "The Saint," respectively). In addition to activities in their clubhouse on West Tenth Street, the members of the Tile Club went on excursions to the Erie Canal, to the shores of Long Island, and to Weir's farm at Branchville. Weir must have painted a number of tiles, but only one survives, the head of a Christmas elf (1878, East Hampton, Guild Hall). On Tile Club jaunts he also did oils: a portrait (private collection) inscribed "Cadmium," his Tile Club pseudonym; *The Daughter of the Tow*

3.3 J. Alden Weir, The Mother, *1884, oil on canvas, 44⅛ × 34¼ in., signed and dated:* JAW '84 *(private collection).*

3.4 Engraving after J. Alden Weir, In the Park, *about 1879, now divided into three separate canvases (see figs. 3.8–3.10) illustrated in* New York Daily Graphic, *March 8, 1879.*

(1879/80, fig. 3.7); a portrait of Arthur Quartley (present location unknown); and *The Tow Girl* (1879/80, fig. 3.8). In its unconventional composition—an attenuated female figure viewed obliquely from below—and its astounding freedom of execution, *The Tow Girl* demonstrates the liberating effect that the Tile Club group had on its members.[6]

By 1878, Weir and his friends Chase, Albert P. Ryder (1847–1917), William Gedney Bunce (1840–1916), and George Maynard (1843–1923), among others, had founded the Art Club, which was "intended to include the progressive art elements of the city."[7] The group met informally in each other's studios until 1883, when they moved into their own headquarters on Sixth Avenue. Although their exact activities have not come to light, they are known to have sponsored a Velázquez evening, when they and their guests gathered to discuss the large collection of photographs of that artist's works owned by Chase.[8] When the Society of Painters in Pastel was organized in 1883, Weir was listed as being among its seven founding members, although he did not show in the organization's first exhibition, which was held the following year.[9] Some of the same artists in the Society of Painters in Pastel, among them Weir, Bunce, Robert Blum (1857–1903), Edwin H. Blashfield (1848–1936), and H. Bolton Jones (1848–1927), founded yet another art organization, one dedicated to pen-and-ink drawing.[10] In 1884, Weir was elected a member of the American Water Color Society.[11] Few of these clubs were continuous in their existence or in their activities, but they nevertheless provided a forum in which the young artists could work together informally, profiting from mutual support that was especially invaluable in the first years after their return from Europe.

Weir soon followed his father and his brother John into their avocation of teaching. By

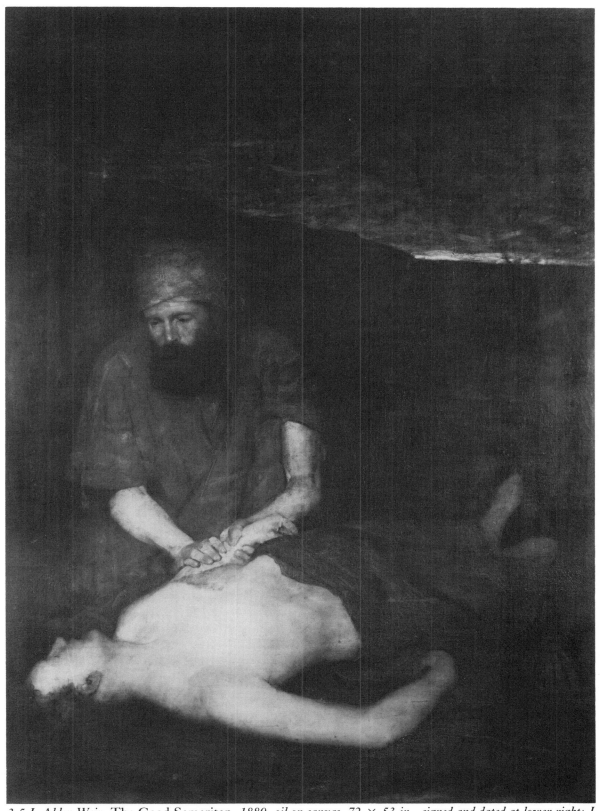

3.5 J. Alden Weir, The Good Samaritan, *1880, oil on canvas, 72 × 53 in., signed and dated at lower right: J. Alden Weir/1880 (Windham, Connecticut, St. Paul's Episcopal Church).*

3.6 Detail of J. Alden Weir, The Good Samaritan *(fig. 3.5).*

1878 he had taken over Eaton's antique and life classes mornings at the Cooper Union School of Design for Women;[12] he also conducted private classes in his studio during the winters of 1881/82 and 1882/83.[13] In addition, he joined the Art Students League, a teaching organization of artists and art students at whose monthly receptions the members took turns displaying their latest efforts. (In January 1880 Weir's work, including a landscape, was exhibited along with the decorative work of Charles C. Coleman [1840–1928].)[14] Weir gave an informal lecture to a composition class conducted by Thomas W. Dewing (1851–1938) at the League during the winter of 1881/82, and by 1885 he was a regular teacher there.[15] Although teaching absorbed much time he could better have spent on his own work, it did provide him with a regular source of income.

Figure Paintings

Weir's work during those early years continued to reflect his Paris training. His works of the late 1870s and the 1880s are filled with reminders of his favorite old masters, a fascination with the art of the past that was characteristic of many artists who had studied abroad, particularly those who had been trained in Munich. Weir's friendship with Duveneck and Chase must have reinforced this influence, which is particularly visible in Weir's portraits and

3.7 J. Alden Weir, Daughter of the Tow, *1879/80, oil on canvas, 17½ × 13½ in., unsigned (private collection).*

figure paintings. While none of his portraits borrow directly from old-master sources, the format of many of them can be traced to those in paintings he had seen in Europe. *Helen Weir Sturgis* (about 1878, fig. 3.9) recalls the early work of Frans Hals in the three-quarter, frontal pose of the figure; in its dark tonalities; and in its precise treatment of detail, which can be particularly well seen in the delicate fern. Weir's model is drawing on her gloves, and he emphasizes the gesture, thus imbuing it with an implicit movement. The portrait of Mrs. Sturgis, who was Weir's sister, could be compared to any number of female portraits by Hals, such as *Catharina Both van der Eem, wife of Paulus Beresteyn* (Paris, Musée du Louvre) or *Aletta Hanemans, wife of Jacob Pieterz. Olycan* (1625, The Hague, Mauritshuis).[16] Hals may also have been Weir's source for his portrait of *George Maynard* (about 1882, fig. 3.10). Executed on the occasion of Maynard's election as an associate member of the Academy, the subject is shown seated in a chair placed on an angle to the picture plane, resting his arm on the rounded chairback, and turning to face the viewer. The relaxed pose and Maynard's direct gaze make this a particularly telling portrait. Weir's composition may have been inspired by the one that Hals introduced in *Isaac Abrahamsz. Massa* (Toronto, Art Gallery of Ontario) and later explored in a number of male portraits, including those of two artists, *Frans Post* (Mrs. David Corbett) and *Portrait of a Painter Holding a Brush* (early 1650s, New York, The Frick

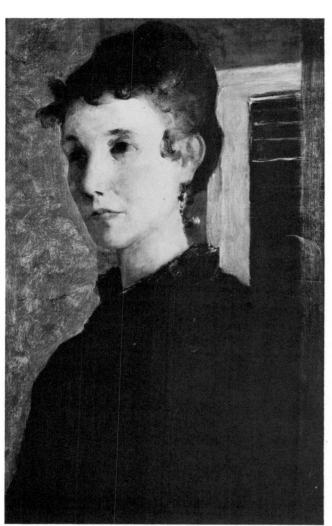

3.8 J. Alden Weir, The Tow Girl, *1879/80, oil on canvas, 20 × 12 in. (New London, Connecticut, Lyman Allyn Museum, Frank Loomis Palmer Fund, 1944).*

3.9 J. Alden Weir, Helen Weir Sturgis, *about 1878, oil on canvas, 49 × 36 inscribed at lower right:* J. ALDEN WEIR/PER D. WEIR *(Chattanooga, Tennessee, Hunter Museum of Art, Gift of M. R. Schweitzer, 1973).*

Collection).[17] *The Orange Ribbon (The White Cravat)* (1890, color plate 2), showing Weir's daughter Caro in a somber dress with a large white cravat around her neck, recalls several of Hals's portraits. Caro's studied frontal pose, especially the placement of her hand on her hip, her elbow raised, resembles that of Hals's models in such works as *Portrait of a Man* (about 1650–52, New York, The Metropolitan Museum of Art).[18] The Hals portrait belonged to the New York collector Henry Gurdon Marquand prior to his presenting it in 1890 to The Metropolitan Museum of Art, and, since Weir sometimes advised Marquand on purchases for his collection, he was probably familiar with it. Hals's influence can also be noted in a painting that Weir planned immediately after his student trip to Holland but never actually executed. On February 28, 1875, he wrote to his father about the picture, which he proposed to submit to the Centennial Exhibition in Philadelphia the following year. "What I have been thinking of was a group of the students here, those of character and promise; there are some fine heads among them and I think I could make an interesting group. I made a sketch which the students seemed to like."[19] In considering that group portrait, it seems logical that Weir

9. J. Alden Weir, *Olin Levi Warner*, about 1889, oil on canvas, 21 1/4 x 17 in., unsigned (New York, The National Academy of Design).

16. J. Alden Weir, *Anna and Caro in the Twelfth Street House,* 1887, pencil, watercolor, and gouache on paper, 17 1/2 x 13 1/4 in. (sight), signed and dated at lower left: J. Alden Weir/1887 (private collection).

9. J. Alden Weir, *Olin Levi Warner,* about 1889, oil on canvas, 21 1/4 x 17 in., unsigned (New York, The National Academy of Design).

10. J. Alden Weir, *Two Dogs,* 1885, watercolor on paper, 12 1/2 x 18 3/8 in. (sight), signed and dated at lower left: J. Alden Weir/85 (private collection).

11. J. Alden Weir, *Silver Cup with Roses,* 1882, oil on canvas, 12 x 9 in., inscribed on the rim of the chalice (with trompe l'oeil shadows, as if etched): To Anna Dwight Baker from J. Alden Weir, and on the body of the cup: May 18th/1882 N.Y. (Thyssen-Bornemisza Collection, Lugano, Switzerland).

12. J. Alden Weir, *Flowers,* early 1880s, watercolor and gouache on paper, 14 x 20 1/8 in., signed and dated at lower left: *J. Alden Weir* (private collection).

13. J. Alden Weir, *Roses with a Glass Goblet and a Cast of Giovanni Bologna's "Venus After the Bath,"* 1884, pencil, watercolor, and gouache on paper, 17 7/16 x 12 1/8 in. (sight), signed at lower left: J. Alden Weir/84 (New York, jointly owned by The Metropolitan Museum of Art and Erving Wolf Foundation).

14. J. Alden Weir, *Flowers on a Window Sill*, 1884, pencil, watercolor, and gouache on paper, 19 1/4 x 13 1/4 in. (sight), signed and dated at lower left: *J. Alden Weir/'84* (private collection).

15. J. Alden Weir, *Anna Sewing,* 1885, pencil, watercolor, and gouache on paper, 12 x 9 in. (sight), signed and dated at lower left: J. Alden Weir/1885 (private collection).

16. J. Alden Weir, *Anna and Caro in the Twelfth Street House*, 1887, pencil, watercolor, and gouache on paper, 17 1/2 x 13 1/4 in. (sight), signed and dated at lower left: J. Alden Weir/1887 (private collection).

3.10 J. Alden Weir, George Maynard, *about 1882, oil on canvas, 30 × 25¼ in., inscribed on the reverse:* G. W. Maynard/by J. Alden Weir *(New York, National Academy of Design).*

would have planned to follow the example of Hals's civic-guard portraits, which he had copied (1874/75, fig. 2.37).

Weir's emulation of Hals was most demonstrable in his major painting, *In the Park* (about 1879, see fig. 3.4), which was divided into several smaller and less controversial canvases after its exhibition at the Society of American Artists in 1879. Three fragments of the composition are known: *Wyatt Eaton* (fig. 3.11), *The Flower Seller* (fig. 3.12), and *Union Square* (fig. 3.13).[20] Only two of Weir's figures in the original *In the Park* group possessed the elegance usually associated with academic painting during the period. These were the seated man (actually the artist's friend Eaton) reading a newspaper, and the pretty young woman who advanced toward him from the opposite side of the picture. The two were approached by several figures, all of whom represented the lower echelons of New York society. A small girl selling flowers stood between Eaton and the woman; behind them were three male figures. In the center of the composition, directly behind the flower seller, was an elderly blind beggar who carried a cane and wore a sign announcing his sightless condition. Two additional male figures flanked the pretty young woman: on her right, a middle-aged man with a sack; on her left, a young man who read from the circular he held. In the distance, Weir painted an urban

3.11 J. Alden Weir, Wyatt Eaton, *about 1879, oil on canvas, 31¼ × 18⅛ in., signed at upper left:* J. Alden Weir *(Washington, D.C., National Museum of American Art, Smithsonian Institution, Gift of William T. Evans, 1915).*

3.12 J. Alden Weir, The Flower Seller, *about 1879, oil on canvas, 40⅞ × 22⅝ in., signed at upper left:* J. Alden Weir *(New York, The Brooklyn Museum, Gift of George A. Hearn, 1911).*

3.13 J. Alden Weir, Union Square, *about 1879, oil on canvas, 30 × 25 in., signed at lower right:* J Alden Weir *(New York, The Brooklyn Museum, Museum Collection Fund, 1926).*

view—tall tenements, a fence, and a few trees. The background probably resembled the view of buildings in the street scene, *Snowstorm in Mercer Street* (1881, fig. 3.14). Several aspects of Weir's composition related closely to Hals's genre scene *The Merrymakers at Shrovetide* (fig. 3.15).[21] Weir had seen the painting during his student years; it was shown in an 1874 exhibition he attended at the Palais du Corps Législatif in Paris. A similar subject, *Young Man and Woman in an Inn (Jonker Ramp and His Sweetheart)* (1623, New York, The Metropolitan Museum of Art),[22] was in the well-known collection of Adriaen van der Hoop which Weir visited during the winter of 1874/75. Obviously impressed by its adventurous, active composition, he made a quick sketch (Caroline P. Ely and Ann Ely Smith) of it at the time. Both Hals paintings depict groups of figures in a constricted space and on a shallow foreground stage. Weir almost duplicated the arrangement of the figures in *The Merrymakers at Shrovetide* in the right side of his composition of *In the Park*, where he surrounded the beautiful young woman with male figures that in Hals's work are revelers. Hals also exerted some influence on

3.14 J. Alden Weir, Snowstorm in Mercer Street, *1881, oil on wood, 23¾ × 15½ in., signed at lower left: J. Alden Weir (private collection).*

3.15 Frans Hals, Merrymakers at Shrovetide (The Merry Company), *oil on canvas, 51¾ × 39¼ in., signed (on flagon): fh (New York, The Metropolitan Museum of Art, Bequest of Benjamin Altman, 1913).*

Weir's style. The extant fragments of the picture are executed in a bold, fluid manner, making frequent use of the strongly contrasting colors that typify Hals's palette. *Laughing Boy* (about 1879, fig. 3.16), a study for the figure on the far right of Weir's composition, suggests that he may have turned to his quick pencil sketches of some of Hals's other paintings in developing his individual figures for *In the Park*. The painting style and the arrangement of the figure resemble any number of single male figures then attributed to Hals (although some were later discovered not to be his), from which Weir made copies (1874/75, Caroline P. Ely and Ann Ely Smith, and fig. 3.17). These included *The Serenade* (Amsterdam, Rijksmuseum), which was actually by Judith Leyster, and *The Fool* (Amsterdam, Rijksmuseum), a copy by an unknown artist after Hals's *Lute Player* (Paris, Baron Alain de Rothschild).[23]

Why would Weir have chosen Hals as his model for a scene so evidently drawn from contemporary life? The answer lies partly in Hals's subject matter as it was interpreted in the late nineteenth century, primarily in the writings of Thoré-Bürger (Théophile Thoré), the art critic and connoisseur who in the 1860s rescued Hals from oblivion. Thoré-Bürger argued for the acceptability of contemporary subjects in the art of both the seventeenth and nineteenth

3.17 *J. Alden Weir, copy, 1874/75, after a copy, artist unknown (Amsterdam, Rijksmuseum), of Frans Hals,* Lute Player *(in the collection of the Baron Alain de Rothschild, Paris), pencil on paper, 3⅝ × 3 in., inscribed by Weir at lower middle: F. Hals (Caroline P. Ely and Ann Ely Smith).*

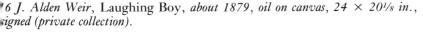

J. Alden Weir, Laughing Boy, *about 1879, oil on canvas, 24 × 20⅛ in., signed (private collection).*

centuries. According to Frances Suzman Jowell, who has explored this subject in depth:

> Bürger places great importance on the fact that Hals' images were drawn from the people around him and his interpretation of Hals depended on assumptions about the naturalism of Hals' paintings, naturalism as Bürger understood the term. He assumed that Hals painted scenes from contemporary life around him, capturing the expressions and moods, gestures and movements of people as they appeared in life, in all their variety, without the trappings of allegorical concerns, and free from reference to other pictorial images or stereotypes.[24]

Today's scholars have presented a convincing argument for iconographic meaning in Hals's pictures, but Thoré-Bürger and his contemporaries ignored the possibility of that content. To them, gestures and accessories were simply elements conceived in nonchalance and happenstance; the paintings, mere scenes of everyday life in seventeenth-century Holland. Weir undoubtedly shared their misconception, as evidenced by a somewhat unfortunate poem he wrote in praise of the master. In comparing the northern Hals to the southern painters Titian and Tintoretto, who had been "spurred on with encouragement to the height which they gained," Weir observed that "you, great Frans Hals, have reared here in your art / Among a people where poetry shares not a part."[25] Weir, who greatly admired the seemingly everyday quality of Hals's works, saw it as an outgrowth of the Dutch middle-class environment in which Hals labored. His ideas about the origins of Hals's subjects and painting style had probably been formed by Taine's lectures on the history of art at the École des Beaux-Arts, for Taine had developed a theory that an artist's ambience was a powerful determinant in shaping him, and that there was a direct causal relationship between ambience and painting.[26]

Hals was not the only seventeenth-century master whose paintings influenced the development of Weir's figure style during those early years. Works like his *Portrait of a Child* (1887, color plate 3) show that he continued to study old-master paintings until late in the decade. This portrait of Caro was inspired by such works as Sir Anthony Van Dyck's *Portrait of a Young Girl* (Antwerp, Koninklijk muzeum van schoone kunsten), which Weir had copied (1874/75, fig. 2.35) during his student years, and his study of Rembrandt may have spurred his interest in a more intimate form of portraiture. His portrait of his mother (about 1885, fig. 3.18) bears a strong resemblance to Rembrandt's *Portrait of an 83-Year-Old Woman* (1634, London, National Gallery), which Weir had copied in 1877 or 1881 (fig. 3.19). The frontal, bust-length pose, austere black-and-white costume, and light green backdrop of Rembrandt's portrait are duplicated in Weir's. Weir's *Self-Portrait* (1886, color plate 4), with its dramatic lighting and rich paint application, must have been affected by Rembrandt's style of portraiture. Not just the composition but the sitter's serious expression and intense gaze are particularly reminiscent of Rembrandt's self-portraits, such as the one in the Mauritshuis collection that Weir had copied in 1874/75 (fig. 2.39). Even some of Weir's more bravura paintings are replete with old-master borrowings. In *Boy Polishing a Brass Jug* (late 1870s–early 1880s, fig.

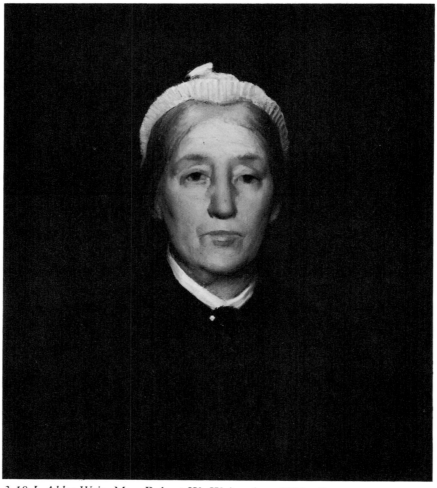

3.18 J. Alden Weir, Mrs. Robert W. Weir, *about 1885, oil on canvas, 24 × 20 in., unsigned (California, Los Angeles County Museum of Art, Gift of M. R. Schweitzer Gallery, 1972).*

3.19 J. Alden Weir, copy, 1877 or 1881, after Rembrandt, Portrait of an 83-year-old woman *(London, National Gallery), oil on canvas, 23⅞ × 20 in., unsigned, canvas stamp:* PREPARED BY / WINSOR & NEWTON, / 38 RATHBONE PLACE, / LONDON *(Charles Burlingham, Jr.).*

3.20), the figure's hairstyle, costume, and facial type, as well as its placement close to the picture plane, could have been inspired by elements in works by Spanish painters—for example the figures in Velázquez's *Waterseller* (about 1619–20, London, Wellington Museum) and *Two Young Men at a Table* (about 1622, London, Wellington Museum).[27]

The effect that the Italian Renaissance painters had on Weir's work is not as easy to measure, although a painting such as *The Black Lace Dress* (1885, fig. 3.21) suggests that Weir had studied Renaissance portraits closely. Like many quattrocento sitters, the model is shown in profile, silhouetted against a patterned tapestry background. The gesture of her raised hand is self-contained; her gaze, contemplative. Among Weir's genre scenes, the most obvious example of the Italian influence may be in *Children Burying a Bird* (1878, color plate 1). Weir seems to have begun work on this picture during the summer of 1878, when he was once again painting in the French countryside at Cernay-la-Ville. He wrote to his father about the picture, "in which I have sought for expression & inspired myself much by the recollection of certain primitives which I saw when I was in London last."[28] The influence of Weir's study of Italian and, perhaps, Flemish primitives can be seen in many aspects of this picture—in the tight, highly finished paint application, the delicate jewellike colors, and the mannered figure style. Weir's figures assume contrived poses, which he has orchestrated self-consciously. As a comparison between the kneeling little girl and the study for her head (1875, fig. 2.30) shows,

3.20 J. Alden Weir, Boy Polishing a Brass Jug, *late 1870s–early 1880s, oil on canvas, 25⅛ × 29⅞ in., unsigned (private collection).*

Weir has idealized the features of his models in order to intensify their expressive power. This emotional quality lends a heroic note to the children and their sad task.

The influence of Jules Bastien-Lepage on Weir's work is readily seen in *Children Burying a Bird*. Features in it that are typical of Bastien's paintings are the high horizon line, which forces the viewer to confront the figures posed on a shallow stage in the foreground; the cool, silvery palette; and the transported expressions of the figures' faces. Further, Bastien often depicted scenes that endowed the life of the peasant with spiritual or emotional significance; here too Weir has followed his example. On his 1878 trip to France, Weir undertook two other peasant subjects, whose whereabouts are no longer known: *The First Step*, which depicted a child beside a woman churning butter outdoors, and *Interior of a Carpenter's Shop*, which showed a carpenter at work at his bench, his head silhouetted in the light of the window.[29] These would likely have demonstrated Weir's regard for Bastien the artist equally strongly.

Bastien influenced any number of Weir's figure paintings during the late 1870s and early 1880s. The pose of the girl in Weir's *Daughter of the Tow* (about 1880, fig. 3.7) is like that of the principal figure in Bastien's *La Chanson du Printemps* (about 1874, Verdun, Musée de la

3.21 J. Alden Weir, The Black Lace Dress, *1885, oil on canvas, 36 × 30 in., signed and dated at upper right: J. Alden Weir—1885 (private collection).*

Princerie), which Weir would have seen at the Salon of 1874. Weir has copied Bastien in choosing an outdoor, sun-filled setting; he also emulates the light colors often associated with Bastien's outdoor work. Even Weir's allegorical paintings were strongly affected by Bastien's example. The figures in Weir's *Death* (1886; fig. 3.22), an illustration for a poem by Robert Burns Wilson, and in *The Open Book* (1891, Washington, D.C., National Museum of American Art)[30] are both plainly based on Bastien's allegorical figures—for example, his *Muse* (1875–76, fig. 3.23)—and on contemplative figures in such peasant paintings of his as *Joan of Arc* (1879; fig. 3.24) and *Les Foins* (about 1878, Paris, Musée du Louvre). In both *Death* and *The Open Book*, Weir borrows the compositional device that is characteristic of almost all Bastien's landscape settings—a horizon that rises vertically nearly to the upper edge of the canvas. Weir uses this feature also in his own landscape work. Beginning with *Lengthening Shadows* in 1887,[31] the high horizon line appears in many of his pictures of the rocky Connecticut countryside. Again taking after Bastien, he often silhouettes trees or buildings against the lightened sky.

3.22 J. Alden Weir, Death, *1886, pencil and ink, grisaille gouache on paper, 8³⁄₈ × 5³⁄₈ in., signed at lower left: J. Alden Weir. fecit. 1886. (Provo, Utah, Brigham Young University.)*

23 Jules Bastien-Lepage, The Muse, *about 1875–76, oil, signed at lower ʔt:* BASTIEN-LEPAGE *(Helsinki, The Art Museum of the Ateneum).*

3.24 Jules Bastien-Lepage, Joan of Arc, *1879, oil on canvas, 100 × 110 in., signed, dated, and inscribed at lower right:* J. BASTIEN-LEPAGE/DAMVILLERS—Meuse/*1879 (New York, The Metropolitan Museum of Art, Gift of Erwin Davis, 1889).*

Such commissioned portraits of Bastien's as *Portrait de M. Wallon* (about 1876, fig. 3.25) affected many of Weir's more formal portraits. In *Robert W. Weir* (1878, fig. 3.1), for instance, Weir has painted his seated father in a three-quarter-length pose, his gaze directed at the spectator and his hands shown in a natural, relaxed manner. Weir has produced a realistic portrait that, as Bastien's do, concentrates on the sitter's facial expression; setting and costume are given relatively little attention. Bastien chose a more striking composition for his *Portrait de Mme. Sarah Bernhardt* (1879, Montpellier, Musée Fabré) and this Weir used as his model in *Flora (Carrie Mansfield Weir)* (1882, color plate 5), which presents Weir's sister as a nineteenth-century version of the Roman goddess of flowers. The model is shown in a profile pose similar to Bernhardt's (although facing in the opposite direction). The actress wears a shimmering, light-colored dress, and so does Carrie, who is posed close to the picture plane and in front of a flat, reflective backdrop, slightly gray in color. Carrie is surrounded by a still life—a garland of mostly white and pale yellow roses and a tall silver cup—which repeats the light colors and glistening paint application of both backdrop and costume. The sitter's face and hands are emphasized; they are the only warmly colored, fully modeled areas on the canvas. In his Bernhardt portrait, Bastien continued the experiment with a narrow range of grays and whites that he had started in *La Communiante* (about 1875, Tournai, Musée des Beaux-Arts), a portrait of a young girl wearing the white dress and veil of her first communion. At Bastien's request, Weir had made a copy of *La Communiante* (1876, present location unknown), and he certainly saw the portrait of Sarah Bernhardt, if not at the Salon of 1879 then at an exhibition at Grosvenor Gallery in London the following year.[32] These works unquestionably inspired the lighter palette and unusual composition of Weir's *Flora*. Later, Bastien's *Communiante* served as the inspiration for Weir's three-quarter-length portrait of Caro (1887, fig. 3.26), which shows the little girl in a white dress and coat and posed in an almost identical frontal position. In his picture, however, Weir has used a bright red background, which lends a warm color note absent in Bastien's.

3.25 Jules Bastien-Lepage, Portrait of M. Wallon, *about 1876, oil (France, Musée de Versailles)*.

Weir's friendship with Bastien remained strong until the artist's early death. He probably saw Bastien in Paris in 1878 and 1879; the following year he visited Bastien's family at Damvillers and purchased the artist's *Joan of Arc* (1879, fig. 3.24) for Erwin Davis. It must have been in those years that Weir and Bastien discussed buying a house in the French countryside where they could work together.[33] Weir did not see Bastien again until 1883, although they continued to correspond and Weir, as he mentioned, often saw Bastien's works in exhibitions.[34] In 1883, he invited Bastien to visit him in New York, where they planned to paint together in Weir's studio. Bastien predicted at that time a great future for art in America. "America is in an exceptional position for forming an original and unconventional school of painting. She is not fettered by tradition as we are," he told an interviewer.[35] The proposed visit apparently never took place, since Bastien's health was declining rapidly. He died in 1884, a staggering loss to Weir, who considered him his closest European friend. (Bastien's death accounted largely for Weir's diminishing interest in foreign travel.) A month later, Weir presented a lecture on Bastien at the Art Students League and in 1887 he joined with Millet and Saint-Gaudens to collect American contributions to a fund for erecting a commemorative statue to Bastien at his village, Damvillers.[36]

3.26 J. Alden Weir, Caro, 1887, oil on canvas, 24¼ × 20⅛ in., signed at upper left: J. Alden Weir—87 (private collection).

In the early 1880s, Weir was painting peasant pictures that were far more conservative than those Bastien was doing in the same period. Weir's dark palette and rich paint application attests that he was again finding inspiration in the work of the Anglo-American artist Robert Wylie, who had died in 1877.[37] Weir's *Milkmaid of Popindrecht* (1881, fig. 3.27), painted during a summer visit to Holland, is one of his most ambitious peasant subjects. It was exhibited in 1882 at the Academy, where it was cited as "one of the best pieces of work he has ever shown" and praised as containing "little of the immature quality of some of his early work."[38] The model, clearly a member of the Dutch working class, is shown leaning against a wooden door, her left hand placed stolidly on her hip. Dressed in picturesque Dutch costume, the young woman is posed on a narrow, foreground stage and surrounded by glistening brass pots. Her pose and placement recall that of Weir's model in *The Oldest Inhabitant* (1875/76, fig. 2.31); *The Mother* (1884; fig. 3.3) employs some of the same devices. In the latter, the principal figure, a young mother in peasant dress, sits beside the cradle that holds her baby. She grasps a book, presumably a prayer book, in her right hand, and, with her left, makes a gesture that leads the viewer's attention to her face and its peaceful expression. Both the mother and the cradle are positioned directly confronting the spectator in the foreground

3.27 J. Alden Weir, The Milkmaid of Popindrecht, *1881, oil on canvas, 76½ × 51 in., unsigned (Provo, Utah, Brigham Young University).*

on a shallow stage. These are the last of Weir's European subjects; even *The Mother* may have been done from an oil sketch of a child (1874, Provo, Brigham Young University) and from a drawing, *The Little Sabot* (1882, Provo, Brigham Young University), both of which Weir had done earlier. Shortly after 1883, when he made his last important European trip, this type of subject matter disappeared from his work forever.

Weir undertook at least one important religious painting in the 1880s, *The Good Samaritan* (1880, fig. 3.5). The painting shows the Samaritan leaning over a half-clad man in the foreground and looking out into the space beyond the picture plane. The two figures are linked by the Samaritan's gesture: with both hands he grasps the limp arm of the unconscious traveler. The theme was a common one in French art of the period; Weir's arrangement of the two characters is not unlike that in a painting by Théodule-Augustin Ribot (1823–1891) of the same subject (about 1870–75, Pau, Musée des Beaux-Arts).[39] Weir has placed his recumbent figure in the foreground, diagonal to the picture plane, in a manner that recalls Gérôme's earlier depictions of dead or dying figures in such paintings as *The Death of Caesar* (1867, fig. 2.9) and *Death of Marshal Ney* (1868, England, Sheffield City Art Galleries). The similarity in

Weir's and Gérôme's paintings was obvious to their contemporaries: when *The Good Samaritan* was exhibited at the Society of American Artists, in 1880, one reviewer noted that Weir's placement of the traveler "compels a strong foreshortening, like that of the dead Caesar in Gérôme's well-known picture."[40]

Since *The Good Samaritan* is the only major religious painting Weir is known to have painted, a natural question is: Why did the artist embark on such a subject at this stage in his career? Some tentative answers come to mind. *The Good Samaritan* offered Weir an opportunity to depict a partly nude figure, something he had wanted to do since his student days. The inclusion of this figure, as well as the presentation of a meaningful subject done on a large scale, made the painting an appropriate choice for submitting to the Society of American Artists's 1880 show, where many members of the Society exhibited pictures featuring nude and partly nude figures.[41] Weir's Samaritan appears to be a portrait of Albert Pinkham Ryder (fig. 3.6), a close friend of his and a founding member of the Society. Through Ryder, Weir probably knew Robert Loftin Newman (1827–1912), a French-trained painter who made a specialty of religious subjects. He may have inspired this exploration of Weir's of a religious theme.[42]

Weir also painted at least two allegorical subjects at around the same time: *The Muse of Music* (1881/84, fig. 3.28) and an unidentified painting of a woman dressed in classical costume and wearing a crown that is featured in a photograph (about 1883, Provo, Brigham Young University) of Weir's studio at the Benedick, a newly opened studio building where many of the younger artists worked. Weir spent an unusual length of time on *The Muse of Music*. It was exhibited as *Music* at the Society of American Artists in 1881, when one writer criticized the artist's choice of model. "We make no objection to his passing by Beauty, but if we agree to that sacrifice we have a right to insist on character as the only substitute," he commented.[43] Perhaps as a result, the man who had purchased *The Muse of Music* demanded that the head be repainted. Weir responded, "As I have decided to do no more than I have done, it may remain in my possession."[44] Relenting the following year, he began to rework the picture, making extensive changes in the head. He reduced its overall size, softening and idealizing the features and altering the hair and crown. *The Muse of Music* nevertheless remained unsold until 1884, when it was purchased by Ichabod T. Williams, who displayed it in the newly renovated music room of his New York residence.[45] Weir's picture is one of many nineteenth-century allegorical paintings of the Muses. He was probably acquainted with Joseph Fagnani's series, *The Nine Muses*, which was exhibited in New York during his youth and purchased by The Metropolitan Museum of Art in 1874. The Muse *Polyhymnia* in the series could have suggested some of the accessory elements seen in Weir's picture: the lute the Muse holds and her gesture of placing her hand, one finger extended, against her head. The ultimate inspiration for Weir's picture, however, was Sir Joshua Reynolds's *Sarah Siddons as "The Tragic Muse"* (about 1784, San Marino, California, Henry E. Huntington Library and Art Gallery). Weir admired Sir Joshua wholeheartedly; he studied his works carefully, first from engravings and later, in Europe, from the originals, and his Muse copies the enthroned pose, the gesture, and intense gaze of Reynolds's model.

In the mid- to late 1880s, Weir's figure subjects began to take on a new appearance. He turned to contemporary themes, but instead of the coarse types he had depicted in *In the Park* (about 1879, see fig. 3.4) he chose more intimate subjects: his wife and, later, their daughter Caro. These works are often large-scale in composition, with life-size figures usually occupying the foreground, placed close to the picture plane. Although they are basically academic in conception and execution, they represent a compromise between academic ideals and the more progressive art that had begun to attract Weir's attention around 1880. His pictures of this period correspond to what Albert Boime has described as the *juste milieu* ("middle-of-the-road") art of France's Third Republic. In the late 1870s, responding to the influence of Impressionism, many French painters rejected the tight, highly finished paint application practiced by such academicians as Jean-Léon Gérôme and Jean-Louis-Ernest Meissonier

3.28 J. Alden Weir, The Muse of Music, *1881/84, oil on canvas, 44⅜ × 34½
in., signed vertically at lower right: J. Alden Weir. 82–84 (California, The Fine
Arts Museums of San Francisco, Mildred Anna Williams Collection).*

(1815–1891), and strove for a new technical freedom. While retaining strong draftsmanship,
particularly in their treatment of figures, they sometimes blurred contours and painted
sketchily, especially in background or landscape areas.[47] Not unexpectedly, this French
development had its American counterpart. American painters, trained at the École des
Beaux-Arts and at other Paris schools and well acquainted with contemporary French art,
similarly borrowed their manner of working during the 1880s and 1890s.[48] Weir, already
influenced by the *juste milieu* naturalist Jules Bastien-Lepage, turned to increasingly progressive models for his mid-1880s pictures while struggling at the same time to maintain certain
aspects of his academic style: firm draftsmanship; three-dimensional, anatomically correct
figures; technical virtuosity; and thoughtfully conceived and carefully executed compositions.
By the end of the decade he had adopted a new sort of format, often smaller in scale than
before and more informal in treatment. His painting style became less finished, the contours
less decisive and the modeling less firm. Light and atmosphere were evoked to a more
prominent degree in his works—even in those still-life and figure paintings set indoors. His
palette lightened considerably. These changes were by no means sudden or complete; rather,
his work altered slowly, with dark, highly finished paintings still being painted as late as

1890. But in the main this period can be interpreted as the bridge between the old and the new in his art: he was beginning to take his first tentative steps into the impressionist realm.

The development of Weir's figure style during the 1880s is best demonstrated by his portraits of his wife, Anna Baker Weir. *Anna with a Greyhound* (about 1882, color plate 6) shows Anna in an elegant black dress and hat standing with a greyhound in a wooded landscape. Although painted in the tight, academic style Weir had learned from his mentor, Gérôme, the portrait is a departure in that he has posed his model outdoors. His juxtaposition of dark-clothed figure and green landscape can be compared to earlier French works: Courbet's *A Lady in a Riding Habit—L'Amazone* (late 1856, fig. 3.29), Manet's *Portrait de Madame Brunet* (1860, private collection) and *Woman with Dogs* (about 1862, private collection), or Bastien's series of outdoor portraits, painted in the 1870s, of members of his family.[49] In Weir's *Against the Window* (1884, color plate 7) Anna is depicted in a more relaxed pose; she leans back comfortably in a chair by a window giving out onto an urban view—the skyline of New York on an overcast day. Weir has emphasized the three-dimensionality of his model's face with careful, solid modeling; shadows are particularly evident along her cheekbone and around her eyes. He even draws firm contours around the edge of Anna's face, where the

3.29 Gustave Courbet, A Lady in a Riding Habit—L'Amazone, *1856, oil on canvas, 45½ × 35⅛ in. (New York, The Metropolitan Museum of Art, The H. O. Havemeyer Collection, Bequest of Mrs. H. O. Havemeyer, 1929).*

3.30 J. Alden Weir, Street Scene and Woman in a Café, *probably 1883, oil on wood, 6⅛ × 9¼ in., unsigned (private collection).*

local color of her flesh shows little effect of the surrounding light and air. Only in the still life of yellow roses beside Anna does Weir indulge in some broad, free brushwork. The treatment of these fragile, wilting blossoms, held in a translucent container placed on a window sill, in natural light, is noticeably different from that of the figure. Weir uses broad, flat strokes to suggest the sparkling highlights on the vase and single, rapid strokes to represent entire petals and leaves. In this painting, particularly in the handling of the still-life element, Weir's work reflects the influence of Édouard Manet. A small oil sketch of Weir's (probably 1883, fig. 3.30) shows two different scenes—on the left, a city street scene with a crowd of figures beneath a leaden sky; on the right, a woman seated in an outdoor café. Weir's rapid, summary treatment and his evident concern for the effects of light and atmosphere bear evidence of having been inspired by his study of Manet's style.

When Weir saw Manet's work during his student years, he had been less than enthusiastic. After attending a studio exhibition of Manet's works rejected by the Salon in 1876 he wrote to his father: "His value of color is not bad; this, however, is all I can say of him. His portrait of a man full length has no bones in his leg, which he considers a trifle, as color is the great thing in art, but the French Jury has enough good sense to differ from him on that point."[50] Weir revised his opinion, possibly by 1878, but certainly by 1881, when on a trip to Paris he purchased from Durand-Ruel, an art dealer, two of Manet's paintings, *A Boy with a Sword* (about 1861, fig. 3.31) and *Woman with a Parrot* (1866, fig. 3.32), for Erwin Davis.[51] He then visited Manet's studio, where the artist was holding a reception, and spent some time studying his paintings. There he bought *Marine (Les Marsouins)* (1864, Philadelphia Museum of Art), which, like the two figure paintings, was destined for Davis's collection.[52] Greatly impressed by the works he had studied in Manet's studio, Weir made a copy (about 1881, Provo, Utah, Brigham Young University) of the head of the model in *A Boy with a Sword;* the paintings he did during the early and mid-1880s showed the increasing influence that Manet's style and subject matter were exerting on him. His admiration for Manet, however, seems to have been limited to paintings Manet had done in the 1860s, before his brushwork and subject matter began to reflect those of his impressionist colleagues. Manet's early paintings, done two decades before Weir met him, would have fitted more easily into the academic tradition of Weir's training; it was probably the old-master quality of Manet's work that appealed to him.

In his important picture *In the Park* (about 1879, see fig. 3.4) Weir, in his emulation of Hals, may have been following Manet's example of using explicit old-master models to depict a scene from modern life. Weir developed his contemporary picture in the manner traditionally reserved for significant historical subjects, a device of Manet's. *In the Park* was important not only because it introduced an unconventional subject—lower-class types in an urban environment—but because the subject was conceived and developed in a grand academic manner, complete with references to the art of the past. Weir's unusually progres-

3.31 *Édouard Manet*, A Boy with a Sword, *about 1861, oil on canvas, 51⅝ × 36¾ in., signed at lower left:* Manet *(New York, The Metropolitan Museum of Art, Gift of Erwin Davis, 1889).*

3.32 Édouard Manet, Woman with a Parrot, *1866, oil on canvas, 72 × 50⅝ in.,
signed at lower left:* Manet *(New York, The Metropolitan Museum of Art, Gift of
Erwin Davis, 1889).*

sive approach in this picture could be seen as paralleling that of Manet, who had used old-
master borrowings in his scenes of contemporary life as early as the 1860s. Weir's portrayal of
his friend Eaton as a fashionable man reading a newspaper in Union Square could recall
Manet's inclusion of a number of his friends and colleagues as models in such paintings as
Music in the Tuileries Gardens (1862, London, National Gallery).[53] Weir's composition, with
the figures pressed close to the picture plane, can be found in a number of Manet's pictures,
among them, *Skating* (1877, Cambridge, Fogg Art Museum, Harvard University) and *At the
Café* (1878, Baltimore, The Walters Art Gallery).[54] Even Weir's decision to dismember a
picture that had been unfavorably reviewed and to present the fragments as individual
compositions may reflect Manet's occasional practice, for instance, with *Les Gitanos* (about
1861, now destroyed).[55]

Another painting possibly informed by Manet in its treatment of old-master sources is

Boy Polishing a Brass Jug (late 1870s–early 1880s, fig. 3.20). It can be compared to some of Manet's single studies of young men, such as *The Water Drinker* (about 1861, The Art Institute of Chicago) and *Les Bulles de Savon* (1867/68, Lisbon, Fundação Calouste Gulbenkian),[56] which in turn were inspired by Velázquez and other seventeenth-century realists. Manet's influence can be detected in Weir's painting style in *Boy Polishing a Brass Jug*, where he uses much bolder brushwork, with little of the academic modeling or careful detail usually seen in his early pictures. His palette, mainly black, near-black, gray, and flesh tones, is relieved by the warm, bright colors of the brass jug. While other evidence places Weir's enthusiasm for Manet at a slightly later date, the style, composition, and subject matter of *In the Park* and *Boy Polishing a Brass Jug* suggest that he may have begun to study Manet's work as early as 1878. Weir at that time was nevertheless still very much committed to the academic principles he had learned at the École des Beaux-Arts, and any influence of Manet would have been tempered by that of far more traditional artists, Gérôme and Bastien in particular.

3.33 J. Alden Weir, Anna on the Balcony of Duveneck's Studio, *1883, oil on canvas, 77 × 47 in., unsigned (Provo, Utah, Brigham Young University).*

Traces of Manet's style can be seen unequivocally in several of Weir's figure paintings. *Anna on the Balcony of Duveneck's Studio* (1883, fig. 3.33), painted in Venice, where the Weirs, on their honeymoon, visited Frank Duveneck, is a full-length portrait of Anna Weir standing beside a jardiniere filled with geraniums. For this work, Weir chose the life-size scale and realistic figure style that Manet had used in such paintings as *Woman with a Parrot* (1866, fig. 3.32) and *The Street Singer* (about 1862, Boston, Museum of Fine Arts).[57] Placed close to the picture plane, the figure fills the foreground of the composition; the costume, accessory elements, and setting are minimal. Weir's style, however, remains far more academic than Manet's; his portrait of Anna is carefully drawn and fully modeled. He does not emulate Manet's flattening of forms or his innovative treatment of space; unlike Manet's figure, who stands before a flat, neutral background, Anna's position in space is explicitly marked by the jardiniere, the wall behind her, and the view of the balcony beyond.

During the late 1880s Weir explored a subject—the contemplative woman—that fascinated many of his contemporaries, among them Thomas Wilmer Dewing (1851–1938), William Merritt Chase, and Robert Reid (1862–1929). For these artists, the activities of the female figure assumed less importance than her thoughts and emotions. Women, who at mid-century had been most often shown engaged in simple domestic tasks, were now represented thinking, reading, or playing musical instruments. They were endowed with a new intellectual complexity. Weir's paintings of this sort, done between 1885 and 1890, show Anna in a variety of contemplative attitudes that convey feelings or moods. In a sense, they are more

3.34 J. Alden Weir, A Reverie, *1886, oil on canvas, 20 × 25⅞ in., unsigned (private collection).*

3.35 J. Alden Weir, The Miniature, *1888, oil on canvas, 23½ × 19⅝ in., signed and dated at lower right: J./Alden./Weir./1888 (Huntington, New York, Heckscher Art Museum).*

fully developed versions of the *tête d'expression* exercise that Weir practiced during this years at the École des Beaux-Arts.[58] *A Reverie* (1886, fig. 3.34) even duplicates one of these assignments—*La Réflexion* (reflection or thought).[59] A bust portrait of Anna, *A Reverie* shows her leaning her head on her hand; she is suported by her elbow, which rests on a pillow. In order to focus our attention on the model and her expression, the artist has posed her close to the picture plane, eliminating any suggestion of setting. *The Miniature* (1888, fig. 3.35) is even more advanced a composition: Anna, who is seated in profile, turns her head to look out at the viewer. She holds a miniature and she seems to be contemplating its subject, presumably a loved one. In *At the Piano* (about 1890, fig. 3.36), Anna seems oblivious to the instrument behind her; again, she is lost in thought. In *Reading* (1890, fig. 3.37), Anna is shown in a dark interior; only a thin shaft of light through what may be either an all-but-closed curtain or door illuminates the scene. She reads quietly, a dog (one of the Weirs's many) draped across her lap.

Weir explores the effects of artificial light in *Anna by Lamplight* (late 1880s, fig. 3.38). In this unfinished picture, Caro joins her mother at a table where a shaded lamp casts pink and red highlights on a white cloth. Weir's paint application and choice of subject in this picture resemble those of John Singer Sargent's mid-1880s interiors, where color is applied in long,

3.36 J. Alden Weir, At the Piano, *about 1890, oil on canvas, 47¼ × 39¼ in.,*
unsigned (New York, Hirschl & Adler Galleries).

3.37 J. Alden Weir, Reading, *1890, oil on wood, 16 × 11½ in., signed*
and dated at upper left: J./Alden Weir/1890 (private collection).

feathery brushstrokes. In *The Christmas Tree* (1890, color plate 8), which represents Caro
holding a doll, Weir exploits the effects of artificial light more dramatically. The folds of
Caro's white dress have cool blue shadows, and the evergreen beside her shimmers with
glowing pink candles and glistening ornaments. In these works Weir evinces a more individual painting style, composition, and choice of subject matter; his figure paintings of the
late 1880s, as a whole, are far less derivative than those he had executed earlier in the decade.
    The greatest of Weir's figure paintings during the period 1885 to 1890 is *Idle Hours* (1888;
fig. 3.39), which won an award in the Prize Fund Exhibition of 1888. It was subsequently
purchased by the exhibition's organizers, who presented it to The Metropolitan Museum of
Art.[60] At first glance, the picture appears to mark a more progressive direction for Weir; he
shows a new interest in the effects of natural light, with Anna and Caro posed in front of a
window covered only by sheer white curtains, their white dresses reflecting the light that
pours in behind them. Weir's palette is far lighter in key; his brushwork, while carefully
confined within contours, is somewhat broken, with repeated, even strokes of color laid on
side by side. Nonetheless, *Idle Hours* was conceived and executed in the academic manner that
Weir had learned under Gérôme at the École: his models are arranged in a carefully balanced
pyramid—Anna's dress and her extended right arm and Caro's dress create two diagonals that

3.38 J. Alden Weir, Anna by Lamplight, *late 1880s, oil on canvas, 16⅛ × 20⅛ in., unsigned (private collection).*

direct our line of vision to the triangle's apex, the hanging birdcage centered above the two figures. Each figure is formed in an individual triangle counterpoised to the other, and the two are joined by Anna's outstretched left arm and Caro's guitar, which overlap, directly beneath the birdcage, in the center of the well-planned composition. In preparation for this painting, the artist made a rough drawing (Brigham Young University) and an oil sketch (private collection) for the figure of Anna, as well as a highly finished drawing for the entire composition (1888, fig. 3.40). The latter was actually squared for transfer and then cut into no fewer than thirty-six squares, each of which was used for drawing one segment of the composition onto the canvas.[61] Sometimes Weir has divided these small squares even further, usually along difficult contours such as the line of the child's hair and shoulder, so that the preliminary drawing could serve as a guide in his work on the finished painting.

During the late 1880s, Weir created a number of portraits of friends and models that are done on a smaller scale and in a more informal manner than those he did earlier in the decade. The distinct portrait styles of the two periods are best illustrated in Weir's repeated depiction of his friend the sculptor Olin Levi Warner (1844–1896). The first one (1879/80, fig. 3.41) may have been painted at the same time that Warner was modeling his well-known bust of Weir (1880, fig. 3.42).[62] Like the portraits of Robert Weir (fig. 3.1) and George Maynard (3.10), this work shows a three-quarter view, dignified and natural, of the seated subject.

3.39 J. Alden Weir, Idle Hours, *1888, oil on canvas, 51¼ × 71⅛ in., signed and dated at lower right: J. Alden Weir—1888 (New York, The Metropolitan Museum of Art, Gift of Several Gentlemen, 1888).*

3.40 J. Alden Weir, Drawing for "Idle Hours," *1888, pencil, black and white chalk on gray paper, 13⅝ × 18½ in., unsigned (private collection).*

3.41 *J. Alden Weir,* Olin Levi Warner, *1879/80, oil on canvas, 36 × 29 in., signed and inscribed: To my friend/——[Olin] L. Warner/Weir (New York, American Academy of Arts and Letters).*

Warner looks intently off to the side as if something has attracted his attention; grasping the arm of the chair with his right hand, he gestures emphatically with his left. This is a formal portrait that belies the intimacy between the artist and his model; it too is executed in the academic style Weir had learned at the École. The second portrait of Warner (about 1889, color plate 9) must have been painted at Warner's request when he was elected an associate member of the National Academy of Design in 1889. Weir has focused in on his subject, choosing a bust-length composition that enables him to concentrate on Warner's expressive face and on his hand, placed prominently as a reminder of his creativity. He is posed in front of an unidentified relief sculpture not unlike those that appear in Weir's still lifes of the period, but probably here an original work by Warner. Weir's precise academic style has been transformed: totally eliminating contours and lines in this later portrait, he has applied his color in long, feathery strokes that suggest that the sitter is surrounded by light. Some areas are most summarily treated, particularly the hand, which is shown in a few broad strokes of pigment.

Weir's portrait of Robert Minor (1889, fig. 3.43) was also painted to satisfy the sitter's election requirements at the Academy; it shares the same immediate presentation and loose,

3.42 Olin Levi Warner, J. Alden Weir, *1880, bronze, height: 22½ in., inscribed on reverse: Alden Weir (New York, The Metropolitan Museum of Art, Gift of The National Sculpture Society, 1898).*

3.43 J. Alden Weir, Robert Minor, *1889, oil on canvas, 22 × 18 in., signed at upper right:* J. Alden Weir—1889 *(New York, National Academy of Design).*

fresh brushwork. Here, however, Weir's palette has begun to lighten, and the background of the painting is a surprising bright green. In some female portraits from this period—for example, *Anna Looking Down* (about 1890, fig. 3.44)—Weir utilizes the same sort of informal composition and broad paint application; the figure is surrounded in light in a moist, almost tangible atmosphere. His tendency toward smaller, more intimate portraits executed in a more progressive style did not affect all his work during this period. His portrait of the actor John Gilbert (about 1888, The Players Club, New York) is painted in a style reminiscent of that of his earlier portraits. Since this was a commission rather than a painting of a close friend or family member, Weir may have decided to revert to an earlier and less controversial style.

While Weir could hardly be described as an animal painter, he did produce a number of "animal portraits" of the family dogs—Jags, Bush, and Gyp—as well as several interior scenes with dogs. Done both in watercolor and oil, these seem to date between 1885 and 1887. *Hunter's Dog and Gun* (1885, fig. 3.45) shows a dog asleep beside a simple country chair against which is propped his master's gun. The watercolor scene is set inside a barn, with hay on the floor and a view of the distant landscape through an open door. In another watercolor, *Two Dogs* (1885, color plate 10), Weir established the format typical of most of his work in this

3.44 J. Alden Weir, Anna Looking Down, *about 1890, oil on wood, 15¾ × 11¾ in., unsigned (private collection).*

genre. The dogs lie on a hearth rug in front of a blazing fire. They are surrounded by glistening brass objects: a cauldron, a skimmer, fireplace tools, a bed warmer. Two other watercolors, *Three Dogs* (1887, private collection) and *After the Hunt* (1887, present location unknown), are similar in subject and composition. The only two oil paintings of animals in interiors are fluidly painted with dark, rich colors. One of these, *My Own Fireside* (1886, fig. 3.46), probably the picture *After a Day's Run,*[63] resembles the watercolors in composition, while the other, *Fireplace with Dogs* (about 1886–87, Kennedy Galleries), is the only one of the dog pictures organized on a vertical format. These watercolors and oils represent a charming but isolated tangent in Weir's career.

Throughout the 1880s, Weir continued to explore the expressive possibilities of the figure, making good use of the training he had received at the Ecole des Beaux-Arts in the previous decade. He attempted literary, historical, religious, or allegorical subjects only rarely. Rather, he looked for subjects in the world around him—first, among the peasants of France and Holland and the poorer members of New York society and, later, among his friends and family members. In the latter pictures, Weir's individual style began to emerge;

3.45 J. Alden Weir, Hunter's Dog and Gun, *1885, watercolor and white gouache on cream paper, 501 × 456 mm., signed at lower left: J. Alden Weir—85 (Cambridge, courtesy of the Fogg Art Museum, Harvard University, Grenville L. Winthrop Bequest).*

his experiments in them prepared him for innovations in a series of life-size figure paintings that he would undertake during the 1890s.

Still Life

In his first years back in New York, Weir began to establish a reputation as a painter of still life, an important genre for him until the early 1890s.[64] He had done some still lifes in Paris, mainly kitchen subjects, strongly influenced by the old masters, but they were intended as studio exercises rather than as exhibition pieces. There are no securely dated still lifes until 1880 (although Weir likely turned his attention to this genre by 1877), but by 1884, he

3.46 J. Alden Weir, My Own Fireside, *1886, oil on canvas, 16 × 24 in., signed at lower right: J. Alden Weir 86 (California, San Diego Museum of Art).*

had produced a series of large-scale arrangements of flowers and decorative objects. These works, like those he would have seen each year at the Paris Salon, were conceived as major exhibition pieces, and they were undoubtedly influenced by the still lifes of such successful European painters as the Belgian Jean-Baptiste Robie (1821–1910) or the French Blaise Desgoffes (1830–1901). Around 1884, Weir's still-life work began to take on a new character. While continuing to do floral still lifes, he returned to kitchen subjects—decorative plates and vessels, fruit, even dead game. Rarely exhibited, they were far more intimate in scale and less grandiose in composition than the earlier ones. In treatment and subject, these works of the mid- and late 1880s resemble paintings done two decades earlier by Manet and by less progressive realists such as Antoine Vollon (1833–1900), Eugène-Louis Boudin (1824–1898), Ignace-Henri-Jean-Théodore Fantin-Latour (1836–1904), and François Bonvin (1817–1887), all of whom were affected by the contemporary revival of interest in the informal game and kitchen still lifes of the eighteenth-century master Jean-Baptiste-Siméon Chardin.

In the late 1880s and early 1890s, Weir began to react to the influence of Impressionism, one of the first Americans to do so. His tabletop still lifes reveal a growing interest in the effects of light and atmosphere, and he began to paint flowers out-of-doors. Thus his approach to still life proceeded in the same direction as had his work in other genres. He began with the study of the old masters, worked in an academic style, and then responded to a series of increasingly more advanced realist influences, finally turning to the impressionist style that would dominate all his art in the 1890s. This development can only be established within general periods, for not many of his still lifes are actually dated or easily datable. Further, his still lifes do not develop smoothly: there are often unexpected experiments that predate the

eventual direction of his work in this genre; at the same time, there are pictures that return to
subjects or styles that he had supposedly rejected decades earlier.

When Weir began to paint the floral still lifes that became one of his favorite subjects
during the early 1880s is not exactly known—two of them may have been done before 1880.
Flowers: Roses in a Silver Bowl on a Mahogany Table (probably 1877–80, fig. 3.47) shows on a
dark but highly polished mahogany tabletop a silver bowl containing a tight bouquet of mixed
flowers, among them lilacs and roses, spotlighted against a flat, dark background. The simple
backdrop and conventional composition—the vase of flowers centrally placed—recall the
work of George Cochran Lamdin (1830–1896) and other American still-life painters of the
period. Weir's work here still lacks the misty, palpable atmosphere and suggestive light
effects that later endow his floral still lifes with such grace. An inscription on the reverse of
Lilacs in a Canton Bowl (probably 1879, fig. 3.48) dates that painting. It is a far more individual
composition: the bowl and its contents, viewed obliquely from below, are cropped abruptly.
As a result, the still life is seen without any reference to the ground or other support, and it
appears to press against the picture plane. The fragmentary quality of *Lilacs in a Canton Bowl*
is such a change from Weir's other still-life paintings that it is tempting to speculate that the
painting has been cut from a larger and presumably more complete composition. That
theory, however, is disproved by an examination of the wooden panel on which it is painted,

3.47 J. Alden Weir, Flowers: Roses in a Silver Bowl on a Mahogany Table,
probably 1877–80, oil on canvas, 24 × 20 in., unsigned (private collection).

3.48 *J. Alden Weir*, Lilacs in a Canton Bowl, *probably 1879, oil on wood, 7⅞ × 10 in., inscribed on the reverse: Painted by/Julian Alden Weir/1879 (Provo, Utah, Brigham Young University).*

whose edges, beveled around all four sides in a manner typical of Weir's panel paintings, give no indication of having been cut down.

Still Life in the Studio (about 1877–80, fig. 3.49), probably set in Weir's New York studio in the Benedick building, is one of the earliest of his paintings in the genre.[65] Two photographs of his studio (about 1883, Provo, Utah, Brigham Young University) show many of the objects depicted here—the cylindrical, dome-topped brass lantern with decorative piercing; the baluster-shaped blue and white oriental vase; and the spinning wheel. In the painting, the lantern and the vase, along with a brass cauldron, a pewter plate, a brass bowl, and some flowers, are arranged on top of a simple wooden table placed at an angle to the picture plane. The shallow space and the vertical wall behind the objects are crowded with paintings, presumably Weir's. Of those on the left, none are actually visible; one is cropped so that only the lower edge of the frame is included in the composition, and the other is turned away from the viewer so that only the blank canvas and the wooden stretcher and keys can be seen. On the right are three pictures, only one of which is readily recognizable—Weir's copy (1877 or 1881, private collection) after *Mrs. Siddons*, by Thomas Gainsborough (1783/85, London, National Gallery).[66] Weir's still life may be viewed as the artist's statement on his life after returning from Europe. Certain paintings and props have been placed aside: the copy after Gainsborough and the spinning wheel so prominently featured in his major peasant painting, *Interior—House in Brittany* (1875, fig. 2.15); these may represent the type of painting he had done while abroad. Other subjects, elaborate decorative objects, have been moved to the forefront, suggesting the new position that still life has assumed in Weir's career. Whatever his intent, *Still Life in the Studio* is exceptional among Weir's early paintings in the genre. Its horizontal format and conspicuous interior setting, which almost overwhelm the objects' arrangement, are never to be repeated in Weir's later work. The awkwardness of the picture, with its illogical spatial relationships and mannered repetition of rounded forms, is soon to be replaced by graceful arrangements in which soft blossoms play a more prominent part.

Weir's style and choice of still-life subject matter were inspired by the success of contemporary flower painters at home and abroad. While in Paris, Weir had the opportunity to

3.49 J. Alden Weir, Still Life in the Studio, *about 1877–80, oil on canvas, 30 × 48¼ in., signed at lower left: Julian Weir (New Haven, Connecticut, Yale University Art Gallery, Gift of John F. Weir).*

study many examples of contemporary still-life painting at the annual Salon. To reconstruct the Salon as Weir saw it is impossible, but by examining the catalogues and reviews of the exhibitions of the period several generalizations can be made about the still-life painters whose work he would have seen. Not many of those exhibiting at the Salon seem to have been trained in the conventional manner; no teacher at all is listed beside some of the names in the Salon catalogues. The Lyons school of still-life painting was heavily represented, its most prominent members being Simon Saint-Jean (1808–1860) and Jean-Étienne (known as Joanny) Maisiat (1824–1910), both of whom produced floral still lifes in a somewhat conservative style. A wide variety of subjects were exhibited: fruit, decorative objects, and, most often, flowers. These were pretentious still lifes, complicated in composition and large in scale. In spite of the humble position to which the genre was relegated by most academic artists of the period, it obviously remained popular, attracting such progressive artists as Fantin-Latour, for one.

In the America of the 1870s and 1880s, flower painting was enjoying a revival in which Weir and a multitude of his contemporaries, among them Chase and Emil Carlsen (1853–1932), participated. It offered them a means of exploring solutions to technical and formal problems; still life, traditionally a less esteemed genre, was not encumbered by the academic restraints applied to more conventional subjects. For Weir and his colleagues, romantic flower painting had unquestionably replaced the closely observed, bountiful still lifes of fruit and vegetables popular at mid-century; their bouquets of flowers were loose and open, with blossoms and petals scattered on a tabletop support in soft contrast to the surfaces and textures of the vessels that hold them. Led by John La Farge (1835–1910), a French-trained painter then the most influential still-life artist in America, this generation of painters produced paintings that became more subjective and expressive. They no longer strove for truth to nature but for the evocation of a mood, so that the still-life elements depicted became not an end in themselves but a means for expressing ideas and emotions. For their purposes, delicate floral subjects, often roses or peonies, shown in informal arrangements in and around antique or precious decorative objects, were an ideal theme.

Between 1880 and 1884 Weir painted a series of large-scale floral still lifes of which *Still Life: Peonies* (1881, fig. 3.50) is typical. All are vertical in format, a feature often emphasized by the use of tall, slender vases and by columnar or pyramidlike floral arrangements. The compositions are always complicated, showing several different kinds of flowers or several different kinds of vases, with the flowers usually brightly lit and set against a darkened background. Weir began to develop this format in several paintings dated, or datable, to 1880 and 1881. The earliest of these may be *Roses* (probably 1880, fig. 3.51). Here Weir masses fragile blossoms and antique objects—a German faïence jug, a crystal goblet, and a Chinese figurine—in a triangular arrangement against a dark, mottled background.[67] As he continued to expand on this compositional scheme, he added a sculptural relief as a foil for his floral arrangements, an accessory that made its first appearance in *Les petites roses* (1880, fig. 3.52), where its presence is minimized by its background placement, cast in shadow. The background of *Flower Piece* (1882, fig. 3.53) contains a similar relief, but Weir has embellished this

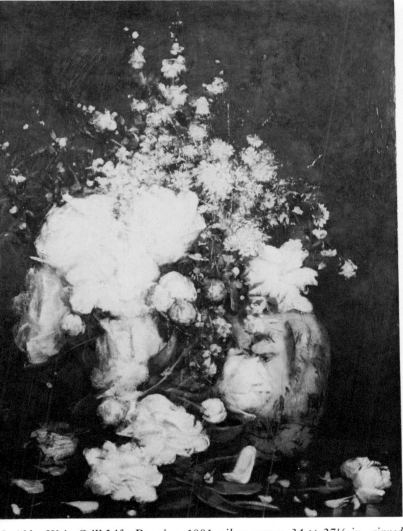

J. Alden Weir, Still Life: Peonies, *1881, oil on canvas, 34 × 27¼ in., signed [and d]ated vertically at lower right: J. Alden Weir (underscored) 1881 (private [collec]tion).*

3.51 J. Alden Weir, Roses, *probably 1880, oil on canvas, 24 × 16 in. possibly signed and dated: J. Alden Weir 80 [?] (Andover, Massachusetts, Phillips Academy, Addison Gallery of American Art).*

3.52 J. Alden Weir, Les petites roses, 1880, oil on canvas, 35¾ × 23¾ in., signed and dated at lower left: J. Alden Weir—/1880 (New Paltz, New York, Huguenot Historical Society).

3.53 J. Alden Weir, Flower Piece, 1882, oil on canvas, 29⅝ × 21⅝ in., s and dated at lower right: J. Alden Weir 1882 (Oregon, Portland Art Museum, of Henry L. Corbett, Elliott R. Corbett, and Hamilton F. Corbett, in memo their mother, Helen Ladd Corbett, 36.130).

composition with a profusion of flowers—four different vases full of them. As in other compositions undertaken by Weir in the early 1880s, the flowers and decorative objects are tightly grouped in a pyramid form and spotlighted so that the relief in the upper right corner is thrown into shadow. In *Still Life with Flowers* (1881, fig. 3.54) Weir introduced the compositional format that he would use in his most accomplished flower paintings: flowers placed in tall, narrow vases arranged in front of a flat, dark wall. The triangular arrangement of the earlier compositions is retained, but now Weir achieves a greater verticality. The attenuated vases are almost top-heavy; the flowers are invested with a greater visual weight than the vessels that hold them.

Two of these large-scale, floral still lifes were exhibited together at the Society of American Artists in 1884: these were *Roses* (1883–84, fig. 3.55) and *Flowers and Chalice* (present location unknown), in which Weir used an almost identical composition.[68] In the upper background of both he placed a relief; in the foreground, a floral arrangement of open peony blossoms, with wilted petals scattered across the tabletop. In spite of the central placement of both reliefs, the artist has created an asymmetrical composition by adding on the right a tall element—another vase of flowers in the first painting; a standing cup of embossed silver in the second. The relief sculptures shown in these paintings are well-known Florentine Renaissance objects that would have been readily recognizable to Weir's contemporaries—a Madonna and Child by Andrea della Robbia and St. John the Baptist by Desiderio da Settignano.[69] The choice of these reliefs as still-life motifs and their prominent placement within these two compositions must be intentional, but since Weir did not comment on these works, their significance is only conjectural. Obviously, in these and other still lifes containing antique sculpture and decorative objects Weir attempts to associate his art with the great art of the past, returning to the art of the Italian Renaissance that he had studied all his life and considered his model.

The deliberate inclusion of references to major artistic achievements may also have been an attempt to elevate still life from its lowly position in the academic hierarchy. Weir was well aware of the traditional attitude, which placed the genre near the bottom of the list of possible subjects. Only copies were less·esteemed. He was a great admirer of the writings of Sir Joshua Reynolds, however, and Reynolds had declared that "even the painter of still life . . . deserves praise in proportion to his attainment; because no part of this excellent art, so much

3.54 J. Alden Weir, Still Life with Flowers, *1881, oil on canvas, 24 × 20¼ in., signed at lower right: J. Alden Weir 1881 (private collection).*

3.55 J. Alden Weir, Roses, *1883–84, oil on canvas, 35½ × 24¾ in., signed at upper right: J. Alden Weir (Washington, D.C., The Phillips Collection).*

the ornament of polished life, is destitute of value and use." According to Reynolds, the aspiring painter should not devote himself totally to still life; instead, he should begin "by aiming at better things." If the artist "is obliged to descend lower, he will bring to the lower sphere of art a grandeur of composition and character, that will raise and ennoble his works far above their natural rank." In still-life paintings like *Roses* and *Flowers and Chalice*, Weir may have been striving for just such a grandeur.[70]

In his choice of objects and, in a sense, in their arrangement, Weir relied on several earlier artistic traditions. His works can be related to the seventeenth-century Flemish artists who painted wreaths and garlands of flowers around simulated sculptures or paintings of venerated images, most often a Madonna and Child. The most prominent of these artists were Jan Brueghel and Daniel Seghers. While the former depicted flowers in circular wreaths, the latter sometimes placed his flowers in somewhat irregular bunches, creating a more dramatic composition with strong light and dark contrasts. Weir would likely have seen examples by these two artists and by their many followers (who included Jan van Thielen, Joris van Son, Jan van Kessel, Alexander Coosemans, and Nicholaes van Veerendael) on his student trip to Holland and Belgium and in the galleries and museums of Paris.[71] He would also have been aware of the revival of this sort of subject then in progress in Lyons, France's leading provincial center for still-life painting, for he probably saw the works of several of the Lyons artists at the Paris Salon. Simon Saint-Jean, Apollinaire-Louis Sicard (1807–1881), and Pierre Chabal-Dussurgey, known as Pierre-Adrien Chabal (1819–1902), are among the artists who painted vertical still lifes emulating their seventeenth-century Flemish predecessors.[72] (A recent interpretation of Brueghel's paintings of flower wreaths around depictions of the Madonna and Child may offer some insight into the meaning of Weir's flower paintings. David Freedberg[73] has demonstrated how Brueghel's wreaths both enhanced the value of the images they surrounded and set them apart from everyday reality, stressing their supernatural role so that they became objects of homage. These paintings can also be associated

3.56 J. Alden Weir, Still Life: Roses, *1882, oil on wood, 14⅛ × 10 in., signed and dated at lower left: J. Alden Weir/1882 (Canajoharie, New York, Conajoharie Library and Art Gallery).*

with the Italian tradition of inserting venerated images into larger paintings done in a later era. The reliefs in Weir's paintings, clearly valued and much admired, are also set apart by flowers. The artist and the spectator are paying tribute to what the simulated relief represents artistically and thematically.)

Weir's early still-life paintings must be considered in the type of decorative setting that they were intended to occupy. Many of them—certainly *Roses* (1883–84, fig. 3.55) and *Flowers and Chalice*—were sold, if not commissioned, by Cottier and Company, a decorating firm with branches in Paris and London which had opened a New York office in 1873. It also sold and exhibited paintings by Weir and his friends Bunce and Ryder, among others.[74] Weir undoubtedly met Daniel Cottier and his partner James Inglis soon after his return from Paris. Their taste in interior decoration may have helped to shape Weir's choice of subject and the composition of his still lifes. Cottier's interiors featured a variety of antique European and oriental decorative objects; these were liberally mixed with modern pieces and displayed on mantels and on hanging shelves in rich, crowded, somewhat somber rooms. Weir's still lifes were obviously well-suited to this kind of setting. The combination of flowers and decorative objects seen in *Roses* could easily have been encountered in such an interior, on a table or, more likely, on a mantelpiece.[75]

During the early 1880s, while Weir was engrossed in his large floral still lifes, he began to paint a few more intimate compositions that anticipate the direction his still-life work would take at the end of the decade. These were generally not exhibition pieces but works painted for friends. In *Silver Cup with Roses* (1882; color plate 11), a bowl and pitcher filled

3.57 J. Alden Weir, Roses, *1884, oil on wood, 8 × 10 in., unsigned (Mark Carliner).*

with flowers are placed in front of the standing silver cup that appears in many of Weir's early still lifes. Here, however, the artist has added to it an inscription, complete with trompe l'oeil shadows to heighten the engraved effect, that reads, "To Anna Dwight Baker from J. Alden Weir/May 18th/1882 N.Y." The still life was a birthday present for Anna, who would become Weir's wife less than a year later.[76] Similar in composition, *Still Life: Roses* (1882, fig. 3.56) is executed on a smaller scale and with greater freedom; this painting was once owned by Weir's friend Carlsen.[77] *Roses* (1884, fig. 3.57),[78] Weir's wedding gift to the architect Stanford White, shows the flowers filling a simple porcelain vase; it is almost a vignette from the foreground of another *Roses* (1883–84, fig. 3.55), Weir's most spectacular still life. The more modest still lifes are painted in the same style as Weir's larger ones. He uses an extremely dark palette, with pigment applied particularly richly in the blossoms, which are built up so thickly that they almost project from the picture surface. This heavy paint application became such a hallmark of Weir's technique that when his still lifes were parodied in a New York exhibition in 1883, the flowers were created by applying "masses of white paper . . . to the canvas" and painting it over.[79] One still life from the early 1880s is an exception. *Flowers: A White Bowl Filled with Dandelions* (1882, fig. 3.58) is painted in a brighter palette, with pigments far more thinly applied. The painting is remarkable in its simplicity: dandelions placed haphazardly in a polychromed faïence bowl spill over onto the tabletop. The support and background are austere. The composition, with its central vessel and

3.58 J. Alden Weir, Flowers: A White Bowl Filled with Dandelions, *1882, oil on panel, 16 × 21 in., signed at upper right: J. Alden Weir/'82 (private collection).*

unadorned setting, recalls that in earlier still lifes by Fantin-Latour—for example, *Chrysan-themums* (1872, private collection).[80]

Some of Weir's simple still lifes may have been composed with a specific meaning, particularly in one that can be seen as a statement about an artist whom Weir admired. *Still Life (Silver Chalice, Japanese Bronze, and Red Taper)* (about 1884–89, fig. 3.59)[81] shows a group of decorative objects arranged on a tabletop in front of a painting, whose frame bears Weir's signature, and a matted grisaille, on which James Abbott McNeill Whistler's characteristic butterfly and signature are visible. Whistler's signature receives dramatic emphasis by its position on a white ground in the middle of an otherwise flat, blank area of the composition. The grisaille is cropped, but it is most likely a photograph of a self-portrait of Whistler mounted and signed by the subject. Friendship tokens such as these were commonly exchanged by artists during the period. Weir owned just such a momento (Caroline P. Ely and Ann Ely Smith) of his acquaintance with Whistler, whom he met briefly in London in 1877 and 1881 and who was soon exerting a strong influence on him, especially on his work in pastel and printmaking.[82] The reference to Whistler is reinforced by Weir's emulation of his painting style: he abandons his usual rich impastos and opaque pigment in favor of Whistler's

3.59 J. Alden Weir, Still Life (Silver Chalice, Japanese Bronze, and Red Taper), *about 1884–89, oil on canvas, 17 × 11¾ in., signed at upper right: J. Alden Weir (Professor and Mrs. Robert N. Ganz).*

3.60 J. Alden Weir, A Bit of Blue, *by 1889, oil on wood, 7½ × 5⅛ in. signed at lower left: J. Alden Weir (Mr. and Mrs. Alvin L. Snowiss).*

thin paint application. In some areas, the canvas is completely exposed; in others, it is so lightly covered that its weave remains clearly visible. Except for the bright red taper, Weir's palette is limited to the subtle tonal variations characteristic of Whistler's work.

By the mid-1880s, Weir was painting only smaller, more intimate, still lifes, informal compositions consisting of kitchen items and a few flowers or pieces of fruit almost casually arranged. Less extensively exhibited and reviewed, these works suggest that still-life painting had begun to occupy a less important place in Weir's career. The reasons for the new character of Weir's still lifes are manifold. He was still seeking inspiration in the art of the past, but his attention had turned to the still lifes of Chardin, whose work had enjoyed a resurgence of popularity in France during the 1850s and 1860s.[83] Americans trained abroad absorbed the enthusiasm for him, so that by 1880 several of Weir's friends, most notably Chase and Carlsen, had been strongly influenced by the great French painter.[84] Chardin must have been Weir's model in two miniaturistic still lifes that he did on wood panels between 1885 and 1889. In *A Bit of Blue* (by 1889, fig. 3.60) and *Dutch Greybeard Jug* (1885, fig. 3.61) Weir greatly simplifies his composition, creating a stark arrangement of a limited number of objects on a bare tabletop in front of an unadorned, neutral-colored wall. He seems to have selected and placed these objects with a greater awareness of their formal qualities, particularly their shapes. A big-bellied stoneware jug stands almost in the center of composition,

3.61 J. Alden Weir, Dutch Greybeard Jug, *1885, oil on wood, 7½ × 6 in., signed and dated at middle right: J. Alden Weir 1885 (private collection).*

3.62 J. Alden Weir, The Delft Plate, *1888, oil on wood, 22 × 13¾ in., signed at upper left: J. Alden Weir / 1888 (Abraham Shuman Fund, courtesy, Museum of Fine Arts, Boston).*

with a single blossom lying on each side of it on the table. The symmetry is affected only slightly by the oil lamp hanging on the wall to one side. In spite of the flowers and petals cast across the tabletop as a reference to a human presence, *Dutch Greybeard Jug* suggests the timeless spirit of Chardin's work. *A Bit of Blue* combines a Chardinesque metal urn on a stand with a few flowers in a pretty blue and white cup.[85] The stability of *Dutch Greybeard Jug* has here been replaced by a more active composition—the principal object is placed off-center, with much of the still life occupied by the blank wall above the cup. The lid of the urn is precariously balanced, and a flower and some petals, which have presumably fallen from the cup, lie on the table. The composition is one that invites the eye to wander from object to object.

Weir's interest in Chardin was heightened by his enthusiasm for the work of Édouard Manet, who was a leading exponent of the Chardin revival in France. When Weir called at Manet's studio, he did not buy any of his still lifes, but they were undoubtedly among the paintings he studied during his visit. Judging from the development of Weir's still-life style during this period, he would have been impressed primarily by Manet's still lifes from the 1860s, the particular period of his work that also exerted great influence on Weir's figure style. *The Delft Plate* (1888, fig. 3.62), Weir's first regular-scale kitchen subject, can be compared to Manet's *Still-Life—Salmon* (1869, Shelburne, Vermont, Shelburne Museum), which Weir could have seen when it was on view in the impressionist show held in New York in 1886, first at the American Art Association and then at the National Academy of Design.[86] Although Weir's composition is vertical and Manet's is horizontal, Weir employs many of Manet's devices. The elements of Manet's *Still-Life—Salmon* are tightly grouped in a pyramid, with some of the objects tilted or placed so close together that there seems hardly enough space to accommodate their volume. Diagonal lines enliven the composition of Manet's work (and Weir's); these are most noticeable in both still lifes in the placement of the knife, which leads the viewer's eye into the picture space, and in the lower left, where the edge of the cloth ends or is folded back to reveal the table below. Weir's painting technique in *The Delft Plate*

3.63 *J. Alden Weir,* Vase and Roses, *late 1880s, oil on canvas, 12 × 14 in., unsigned (Dr. and Mrs. John J. McDonough).*

also owes much to Manet, particularly in the fluid brushwork, the summary treatment of reflective surfaces like the tankard's, and the use of neutral shades varied subtly in tone, with occasional color notes added. The stark white tablecloth and the dark brown background serve as foils to the brilliant yellow and orange peaches and the bright red honeysuckle.

In his floral still lifes of the late 1880s Weir paints even more casually arranged bouquets of flowers; these are composed of far fewer blossoms and show less variety in color and type. One of his simpler, more informal still lifes is *Vase and Roses* (late 1880s, fig. 3.63), which shows a plain tabletop with two roses in front of an empty vase. Weir has created a sense of immediacy; it is as though an unseen hand is about to place the flowers in the vase. In his earlier works, petals or flowers appear to have tumbled from a completed bouquet; in this case, the actual creation of the arrangement is interrupted. In *Vase and Roses*, Weir is again preoccupied by the effects of light and atmosphere. The hard reflective surface of the vase is contrasted with the soft, moist petals and leaves of the roses in front of it. In his *Roses* from those later years (about 1882–90, fig. 3.64), the flowers are simply strewn on the tabletop: the unadorned surface, neutral background, and sense of atmosphere again recall still lifes by Manet. Also similar to Manet's works in style, composition, and treatment are *The Dutch Shoe* (1890, fig. 3.65), painted with a palette knife in silvery colors, and *Fruit* (about 1888, fig. 3.66), where a bough of leaves and tomatoes is hung on a wall above a pile of ripe (and overripe) tomatoes on a tabletop. *Pheasants* (by 1889, fig. 3.67) is painted in a more advanced style: it is only sketchily finished. Weir, in an obvious attempt to create a rough paint surface, has applied his pigment not only with a brush but also with his palette knife.

Weir seems to have lost interest in still-life painting by about 1890. Although still lifes continue to appear sporadically during the 1890s and the early 1900s, they represent a relatively minor part of his oeuvre. Nevertheless, still life had performed an important

3.64 J. Alden Weir, Roses, *about 1882–90, oil on canvas, 9½ × 14¾ in., signed at lower left: J. Alden Weir (Mr. and Mrs. Raymond J. Horowitz).*

3.65 J. Alden Weir, The Dutch Shoe, *1890, oil on wood, 21 × 15 in., signed and dated at upper right: J. Alden Weir/1890 (private collection).*

3.66 J. Alden Weir, Fruit, *about 1888, oil on canvas, 21⅛ × 17¹³/₁₆ (New York, The Metropolitan Museum of Art, Gift of Robert E. Tod, exchange).*

function for Weir during the 1880s, for it was in that humble genre that he solved many of the formal and aesthetic problems he was encountering in his work of those years.

Landscapes

Weir had painted landscapes during his student days, but they had been mainly as studies for backgrounds in his figure paintings—*Harvesters in Brittany*, for instance, for which one study survives (1874, fig. 2.15). Many of his early landscapes, done during the late 1870s and early 1880s, continue to represent European views, because it was usually on his summer trips abroad that Weir took the opportunity to paint in the countryside. *A French Homestead* (probably 1878, fig. 3.68) was likely painted on a return visit to Cernay-la-Ville and *Mill at Dordt* (1881, fig. 3.69) in Holland, where Weir painted with his friend Twachtman and his brother John, who in 1881 had finally succeeded in making his long-hoped-for trip to Europe

3.67 *J. Alden Weir,* Pheasants, *1889, oil on wood, 17³/₄ × 30 in., signed and dated at upper left:* J.A.W./'89. *(Hartford, Connecticut, Wadsworth Atheneum, Gift of Mrs. Edward Young Stimpson).*

with Julian. In composition and style both paintings deviate little from the academic landscape style then popular in France. They are carefully chosen views with recognizable focal points—the farm building in one, the windmill in the other—and elements such as grazing goats or gliding birds included for visual interest. *A Brittany Village* (late 1870s or early 1880s, fig. 3.70) represents a rural village with far greater realism both in composition and in treatment; the work recalls similar subjects painted by Bastien-Lepage, whose *Goose Girl* (Philadelphia, Philadelphia Museum of Art, Johnson Collection) could easily have inspired this picture.

While in Paris as a student and later as a visitor, Weir had certainly been exposed to the French landscape style of the Barbizon school. In 1878, after seeing an exhibition of paintings by Pierre-Etienne-Théodore Rousseau (1812–1867), Jean-Baptiste-Camille Corot (1796–1875), Charles-François Daubigny (1817–1878), and other Barbizon artists, he had written to his parents: "To see these works one is really inspired to go to work immediately. The simplicity and truth of these men makes one love art and want to get to work."[87] Although Weir visited Barbizon during his Paris years, it was not until later that those artists seem actually to have influenced him: his commitment to the Barbizon style appears to date from the early 1880s, and may even have been stimulated by his friendship with several older American artists who specialized in landscape painting—Albert Pinkam Ryder, George Inness (1825–1894), and Robert C. Minor (1840–1904). During the late 1870s Weir and Ryder were part of the circle of artists around the art gallery Cottier and Company, which often sold French Barbizon and Dutch Hague School landscape paintings. Both Inness and Minor had already visited Barbizon, and had come home with a deep appreciation for the artists who painted there. While Weir may have met Inness first through his father, Robert, he saw him in Paris and came into contact with him again in New York through the Society of American Artists and other art organizations. Weir may have joined Minor in Keene Valley in the

3.68 J. Alden Weir, A French Homestead, *probably 1878, oil on canvas, 20¹/₁₆ × 24 in., signed at lower right: J. Alden Weir (New York, The Brooklyn Museum, Gift of Alfred W. Jenkins, 1929).*

Adirondacks in 1882;[88] he was well-acquainted with Minor's poetic landscapes, which were executed in a rich, dark palette with their pronounced brushwork sometimes enhanced by the use of the palette knife. Weir's *Haystacks, Shepherd, and Sheep* (probably 1884, fig. 3.71) is similar to Minor's *A Hillside Pasture* (Washington, D.C., National Museum of American Art) in its subject, an evocative rural scene; in its palette; and in its composition, where the action is focused in the middle ground and the foreground is simply filled with rocks and grass. Later in the decade, in works such as *A Belt of Wood* (1888, fig. 3.72), Weir shows an informal, apparently unpremeditated composition—a view of trees, grass, and sky—with no detail or action to distract from the observation of nature. He achieves a rougher paint surface by building up some areas with a palette knife, with results most obvious in the cloud-filled sky. During the late 1880s Weir became more interested in creating a tactile paint surface, which he achieved by means of a palette knife or by dragging the wooden end of his brush repeatedly over the surface of the picture. This treatment is evident even in more conventional landscapes like *A Connecticut Farm* (about 1886, fig. 3.73).

The strongest influence on Weir's landscapes of the late 1880s was unquestionably

3.69 *J. Alden Weir,* Mill at Dordt, *1881, oil on canvas, 34½ × 24¾ in., unsigned (private collection).*

Twachtman's.[89] The two artists had become friends a decade earlier. Fresh from their studies abroad, they had both joined the Society of American Artists and had made excursions with the Tile Club. They had friends in common in such artists as Chase and Duveneck. Weir joined Twachtman and his wife on part of their honeymoon trip in Europe, and the two artists painted together in Holland. For much of the years 1882 to 1887, Weir and Twachtman were separated—Twachtman and his wife returned to their native Cincinnati for the birth of their first child, then Twachtman studied in Paris between 1883 and 1885, next he painted a cyclorama in Chicago in the winter of 1886/87. Finally, in 1888, he joined Weir at Branchville.[90] Weir, who had been painting landscapes in a desultory fashion, began to focus on the genre with new enthusiasm, and along with Twachtman he explored its expressive possibilities. It was probably around this time that Weir created a series of small-scale studies of the landscape around his farm. In these pictures he invariably chose the gray, overcast days of the late autumn, winter, and early spring. Melancholy in mood, the paintings borrow Twachtman's delicate tonal palette. Unlike Weir's earlier landscapes, which are often painted in fairly strong colors with definite contrasts of light and dark, the later ones are done in muted tones, all of which are kept within a narrow range of values. In *Autumn*

3.70 J. Alden Weir, A Brittany Village, *late 1870s or early 1880s, oil on canvas, 19 × 24 in., inscribed and signed at lower left:* To my friend J. A. Valentine/J Alden Weir 1885/Hotel———of Brittany *(Dr. Helen E. Peixotto).*

Landscape (about 1888–90, fig. 3.74), Weir uses subtle value variations to establish spatial relationships within the picture. The double tree in the foreground, for instance, is slightly more darkly colored than are the trees in the distance. Weir's *Early Spring at Branchville* (about 1888–90, fig. 3.75) and Twachtman's *End of Winter* (after 1889, fig. 3.76) show how similarly the two artists were developing. Both have selected the transitional moment when the frozen landscape has begun to thaw; there is the slightest hint of regeneration in the vegetation. The evanescent changes in season, light, and weather conditions constitute the subject matter of these pictures; little actually happens, and even the few buildings and stone walls included are relegated to the middle distance, where they are obscured by foliage and mist. Weir has also absorbed something of Twachtman's sense of design. He now leads us into his composition on a strong diagonal, which disappears at a relatively high horizon line. The tree trunks and limbs, still bare from winter's chill, are silhouetted against the pale gray sky and the flat, slightly darker shapes of the distant foliage. The light calligraphic brushstrokes used in the trees and the broken touches of color representing the grass in the foreground are particularly reminiscent of Twachtman's more innovative painting style.

Weir's *Autumnal Days* (about 1890, present location unknown) was inspired by works like Twachtman's *Arques-la-Bataille* (1885, New York, The Metropolitan Museum of Art). In

3.71 *J. Alden Weir,* Haystacks, Shepherd, and Sheep, *probably 1884, oil on canvas, 29 × 36 in. (Provo, Utah, Brigham Young University).*

3.72 *J. Alden Weir,* A Belt of Wood, *1888, oil on wood, 14¾ × 26 in., signed at lower right:* J. Alden Weir '88 *(Stephen C. Clark, Jr.).*

3.73 *J. Alden Weir,* A Connecticut Farm, *about 1886, oil on canvas, 34 × 45 in., signed at lower right: J. Alden Weir (New Jersey, Princeton University, The Art Museum, Gift of A. E. McVitty).*

3.75 *J. Alden Weir,* Early Spring at Branchville, *1888–90, oil on canvas, 20¼ × 25¼ in., signed at lower left: J. Alden Weir (private collection).*

Autumnal Days, Weir follows his friend's example in developing his composition: the landscape, divided into bands of tonal color, rises to an elevated horizon behind a screen of delicate tree trunks. Most of Weir's paintings, however, are far more realistic than Twachtman's; they remain a record of a particular locale. Even in works such as his *Lengthening Shadows* (1887, fig. 3.77), where the composition seems to have been determined by considerations of design, Weir represents a specific hillside, specific trees. Further, his painting style in all these landscapes retains some element of his academic training. The contours of the objects depicted, for example, remain firm, and are never dissolved as Twachtman's sometimes are.

These tentative efforts in landscape painting prepared Weir for more innovative developments when, in the summer of 1891, he began to work in a style more directly influenced by French Impressionism.

3.74 *J. Alden Weir,* Autumn Landscape, *about 1888–90, oil on wood, 14¾ × 18 in., signed at lower left: J. Alden Weir (private collection).*

3.76 John H. Twachtman, End of Winter, *after 1889, oil on canvas, 22 × 30⅛ in., signed at lower right: J. H. Twachtman (Washington, D.C., National Museum of American Art, Gift of William T. Evans, 1909).*

By the end of the 1880s Weir had achieved a certain reputation and was enjoying some commercial success in New York. He was elected an associate member of the National Academy in 1885. At the annual meeting of the Academy's members that year he got thirty-five votes, three more than the required thirty-two and more than any other candidate except for J. Francis Murphy, who received an equal number.[91] The following year Weir was made an Academician, the highest level of membership that the National Academy bestowed on its members. His election was secured after a reconsideration vote, for only one of the candidates, Weir's friend Arthur Quartley, who died the following year, was elected on the first ballot.[92] Like all newly elected Academicians, Weir was required to present a diploma work, one which was typical of his artistic achievements. He submitted *Mary Joyce* (1882, New York, National Academy of Design), a picture of a girl looking with downcast eyes at a few small flowers she holds in her hand. Its sentimentality, strong anecdotal quality, and careful finish ally it to works that Weir had exhibited at the Academy earlier in the decade; in this sense, it is an appropriate choice for his diploma piece. However, when *Mary Joyce* was presented to the Academy in 1887,[93] it had been painted five years earlier and hardly represented Weir's most recent work. There must have been a number of paintings then in his studio which were both newer and more impressive. The apparent casualness with which *Mary Joyce* was selected suggests that Weir may have been unconcerned about the impression his diploma work would make at the Academy. In 1888 he sent a far less conventional

3.77 J. Alden Weir, Lengthening Shadows, *1887, oil on canvas, 20¾ × 25 in., signed at lower left: J. Alden Weir—1887 (Dr. and Mrs. Demosthenes Dasco).*

picture, *Idle Hours* (1888, fig. 3.39), to the Prize Fund Exhibition, where it won an award. The following year, the sale of his and Twachtman's oils and pastels at the Ortgies Gallery, even if not totally successful financially, brought a large segment of his work before the public for the first time. A few of the landscapes and the pastels in this exhibition showed that his work was beginning to react to French Impressionism. For Weir, the summers of 1890 and 1891 were his turning point. When his Branchville work, displaying the results of his first experiments in Impressionism, was shown at the Blakeslee Galleries in January 1891, he was immediately perceived as a convert to the new style.

4

Works in Secondary Mediums:
Watercolors, Pastels, and Prints

THROUGHOUT HIS CAREER J. ALDEN WEIR WORKED IN A VARIETY OF MEDIUMS, BUT during the 1880s and 1890s his work in watercolor, pastel, and printmaking assumed a new importance for him, as evidenced by the diverse examples he exhibited in the major annuals and expositions, as well as in the one- and two-man shows he held in 1893, 1895, and 1897. His work in the secondary mediums certainly contributed to his development as a painter: in them he was able to experiment more freely; to try subjects, compositions, and effects that the academic realm of oil painting inhibited; and to adopt for the first time most of the innovations that would become characteristics of his impressionist style—rough surfaces, broken brushstrokes, lighter colors, and more informal, seemingly spontaneous compositions. It could even be said that his new style in oil painting was the result of his work in these other mediums.

Watercolors

Weir had probably worked in watercolor from his earliest days in his father's studio, but in the 1880s that medium assumed an independent role in his development. He exhibited large, highly finished watercolors frequently, beginning at the American Water Color Society in 1880, when one critic observed that "unless error is made, this is the first time that Mr. Weir shows water-colors."[1] Weir was nominated for membership in the Society as early as 1882, but was not actually elected until 1884.[2] Almost every year from 1880 until 1890 he exhibited several works in the Society's annuals, which were held at the National Academy of Design. In 1883, Weir's watercolors were featured at H. Wunderlich & Co. in New York along with some by Régis Gignoux, a French artist who had worked in America, and, in 1884, Weir had his own one-man show of watercolors at Doll and Richards, in Boston.[3]

Few of Weir's student watercolors survive. He often colored his sketches after the old masters with watercolor, however, and must have carried that medium's eminently portable materials with him when he went out in the French countryside in the summers. *Fountain in the "Halls" of the Latin Quarter, Paris* (1875, fig. 4.1), inscribed "Paris April 29th 1875," is an example of the style Weir was developing in Paris during the 1870s. He has chosen a view in

4.1 J. Alden Weir, Fountain in the "Halls" of the Latin Quarter, Paris, *1875, pencil, pen and ink, and watercolor, 6⅝ × 9⅝ in. (sight), signed, dated, and inscribed at lower right:* Paris April 19ᵗʰ 1875/JAWeir *(present location unknown).*

which the solidity and architectonic shapes of the buildings give structure to his composition. In spite of the presence of a few figures, the scene is static; little effort has been made to suggest the movement and bustle of city life. Weir has worked in an academic manner: each form has been outlined carefully, the underlying pencil and pen-and-ink drawing is still visible, and the colors have been applied in translucent washes that cover the surface of the paper.

Soon after his return to New York in 1877, Weir painted a watercolor bust portrait of his father (probably 1878, fig. 4.2), which may have been done in preparation for his oil portrait of Robert (1878, fig. 3.1). The watercolor focuses almost exclusively on the sitter's face, his clothing and the background merely suggested by broad washes of color. The artist has used repeated strokes, sometimes heightened with gouache, to represent the fine wrinkles at the corners of his elderly father's eyes and mouth, the circles under his eyes, and the wisps of white hair on his head and chin, all of which are faithfully delineated. Weir's success in capturing the appearance and the pensive mood of this sitter notwithstanding, he attempted such conventional portraits in watercolor only rarely. Many of the bust-length figures he did in that medium are generalized by the sitter's demeanor and by the addition of accessory elements—a portrait of Anna contemplating a single blossom; one of Caro, her eyes filled with tears, holding a toy pail.

By 1881, Weir had already begun to experiment with a new and more dramatic water-color style, which is exemplified by his *Port Jefferson* (1881, fig. 4.3).[4] Here the preliminary drawing, neither as controlled nor as complete as that of *Fountain in the "Halls" of the Latin*

4.2 J. Alden Weir, Robert W. Weir, *probably 1878, watercolor on paper, 21¼ × 14½ in. (sight), unsigned (private collection).*

Quarter, Paris (1875, fig. 4.1), is obscured by the extensive use of gouache—strong opaque blacks, for the most part. Black is used to fill in several forms, mainly the hulls of two docked boats; to outline the vertical poles along the shoreline; and, applied more delicately, to define such details as the rigging in the ships and the wire strung between the poles. The watercolor application is animated; there are striking light and dark contrasts, and the medium's expressive possibilities have been exploited in a variety of ways. Weir's washes are less evenly applied—in some places the white of the paper shows through; elsewhere, it is covered by the color. The artist has caused some of his washes to bleed freely into the surrounding color, as is particularly evident in the sky, where dark clouds run into lighter areas that in turn blend with the hills of the horizon below them. In other areas, the washes have been allowed to dry into definite edges, creating dark, ragged lines. Weir, using a relatively dry brush, has applied an erratic series of sharp strokes to add dark accents on top of the washes. This free, unconventional technique has an effect on the watercolor's final appearance: it results in an image that in the richness of its paint surface emulates an oil painting.

Weir used a similar approach in several genre scenes he did during the early 1880s; these depict men engaged in work, a departure from his characteristically elegant subjects. Among

4.3 J. Alden Weir, Port Jefferson, *1881, pencil, watercolor, and gouache on paper, 6³/₄ × 9³/₄ in. (sight), signed and dated at lower right:* J. Alden Weir/1881 *(Oregon, Portland Art Museum, Gift of Mr. and Mrs. William M. Ladd).*

them are interior scenes of a cook standing before a stove (early 1880s, fig. 4.4) and two men laboring in a barn or a blacksmith's shop (1881, fig. 4.5). The latter demonstrates Weir's development of a less descriptive watercolor technique: he has represented the character of the somber, crowded interior without enumerating the details of its contents. The deep, rich colors and Weir's free brushwork are particularly appropriate for such a realistic scene. Although Weir's style in these two genre scenes and in *Port Jefferson* is somewhat individual, its origins can be found in the work of several artists whose work he admired. The subject and treatment of his harbor scene, particularly his extensive use of black to unify the composition, can be compared to Twachtman's oils of the late 1870s and early 1880s.[5] Weir may also have been inspired by the watercolors of Édouard Manet, who in the 1870s had done a number of beach and coastal views in which black, often applied with a dry brush, was used in combination with transparent washes.[6]

Weir continued to use black in his watercolors, but it gradually assumed a less important place in his palette. In *On the Avon* (1883, fig. 4.6), he has moved his model outdoors: his wife, Anna, is shown in a rowboat along a riverbank in Stratford-on-Avon, England, which the Weirs visited on their honeymoon. The artist demonstrates here his greater interest in the ephemeral quality of light and atmosphere. He presents the reflection of the trees, the fence, and the boat in the quiet, mirrorlike water and, along the left side, has skillfully suggested the shadow of the massive tree in the foreground. Much of the effect is achieved through the use of pale transparent washes, but by adding calligraphic strokes of black pigment to the limbs and foliage of the tree he has enhanced the visual interest of the scene.

4.4 J. Alden Weir, Man at the Stove, *early 1880s, pencil, watercolor, and gouache on paper, 8⅞ × 5⅛ in. (sight), signed at lower right:* J. Alden Weir *(Provo, Utah, Brigham Young University).*

4.5 J. Alden Weir, Men at Work in an Interior, *1881, pencil, watercolor, and gouache, 9⅝ × 6½ in. (sight), signed and dated at lower left:* J. Alden Weir/1881 *Provo, Utah, Brigham Young University).*

At the American Water Color Society, Weir began in 1882 to exhibit some of his most beautiful watercolors, those depicting still-life subjects. Among the earliest is *Flowers* (early 1880s, color plate 12), which shows a bouquet tossed casually on the ground. The subject's presentation was unusual for Weir, for he was then developing in his oils a still-life composition that characteristically featured at least one decorative vase filled with elaborate arrangements of flowers. In the watercolor, however, he was observing a tradition established in mid-century America by followers of the English Pre-Raphaelites, who showed still lifes in their natural setting, outdoors. In *Flowers*, a few brilliant red blossoms, perhaps poppies, and several kinds of delicate white flowers are placed on a dark brown ground. Their coloration is emphasized by strong lighting and by the use of opaque white highlights, which define the individual petals of some of the flowers, such as the daisy in the center foreground. Weir is still working in rich colors, highly contrasted, and using gouache extensively.

In *Roses with Glass Goblet and a Cast of Giovanni Bologna's "Venus After the Bath"* (1884, color plate 13), Weir applies some of the same techniques to a tabletop arrangement of antique objects and delicate, wilting flowers. This was the sort of subject that caused one reviewer to

4.6 J. Alden Weir, On the Avon, *1883, pencil, watercolor, and gouache on paper, 6½ × 9½ in. (sight), inscribed and dated at lower right: Stratford on Avon/May 26ᵗʰ/83 (Provo, Utah, Brigham Young University)*

comment that Weir's work had "a charm of spirituality and the suggestion of decay which belongs rather to Old World art than to New."[7] Weir has achieved an even greater textural richness: the surface of the paper has been covered with washes, which have then been highlighted with white and pale gray gouache applied in a distinct linear manner. He uses the two techniques in order to differentiate between the surfaces and the textures of his models—the glistening transparency of glass, the reflective metal surfaces of the silver tankard and the bronze statuette, and the soft, pliable petals of the yellow roses. In *Flowers on a Window Sill* (1884, color plate 14), Weir shows more interest in the effects of natural light. The flowers are held by clear glass vessels placed in front of a window through whose panes an urban view, probably of New York, is visible. Weir's palette has been clarified; the dark, opaque colors evident in his earlier work have been replaced by lighter tones applied in washes, with gouache used sparingly, usually just in the highlights.

In all these still lifes Weir was inspired by John La Farge, who in the 1870s and 1880s was creating and exhibiting a large number of still lifes in watercolor, many of which juxtaposed flowers and antique decorative objects.[8] La Farge's *Still Life with Chinese Vase of Roses* (about 1878–79, fig. 4.7), exhibited at the American Water Color Society in 1879, is executed with the wide range of techniques that Weir was soon to employ—broad washes in some areas, heavy gouache in others. La Farge's sensitivity to the coloristic qualities of light and to the vaporous atmosphere surrounding his models must have been a major factor in the transformation of Weir's palette, which remained somber but in which black gouache became gradually less prominent. The emphasis that La Farge placed on watercolor within his own

4.7 John La Farge, Still Life with Chinese Vase of Roses, *about 1878–79, watercolor on white paper, 16⅛ × 16 in. (Cambridge, courtesy of the Fogg Art Museum, Harvard University, Grenville L. Winthrop Bequest).*

oeuvre may also have had an effect on Weir, who around this time began to undertake larger and more finished watercolors, and to exhibit them more often as independent works of art.

Perhaps the most impressive of Weir's watercolors are those he did with his wife, Anna, as his model. The earliest show Anna in picturesque costumes: in *Sunday Morning* (1883, fig. 4.8) she wears a peasant dress and cap; the prayer book she carries and her devout expression suggest that she is on her way to a religious service.[9] The life-size scale of the work and the technique Weir used in painting it—gouache applied in an even and highly finished manner— seem to be unique in his work. *Anna Seated* (1885, fig. 4.9), which evokes a nostalgia for the past, portrays Mrs. Weir in an old-fashioned, Empire dress, seated in a painted chair of the same period.

The most effective of the watercolor series are the domestic scenes that show Anna, in contemporary clothing, engaged in quiet, contemplative tasks—sewing or reading—or simply musing. The earliest may be *Anna Sewing* (1885, color plate 15), in which she sits working in front of a window only partly covered by sheer curtains. Sunlight streams in, illuminating Anna's dress, hand, and the white material on which she sews. Weir has planned his setting carefully: each element has been selected for the part it plays in structuring the composition— the shutter, the window mullions, the framed and matted picture, and the high-backed chair create a pattern of horizontal and vertical lines around the figure. *In the Library* (late 1880s, fig. 4.10) is one of the largest of the series. Anna and Caro are shown seated in a darkened interior, with dramatic lighting, perhaps from a window on the left, creating strong light and shadows. The child is engrossed in her book, but the mother is evidently distracted—a letter lies on her lap, its envelope has fallen at her feet. Anna's gestures suggest depression or

. *Alden Weir,* Sunday Morning, *1883, pencil, watercolor, and* *he, on paper, 47½ × 30 in. (sight), signed with a monogram and* *at lower left:* JAW 83 *(private collection).*

4.9 J. *Alden Weir,* Anna Seated, *1885, pencil and watercolor on paper, 13¼ × 9¼ in. (sight), signed and dated at upper left: J. Alden Weir/'85 (private collection).*

sorrow: her right hand rests limply on the arm of her chair; her left hand supports her head. The artist has returned here to the dark palette that characterized his earlier watercolors, perhaps to reinforce the scene's sober mood. In spite of the low lighting, Weir continues to explore the effects of natural light falling on the figures and their setting.

Anna and Caro in the Twelfth Street House (1887, color plate 16) is a more complicated composition. Seated in the foreground, Anna turns her glance from the letter in her lap to the far end of the room, where Caro is looking out a window at a nearby building. The placement of the figures—Anna in the right foreground and Caro in the left distance—establishes a delicate balance between the two. Weir's use of cropping, particularly of the fireplace fender on the left and of Anna on the right, together with his treatment of space (a highly polished floor seems to recede up rather than back to the open window) suggest that he had already

4.10 J. Alden Weir, In the Library, *late 1880s, pencil, watercolor, and gouache on paper, 30¾ × 20½. (sight), unsigned (private collection).*

begun to study the compositional devices of the French Impressionists. His format could be compared to that of Gustave Caillebotte's oil painting *Les raboteurs de parquet* (1875, Paris, Musée du Louvre, Galerie du Jeu de Paume), which was exhibited in New York in 1886, only a year before Weir did this watercolor.[10] Caillebotte's use of rich, dark oil pigments and his ability to represent cool natural light with sharp contours and firm lines may also have influenced Weir. Nevertheless, in *Anna and Caro in the Twelfth Street House,* as in other of his watercolors of the period, Weir's colors are precisely rendered without losing their clarity and freshness. His style has become more English than French; a development that was likely the result of his admiration for Edwin Austin Abbey (1852–1911), a leading American water-colorist in the 1880s who later settled in England.[11] Weir had known Abbey since the late 1870s, when they were both members of the Tile Club, and he was certainly familiar with Abbey's watercolors, which were painted in the English manner and exhibited regularly at the American Water Color Society. Abbey's *An Old Song* (1885, fig. 4.11), a historical genre scene set earlier in the century, offers an Anglo-American counterpart to Weir's contempo-rary subjects. Both artists work in a controlled, highly finished style, using natural light to clarify three-dimensional forms and lavishing attention on accessory elements so masterfully

17. J. Alden Weir, *The Letter*, 1890, pencil, watercolor, and gouache on paper, 30 1/4 x 20 1/4 in., signed and dated at lower left: J. Alden Weir—1890 (private collection).

18. J. Alden Weir, *Feeding the Chickens, Branchville,* early 1890s, pastel on paper mounted on canvas, 20 1/8 x 24 1/4 in., unsigned (private collection).

19. J. Alden Weir, *The Ice House,* pencil and pastel on paper, 11 3/4 x 9 in. (sight), unsigned (private collection).

20. J. Alden Weir, *Branchville Pond*, pencil and pastel on paper, 8 13/16 x 9 3/16 in., unsigned (private collection).

21. J. Alden Weir, *The Windowseat*, 1889, pastel and pencil on paper, 13 1/4 x 17 1/2 in. (sight), signed and dated at lower right: J. Alden Weir/1889; and at upper right: J. Alden W——(private collection).

22. J. Alden Weir, *The Tulip Tree, Branchville*, pencil, watercolor, and pastel on paper, 13 1/4 x 9 1/2 in. (sight), unsigned (private collection).

23. J. Alden Weir, *The Laundry, Branchville*, about 1894, oil on canvas, 30 1/8 x 25 1/4 in., signed at lower right: J. Alden Weir (private collection).

24. J. Alden Weir, *The Red Bridge,* about 1895, oil on canvas, 24 1/4 x 33 1/4 in., signed at lower left: J. Alden Weir (New York, The Metropolitan Museum of Art, Gift of Mrs. John A. Rutherfurd, 1914).

4.11 Edwin Austin Abbey, An Old Song, *1885, watercolor and pencil on paper, 27½ × 47½ in. (sight), signed and dated at lower left: E. A. Abbey/1885. (New Haven, Connecticut, Yale University Art Gallery).*

represented that their surfaces and textures bear little evidence of the brushwork that has created them.

Anna Dwight Weir Reading a Letter (about 1890, fig. 4.12), an unfinished watercolor, reveals a great deal about Weir's working method. In it the artist has completed the background—the shuttered window, the floral arrangement on the sill, and the framed pictures— but he has only begun work on the figure. Anna, whose head and shoulders are finished, is otherwise sketched in pencil, with lightly drawn contours defining her hand and arm and less definite lines suggesting the folds and decoration of her dress. From this watercolor it is obvious that Weir did not develop all parts of his composition evenly as he worked; instead, he seems to have almost completed one area before moving on to the next. He probably finished the background of *Anna Dwight Weir Reading a Letter* first, and then began on the figure, working from top to bottom, before stopping in the middle of his task. Some areas are covered only with a transparent wash, a step that would precede the application of smaller, more distinct strokes of color to delineate details.

The most ambitious watercolor in this series—*The Letter* (1890, color plate 17)—shows Anna, pen in hand, as she pauses in writing a letter; Caro, seated at her feet, is absorbed in a toy. The artist lavishes attention on surfaces and textures, re-creating the soft pink of Anna's dress, the dark green foliage of the still life beside her, and the rich pattern of the tapestry behind her. This was the last of Weir's domestic genre scenes and the culmination of his use of a large scale in the watercolor medium.

Around the same time that Weir was painting his domestic scenes, he was using their elaborate interiors as settings for occasional watercolor pictures of his dogs, which were usually shown resting in front of a hearth. In *Two Dogs* (1885, color plate 10), he has gone to great lengths to represent the surfaces and textures of his models and their surroundings. The gleaming brass of the cauldron and the fireplace tools, the individual hairs of the dogs and the

4.12 J. Alden Weir, Anna Dwight Weir Reading a Letter, *about 1890, pencil, watercolor, and gouache on paper, 12½ × 9¼ in., unsigned (New York, The Metropolitan Museum of Art, Mr. and Mrs. Norman Schneider Gift, 1966).*

fur hearth rug, and the rough bark of the wood in the fire are all depicted realistically through a skillful application of washes punctuated by delicate strokes of contrasting colors, often enhanced by gouache.

In the late 1880s and early 1890s, when Weir's watercolor palette was somewhat somber and his technique restrained, he did relatively few landscapes and exhibited even fewer. His technique in *Hillside with Wheat* (late 1880s, fig. 4.13) resembles that in other subjects he was doing around the same time. Over transparent washes he has applied fine strokes to represent the individual blades of wheat in the foreground; such detailing is minimal in the background, where the foliage of the trees is represented with repeated layers of wash. In *Farmer with Oxen* (about 1890, fig. 4.14), he places the figure and the oxen in the foreground, where they act as the focal point. In this watercolor his technique becomes more animated: his washes are enhanced by varied strokes of color, with accents applied with a relatively dry brush in the tree trunks and the stone wall in the distance. In *Man on a Quai, Paris* (probably 1889, fig. 4.15), he added watercolor washes and some gouache to a quick pencil sketch of the river

4.13 J. Alden Weir, Hillside with Wheat, *late 1880s, pencil, watercolor, and gouache, 14 × 9 3/4 in., unsigned (private collection).*

4.14 J. Alden Weir, Farmer with Oxen, *about 1890, pencil and watercolor on paper, 6⅞ × 11 in. (sight), unsigned (private collection).*

4.15 J. Alden Weir, Man on a Quai, Paris, *probably 1889, pencil, watercolor, and gouache on paper, 6³/₈ × 9¹/₄ in. (sight), signed at lower left: J. Alden Weir (private collection).*

4.16 J. Alden Weir, Mending the Stone Wall, *late 1890s, pencil, watercolor, and gouache on paper, 11⁷/₈ × 11¹/₄ in. (sight), signed at lower left:* J. Alden Weir *(private collection).*

Seine. As his perception of the medium shifts, his watercolors begin to lose the clarity and pellucidity of his earlier efforts: in *Mending the Stone Wall* (late 1890s, fig. 4.16), for instance, the surface of the watercolor has been reworked repeatedly, wash applied on top of wash, often with some body color added, resulting in an effect that no longer seems spontaneous.

During the late 1890s, Weir experimented more freely with gouache, creating works in which line, color, and design took precedence over representation. The striding hunter and his dog are lost in a pattern of color in *The Hunter* (1895–1905, fig. 4.17). The man, barely visible in the upper middle of the composition, is viewed through an intricate screen of trees, one of which is pressed close to the picture plane. Short rapid strokes, many of them heightened with white gouache, increase the work's textural quality. The composition is flattened and presented as a two-dimensional pattern, and the horizon is raised to the upper edge of the paper, so that we are forced to read upward rather than backward in space. In *Rabbits by a Pond* (late 1890s, fig. 4.18), Weir shows in gouache a screen of slender trees whose trunks are reflected in the water below. The density increases from the foreground, where much of the paper is allowed to show through to suggest the frozen surface of the water; to the middle ground, where the trees themselves are more solidly painted; to the distance, where a view of the forest and its surrounding hills is represented by heavy lavender gouache. The strong design, especially in the repetition of forms, and the use of unrealistically pale colors make this a highly decorative picture.

4.17 J. Alden Weir, The Hunter, *1895–1905, pencil, watercolor, and gouache on paper, 7³/₈ × 9¹/₄ in. (sight), unsigned (private collection).*

4.18 J. Alden Weir, Rabbits by a Pond, *late 1890s, pencil and gouache on paper, 9½ × 7⅜ in. (sight), unsigned (Provo, Utah, Brigham Young University).*

Weir continued to work in watercolor until the end of his career. Indeed, the medium was one that he turned to more often as he aged; its small scale and informality made it suitable for his later years, when poor health sometimes prevented his undertaking more ambitious works in oil. *Kingsworthy* (1913; fig. 4.19) is typical of his late watercolors. He most frequently chose landscape subjects then, usually scenes where the sky, trees, and water gave him an opportunity to represent the changing effects of weather. His watercolors were less fragmentary in appearance; little of the paper remained uncovered. In general, he used clear washes and relatively little gouache. He applied his colors in broken strokes, which were long and somewhat flaccid; gone were the delicate, small strokes that had enlivened his earlier work. His palette was extremely pale, often cool in tone. Nonetheless, he occasionally regained the energy of his earlier watercolor style. In *Wolvesley Castle* (probably 1913, fig. 4.20), for instance, where the stonework of the ruined castle and the foliage of the trees behind it are depicted by a layer of broken brushwork applied over translucent washes, the elderly artist once more recaptures the flare and vitality of his younger days.

4.19 J. Alden Weir, Kingsworthy, *1913, pencil and watercolor on paper, 8½ × 11½ in. (sight), signed at lower left: Kingsworthy J. Alden Weir (private collection).*

4.20 J. Alden Weir, Wolvesley Castle, *probably 1913, pencil and watercolor on paper, 13½ × 9⅝ in. (sight), signed at lower right: J. Alden Weir (private collection).*

Pastel

The development of Weir's work in pastel, which reached its peak in the late 1880s and the 1890s, is difficult to trace. Few of his pastels are signed and fewer are dated; many of the works are small and informal and were done only for his own satisfaction. Weir exhibited with the Society of Painters in Pastel in 1888, 1889, and 1890, and eight of his pastels were included in the exhibition and sale he and John H. Twachtman held in 1889.[12] No chronology can be assembled from his infrequently exhibited examples; the works he showed can rarely be identified, for their subject matter and titles are similar and they were not accorded the critical attention usually given to his larger and more finished works of art.

It can be assumed that Weir first turned seriously to pastel during the 1880s, when the medium was enjoying a revival in the United States.[13] In 1883, he was listed as one of the founding members of the Society of Painters in Pastel, although he did not participate in their first exhibition, which was held in the following year.[14] His active use of pastel probably dates to the summer of 1888, when he and Twachtman worked together at the Weir farm at Branchville, Connecticut. A major cause of his interest, however, was a large group of pastels shown in the exhibition of French impressionist works brought to New York by Durand-Ruel in 1886. At this landmark exhibition Weir probably saw pastels by such artists as Hilaire-Germain-Edgar Degas (1834–1917), Pierre-Auguste Renoir (1841–1919), Claude Monet (1840–1926), and Berthe Morisot (1841–1895). He was also familiar with the pastels of James Abbott McNeill Whistler, whose work was featured at a major exhibition at H. Wunderlich & Co. in 1889. Whistler had already influenced several Americans in Weir's circle, Twachtman, William Merritt Chase, and Robert Blum, for example, all of whom either knew his work or had met him on their trips to Europe.

Pastel, essentially colored chalk mixed with gum for binding and molded into sticks, can be used in a variety of ways. It can be applied in a thick layer to achieve an effect not unlike that of an oil painting or it can be used sparingly to create a work that more closely resembles a drawing. *Feeding the Chickens, Branchville* (early 1890s, color plate 18), is a rare example of Weir's use of the former method. He has applied his pastel heavily to create a surface like an oil painting's, and then added lighter touches of color in chalky, linear strokes that are most evident where the dark crowns of the trees are silhouetted against the lightened sky. Most of Weir's pastels, however, fall into the latter category; they are unequivocally drawings. He usually begins by making pencil guidelines that define the principal masses of the composition, and applies to this framework the color, usually in broken strokes made with the tip of the pastel, but occasionally in broader areas produced by dragging the full length of the stick across the paper. *Connecticut Fields* (fig. 4.21) exemplifies his technique. Weir has drawn a number of pencil lines to indicate the placement of the clouds, the hills, and the edge of the meadow in the middle distance; even the outlines of the bushes have been drawn in first, not with firm, continuous contours but with soft, broken outlines. Color has been added, though not to the entire surface of the paper; the area left blank serves as a part of the composition. As in most of his pastels, Weir here uses a subtly colored paper, which lends a unifying tone to the work. A similar approach can be seen in *Conanicut Island* (about 1894, fig. 4.22), where crisp pencil outlines surround the wharf and the beached boats, and pastel is used sparingly, except in the brilliantly colored water represented by long strokes of white and azure blue.

Much of Weir's pastel style in landscape has been borrowed from Twachtman's, who seems to have experimented with the medium as early as 1885. In *The Edge of Webb Farm* (fig. 4.23), Weir follows Twachtman in the choice of support (a bluish-gray-toned paper) and in technique, which favors delicate linear effects. Weir has also developed a typical Twachtman composition: the forms depicted in detail are massed in the middle distance, with the foreground left almost empty and the sky only suggested. This effect is evident in Twachtman's pastel *Trees in a Nursery* (about 1885–90, fig. 4.24), where the focal point is a copse of trees in

4.21 J. Alden Weir, Connecticut Fields, *pencil and pastel on gray paper, 11⅛ × 16¾ in. (sight), unsigned (private collection).*

4.22 J. Alden Weir, Conanicut Island, *about 1894, pencil and pastel on paper, 7⅞ × 10¼ in. (sight), signed at lower middle:* J. Alden Weir *(private collection).*

4.23 J. Alden Weir, The Edge of Webb Farm, *pencil and pastel on light gray paper, 8 × 10⅝ in. (sight), unsigned (private collection).*

the middle ground, and sketchy rows of trees alternate with blank areas of paper in the foreground. In *The Edge of Webb Farm* Weir has represented rocks, grass, and bushes in the middle ground with an intricate linear pattern of pastel; in the foreground, the paper has been left nearly blank; in the distance, the sky has been shaded slightly with white chalk.

Weir often uses white or high-keyed colors in his pastels, not only to represent highlights but also to outline the silhouette of dark forms against lighter areas. Along the horizon line of *The Edge of Webb Farm*, for example, he has sketched in the crowns of several trees that are defined less by their contours as by the lightened sky behind them. His use of toned paper has heightened the effect, increasing the contrast between the pastel and its support. The same device is seen more dramatically in *The Ice House* (color plate 19), where the gray paper establishes the dark areas of the composition, mainly the slender trunk of the foreground tree and the forest behind it. The artist then adds the high-keyed colors—white on the walls of the icehouse and in the sky; brilliant greens in the grass and foliage. The gray-toned paper serves a similar function in *Branchville Pond* (color plate 20), with some lighter touches of blue, green, and yellow for a rocky knoll in the foreground and, in the middle distance, blue and green for the trunks of the silhouetted trees, the forest, and its reflection on the surface of the pond. The pale blue of the sky and the water below is lightened still further by strokes of pure white chalk to create clouds in the sky and highlights in the water.

Weir's use of white is best illustrated by *The Windowseat* (1889; color plate 21), which he exhibited at the Society of Painters in Pastel in 1890. Described at the time as a "graceful

4.24 John H. Twachtman, Trees in a Nursery, *about 1885–90, pastel on paper, 18 × 22 in., unsigned (Mr. and Mrs. Raymond J. Horowitz).*

modulation of white tones,"[15] it features the artist's wife, Anna, clad in a simple white dress and seated beside a window, her book and a flower laid aside as she gazes out into the green landscape beyond. This is a quiet scene, devoid of action; the artist concentrates instead on the effects of light. The cool darkness of the room is relieved by the brilliant sunlight, which streams in through the leaded windows and illuminates the unadorned walls and the soft folds of the model's dress. Anna, posed on a narrow foreground stage, is pressed between the picture plane and the wall immediately behind her; in a sense, she is reduced to another design element in a pattern of light and dark. This pastel, executed on a trip to England in the summer of 1889, may have been inspired by Weir's study of Whistler's work, which he would likely have seen in that artist's exhibition in New York the previous March. One of Whistler's oils—*Symphony in White, No. 1: The White Girl* (1862, Washington, D.C., National Gallery of Art)—had been shown in New York in 1881 and could have sparked Weir's exploration of the subtle nuances in tones of white.[16] Weir's pastel recalls his earlier oil experiments in shades of white; most notably *Flora: Carrie Mansfield Weir* (1881, color plate 5). In *The Windowseat*, however, the lack of finish, even in areas of the figure's face and hands, makes this a more daring effort, and one which the artist probably would not have presumed to attempt in oils.

Since landscape was by far the most common subject for Weir's pastel work, he occasionally did pastels of figures posed outdoors, especially when he was exploring similar subjects in oil in the 1890s. *Girl Standing by a Gate* (1896, fig. 4.25), far more highly finished than Weir's landscapes, is typical. In it he has used pencil to outline and model forms, particularly the stone wall, the wooden gate, and the figure. His pencil lines, drawn sharply, are short and fairly stiff. The only area that receives his usual free treatment is the landscape in the distance, where tree trunks and foliage are loosely suggested by a few quick strokes. Even the choice of subject is more anecdotal than is common in Weir's work of the period. The simple costume of the model, the full bucket at her feet, and the stool resting on top of the stone wall indicate that this is a milkmaid who has paused in her labors. In subject and technique, *Girl Standing by a Gate* recalls the pastels of Jean-François Millet (1814–1875), whose work seems also to have influenced Weir's oil paintings of the 1890s. The technique

4.25 *J. Alden Weir,* Girl Standing by a Gate, *1896, pencil and pastel on paper, 13¾ × 9½ in., signed at lower right: J. Alden Weir '96 (Bellevue, Washington, Michael R. Johnson, Inc.).*

4.26 J. Alden Weir, Woman in a Garden, *1900–1905, pencil and pastel on paper, 7¼ × 9⅞ in. (sight), unsigned (private collection).*

Weir used in this pastel—a distinctly linear application of color in short rapid strokes over a dark preliminary drawing with the bare paper often permitted to show through—is typical of Millet's pastels as early as the 1850s.

Woman in a Garden (1900–1905, fig. 4.26) shows a new, less restrained technique that Weir adopted in his pastels at the turn of the century. As always, he began with a pencil sketch, but now his outlines are far more fragmentary; the figure is suggested by a few cursory strokes and the contour of the bed of flowers, the focal point of the composition, by a few irregular broken lines. At the same time, his pastel application has become heavier, with some areas, notably the flowers and the forest beyond, represented in dense, grainy pastel.

The only known Weir still life executed in pastel is one of his most ambitious efforts in that medium. Executed on a relatively large scale, *Vase of Roses* (late 1880s, fig. 4.27) is one of the few pastels in which he attempts to cover the surface of the paper evenly. The bare paper shows through in some areas, most noticeably in the highlight on the vase, but the support is largely concealed by delicate strokes of color. The treatment of the wilting pink and yellow roses and the translucent vessel that holds them demonstrates Weir's ability to surround three-dimensional objects with light and atmosphere.

Pastel had a far-ranging effect on Weir's work in all mediums. It enabled him to experiment with high-keyed colors and with brilliant whites; these tones soon occupied a more prominent place in his palette in oils. By working in pastel he could create the richer, more variegated surfaces that by 1900 would be common in his oil paintings. Further, the dry

4.27 J. Alden Weir, Vase of Roses, *late 1880s, pastel on paper, 16 × 14 in., signed at lower right: J. Alden Weir (Mr. and Mrs. Ralph Spencer).*

chalky surface created by his soft application of pastel also affected his application of paint in his oils, where he often strove for a similar effect in spite of the more fluid character of that medium. The most visible result of Weir's tentative explorations in pastel, however, was a greater freedom in his approach to his subjects, particularly his landscape subjects, and an attendant release from the academic constraint of finish.

Mixed Mediums

By the 1890s, Weir's work in watercolor and pastel had led him to combine the two. His work had been developing along parallel lines in both mediums, as attested by his greater freedom of application, more richly textured surfaces, and more frequent use of high-keyed colors, particularly the brilliant whites.

The combination of mediums is most often seen in Weir's landscapes. In *The Tulip Tree, Branchville* (color plate 22), he first applied broad washes of watercolor to establish the major masses of the composition: the blue of the sky, the cool gray shadows of the foliage, and the lavender shadow in the center foreground. Next, he went over the surface of the paper with pastel, working in short, delicate strokes to capture the effect of light falling on the leaves of the tulip tree. The sky's pale blue is balanced by the green of the tree; the contours dissolve in overlapping blue and green strokes. Here, more than in other works, Weir closely follows the tenets of the French Impressionists.

By using watercolor and pastel together, Weir was able to create the effects for which he was striving in the individual mediums, but with far greater ease. These are the works that most closely resemble oil paintings in appearance; in them Weir was able to experiment unconstrainedly with the colors and surface textures that would soon appear in his oils.

Prints

Weir produced over 140 prints, mainly etchings and drypoints, in editions of varying sizes, some in only a few impressions.[17] Many of Weir's etchings are identified with a monogram or signature in the plate, but few are actually signed by the artist. (Those pulled by the artist's daughter Caroline Weir Ely after his death are signed with her initials.)[18] He is reported as saying late in his life that he had worked as an etcher "for a period of about eight years," but not as specifying which years they were.[19] He dated few of his prints and he kept no record of them, with the result that a variety of dates for his printmaking activity have been proposed: for his initial work, as early as 1885; for his last, as late as 1894. Most scholars, however, have agreed that Weir's interest in printmaking was strongest from about 1887 to 1893.[20]

The boundaries of Weir's printmaking activities may not be so clear-cut, for his interest in the medium was certainly aroused well before 1885. As a young man, he probably studied his father's fine collection of prints.[21] His father may even have offered him some rudimentary instruction in etching, for during the 1820s, Robert had worked in the medium, copying "some of Rembrandt's etchings so close as to be with difficulty detected."[22] Julian may also have seen an important exhibition of French etchings, held at the Derby Gallery in New York in 1866, that had been organized by Alfred Cadart, the Paris publisher. In Paris, in 1875, Weir took at least one lesson in etching (where and from whom are unknown), and was pleased with the results. As he wrote to John, "This evening [I] got a proof which although bad [is] so much better than I had expected I will feel encouraged to go on with it."[24] When he returned to New York in 1877, etching was enjoying a revival; the New York Etching Club was established that same year.[25] While it is known that its members gathered together in each other's studios in the early days to etch and pull plates, no record of the membership exists until 1882, when the club held its first major exhibition, at the National Academy of

Design. Weir was listed among the club's New York members that year and the next (though he did not exhibit), but not again until 1893, when he renewed his membership after a lapse of ten years. He must have been etching in the earlier period, for such a small and select group would hardly have accepted him as a member if he was not yet working in the medium. Several of his friends, among them Twachtman, William Merritt Chase, Wyatt Eaton, and Charles Adams Platt (1861–1933), were already experimenting in etching at the time, and Weir himself may have begun and then stopped, resuming later in the decade. There is no real explanation for the hiatus, nor is it known which, if any, of his plates could have been executed during the early 1880s. A number of factors could have diverted his attention from the medium between 1883 and about 1887: Twachtman, who seems to have been instrumental in encouraging Weir's etching, was no longer in New York; Weir's family and professional responsibilities, including a heavy teaching load, may have distracted him; and he did not then have his own press, which would have discouraged him. It is equally possible that Weir continued to etch on an occasional, informal basis throughout the 1880s, but that he preferred not to exhibit until he gained more experience. After the late 1880s, when he brought his prints before the public for the first time, he continued to exhibit widely until at least 1895; he may have continued to etch and pull plates later than has been suggested. He began to display his work at the New York Etching Club in 1888; in 1892, he contributed eighteen prints to the club's show, and the following year, twelve. In 1893, he sent more than forty etchings and drypoints to the World's Columbian Exposition in Chicago. That same year he took part in an exhibition at the American Art Association that showed his work and Twachtman's together with that of Claude Monet and Paul-Albert Besnard (1849–1934). Weir's etchings, over seventy of them, some in more than one state, far outnumbered his oil paintings and were received with much more enthusiasm. In 1895, an exhibition of his work at H. Wunder-lich & Co. included fourteen etchings, which were praised for their "effect of mass by line." Judging by the number of etchings he showed and by the importance of the exhibitions in which they were included, it is clear that as late as 1895 Weir still considered printmaking a major form of expression.[26]

Weir likely began his printmaking career by making reproductive etchings; one (probably after 1882, West Point Museum Collections, United States Military Academy) after a version of Robert Weir's painting *Santa Claus, or Saint Nicholas*, may have been among the first of them.[27] It is typical of all Weir's reproductive prints: the entire plate is etched, with little or no blank paper in evidence; the parallel hatching lines are short, regular, and close together; and detail is emphasized. Even after 1887, when Weir began to etch in earnest, he still did a number of reproductive prints. He copied *Portrait of Lucas Vorsterman*,[28] an etching by Sir Anthony Van Dyck, as late as 1888, yet another example of his lifelong dependence on the old masters for inspiration. Many of his reproductive prints are after his own work, re-creations of his compositions in other mediums. His *Portrait of Mr. Delano*[29] duplicates his oil painting *Warren Delano* (1880, Hyde Park, New York, Home of Franklin D. Roosevelt, National Park Service); *Oriana*[30] is after the oil painting of the same title (Northampton, Massachusetts, Smith College Museum of Art). His two etchings of dogs sleeping on a hearth, done during the late 1880s, reproduce his watercolors *Three Dogs* (1887, private collection)[31] and *Two Dogs* (1885, color plate 10).[32] These reproductive works presumably date early in Weir's experience as an etcher, before he was sufficiently confident of his command of the medium to undertake original compositions.

Weir's original etchings were often developed from preliminary drawings, of which enough survive to suggest that they were a standard feature of his working procedure, especially for figure subjects. For *The Lesson* (about 1890, fig. 4.28),[33] he first made a pencil drawing of the composition (about 1890, fig. 4.29); it appears, of course, in reverse to the finished etching. The border around the edge of the drawing (which corresponds to the size of the plate) and the strong hatching to represent shadowed areas mark this as a printmaker's working drawing. There is little detail; Weir seems merely to have been plotting the strong light and dark contrasts that create such drama in the finished etching. The verso of the

4.29 *J. Alden Weir, Drawing for "The Lesson," about 1890, pencil on paper, 10 × 6⅛ in., unsigned (Provo, Utah, Brigham Young University).*

28 *J. Alden Weir, The Lesson, about 1890, etching, 6¹⁵/₁₆ × 4⅞ in. ate), signed in plate at lower right:* J.A.W. *(private collection).*

4.30 *J. Alden Weir, Tracing on the verso of drawing for "The Lesson," about 1890, carbon and pencil, 10 × 6⅛ in., unsigned (Provo, Utah, Brigham Young University).*

drawing (about 1890, fig. 4.30) reveals the next step in Weir's preparatory process: he must have placed the drawing right side up (fig. 4.29) on the glossy side of a piece of carbon paper, and traced its principal contours; they would have been reversed on the other side of the drawing, showing him how his composition would appear etched and printed. (The printed image of any etching is the mirror image of its plate.)

He used a slightly different working method in his drypoint *On the Piazza* (fig. 4.31).[34] He began as usual with a pencil drawing (fig. 4.32), over which he placed a piece of transparent tracing paper. He then traced the principal lines of the drawing onto the paper (fig. 4.33), which, when held up to the light and viewed from the reverse, would allow the composition to be assessed as to its appearance when printed—again, the mirror image of the original drawing.

4.31 J. Alden Weir, On the Piazza, *drypoint, 4 × 4¹⁵/₁₆ in. (plate), unsigned (Washington, D.C., Library of Congress).*

Some of Weir's small landscape etchings, for instance, *Bas Meudon No. 2* (1889, fig. 4.34),[35] and some of his city scenes, such as *Adam and Eve Street* (1889),[36] which seem to have been done on the spot with little or no preparatory work, show the influence of Weir's friend John Twachtman. Twachtman was already etching when Weir accompanied him and his wife, Martha, on their honeymoon trip through Holland. Weir would probably have watched them work, for both of them created and exhibited prints during the early 1880s.[37] Twachtman is said to have carried copper plates and an etching needle in his pocket so he could make informal landscapes on his travels through the countryside.[38] Weir picked up the habit: "It was so easy to carry about in one's pocket a half dozen plates which would fill up

4.32 J. Alden Weir, Drawing for "On the Piazza," *pencil on paper, 4⁷/₁₆ × 5¹/₂ in., unsigned (Provo, Utah, Brigham Young University).*

4.33 J. Alden Weir, Tracing of drawing for "On the Piazza," *pencil and pen and ink on paper, 4⁹/₁₆ × 5¹/₈ in, unsigned (Provo, Utah, Brigham Young University).*

4.34 J. Alden Weir, Bas Meudon, No. 2, *1889, etching, 3⅞ × 5⁵⁄₁₆ in. (plate), signed in plate at lower right:* J.A.W. *(private collection).*

odd moments," he reminisced in 1911.[39] *Bas Meudon No. 2* is a good example of the small, informal sort of piece that resulted from such casual efforts: it is not a highly finished work with a well-planned composition and careful hatching but almost a sketch, with long rapid lines suggesting the clouds, the foliage, and their reflection in the water. Many of Weir's landscape etchings, among them *The Wooden Bridge*[40] and *The Stone Bridge,*[41] follow the format typical of Twachtman's work in every medium: landscape elements massed in the middle distance; the sky and the foreground less fully finished.

Weir's prints also owe much to those of Whistler. After visiting Whistler in London on his way home from Paris in 1877, Weir had gone to the British Museum to study his prints and had commented on their wide range of quality, "some of which are certainly remarkably fine and more decidedly bad." He continued: "In etching he always manages to get a good tone, which I believe [to be] a great deal in etching."[42] Weir nevertheless at that time considered Whistler's etchings "child's play" compared to Albrecht Dürer's woodcuts and engravings, but he must have revised his opinion during the early 1880s. By then he would have seen examples of Whistler's work on his trips to Paris and London and at exhibitions held by the New York Etching Club and at H. Wunderlich & Co., which showed Whistler's Venetian etchings and drypoints in 1883.[43] Weir borrowed heavily from Whistler for his printmaking style: his *Blacksmith Shop* (1889?, fig. 4.35)[44] is a subject of the kind that had long fascinated Whistler. As in many of Whistler's plates, there is much white space in the foreground, where objects have been merely outlined; the dense hatching and darkened areas are concentrated in the middle ground immediately surrounding the blacksmith, the focal point of the composition. Weir may also have acquired his taste for nocturnal subjects from Whistler; following his example, Weir lit his scenes with artificial light in such prints as *By Candlelight*[45] and *The Evening Lamp.*[46] Whistler may also have inspired some of Weir's more intimate subjects—women and children reading or sitting quietly;[47] domestic genre scenes, usually depicting Weir's wife, Anna, and their daughter Caro—that utilize some of the same formal devices seen in Whistler's work. In his *Gyp and the Gipsy* (1890, fig. 4.36),[48] for example, Weir places his subject high on the plate and focuses on her head and shoulders, leaving the remainder of the plate blank. He has heeded the advice that Whistler had given his students Walter Sickert (1860–1942) and Mortimer Menpes (1855–1938): to start the drawing at the point of greatest interest and proceed out from it, so that the work could be left off at any point and there would still be a complete picture.[49] Whistler's influence can also be seen

4.35 J. Alden Weir, The Blacksmith Shop, *1889?, etching and drypoint, 10¾ × 7¹³/₁₆ in. (plate), signed in plate at lower right: J. Alden Weir (private collection).*

in Weir's urban views. In city scenes like *The Carpenter's Shop* (1891, fig. 4.37)[50] and *My Backyard No. 2* (1890, fig. 4.38),[51] Weir uses the flat facades of buildings, placed parallel to the picture plane, to limit spatial recession and to create a two-dimensional decorative pattern on the surface of the plate.

4.36 J. Alden Weir, Gyp and the Gipsy, *1890, drypoint, 7¹³/₁₆ × 5⅞ in. (plate), signed in plate at lower left:* J. Alden Weir; *inscribed in the plate at upper right: Caro—1890 (Washington, D.C., National Museum of American Art, Smithsonian Institution, Gift of Brigham Young University, 1972).*

4.37 J. Alden Weir, The Carpenter's Shop, *1891, etching, 7⅞ × 5¹⁵/₁₆ in. (plate), signed in plate on clapboard near lowest step:* J.A.W. *(private collection).*

4.38 J. Alden Weir, My Backyard, No. 2, *1890, etching, 7⅞ × 5¹⁵/₁₆ in. (plate), signed in plate at lower right:* J.A.W. *(Washington, D.C., National Museum of American Art, Smithsonian Institution, Gift of Brigham Young University, 1972).*

Whistler (perhaps through Twachtman) also had an effect on some of the more technical aspects of Weir's etchings. Weir did his own printing on old paper which he collected for the purpose. At times he trimmed the print to its plate mark, leaving only a small tab for his name or monogram—again a practice of Whistler's. Weir may have had Whistler's well-known series of prints of views of London and Venice in mind when he undertook his Isle of Man series—eighteen prints, complete with a title page, and printed in London.[52] They are markedly different in style from his other etchings in that their surfaces are more heavily worked. In *Castle Rushen—Isle of Man* (1889, fig. 4.39),[53] for one, he uses deeper, stronger strokes to create dense blacks that are particularly striking in the boats and their silhouetted masts and rigging. For the buildings behind them, he employs delicate, varied strokes; to suggest the buildings along the shoreline, regularly spaced, overlapping vertical lines. Here, as in many of his Isle of Man landscapes, the sky has not been etched at all; to lend tone to it he has relied on the texture of his paper and on the varying degrees to which he wiped the ink from the plate.

In addition to his etched genre scenes with Anna and Caro, Weir did a series of portraits

4.39 *J. Alden Weir*, Castle Rushen—Isle of Man, *1889, etching, 8³⁄₄ × 11⁷⁄₈ in., signed in plate at lower middle:* J. Alden Weir *(in reverse); inscribed in plate at lower right:* Castle Russian / Isle of Man *(private collection).*

of friends and of members of his family. Although some of them, like *Portrait of John H. Twachtman* (1888),[54] show the subject quietly reading or working in a domestic interior, most of them are austere, focusing almost entirely on the individual's face and the character it expresses. Weir's *Portrait of Theodore Robinson* (fig. 4.40)[55] is one of the most poignant of the latter. He has depicted his friend (an acute asthmatic) in a moment of rest, his sunken eyes closed and his head leaning back wearily on his raised arm. In such portrait etchings as this, Weir continued to adhere to the academic standards of his training: the faces of his subjects are relatively finished, with firm contours and a strong suggestion of modeling.

While etching and drypoint represented Weir's principal printmaking techniques, he did do one engraving and three lithographs. The engraving, *Arcturus* (1893, fig. 4.41),[56] was done as an illustration for *Scribner's Magazine* of May 1893, where it was reproduced with an architectural surround. This is the most studied of Weir's prints: a young boy, wearing only a loincloth, stands on a globe in the center of the composition. In one hand he holds what appears to be an unstrung bow; with the other, he reaches to his shoulder as if to draw an arrow from an invisible quiver. The three stars in the background of the engraving must allude to Arcturus as the brightest star of the northern constellation Boötes. Many of the accessories seem to refer to hunting: an animal's skull and horns, a bandolier that hangs from the horns, and a metal trap suspended from an unseen support. Some features—the elaborately folded drapery encircling the figure and the twisted ribbon floating inexplicably behind

4.40 J. Alden Weir, Portrait of Theodore Robinson, *drypoint, 6⅞ × 5 (plate), unsigned (private collection).*

4.41 J. Alden Weir, Arcturus, 1893, engraving, 8⅞ × 7⅜ in. (plate); unsigned in plate, signed in pencil at lower left: J. Alden Weir (Washington, D.C., National Museum of American Art, Smithsonian Institution, Gift of Brigham Young University, 1972).

him—seem intended as purely decorative. Despite the complexity of the composition and its relatively high degree of finish, the meaning of *Arcturus* remains obscure.

In 1896, just as Weir seemed to be turning away from printmaking, lithography enjoyed a revival. Montague Marks, editor of *The Art Amateur*, organized the American Society of Painter Lithographers, and such painters as G. Ruger Donoho (1857–1916), F. Hopkinson Smith (1838–1915), Henry Ward Ranger (1858–1916), and Weir himself began to experiment in the medium for the first time.[57] Weir executed two lithographs—*Portrait of a Woman Sewing*,[58] a reproduction of an earlier watercolor, and *Woman and Little Girl*,[59] for which he made a highly finished preparatory watercolor in sepia—but both of them lack the immediate freshness of his etchings and drypoints. His final lithograph, *At the Piano*,[60] was done late in his life for a collection of drawings, published by the National Arts Club, that were sold for the benefit of the American Artists' War Emergency Fund.

4.42 J. Alden Weir, Portrait of Miss Hoe, *drypoint, 10 × 6⅛ in. (plate), unsigned (Mr. and Mrs. Raymond J. Horowitz).*

Printmaking was important for Weir only for a brief period of his career, but the period was a meaningful one. His interest in etching and drypoint was strongest during the late 1880s and early 1890s, just when he was beginning to develop an individual, impressionist style. As his *Portrait of Miss Hoe* (fig. 4.42)[61] demonstrates, his experiments with printmaking offered him an opportunity to capture in black and white some of the subtle light and atmospheric effects that he was exploring in color in other mediums. Frances Weitzenhoffer, in the summary of her article on the American impressionist printmakers, has aptly observed: "They translated the principles of Impressionism through the use of lines—short thin lines, nervous staccato lines, rich mellow lines, sometimes lines that are close together to suggest atmosphere or sparkling brilliance. The results are spontaneous works that capture impressions of shifting grace in form and movement, with a touch as light as air."[62] Etching may also have helped to maintain the strong linear quality present in Weir's work even after he began to use the broken brushstrokes of Impressionism: the geometric structure and formal design evident by around 1890 in etchings like *The Carpenter's Shop* (fig. 4.37) were later incorporated into such major landscapes of Weir's as his 1895 *Red Bridge*.[63]

5

Impressionism 1890–1900

WEIR'S CONVERSION TO IMPRESSIONISM WAS NOT EVIDENT IN HIS PAINTING UNTIL around 1890, sixteen years after the French Impressionists' initial exhibition in Paris and four years after their last, but its influence on his work, once seen, would continue until the end of his career.[1] Weir appears to have been one of the first American artists to visit an impressionist exhibition in Paris. He recorded his reaction to it, an unfavorable one, in a letter to his parents on April 15, 1877: "I went across the river the other day to see an exhibition of the work of a new school which call themselves 'Impressionalists.' I never in my life saw more horrible things. I understand they are mostly all rich, which accounts for so much talk. They do not observe drawing nor form but give you an impression of what they call nature. It was worse than the Chamber of Horrors. I was there about a quarter of an hour and left with a head ache."[2]

Weir's 1877 response to the Impressionists, which suggests that he was startled by their work, is surprising, for logically he should have known of them earlier. He was a student in Paris in 1874 and 1876 when paintings by the group had been on view at their well-publicized exhibitions. He had certainly seen the work of Édouard Manet, who was not a participant in the Impressionists' exhibitions but who did create paintings strongly influenced by their precepts.[3] His mentor, Gérôme, was acquainted with both Manet's work and the Impressionists' and commented freely on the movement, though in negative terms.[4] Several friends of his, John Singer Sargent among them, studied with Carolus-Duran, a realist painter who had once moved in Manet's circle.[5] The result of all this presumed exposure to the Impressionists and their work on Weir's painting style was negligible during the 1870s. As a student at the École des Beaux-Arts he was striving for the academic recognition held in contempt by those of the Impressionists whose style flouted the École's rigorous training.

Turning away from traditional art, the Impressionists sought inspiration in new visual sources—photography, popular illustrations, and, especially, the color prints of Japan. They showed their subjects, usually landscapes or scenes of contemporary life, as they appeared at the moment of viewing, and achieved a spontaneous, unpremeditated effect with such compositional devices as cropping, asymmetry, and the placing of figures close to the picture plane. They rejected the elaborate studio procedures of their more traditional colleagues and

188

often painted outdoors, the better to capture transitory qualities of light and atmosphere. They used pure, brilliant colors applied side-by-side or in overlapping broken strokes, a technique that created an illusion of shimmering light and that enabled them to show reflected as well as local color. The bold impasto of their textured paint surfaces and their abolishing of firm outlines were further departures from prevailing standards for a finished painting, and, because they often ignored the conventions of modeling and perspective, their paintings appeared flat.

While Weir the art student was offended and puzzled by these features of Impressionism, Weir the artist gradually became accustomed to progressive French painting, acquiring a more balanced outlook that would prepare him to accept Impressionism around 1890. In Paris, in 1881, he made significant purchases from Durand-Ruel on behalf of an American buyer—one painting by Edgar Degas; two by Manet (1861, fig. 3.31; 1866, fig. 3.32).[6] He then visited Manet's studio and acquired yet another work; Manet's paintings were to influence his development for the rest of the decade. Paintings by the French Impressionists were first seen in large numbers in New York in 1886, in an exhibition shown at the American Art Association and then at the National Academy of Design. They were soon being exhibited in New York fairly regularly. In 1889 Weir again visited Paris, where he probably saw more examples of the style. Most of his knowledge of Impressionism, however, was indirect, coming from friends who had already embraced the style after working or studying in France. During the crucial period of Weir's conversion to Impressionism, these painters—among them John H. Twachtman, John Singer Sargent, Theodore Robinson (1852–1896), and F. Childe Hassam (1859–1935)— encouraged his progress by their example. Twachtman was painting impressionist snow scenes around his home in Connecticut as early as the winter of 1888/89. Hassam, returning in 1889 from four years of study in Paris, settled in New York; his cityscapes, done at home and abroad, strongly exhibit the influence of such French Impressionists as Gustave Caillebotte, Claude Monet, and Camille Pissarro. Sargent arrived in New York in 1890: after visiting Monet at Giverny in 1887 he too had begun painting in an impressionist style. Robinson, who usually spent his winters working in New York, had met Monet in 1887 and visited him each year at Giverny from 1888 to 1892. It was he who provided the most direct connection to the acknowledged leader of French Impressionism and it was he who played the key role in Weir's growing commitment to the style. As Weir was finding his own way as an Impressionist, he relied heavily on Robinson's advice. The two visited exhibitions together and debated aesthetic issues; Weir even read excerpts of Robinson's letters to his pupils at the Art Students League.[7]

Weir, for several reasons other than his less than firsthand knowledge of the style, adopted Impressionism more slowly than did some of his colleagues. He was slightly older and certainly better established than many of his peers, and so more resistant to innovation; academic principles were more deeply imbued in him; and landscape painting, the Impressionists' primary genre, had become a consuming interest of his somewhat late. The development of his impressionist style during the 1890s can be divided into three phases. From 1890 to 1892, he explored the possibilities of the style only cautiously; he lightened his palette, adopted some broken brushwork, and was less formal in his compositions. Landscape assumed a new importance to him. He began several more advanced figural paintings in outdoor settings during the summer of 1891, only to be interrupted by his wife's untimely death. He then turned his attention to a commission to paint a mural for the World's Columbian Exposition, which was to open in Chicago in 1893. Only after he finished the mural did he resume easel paintings, and it was in these that he utilized the impressionist mode more surely, turning for inspiration to Japanese prints, the art form that had so markedly influenced the French Impressionists twenty years earlier. From 1893 to 1895, Japanese prints informed his paintings: his compositions featured cropping, asymmetry, and oblique angles; his figures were treated as flat silhouettes, except for their faces; and pattern assumed a new role in his work. At this period of his greatest achievement in the impressionist style, Weir's concern for the formal qualities of line and color in some of his decorative paintings parallels features of French Post-Impressionism then reaching its height in Paris. By the late 1890s, the pace of Weir's search for a personal impressionist style had slowed, and the dictates of his academic training—strong draftsmanship, firm modeling, and anatomical accuracy in the representation of figures—reasserted themselves with new force.

1890–1892

In 1890, impressionist paintings by American artists appeared in full force at the exhibitions of the National Academy of Design and the Society of American Artists. The following year, Edmund C. Tarbell (1862–1938) showed his *Three Sisters—Study in June Sunlight* (1890, Wisconsin, Milwaukee Art Center Collection) at the Academy's spring exhibition. At its autumn exhibition, William Merritt Chase exhibited an outdoor scene painted in New York's Central Park; Childe Hassam, two views of Manhattan's parks, one set in winter, another in spring; Robinson, two landscapes displaying "a brilliantly natural effect of out-of-doors light and atmosphere."[8] In the 1891 exhibition of the Society, where Hassam showed *Spring Morning in the Heart of the City* (1890, New York, The Metropolitan Museum of Art) and Chase, *An Early Stroll in the Park* (about 1890, New York, Kennedy Galleries), Weir exhibited *The Open Book* (1891, fig. 5.1), prompting one critic to place him among the artists who seemed "to lose courage instead of gaining it."[9] An example of Weir's continuing interest in idealized academic subjects, *The Open Book* represents a draped female figure seated in a sunlit landscape; holding a daisy in her right hand, with her left she marks the place in an open book that

5.1 J. Alden Weir, The Open Book, *1891, oil on canvas, 31³/₄ × 29¹/₈ in., signed at lower left: J. Alden Weir/1891 (Washington, D.C., National Museum of American Art, Smithsonian Institution, Gift of John Gellatly).*

is perhaps Japanese in origin. Allegorical overtones in the picture may have been inspired by Weir's recent interest in Pierre Puvis de Chavannes (1824–1898), one of whose works he had purchased from Durand-Ruel in Paris in 1889.[10] Many aspects of *The Open Book* also recall works by Jules Bastien-Lepage—the virtually square format, elevated horizon line, cool palette, and model's transported expression. Only Weir's treatment of the landscape—in particular, the delicate flowers in the foreground, the shadow cast by an unseen source, and the soft clouds above the crest of the hill—offer any hint of his work's future development.

In style and treatment of subject, Weir's interior scene *In the Livingroom* (about 1890, fig. 5.2) shows evidence of his response to Impressionism, as a comparison with *Idle Hours* (1888, fig. 3.39), a similar domestic subject painted only two years earlier, reveals. *In the Livingroom* depicts Anna with her back to the viewer, a device used by Chase among many other American painters to heighten the intimacy of a composition and to impart to its subject an air of mystery. *In the Livingroom* is not anecdotal; it simply captures a quiet, contemplative moment in the Weirs' home life. This is the same room represented in *Idle Hours*, but the vantage point has been changed in order to create a greater sense of spontaneity. Whereas in the earlier painting the window is placed parallel to the picture plane, now its angle is oblique. In *Idle Hours*, Weir, trying for a consciously balanced composition, poses his figures

5.2 *J. Alden Weir*, In the Livingroom, *about 1890, oil on canvas, 25 × 20 in., unsigned (private collection).*

in interlocking triangles; here, the model and her accoutrements are placed haphazardly. Here too, Weir's painting style enhances the informal quality of the subject; the feathery brushwork, with soft flecks of color, obscures the careful drawing that undoubtedly lies beneath the surface of the painting. Weir's acceptance of Impressionism nevertheless remains tentative: his palette is still restrained and his brushwork is only occasionally broken.

The same ambivalence can be seen in landscapes Weir produced around 1890. While continuing to paint moody, tonal pictures like *Early Spring at Branchville* (1888–90, fig. 3.74), he was introducing into other works some aspects of Impressionism. In *The Farmer's Lawn* (about 1890, fig. 5.3), he roughens the paint surface, applying pigment in broad patches. His palette becomes higher in value, almost pastel, with a chalky quality that will be common in his outdoor work throughout the decade. He establishes areas of light and dark with little equivocation; the edges of the blue and lavender shadows remain clearly defined. In *The Lane* (about 1890; fig. 5.4), Weir begins to break up the paint surface. Some of the broad brushwork seen in *The Farmer's Lawn* is repeated in the foreground of the picture, but smaller touches of color are used to suggest the fresh foliage of early spring, and ridges of impasto represent the irregular surface of the stone wall at the crest of the hill. The palette is even higher in key.

Weir's one-man show at Blakeslee Galleries in January and February of 1891 was billed as including only recent paintings.[11] Of the twenty-three pictures included, at least seventeen were landscapes, many of which cannot now be identified. Two—*Roses* and *Flowers*—may have been still lifes. Only four were figure paintings: *The Christmas Tree* (1890, color plate 8);

5.3 J. Alden Weir, The Farmer's Lawn, *about 1890, oil on canvas, 20¾ × 29 in., signed at lower right: J. Alden Weir (private collection).*

5.4 J. Alden Weir, The Lane, *about 1890, oil on wood, 10¼ × 15¾ in., signed at lower left: J. Alden Weir (Washington, D.C., The Phillips Collection).*

Nasturtiums (about 1890, private collection), a lavender-toned bust portrait of Anna; *A Head,* an unidentified work; and *Drilling Rock* (about 1890, present location unknown), showing a farmer working outdoors. The content of the show reveals the direction of Weir's work during the next decade: still-life painting all but eliminated; figure paintings more often set outdoors; and landscape his principal mode of expression. Weir, in a letter to his brother John, acknowledged that these exhibition paintings marked a break with his earlier work: "Traditions are good things and interesting, but are not these things so much instilled in me that instead of the character and aspect interesting me most, I was hampered by trying to render the things I did not see and unable to get at the things that really existed."[12] His Blakeslee exhibition caused Weir to be hailed as "the first among Americans to use impressionistic methods and licenses successfully," but it was hardly a demonstration of his complete mastery of the style; he had included in it some of the tonal landscapes and Barbizon-inspired paintings he had done during the 1880s. The conservative character of these earlier works may have accounted for the exhibition's success, for after praising Weir's ability to represent "that atmospheric quality, that out-of-doors look which a considerable number of his French comrades have attained from the start," one critic went on to catalogue the ways in which the artist had modified Impressionism. His paintings, "within their limits, [were] faithful transcripts of nature," and "one [did] not need to stand more than a reasonable distance away from them to understand what the painter was aiming at." The writer concluded with the opinion that "Mr. Weir will yet go further and do better."[13]

This he did during the summer of 1891. Weir's impressionist style, perhaps inspired by the paintings his colleagues had recently exhibited, was developing rapidly. He began a group of paintings about which he wrote to John. "I have painted a great many canvasses this summer . . . among the best of my work is in the search of color & I do think it will make my last year's work look pale."[14] His accelerating development can be seen first in his landscapes. Like those he had painted a year earlier, *Early Moonrise* (1891, fig. 5.5) is a tonal picture with a melancholy palette and subtle variations of color in which Weir's use of distinct horizontal bands—the sky, the distant forest, the screen of bushes—all enlivened by a single strong diagonal, the toppled tree in the foreground, is reminiscent of Twachtman's. Weir's paint application is now varied; he uses a thick, heavily laden brush in the background, a finer, drier brush in the screen of bushes, and some light broken brushwork in the foreground. The rough brushwork, the somber palette, and the choice of subject—a still twilight scene—may have been the result of his reexamination of paintings by Barbizon artists, perhaps Théodore Rousseau or Charles-François Daubigny, or by their American followers, for example, Dwight W. Tryon.

Throughout the 1890s Weir tended to paint scenes showing buildings or other solid structures—fences, trellises, bridges, even screens of trees or vines—in decorative interwoven or intersecting lines that both define recessional planes and enhance the works' decorative appeal. Weir undoubtedly learned to use these architectonic shapes from paintings by his friends Twachtman and Robinson, who in turn were inspired by such French Impressionists as Gustave Caillebotte and Claude Monet. In the summer of 1891, Weir painted *The Grey*

5.5 J. Alden Weir, Early Moonrise, *1891, oil on canvas, 34¼ × 24⅝ in., signed and dated at lower right: J. Alden Weir—91 (private collection).*

5.6 *J. Alden Weir*, The Grey Trellis, *1891, oil on canvas, 26 × 21½ in., signed and dated at lower left: J. Alden Weir—91 (private collection).*

Trellis (1891, fig. 5.6), a view of his garden. In the immediate foreground, parallel to the picture plane, are several posts of a trellis in whose midst an empty screen of vertical and horizontal supports recedes on a diagonal. The trellis's geometric pattern is repeated by four tall, leafless tree trunks on the right edge of the canvas and by the fence that bounds the garden in the distance. In this painting, as in other of Weir's early impressionist pictures, broken brushwork is limited mainly to the flowers and foliage, the white flowering tree in the center of the composition in particular. Delicate calligraphic lines, most evident along the contours of the trellis, help define each element. The palette, though lighter, is still somewhat tonal.

The rural theme in *Midday* (1891, fig. 5.7)—the barnyard at Weir's Branchville farm, complete with pecking chickens—is one often chosen by the Barbizon school, but its composition and treatment show Weir's growing involvement with Impressionism. The scene appears fragmentary and spontaneous: a tree, invisible save for one of its limbs that floats unsupported along the upper border, casts a shadow across the foreground. The canvas's most striking feature is the transformation of Weir's painting technique. Broken brushwork is used throughout the picture, although it does not compromise the firmly drawn structure of buildings, fences, trees, and foliage. Weir's palette has brightened considerably. His new

5.7 J. Alden Weir, Midday, *1891, oil on canvas, 34 × 24½ in., signed and dated at lower right: J. Alden Weir '91 (Fall River, Trina, Inc.)*

awareness of color can best be seen in his treatment of shadows—blues and greens for those in the foreground; a cool lavender for one on the red wall of the barn.

The figure paintings from the summer of 1891 are far more advanced. Some are quick sketches executed outdoors in an attempt to record a fleeting effect of light. *Anna Seated Outdoors* (1891, fig. 5.8) is one of these. Working on a small wooden panel, Weir shows his wife silhouetted against a sun-filled landscape. His colors are almost luminous and he eliminates detail. He varies the surface of the picture by using a palette knife for representing Anna's dress and the wooden tip of his brush to create the pronounced striations on the wall of the buildings behind her. Many of the paintings Weir began that summer were larger works that he never finished; the landscape settings were almost resolved, but the models were left as mere sketches. Weir clearly distinguished between those two elements in his working procedure. The settings were done on the site at Branchville or Windham, but the figures were to have been completed the following winter in his New York studio, where he could lavish the requisite care on painting their faces and hands.[15] The arduous training he had received at the École des Beaux-Arts two decades earlier would have suggested this working method. Fate, however, intervened: on January 29, 1892, in the winter when Weir would normally have been finishing these pictures, Anna gave birth to another child, Cora. A week later, Anna was dead of puerperal fever. Weir was devastated. He and Anna had been

5.8 *J. Alden Weir*, Anna Seated Outdoors, *1891, oil on wood, 10⅜ × 7⅝ in., unsigned (private collection).*

inseparable and greatly devoted; she was his model as well as his companion. During the previous few years, while his ideas had become increasingly progressive, she had been unflagging in her support. As Weir wrote to Anna's mother, then on a trip around the world: "When we were first married my income was much larger than it is now, having of late striven for other things in which Anna gave me strength and encouragement, and we were both ambitious, we often talked of the time when we would look back on these hard times and smile at them. Man proposes and God disposes."[16]

The figure paintings from the summer of 1891, painful reminders of a happier time, were abandoned. In spite of their unfinished state, they are extremely important, for they are among the most ambitious of any Weir had then undertaken. Weir's figure compositions differ significantly from those of most of his colleagues; in his, the figures are shown large in scale and relatively close to the picture plane, with the landscape as a mere backdrop. In this regard, the 1891 figure paintings recall those of Mary Cassatt, whose *Family* (about 1886, Virginia, Chrysler Museum at Norfolk), exhibited in New York in 1886, may have inspired

5.9 J. Alden Weir, Family Group, *1891, oil on canvas, 38 × 30 in., unsigned (Provo, Utah, Brigham Young University).*

Weir's *Family Group* (1891, fig. 5.9).[17] Cassatt's use of this sort of composition was certainly the result of her friendship with the French painters Edgar Degas and Édouard Manet, both of whose work Weir also admired. In Weir's *Family Group,* Anna is seated with Dorothy, their one-year-old daughter, in her lap; Caro stands behind her, the figures unified by their poses and the positioning of their heads. The landscape setting appears to be virtually finished in rapid, broken brushstrokes that define the grass and the distant fence, but in the models' faces only Dorothy's features have been added. The dresses are just begun, with a few dark lines on them indicating the shapes of the bodies beneath. Weir's palette is clearer and lighter, the red of the chair complementing the bright green of the landscape.

The Wicker Chair (1891, fig. 5.10) is probably the painting that Weir described in a letter to John as "a portrait of Anna & Caro, which, if I can finish, will be my crowning portrait, outdoors."[18] Again his composition is unusual. The figures are placed asymmetrically: Anna is seated in profile on the left, and directly behind her stands a child (probably Caro), who is cropped by the left edge of the canvas. To represent the setting the artist uses regular broken strokes in a method of application that at times resembles an enlarged version of the dots used by some of the French Post-Impressionists.[19] He was no longer simply adding a veneer of brushwork on top of a conventional drawing; he was now building the sky and foliage, even

5.10 *J. Alden Weir,* The Wicker Chair, *1891, oil on canvas, 38 × 30 in., unsigned (private collection).*

5.11 *J. Alden Weir,* On the Porch, *1891, oil on wood, 26½ × 15¾ in., unsigned (private collection).*

Anna's face, with distinct dots of color. *On the Porch* (1891, fig. 5.11), another picture begun that summer but never completed, shows how daring his palette and paint application had become: bright yellows, reds, and blues are set down in thick mosaic touches.

World's Columbian Exposition

In the months following Anna's death, Weir immersed himself in his teaching activities and prepared his pictures for the spring exhibitions. He departed for Chicago in August of 1892, and spent about two and a half months there painting a large mural (fig. 5.12), twenty-five feet in diameter, for the Manufactures and Liberal Arts Building at the World's Columbian Exposition.[20] He joined a group of eight painters who, under the direction of Frank Millet and his assistant, Charles Yardley Turner (1850–1918), were decorating the four entrances to the building. Each portal was flanked by two vestibules, each of which was covered by a large dome that crowned four pendentives. Weir and Robert Reid, a figure painter from Boston and a fledgling Impressionist, were assigned the decoration of the two vestibules at the south portal.

All the artists working on the decoration for the building chose their own subjects, but from the beginning they agreed to emphasize the pendentives by filling them with figures; after some deliberation they decided that the figures should be approximately ten feet high.

5.12 J. Alden Weir, Mural for the Manufactures and Liberal Arts Building at the World's Columbian Exposition, 1892, representing allegorical figures of Decorative Art, The Art of Painting, The Goldsmith's Art, and The Art of Pottery, oil on plaster, approximately 25 ft. in diameter (destroyed).

The entire group collaborated on solving problems to do with working methods and materials. Weir undoubtedly worked most closely with Reid, for their murals' proximity made it essential that they be related both in theme and in style. Weir's mural (1892, fig. 5.12) shows four allegorical figures: Decorative Art, The Art of Painting, The Goldsmith's Art, and The Art of Pottery. Reid presented similar subjects: Iron-working, Ornament, Design, and Textile Arts. The material to be exhibited in the building (manufactured items) suggested these themes, which celebrated the presence of the arts in industry.[21] Both Weir and Reid depicted allegorical figures in their murals, each one endowed with the attributes of what she represented. Seated in the pendentives, the figures were unified not only by their gestures and by the arrangement of their draperies but also by the decorations, in both murals a standing youth placed over each of the four arches that spanned the pendentives. Weir's youths, joined by banners, held plaques; Reid's held wreaths and palm branches. The centers of the ceilings, colored blue in Weir's mural, opalescent in Reid's, were left unadorned.

An exhaustive amount of preliminary work preceded the actual execution of the murals. So that the artists could work in scale, each was given a model of his vestibule. Weir did dozens of drawings (Provo, Utah, Brigham Young University) in which he planned the overall concept of his mural and the pose of each figure. He began work on the figures by hiring a model and drawing from the nude, as his training dictated, and when he had determined the final composition, he had it photographed and enlarged by a technique perfected by Frank Millet. Finally, he made a preliminary sketch directly on the ceiling, which had been covered with a blue ground chosen to match what would be its finished color. Young artists assisted Weir and his painter colleagues in the mammoth task of painting the actual murals; their work was facilitated by an "atomizer," invented by Millet and Turner, which sprayed color onto the ceiling, covering the surface rapidly and evenly. The entire project was completed in a two-and-a-half-month period, a remarkable achievement, especially for an artist like Weir who lacked previous experience as a muralist.

The effect of this interlude as a decorator, which may have been a lasting one on Weir's development, was certainly notable over the next few years. It confirmed for him the camera's potential as an artistic aid, which could explain some aspects of his mid-1890s figure paintings—for example, the heightened realism of his faces and the use of such compositional devices as cropping, which is a photographic technique. The monumentality of his mural project may have fostered the larger scale soon evident in his figure paintings, and the experience may have inspired his use of silhouetted forms, flat areas of color, and simplified detail.

Weir's sojourn in Chicago created an interruption in his personal life and in the development of his impressionist style, but he soon resumed both with equal vigor. On October 29, 1893, a year after he returned to New York, he married Ella Baker, his first wife's sister. Ella, who had cared for his children since Anna's death, restored a measure of tranquillity to his home. Weir showed his works at many exhibitions in 1893, but the most important one was at the American Art Association, in New York, where his work and Twachtman's was presented in comparison with that of the French painters Claude Monet and Paul Albert Besnard. Critics were dazzled by the French artists' paintings. Said the reviewer for the New York *Sun*: "They overwhelm the spectator at first with a flood of splendid violets and golden yellows. One needs a moment, with something to steady himself by, in order to recover from the shock of this dazzling harlequinade of gay colors."[22] By contrast, the Americans' paintings seemed mild: "While, like Monet, they have striven toward the expression of impressions of landscape and figure, they have looked with soberer eyes. There is none of the splendid, barbaric color that distinguishes the works of the Frenchman. They tend to all-very grays modified by greens and blues quite as silvery."[23] Weir was perceived as being "more extremely impressionistic" than Twachtman.[24] Although Weir and Twachtman were overshadowed by the French artists, the exhibition established them both as leading American exponents of Impressionism. In December, Weir and Twachtman sent a group of their paintings to Boston,[25] where Impressionism was being championed by a number of their younger colleagues—among them Tarbell and Frank W. Benson (1862–1951).

Weir's work was again showing dramatic development. The paintings from the summer of 1891 had held great promise: many of them had been painted outdoors, and they were bold in composition, bright in palette, and unrestrained by the academic conventions of finish. In the winter of 1892/93, Weir had begun to explore in a new, more decorative direction, which was the result not just of his recent experience as a muralist but, perhaps more, of his study of Japanese art, which was soon to permeate every facet of his work.[26]

Japonisme

Weir was deeply influenced by *japonisme*, the enthusiasm for Japanese art and culture that swept Europe during the 1860s and 1870s, America in the 1880s and 1890s.[27] In the mid-nineteenth century, the country had just opened to Western trade, and examples of its decorative arts—fans, bronzes, ceramics, screens—were being studied for new sources of inspiration by artists and artisans. They quickly assimilated the basic features of Japanese style and subject matter, and Eastern forms, motifs, and compositions soon prevailed in Western paintings and interiors. Japanese art, notably color prints, had a profound effect on late-nineteenth-century painting; the French Impressionists had been influenced by it in the 1860s, and so had Whistler. Because his admiration for these artists shaped Weir's style during the century's last decade, Japanese art was a major factor in his work too, an integral part of the character of his own impressionist style.[27]

Weir's graphic work gives ample evidence of his response to the art of Japan. In the early 1890s, probably in 1893 or 1894, Weir sent for Japanese paper, inks, and brushes to Tadamasa Hayashi, a prominent Paris dealer in oriental goods, and he used them to make about seventy drawings of a feather, only one of which, *A Feather* (about 1894, private collection), seems to have survived.[28] When it was exhibited at H. Wunderlich & Co., in 1895, it and other of Weir's more experimental works were condemned as "the first rough, as yet un-thought-out ideas, such as one might jot down on the back of an envelope or on some scrap of paper, between the courses of a dinner or seated in a car or cab."[29] Under the influence of reproductions of Japanese art he had seen in *Le Japon Artistique*, a periodical which he had just purchased from the Paris dealer S. Bing in 1894, Weir also did more completely developed studies in black ink.[30] Weir's *Grape Leaves* (about 1894, fig. 5.13) must have been inspired by reproductions similar to Shumbokou's *Écureuils sur une vigne* (fig. 5.14). In drawings such as *In the Hammock* (about 1894, fig. 5.15) Weir uses Japanesque compositional devices—asymmetry, cropping, a high horizon line, and a geometric grille placed parallel to the picture plane—in an individual manner; graphic images from *Le Japon Artistique* typified by *Famille de pêcheurs*, an ink-and-brush drawing by Hokusai (fig. 5.16), or an untitled drawing by Ittsho (fig. 5.17) also influence the means he employs. Lively, irregularly shaped lines created by the twisting of his brush establish the contours of Weir's figures; the various patterns of the hammock's netting, the floor beneath it, the foliage in the distance, are each suggested by lines. The same technique can be seen in landscape drawings like his *Building and Stone Wall* (about 1894, fig. 5.18), where lines of varying lengths and widths represent a view of his Branchville farm. Weir soon modified this new drawing style, shifting to tiny, broken strokes—dots of various sizes and short, staccato lines—in other landscapes, *A Look Across the Fields* (about 1894, fig. 5.19) for one. In it there are hardly any contours or extended lines, except for faint pencil marks to define the outlines of the composition and a few threadlike tracings for the slender trunks and limbs of the trees. Dots and dashes are applied unevenly across the surface of the drawing—some densely, to suggest dark shadows, others sprinkled lightly across grass-covered meadows—but they join together and are readable when viewed from a distance. This radical technique, even more expressively used in *Ella Making a Wreath* (about 1894, fig. 5.20), where his brushstrokes are elongated and, in some areas, so unevenly applied that they take on an agitated appearance, is limited to Weir's work in black ink and brush, but must have affected his oils. At the least, his uses of ink would have enabled him to

5.13 J. Alden Weir, Grape Leaves, *about 1894, ink wash on paper,
7⁹/₁₆ × 10¹/₄ in., unsigned (private collection).*

5.14 Shumbokou, Écureuils sur une vigne, *reproduced in* Le Japon Artistique *3, no. 17
(September 1889), plate* AHB.

5.15 J. Alden Weir, In the Hammock, *about 1894, ink wash on paper, 9½ × 9¾ in. (sight), signed at lower right:* J. Alden Weir *(private collection).*

explore the visual effect of broken strokes and to learn how to use them to create different tonal values. His interest in such experiments in black and white may have been further engaged by his contemporaneous work in etching and drypoint, where the discipline of working without color had already enabled him to find simple graphic means for suggesting light and atmosphere.

More important than Weir's study of black-and-white reproductions was his fascination with the Japanese color prints that had so influenced the French Impressionists. Weir's enthusiasm for these prints can be established as early as 1893, although he may well have been familiar with them earlier.[31] (He had been friendly with Heromichi Shugio, a Japanese

5.16 *Hokusai*, Famille de pêcheurs, *repro-duced in Ary Renan, "La 'Mangua' de Hokusai," Le Japon Artistique 2, no. 8 (December 1888), p. 98.*

5.17 *Hanabusa Ittsho, one of two drawings reproduced in* Le Japon Artistique *3, no. 15 (July 1889), plate* AHE.

importer, since his Tile Club days.)[32] Parts of Weir's collection of Japanese prints survive in the possession of his family and of Brigham Young University,[33] so it is possible to compare specific prints he owned with the paintings he created.

There are approximately fifty Japanese prints which can be documented as having belonged to Weir. A few have been inscribed with information on their provenance—that they belonged to the artist or to his wife, Ella, or that they were purchased from a well-known nineteenth-century dealer of Japanese objects—but most are stamped with Weir's collector's mark, a small red oval containing his monogram, usually on the back of the print.[34] Since many other prints with a Weir family provenance are now mounted on cardboard, the stamp may be present on them, but obscured. Most of the prints are landscapes that usually include architectural elements such as buildings and bridges. Few are devoted solely to figures, although some contain them. Weir collected nineteenth-century prints primarily, nearly seventy per cent of them by Utagawa Hiroshige (1797–1858). There are also multiple examples by Katsushika Hokusai (1760–1849) and Utagawa Toyokuni I (1769–1825). Some may have been purchased in New York, but others came from Paris, from Hayashi and S. Bing; Weir, perhaps at Shugio's suggestion, wrote to Hayashi as early as December 1893, and their correspondence continued as late as 1900, when Hayashi offered him a book on the

5.18 J. Alden Weir, Building and Stone Wall, *about 1894, ink wash on paper, 6¹/₁₆ × 10 in. (private collection).*

5.19 J. Alden Weir, A Look Across the Fields, *about 1894, pencil, ink and brush on paper, 9⁵/₈ × 14⁵/₈ in., signed at lower right:* J. Alden Weir *(Provo, Utah, Brigham Young University).*

5.20 J. Alden Weir, Ella Making a Wreath, *about 1894, ink wash on paper, 13³⁄₈ × 8¹⁄₈ in. (private collection).*

history of Japanese art published in connection with the Universal Exposition in Paris.[35] Weir's purchases from Bing are even better recorded; in 1894, probably on March 20, he bought seventeen Japanese prints from him.[36] Bing and Weir too remained in contact until at least 1900.[37]

Some information about how Weir became absorbed in these prints survives. Several of his artist friends shared his enthusiasm, among them Robert Blum, who lived in Japan for about two years during the early 1890s, and Theodore Robinson, whose close association with the French Impressionists must have exposed him to oriental art around that same time. Robinson's diary records only some of Weir's activities (those he shared with its author), but it suggests the mounting enthusiasm for Japanese prints among the artists in their circle. Weir's interest may have been sparked in 1893, when he went back to Chicago to visit the World's Columbian Exposition; there he could have seen prints by Hokusai and Hiroshige.[38] He undoubtedly saw the important exhibition of Japanese prints held at Boston's Museum of Fine Arts in the autumn of that year, for he was in the city for his wedding (Twachtman, in

Boston to serve as Weir's best man, mentioned visiting the exhibition).[39] Weir was soon immersed in their study, for after spending Thanksgiving with the artist, Robinson wrote that "W. [is] enthusiastic over some old Japanese prints."[40]

Weir, described by Robinson as "Japanese-mad,"[41] took every opportunity to learn more about the prints during the winters of 1893/94 and 1894/95. He and Robinson attended an exhibition of "a beautiful collection of Japanese things" at Boussod, Valadon & Co., then one of Weir's dealers.[42] A month later Robinson, and most likely Weir, saw a group of Japanese prints that Bing lent to the American Art Association.[43] When the Association sponsored a second exhibition and sale of the prints in January 1895, it was attended by Weir along with his fellow artists Robinson and John La Farge.[44] Weir may actually have helped to arrange another exhibition, displayed in November 1895 at H. Wunderlich & Co., also one of his dealers.[45] Japanese art was even a favorite subject at Weir dinner parties: on April 8, 1894, Robinson joined Heromichi Shugio, Twachtman, and some other artists at the Weirs' home for a discussion of that country's art and literature.[46] Weir went so far as to trade a drawing by Jean-François Millet for what Robinson described as "some very good [Japanese] things."[47] No one could doubt that this mania had completely pervaded Weir's circle of friends.

To isolate the first examples of Japanese influence in Weir's work is, however, difficult, for certain of its aspects merely reinforced tendencies that had existed in his art since the 1880s, exaggerating them and bringing them to the fore. These included a general preference for a high horizon line in landscape paintings and, in figure paintings, the placement of his model in the foreground, close to the picture plane. Twachtman was Weir's closest friend and constant companion, and his views were probably the ultimate reason for Weir's adopting into his work the devices of *japonisme*. Judging from paintings such as *Arques-la-Bataille* (1885, New York, The Metropolitan Museum of Art), Twachtman had begun to assimilate the principles of Japanese art while working in Paris. Later, during the 1890s, he continued to find inspiration in it, using some of its elements to forge a decorative impressionist style that in such works as *From the Holley House* (about 1890–1900, W. David Lindholm Collection) bordered on abstraction.[48] Weir, during the mid-1890s, the period of *japonisme*'s strongest hold on him, also developed a highly decorative landscape style, although his landscapes were always more literal than Twachtman's. Because he was now more concerned with the design and structure of his compositions, he chose scenes with strong focal points, such as buildings or bridges, and he exploited their geometric shapes in his depiction of nature. The contours in his landscapes remained as firm and decisive as those in the prints that had influenced them, and the prints' delicate colors may also have inspired the light palette so evident in much of his work of the 1890s.

A landscape in which the Japanesque bent in his work has just begun to emerge is *The Laundry, Branchville* (1894, color plate 23). Its locale is familiar from earlier landscapes, but its unusual vantage point allows Weir to present the buildings in a fresh and unexpected manner. The horizon line is raised almost to the upper edge of the canvas; space recedes up rather than back. The red building and the white laundry strung on a line in front of it—the focal point of the composition—are relegated to the distant horizon, and most of the painting is devoted to the lime green grass, a few craggy boulders, and several tall, thin trees with scant foliage that seem to float on the surface of the hill like two-dimensional decoration.

None of Weir's landscapes were based on any one Japanese print; rather, they had motifs and compositional elements borrowed from several different prints and reassembled in an often original manner. *U.S. Thread Company Mills, Willimantic, Connecticut* (about 1893–97, fig. 5.21), is an example of this process. The focal point of Weir's composition, the stone bridge leading into Willimantic, is viewed from above, seemingly from the middle of the river. One of the bridge's ends and its supporting arches are cropped, a treatment that could have been suggested by any number of prints in Weir's collection, among them Hiroshige's *Ohashi (Bridge); Sudden Shower at Atake* (1857, private collection), from the series *One Hundred Famous Views of Edo*. In his landscape Weir adds at the far left a slender tree pressed close to

5.21 J. Alden Weir, U.S. Thread Company Mills, Willimantic, Connecticut, *about 1893–97, oil on canvas, 20 × 24 in., signed at lower left: J. Alden Weir (Mr. and Mrs. Raymond J. Horowitz).*

the picture plane, its crown cropped by the upper edge of the canvas, its base and roots eliminated from view. (A smaller tree, apparently detached from all support, floats in the center of the composition.) This is a familiar device in such prints as Hiroshige's *Musa* (about 1838, fig. 5.22). The general format of Weir's landscape—a close-up view of architecture on the left and a panoramic view of the distant landscape on the right—recalls in particular *Snowy Morning at Kioshikawa* (about 1829–32, fig. 5.23) by Katsushika Hokusai. The resemblance between the two works is heightened by Weir's massing of architectonic shapes in his foreground, his cropping its seemingly unsupported elements, and his using a low horizon line. Even the style in which *U.S. Thread Company Mills* is painted owes something to Weir's study of oriental art. The pastel colors surrounded by firm, sometimes dark, boundary lines, the flat walls of the factory buildings, and the distinct, patchy shadows, especially those on the trunk of the large tree at the left, could all have been suggested by Japanese prints in his collection.

Weir's occasional use of Japanesque elements in essentially representational landscapes was only the first stage of his absorption of Japanese principles: in 1894 and 1895 he demonstrated a far more educated understanding of their aesthetics in the paintings he created. *In the*

5.22 *Utagawa Hiroshige,* Musa, *about 1838, from the series* 69 Stations of the Kisokaido, *color woodblock print, signed: Hiroshige ga; publisher: Kinjudo; ex coll.: J. Alden Weir (private collection).*

5.23 *Katsushika Hokusai,* Snowy Morning at Kioshikawa, *about 1829–32, from the series* 36 Views of Mt. Fuji, *color woodblock print, signed: Zen Hokusai iitsu hitsu; publisher: Eijudo; ex coll.: J. Alden Weir (private collection).*

Shade of a Tree (1894, fig. 5.24) is in format one of the most daring of these. A leafy branch silhouetted against a sunny meadow extends across the upper edge of the canvas. Enlarged in scale and pressed close to the picture plane, this single element dominates the composition, casting a shadow on the grass below. The branch also confuses the scale of the rest of the composition, which, in a sense, becomes a flat backdrop behind it. The sky is barely visible above the trees in the distance, but there is little suggestion of recession toward the distance: the painting is read as a series of flat areas of color and pattern—the dark shadow, the

5.24 J. *Alden Weir,* In the Shade of a Tree, *1894, oil on canvas, 27 × 34 in., signed and dated at lower left: J. Alden Weir—1894 (Lincoln, Nebraska Art Association, Sheldon Memorial Art Gallery, University of Nebraska).*

meadow, the fence, the stone wall, and the band of trees. A similar format, which combines an enlarged foreground element with a panoramic view of the distance, can be found in at least one Japanese print owned by Weir—*Azakusa Kinkyuzan* (1856, private collection) from *One Hundred Famous Views of Edo* by Hiroshige.[49] Another print in the same series, *Maples at Mamma, the Tekona Shrine and Tsugi Bridge,* actually shows a leafy branch which could have served as the inspiration for its counterpart's placement in Weir's painting.[50]

In *The Red Bridge* (about 1895, color plate 24) Weir has again chosen a favorite subject among Japanese artists—a bridge, this time viewed from below, thus elevated to the upper edge of the composition. Weir owned Hiroshige's *Maple Trees at Tsuten Bridge* (about 1834, fig. 5.25), which contrasts the geometric, manmade forms of the bridge against the beauty of nature—a stream flowing between the two steep tree-covered hillsides. Such a happy juxtaposition may have caused Weir's response to the freshly painted red bridge that he encountered over the Shetucket River near his wife's family's summer home in Windham, Connecticut. The modern structure had replaced an old covered bridge whose loss Weir regretted until he realized that its successor offered him an ideal subject. Several features of Hiroshige's composition have been repeated in Weir's oil painting: the high horizon, which all but blocks the view into the distance, and the use of diagonal lines to establish the principal

5.25 Utagawa Hiroshige, Maple Trees at Tsuten Bridge, *about 1834, from the series* Famous Places in Kyoto, *color woodblock print, signed: Hiroshige ga; publisher: Eisendo; ex coll.: S. Bing; J. Alden Weir (private collection).*

5.26 Utagawa Kuniyoshi, Twelfth act, *1854, from the Japanese* Kana *copybook version of the Chushingura, color woodblock print, signed Ichiyusai Kuniyoshi ga; publisher: Sano-ya; ex coll.: J. Alden Weir (private collection).*

areas of the composition. Another print, perhaps depicting the twelfth act of the Japanese *Kana* copybook version of the Chushingura (1854, fig. 5.26), may have suggested the grille of tree trunks, branches, and leaves that Weir has added close to the picture plane in his *Red Bridge*. In spite of the distance which must have existed between the trees and the bridge, there is little suggestion of spatial recession. The landscape has been reduced to a flat pattern in which the geometric forms of the pylon and bridge are reflected in the water below. The picture surface is enlivened and unified by the artist's broken brushwork: short, regular strokes that do not obscure forms but rather emphasize their shapes and contours. The introduction of the red color note of the bridge was undoubtedly a result of Weir's close study of Japanese prints.

During the 1890s, when Weir was developing his individual impressionist style, he undertook far fewer figure subjects. He did, however, produce an important series of life-size paintings, which usually depicted his wife and children. Done from about 1893 to 1896, these ambitious works were yet another example of Weir's ability to combine effectively the academic standards of his training and the ideas of his current heroes, the French Impressionists. While Weir continued to represent the faces and hands of his figures with the disciplined realism that had been a characteristic of his paintings for the past two decades, the paintings took on a more decorative appearance—the settings carefully selected for their color and design, the figures usually occupying dominant positions close to the picture plane, the costumes often reduced to flat patterns of brushwork.

Baby Cora (1894, color plate 25) shows Ella Baker Weir, seated on the floor, holding up her stepdaughter Cora.[51] Presumably a record of everyday life in the Weir household, the subject and its treatment rely on Japanese prints: Ella displays the baby in a ceremonial manner, and a more austere setting has supplanted the crowded appearance of Weir's early domestic interiors. The artist has chosen a decidedly vertical format, which he emphasizes by standing Cora on Ella's knees. The figures seem to ascend on the canvas instead of being placed side by side or one behind the other. The eye is led upward by a series of curves that begin with the huge dog in the lower right corner; travel along the hem of Ella's skirt, her knees, and her bent arm; and culminate in the arms of the child, which are raised. The upward thrust is interrupted only by the horizontal line of the wide molding that separates the floor and the wall. Weir's treatment of space defies convention. The floor appears to rise so precipitously that it recedes vertically rather than back. Ella, Cora, and the dog occupy the immediate foreground, but there is no actual space between them and the back wall; this is stressed by the placement of the bright red chair, which seems impossibly close to Ella's head. The figures are reduced to flattened shapes—the dog and Ella are black silhouettes; Cora, a white one. Weir has so consciously manipulated the masses and voids in his composition that their arrangement stretches diagonally from the lower right corner to the upper left. As in Japanese prints, each element of the composition contributes to its geometric structure. Even the colors that Weir has chosen—neutral black, brown, and white, with a single note of brilliant red for the chair—recall the limited palette of some figural prints. The oriental flavor of *Baby Cora* may have been partly inspired by the work of Mary Cassatt, whose color prints Weir particularly admired.[52] *Baby Cora* follows Cassatt's work in this medium not only in the choice of subject (maternal devotion, Cassatt's best-known theme) but also in its style: the use of flat areas of color, the unconventional treatment of space, and the deliberate silhouetting of figures.

In the Days of Pinafores (about 1893/94, color plate 26) demonstrates Weir's interest in the colorful patterns often seen in Japanese prints. Two of his daughters, probably Cora and Dorothy, wear blue-and-white-striped dresses and are posed before a brilliantly colored screen decorated with gold birds. The petticoat of one child and the dresses of both are painted with thick, pronounced strokes; the riotously patterned carpet at their feet, with bold ones applied directly on the canvas's white ground in a geometric design. Other elements of *In the Days of Pinafores* are borrowed from Japanese printmakers. The composition is asymmetrical; although the standing child fills the center of the canvas, the other one is wedged into the right corner, her body cropped by the edge of the canvas. The figures are pushed into the foreground, and spatial recession is limited by the decorative background. The subject matter, while intimate, is treated in the Japanese manner; the deportment of the children, one helping the other to undress, is endowed with ceremony. This combination of oriental objects and influences, the lavish use of various patterns in particular, recalls Whistler's *La Princesse du pays de la porcelaine* (1864, Washington, D.C., Freer Gallery of Art), which Weir considered the best painting in the World's Columbian Exposition of 1893.[53] Weir's bright, strong colors, boldly applied to achieve decorative effects, are also reminiscent of the Nabis then painting in Paris.

In the early 1890s Weir did an important series of life-size figures posed outdoors. The first of these, *The Hunter* (1893, fig. 5.27), is a standard full-length portrait of the artist's nephew Alexander Webb Weir, but Japanese prints of women and their attendants walking outdoors may have served as the inspiration for the others. *An Autumn Stroll* (1894, color plate 27), which shows Ella and Dorothy posed beside a tree, could be compared to a print (about 1815, fig. 5.28) by Utagawa Toyokuni I from Weir's collection. Weir seems to have drawn on several compositional devices in Toyokuni's print, which depicts a courtesan and three attendants walking through a snow-covered landscape. Once again Weir has chosen a vertical format, placing his two-dimensional figures so close together that they appear to overlap. Accessory elements—the tree and its leafy branch—are flattened and arranged to frame the

5.27 J. Alden Weir, The Hunter, *1893, oil on canvas, 70 × 40 in., unsigned (Provo, Utah, Brigham Young University).*

5.28 Utagawa Toyokuni I, Courtesan Strolls in the Snow Together with Her Attendants (*probably one sheet of a triptych*), *about 1815, color woodblock print, signed: Toyokuni 99; publisher: Kaga-ya Kichibei; ex coll.: J. Alden Weir* (*private collection*).

29 J. Alden Weir, Face Reflected in a Mirror, *1896, oil on canvas, 4¼ × 13⅝ in., signed and dated at lower left: J. Alden Weir—1896 Providence, Rhode Island School of Design, Museum of Art, Jesse H. Metalf Fund*).

figures. The landscape setting, like that of the print, is simplified: it is reduced to flat areas of color or decorative pattern created by a heavy, striated paint application. Weir's *In the Dooryard* (probably 1894/95, color plate 28) develops some of these ideas even further.[54] The painting celebrates the renewed harmony of Weir's domestic life: Ella, seated, is surrounded by the artist's children; posed in brilliant sunshine, the happy family is enclosed by the spreading limbs of a tree and united by a swag of foliage that curves across the composition. Ella, dressed in lavender, and the three white-clad girls—Caro, standing behind her stepmother; Cora, on Ella's lap; and Dorothy, approaching with a lamb—are placed in the foreground in an arrangement that rises against a background of verdant green landscape. As in other of Weir's figure paintings, he is here responding not only to the oriental influence but also to the currents in French painting that had already assimilated it. Many factors of *In the*

Dooryard recall, in addition, the work of Puvis de Chavannes, who had earlier attracted Weir's interest and who could well have inspired Weir's large scale, vertical format, chalky palette, and figure treatment. Many of Puvis's paintings, intended as mural decorations for public buildings, represented clear allegorical messages; such may be the case in this painting, where Weir's wife holds grass to feed the lamb—a sign of innocence—held by one of his daughters. The powerful decorative effect of the picture also stems from Weir's own mural work, recently completed at the World's Columbian Exposition, which might have made him more aware of the formal devices needed to create an image that makes a powerful visual statement, even from a great distance.

In *Face Reflected in a Mirror* (1896, fig. 5.29), a painting set indoors, Weir continues to use some of the oriental devices he had employed earlier in the decade, but on a more diminutive scale: although this painting resembles *Baby Cora* (1894, color plate 25) in style, it is less than half its size. The figure is placed far to the side, where she is cropped by the bed post that runs along the right edge of the canvas; the center of the composition is filled by her mirrored reflection. The setting and its furniture are selected and arranged to strengthen the picture's design. Flat areas of neutral color are bounded by the emphatic horizontal and vertical lines of the moldings, window jambs, and mirror frame. These elements define and expand the space shown in the painting—the back wall is pierced by a window that provides a narrow view into a sunlit landscape, and the mirror reveals not only the other side of the model's face but also a view of the room behind her, complete to the four-poster bed and its canopy. The mirrored reflections repeat and vary shapes and patterns—the contour of the model's profile, the busy stripes of her blouse. Édouard Manet and Edgar Degas, among many other French Impressionists, had similarly experimented with the possibilities inherent in mirrors and what they reflected. Weir's treatment of the model and her setting also recalls Whistler's figures in such interior scenes as *Harmony in Green and Rose: The Music Room* (1860/61, Washington, D.C., Freer Gallery of Art).[55]

Landscapes: 1893–1897

As early as the mid-1890s, Weir was doing a number of his best landscapes at the Baker family home in Windham, Connecticut, or in nearby Willimantic, an industrial town then the site of large factory buildings. *Obweebetuck* (mid-1890s, color plate 29) is one of Weir's few early landscapes where figures are accorded a prominent role. Some white-clad women are gathered around a porch in the middle ground; they are elegant figures engaged in leisure-time activities. Much of the painting is devoted to the lawn, which is darkened by the shadow cast by the large tree; porch and house are cropped by the right edge of the canvas. Directly behind the forked trunk of the tree, Obweebetuck, a nearby mountain, rises in the distance. Weir, in applying much of his paint in wide, blockish strokes, has used either a broad brush or a palette knife, with a result particularly obvious in the immediate foreground. The general outlines of the composition have been reinforced with darker lines, applied with a thin brush and a sparing amount of pigment, which can be best seen around the edges of the shadows. The chalky quality characteristic of Weir's landscapes is well demonstrated here, this time to a higher degree, with brilliant white touches evident throughout the picture. The pastel colors used in *Obweebetuck*, especially the pale blues and greens, bring to mind the landscapes of Weir's friend Emil Carlsen, who also lived and worked at Windham.

While *Obweebetuck* celebrates man's enjoyment of the beauties of nature, Weir's views of Willimantic focus on the industrial town's encroachment on the surrounding New England landscape.[56] Weir's depiction of the manifestation of industry is a gentle one: the factories are kept at a distance and the workers are hidden. As in *The Red Bridge* (about 1895, color plate 24), which was painted nearby, he has found quiet beauty in the manmade elements that intrude into the landscape. This approach is all the more surprising given his elder brother's devotion to industrial subjects in such dramatic paintings as *Forging the Shaft* (1877, replica of an 1867 painting, fig. 1.11) and Weir's own portrayal of working figures in such watercolors as *Men at Work in an Interior* (1881, fig. 4.5) and such prints as *The Blacksmith Shop* (1889?, fig. 4.35). Weir's tamed treatment of an industrial subject is actually typical of the American Impressionists, who chose to represent only the elegance of scenes, eliminating or idealizing any ugly elements in them. (Childe Hassam's cityscapes of parks and avenues inhabited by well-dressed New Yorkers are the urban counterparts to Weir's views of this northeastern Connecticut town.)

Of the landscapes done in his impressionist period, now at its zenith, Weir's series of Willimantic paintings are among the most accomplished. Only three of them are dated—the earliest 1893; the latest, 1903—but judged on stylistic grounds and on the 1897 date of the third painting, most of them were probably painted between 1893 and 1897.[57] The earliest Willimantic landscapes seem to be two which view the town across a foreground meadow. In *Willimantic Thread Factory* (1893, fig. 5.30) Weir has massed the geometric shapes of the factories and the surrounding homes into the middle distance.[58] The meadow is left bare, enlivened only by a shadow cast by an unseen tree. The town is bounded above by the horizon line of the hills and below by the stone wall that separates it from the tract of grassland. The principal building, a factory with dozens of windows, dominates the scene. Placed in the center of the composition, parallel to the picture plane, the building's length emphasizes the openness of the landscape view behind it and the horizontal format of the painting. *Willimantic* (about 1893–97, fig. 5.31), an unfinished painting, gives some indication of Weir's working procedure in this series. First, on a flat white ground, he drew in the main

5.30 *J. Alden Weir,* Willimantic Thread Factory, *1893, oil on canvas, 24⅛ × 33½ in., signed and dated at lower left: J Alden Weir—93 (New York, The Brooklyn Museum, John B. Woodward Memorial Fund).*

5.31 J. Alden Weir, Willimantic, *about 1893–97, oil on canvas, 13⅝ × 24⅛ in., unsigned (private collection).*

areas of the composition in pencil, and then began to paint with thinned oils, sketching the major outlines with broad, fluid strokes. Even in the finished picture *Willimantic Thread Factory* (1893, fig. 5.30), Weir's paint application remains broad, with small broken brushstrokes used judiciously, mainly for the trees.

U.S. Thread Company Mills, Willimantic, Connecticut (about 1893–97, fig. 5.21) probably follows next in the series. The most obviously "composed" view of the factory town, it draws heavily not only on Japanese prints but also on contemporary works by Theodore Robinson, then living in New York and exerting a strong influence on his friend Weir. Weir's composition—the elements again massed in the middle ground, but here shown in a bird's-eye view—and his clear colors applied with controlled brushstrokes on a firmly drawn framework recall Robinson's Giverny landscapes, begun around 1888. Robinson was enthusiastic about Weir's paintings of Willimantic: "I liked immensely a Conn. factory town. modern and yet curiously mediaeval in feeling. One feels that Durer would have painted it that way . . . it is tremendously artistic, as is everything Weir puts his hand to. An avoidance of the commonplace, picturesque side of things, that is, the cheap picturesque."[59]

The culmination of the series is *The Factory Village* (1897, color plate 30), which shows a motif familiar from the paintings of such French Impressionists as Claude Monet—industrial buildings, smokestacks, and electrical poles nestled peacefully in a burgeoning landscape. Here, as in *U.S. Thread Company Mills* (about 1893–97, fig. 5.21), Weir juxtaposes foreground elements, principally trees pressed closed to the picture plane, with a panoramic view of the countryside in the distance. Willimantic is seen from above, over trees and bushes and across the reflective surface of the water. The rectilinear lines of the buildings establish the composition, but Weir, conscious though he is of its decorative potential, no longer seems to have manipulated it to achieve a contrived effect as he had in some of his landscapes, *The Red Bridge* (about 1895, color plate 24), for one. Rather, he has responded more to nature as he must have encountered it: the cloud-filled sky, the soft foliage of the trees and bushes in the foreground, the smoke pouring from the stack, and the reflections on the river. His colors are clearer and less pastel than those in some of his decorative pictures of the mid-1890s. His brushwork is varied to create a tactile paint surface, yet the strong draftsmanship so evident in those

5.32 *J. Alden Weir*, Winter Landscape, *1897, oil on canvas, 12 × 18 in., signed at lower right: J. Alden Weir—1897 (Nashville, Tennessee, The Fine Arts Center, Cheekwood).*

previous landscapes remains apparent. While short, broken strokes are used in the foreground, most of his paint is applied in solid blockish strokes.

Weir's study of Japanese prints, which often depict snow-covered landscapes, and his admiration for Twachtman, who had been painting snowbound landscapes since the winter of 1888/89, must have been among his inspirations for embarking on a series of snowscapes, which he did mainly between 1894 and 1897. He likely painted them in "The Palace Car," a small house on runners equipped with an oil stove and having windows on all four sides; this eccentric vehicle permitted Weir to paint in comfort during the coldest weather.[60] In most of Weir's snow scenes—*The Ice Cutters* (1895, private collection), for instance—Weir's palette returns to the subtle colors he had used during the late 1880s, when, working closely with Twachtman, he had painted melancholy landscapes of the changing seasons at Branchville. Few of Weir's snow scenes rely on figures for their effect (even in *Cutting Ice* the workers are relegated to the distance and viewed across a wide expanse of ice and snow); indeed, a meditative aura is invoked by their absence. *Winter Landscape* (1897, fig. 5.32) is inhabited only by two small rabbits, who halt before a fallen tree at the edge of frozen water. By raising the horizon line to the upper edge of the canvas, thus obstructing the view into the distance, Weir has isolated this vignette. The unmodulated surface of the snow and the vertical pattern of the leafless trees, which are cropped beneath their crowns, flatten the landscape, making it appear remarkably two-dimensional. The decorative effect of *Winter Landscape* is heightened by Weir's palette of mostly white and neutral grays and beiges, with touches of pale salmon color in the few leaves remaining on their branches.

1897–1900

In the late 1890s, Weir's work took an increasingly traditional direction. He continued to work outdoors on his landscapes, but his style and subjects were subtly altered: he moved slowly away from the radical compositions of the mid-1890s; draftsmanship once again gained equal footing with color in his art; and he worked more laboriously on his exhibition canvases, now larger and more highly finished. These renewed conservative tendencies are particularly apparent in some scenes of rural life, usually farmers with domestic animals, which Weir painted in 1897 and 1898. His subject matter, a departure from those represented by other American Impressionists, recalls works by French painters—academic artists like Jules-Adolphe-Aimé-Louis Breton (1827–1906) and Barbizon painters like Jean-François Millet—but the figures are now represented with a sweetness rarely found in the works of those vigorous advocates of realism. In Weir's rural scenes, the treatment, especially the greater detail combined with the steady, broken brushwork and hardened contours, parallels that in works by those French painters who continued in a modified impressionist style long after the movement had lost its momentum. Weir's *Noonday Rest* (1897, fig. 5.33), for example, shows two farmers eating their midday meal in the shade. Their tools put aside, they recline on a

5.33 J. Alden Weir, Noonday Rest, *1897, oil on canvas, 39½ × 50 in., signed at lower right: J. Alden Weir—1897/—Branchville Conn. (Philadelphia, Pennsylvania Academy of the Fine Arts, Gift of J. G. Rosengarten, Isaac H. Clothier, Dr. Francis W. Lewis, and Edward H. Coates, 1898).*

wooded hillside, punctuated by slender tree trunks, that rises to a narrow band of sky. On the opposite side of the canvas, two oxen have been unharnessed from their cart and stand idle. *Ploughing for Buckwheat* (1898, fig. 5.34) represents a farmer, armed with a whip, taking his oxen to plough a field; incongruously, a child sits in the foreground carefully arranging lines of small rocks, the very elements that would obstruct the famer's task. Among Weir's landscapes these paintings are large, about three feet by four; their size and degree of finish suggest that they took the artist an unusually long time to complete, an impression that Weir's correspondence confirms. Of *Ploughing for Buckwheat*, he wrote to his friend Charles Erskine Scott Wood: "I have just finished a rather large canvas which I hope you will see. It is a New England farmer and if I can get another week of sunlight I can complete it. I have had it on hand for two years and [it] is pretty well considered, but these large canvasses take ten times the time a small canvas does and are ten times as interesting."[61]

5.34 J. Alden Weir, Ploughing for Buckwheat, *1898, oil on canvas, 48½ × 33¾ in., signed at lower left: J. Alden Weir—/Branchville—Conn. (Pittsburgh, Pennsylvania, Carnegie Institute, Museum of Art.)*

Similar trends of conservatism can be seen in Weir's ambitious figure paintings of the late 1890s. In composition and outdoor setting some of them resemble pictures he had done earlier in the decade, although now, at its end, they would have been considered far less radical. In both *The Donkey Ride* (1899/1900, color plate 31) and *In the Sun* (1899, color plate 32), his format is familiar: the life-size figures, pressed close to the picture plane, fill the canvas; the landscape setting, its horizon eliminated or raised to the upper edge of the canvas, serves as a backdrop. There is, however, a new rigidity not unlike that seen in *Noonday Rest* (1897, fig. 5.33) and in other of Weir's rural scenes. In *The Donkey Ride*, particularly, patterns and textures are represented with unprecedented clarity in tight, regularized brushstrokes. The artist's daughters Cora and Dorothy posed outdoors for *The Donkey Ride*, but in spite of the charm of the models and their setting, the picture lacks spontaneity. Like the rural landscapes, this was a work completed slowly and carefully, perhaps over two summers.[62] Certain elements create gay patterns—the fence and the clouds in the landscape, the donkeys' shaggy coats, the girls' dresses—but the faces of the figures are, unquestionably, realistic portraits. *In the Sun*, which shows Dorothy seated outdoors, is a less recognizable portrait: she

5.35 J. Alden Weir, Ella Baker Weir, *pencil on paper, 12⅞ × 8⅞ in. (sight), signed at lower left:* J. ALDEN WEIR—1898 *(private collection).*

5.36 J. Alden Weir, Cora Weir, *pencil on paper, 12⅞ × 8⅞ in. (sig inscribed at upper left:* CORA WEIR/1898; *signed at lower right:* J. ALD WEIR *(private collection).*

no longer looks out at the viewer; her gaze is downcast, her attention focused on a flower she has plucked from several that grow in the foreground. Her features, like those of the studio models Weir was depicting at the time, have been idealized. *In the Sun* is a decorative exercise in which Weir's early mastery of taut, controlled line reasserts itself. In 1898, just before embarking on these paintings, Weir had executed a series of drawings that have an almost Ingres-like quality; portraits of family members, among them Ella (1898, fig. 5.35) and Cora (1898, fig. 5.36), they demonstrate his enduring ability as a draftsman. The same hard linearity continues to appear in his oils of the period, but fewer and fewer of his works are of identifiable subjects.

In his treatment of studio models painted at the turn of the century, Weir followed the same pattern: a renewed academicism first, followed by less convincing characterization that moved gradually toward idealization. *Lady in Front of a Fan Window* (late 1890s, fig. 5.37) repeats compositional devices that Weir had used earlier in the decade, but his figure is represented with a new precision that is particularly visible in the woman's smooth, carefully modeled face. *The Gray Bodice* (1898, fig. 5.38) is said to depict the sister of Henry Dixey, a well-known actor. Her features have been portrayed with a power that had been lacking in Weir's work since Anna's death, six years earlier. Only the title, which addresses the subtle color harmonies of the picture, and the decorative treatment of the model's costume remove

5.37 J. Alden Weir, Lady in Front of a Fan Window, *late 1890s, oil on canvas, 20⅛ × 24½ in., unsigned (private collection).*

5.38 J. Alden Weir, The Gray Bodice, *1898, oil on canvas, 30¼ × 25¼ in.,
signed and dated at upper left: J. Alden Weir (Illinois, The Art Institute of Chicago,
Friends of American Art Collection).*

the painting from the realm of portraiture. In a painting done the previous year, *The Green
Bodice* (about 1897, fig. 5.39), Weir depicted the same model, but in a composition of mirrored
images that he had used so successfully in *Face Reflected in a Mirror* (1896, fig. 5.29): the model
is shown off to the side, her face in profile; most of the canvas is devoted to the reflection of
her face in the looking glass. In *The Green Bodice* Weir introduced the waist-length, life-size
format and contemplative mood that would soon typify his figure subjects. Accessories, here
the large hat tipped at a rakish angle and the soft feather boa, assume a new prominence both
in the composition of the painting and in the titles Weir gave them. In *The Orchid* (1899, fig.
5.40), the model's features have lost their particularity; her personality is concealed by the
downward cast of her eyes, which gaze fixedly on the stylized orchid she holds. The pattern
now has even greater importance, but seems hardened and somewhat contrived; the vibrant,
fresh brushwork in evidence as recently as 1898 in works like *The Gray Bodice* has been
replaced by a surface heavily worked, sometimes striated with the wooden end of the artist's
brush. In *The Yellow Turban* (1900, fig. 5.41), the model turns her face from the viewer. The
intimate character of her pose and the quiet mood of the picture anticipate the figure paintings
Weir would do during the early years of the twentieth century.

25. J. Alden Weir, *Baby Cora*, 1894, oil on canvas, 70 x 40 in., inscribed at upper right: BABY CORA; signed and dated at lower left: J. Alden Weir—1894; dated on the dog's collar: 1894 (Cora Weir Burlingham).

26. J. Alden Weir, *In the Days of Pinafores*, about 1893/94, oil on canvas, 34 1/8 x 27 1/8 in., signed at lower left: J. Alden Weir (private collection).

27. J. Alden Weir, *An Autumn Stroll,* 1894, oil on canvas, 70 x 40 in., unsigned (Provo, Utah, Brigham Young University).

28. J. Alden Weir, *In the Dooryard*, probably 1894, 80 1/8 x 47 1/8 in., unsigned (private collection).

29. J. Alden Weir, *Obweebetuck*, mid-1890s, oil on canvas, 19 1/2 x 23 1/4 in., unsigned (private collection).

30. J. Alden Weir, *The Factory Village*, 1897, oil on canvas, 29 x 38 in., signed and dated at lower left: J. Alden Weir 1897 (New York, jointly owned by Cora Weir Burlingham and The Metropolitan Museum of Art).

31. J. Alden Weir, *The Donkey Ride*, 1899/1900, oil on canvas, 49 x 38 in., unsigned (Cora Weir Burlingham).

32. J. Alden Weir, *In the Sun,* 1899, oil on canvas, 34 x 26 7/8 in., signed and dated at upper right: J. Alden Weir/'99 (Provo, Utah, Brigham Young University).

5.39 *J. Alden Weir*, The Green Bodice, *about 1897, oil on canvas, 33¹⁵/₁₆ × 24³/₄ in., unsigned (New York, The Metropolitan Museum of Art, Gift of George A. Hearn, 1906).*

The Ten American Painters

Impressionism was a widely practiced and accepted style by the late 1890s, and Weir and his impressionist friends were meeting less resistance in exhibiting their work. Earlier in the decade some of the artists' more advanced paintings had been deemed inadmissible to the established annual exhibitions; rejection by the Society of American Artists, originally founded as a liberal exhibition group, had been the most disturbing. Even when their works had been accepted, they had been displayed in crowded rooms side by side with those by painters of diverse aesthetic persuasions. In 1897 this sort of attitude caused ten disgruntled painters to resign from the Society and to establish their own exhibition group, which was eventually known as The Ten American Painters.[63] Its membership was composed mostly of New York painters from Weir's circle—Twachtman, Hassam, Robert Reid, Willard L.

5.40 J. Alden Weir, The Orchid, *1899, oil on canvas, 24½ × 20¼ in., signed at upper left: J. Alden Weir (San Marino, California, Henry E. Huntington Library and Art Gallery).*

Metcalf (1858–1925), Thomas W. Dewing (1851–1938), and Weir himself—with the addition of four Boston artists, Edmund C. Tarbell, Frank W. Benson, Joseph R. De Camp (1858–1923), and the muralist Edward E. Simmons (1852–1931). There were already close ties between the artists of the two cities, several of whom, among them Hassam and Metcalf, were New Yorkers who had been reared in the Boston area. Others had studied in Paris at the same time or had worked together on decorative projects for the World's Columbian Exposition or the Library of Congress; still others were acquainted through their participation in annual shows, not only in Boston and New York but as far afield as Pittsburgh, Chicago, and St. Louis. Membership in what ended as "The Ten" was determined in one case by fate—Robinson, who in the early 1890s led the opposition to the conservative element in the Society of American Artists, had died in 1896—and in others by choice, for Abbott H. Thayer (1849–1921) and Winslow Homer (1836–1910) had declined the group's invitation. The members of The Ten did not have a cohesive aesthetic philosophy; they were united mainly by a desire to exhibit their work under sympathetic conditions. Nonetheless, they had some common experience: nearly all had studied in Paris (De Camp, a notable exception, had been trained in Munich), and all were mature men who had already achieved artistic recognition and success. Often identified as an impressionist organization, The Ten was actually a

5.41 J. Alden Weir, The Yellow Turban, *1900, oil on canvas, 24³/₈ × 20¹/₄ in., signed at upper left: J. Alden Weir/1900 (private collection).*

loosely knit group whose members explored a variety of individual styles and subjects, a point underscored by their asking Homer, then a painter of dramatic coastal views, and Thayer, whose moralistic paintings depict idealized women and children, to join them.

The Ten had no officers, no official constitution, no jury; the space available for its shows was simply divided evenly among the members. Each artist's work—a few examples of what he considered the best of his recent production—was isolated and exhibited as a separate display, sometimes with one painting as a focal point and others arranged around it. In a sense, the exhibitions of The Ten were a series of small one-man shows. The galleries were prepared carefully for the installation of the pictures, at least in the group's early years. In 1898, the walls were painted red, most likely a deep terracotta color, and then covered with cheesecloth, the seams of which were hidden by gilt battens. The floor was concealed by cocoa-colored straw matting. The cheesecloth would have heightened the color of the walls, enhancing the exhibitors' frequent use of white and light pastel colors. Apparently floating in light and atmosphere on a variegated, seemingly penetrable surface, the paintings were exhibited in an approximation of the conditions they were intended to depict.[64] This setting, ultimately Japanese in inspiration, was of the austere type initiated by Whistler, who twenty years earlier had advocated that exhibition galleries be designed in a manner sympathetic to the works displayed in it.

With the exception of Twachtman, who died in 1902 and was replaced by William Merritt Chase, the original members of The Ten continued to exhibit together for twenty years, finishing up with a retrospective held in Washington at the Corcoran Gallery of Art in the winter of 1918/19. Although Hassam claimed credit for beginning the organization, Weir and Twachtman seem to have been its motivating force. In The Ten's first exhibition, which was held at Durand-Ruel Galleries, Weir showed the largest number of paintings—eight—all of them recently completed and reflecting the current directions in his art. Among his landscapes were *Noonday Rest* (1897, fig. 5.33) and *The Factory Village* (1897, color plate 30); among his figure paintings, *The Green Bodice* (about 1897, fig. 5.39) and *The Gray Bodice* (1898, fig. 5.38).

For the most progressive of his impressionist pictures Weir received a mixed critical response; few sold, although later, as he began to modify and soften his impressionist style, he achieved greater recognition. (In 1896, his painting *The Old Rock* [about 1895, New York, William Doyle Galleries, Inc., 1983], won a prize at the annual exhibition of the Boston Art Club. The following year an exhibition of Weir's paintings and pastels was held in New York at Boussod, Valadon & Co.) His comparatively recent success and its attendant financial security permitted him to stop teaching early in 1899 and devote himself entirely to painting. The twentieth century ushered in a period of tremendous artistic upheaval. During its first decade, Robert Henri and his realist followers would challenge the power of the academic establishment just as Weir and his contemporaries had done thirty years earlier. Modern painting—Fauvism and Cubism—would emerge in Europe and come to America, styles whose radical precepts represented a revolution against the aesthetic standards so thoroughly inculcated in the artists of Weir's generation. These developments would leave Weir untouched. At last choosing to remove himself from the mainstream of modern innovation, he would continue to find his inspiration in Impressionism, painting pictures that were exquisite, albeit unaffected by the ongoing current.

6

The Later Years
1900–1919

IMPRESSIONISM HAD BEEN GENERALLY ACCEPTED IN AMERICA FOR SOME YEARS WHEN Weir's personal approach to the style, now confident and unchallenged, became more lyrical. That was after 1900, his period of greatest success and recognition. He displayed his paintings in all the major annuals, most notably in the exhibitions of The Ten American Painters, and held one-man shows in New York in 1907 and 1908. In 1911/12, a retrospective exhibition of his paintings traveled to Boston, New York, Pittsburgh, Buffalo, and Cincinnati. He served on juries, not just at the Academy but for such major exhibitions as the Carnegie International in Pittsburgh and the Panama-Pacific Exposition in San Francisco. From 1900 until his death in 1919, hardly a year passed without his winning a medal or an award. Even within his lifetime his works were being collected by American museums—The Metropolitan Museum of Art, in New York; the Pennsylvania Academy of the Fine Arts, in Philadelphia; the Rhode Island School of Design, in Providence; the Buffalo Fine Arts Academy; and the Cincinnati Art Museum. The Musée du Luxembourg in Paris also acquired one of his paintings, *Jeune femme* (about 1898, Paris, Musée d'Orsay).

During these last years of his career, landscape was unquestionably his principal mode of expression. Except for a few large canvases he did around 1910, most of his landscapes were less obviously composed than the Japanesque paintings he had undertaken during the 1890s. Some, like *A Glimpse of the Sound* (1902, fig. 6.1), display a new informality: they are light and airy, and they are done with loose brushwork and pale colors, usually soft shades of blue, yellow, and green. Painted in Connecticut, usually at Branchville or Windham, long his favorite summer haunts, the landscapes seldom include figures; when they do, as in *A Day in June* (about 1903, fig. 6.2), the figures are just incidental elements in an expansive setting. Around 1903, Weir did a number of landscapes in which he blocked the distant view, often with a screen of trees, using their trunks and limbs to establish a strong linear pattern. One of these, *Visiting Neighbors* (about 1903, fig. 6.3), is exceptional in the prominence given to its model—the artist's daughter Cora, who stands with one of the Weir's donkeys. The view into the distance is blocked by the dense forest, which is represented by regular, short brushstrokes in a tapestry of textures and colors. In *The Birches* (1903, Dr. and Mrs. John J.

6.1 J. Alden Weir, A Glimpse of the Sound, *1902, oil on canvas, 20 × 24 in., signed and dated at lower right: J. Alden Weir/1902 (New Jersey, Montclair Art Museum, Gift of William T. Evans, 1915).*

McDonough), the trees are placed in the middle ground, leaving a foreground stage occupied by rocks, foliage, and two grazing cows. In *Path in the Woods* (about 1903, fig. 6.4), the view is even more restricted, since the trees depicted stand on a rising hillside. The controlled brushwork, applied with stiffer and more even strokes, seen in these paintings and in works like *The Barns at Windham* (about 1905, fig. 6.5) and the harsher palette used in such paintings as *Suburban Village*, actually a view of Windham (about 1902–1905, fig. 6.6), demonstrate how Weir's late career was influenced by Childe Hassam, who, like Weir, had struggled to win acceptance for his impressionist work in the 1890s. Theodore Robinson and John H. Twachtman, both of whom had encouraged Weir in formulating his individual impressionist style, had died—the former in 1896, the latter in 1902—and Weir had to forge new alliances, usually with artists who like himself were practicing in a less venturesome manner.

In many of Weir's late landscapes, he simply returns to compositions and styles he had explored before. Such paintings as *Upland Pasture* (about 1905, fig. 6.7) and *Danbury Hills* (about 1905, fig. 6.8), scenes around his Branchville farm, recapture the spirit of his earlier work. In *Upland Pasture*, the high horizon, the trees silhouetted on the crest of the hillside,

6.2 *J. Alden Weir,* A Day in June, *about 1903, oil on canvas, 23³/₈ × 31³/₄ in., signed at lower left: J. Alden Weir (Illinois, The Art Institute of Chicago, Walter H. Schulze Memorial Collection, 1941).*

and the strongly patterned shadows are features common in such late 1880s landscapes as *Lengthening Shadows* (1887, fig. 3.77); *Danbury Hills*, in its open panorama and clustering of elements in the middle ground, recalls some of his Willimantic scenes of the mid-1890s. Most of Weir's twentieth-century landscapes, by contrast, are more informal glimpses of the Connecticut countryside, with little activity and with landmarks recognizable only to those who frequented the area. *The High Pasture* (about 1905, fig. 6.9) and *Afternoon by the Pond* (about 1908–1909, fig. 6.10) are quiet pictures in which shadows and sunshine, trees and foliage, create rich patterns that are emphasized by bold brushwork. In *The Border of the Farm* (about 1909, fig. 6.11), a figure feeding the blazing fire in the foreground is lost in the broken strokes that represent the swirling smoke, the stone wall, the leaves and trunks of the trees.

Weir took a new, more romantic direction in his landscapes of 1905–1910: he depicted more intimate views of nature, often a quiet woodland interior, sometimes populated with figures to add an anecdotal or literary meaning. Childe Hassam, in paintings like *The Bathers* (1903, Wisconsin, Milwaukee Art Center Collection), may have inspired Weir's choice of subject in *Early Morning* (about 1906, fig. 6.12). Several features of the painting, principally the dim illumination, the idealized figures, and the heavy paint application, bring to mind the arcadian landscapes Weir's friend Albert Pinkham Ryder had painted during the 1880s and 1890s, as does Weir's *Pan and the Wolf* (about 1907, fig. 6.13), which represents a confrontation between the Greek god of pastures and flocks and the predatory animal. There is little

6.3 J. Alden Weir, Visiting Neighbors, *about 1903, oil on canvas, 24³/₈ × 34¼ in., signed at lower right: J. Alden Weir (Washington, D.C., The Phillips Collection).*

drama in this scene: the figures are small; they are relegated to the lower right corner of the composition; and they are almost lost in the pattern of broken brushwork. In *The Haunt of the Woodcock*, sometimes called *Driving the Cows Home* (about 1906, fig. 6.14), a mounted farmer is about to enter a field to round up his cows; this is a modern-day Pan shown in harmony with the landscape and the animals that inhabit it. Weir now begins for the first time to experiment with strong backlighting: in the middle ground, the forked trunk of the tree and its leafy crown are silhouetted against the lightened sky. Weir uses this effect more dramatically in *Moonlight* (about 1907, fig. 6.15), a nocturne in which he works in shades of blue, building up the paint surface with short broken strokes. Only the contours of the tree trunks are firmly drawn; their foliage is blended into the sky. *Lantern Light* (about 1907–10, fig. 6.16) is a murky landscape illuminated only by the brilliant light carried by a single, barely visible wandering figure. *Foggy Morning* (about 1907–10, fig. 6.17), executed on a large scale, was a major painting that Weir never brought to completion. A roseate moon glows behind a tree and casts warm, pink highlights on a flock of sheep gathered in the foreground. A natural effect has been exaggerated in order to lend mood to the scene. These romantic pictures are almost mystical in feeling, a departure from Weir's usual treatment of sunlit landscapes and one that may have been inspired by tonalist artists like Birge Harrison (1854–1929) who worked in a limited palette, often tones of blue, to represent landscapes in which detail was minimized and lighting manipulated in order to convey a feeling. Around the same time, atmospheric nocturnal landscapes were also being painted by many of Weir's contemporaries, among

6.4 J. Alden Weir, Path in the Woods, *about 1903, oil on canvas, 26 × 21¼ in., signed at lower right: J. Alden Weir (Ohio, The Cincinnati Art Museum, Dexter Fund).*

them the Impressionists Emil Carlsen and Childe Hassam, and by that chronicler of the American West Frederic Remington (1861–1909), who was Weir's neighbor in Connecticut.

Weir's interest in nighttime effects extended from these delightful rural scenes to views of New York City that he painted from his studio window. Weir did but two of these—*The Bridge: Nocturne (Nocturne: Queensboro Bridge)* (about 1910, fig. 6.18) and *The Plaza: Nocturne* (1911, fig. 6.19)—but they demonstrate his enduring commitment to a working method of careful preliminary study. As he wrote to Charles Erskine Scott Wood, "Of course none of it could be painted direct, having had to make studies—memorandum to use the following day. The thing itself was so beautiful I had to get the big notes which as you know, are terribly subtle."[1] Each of the two works is a carefully planned picture where light and dark areas create the geometric pattern that is the composition's structure. The principal color in both paintings is a deep blue, with the silhouettes of buildings barely suggested and the emphasis given to the yellow and white lights of the city—windows, street lights, carriage lights— glowing and reflecting against the solid forms around them. Although firmly based on observation, the nocturnes do not represent every detail of the city's appearance, but only capture the essence of its vital nightlife. By setting his subjects after dark, Weir was able to present the city as a beautiful, perhaps even mysterious, place. His two nocturnes offer a strong

6.5 J. Alden Weir, The Barns at Windham, *about 1905, oil on wood, 23⅛ × 33½ in., unsigned (private collection).*

6.6 J. Alden Weir, Suburban Village, *also known as* Windham Village, *about 1902–1905, oil on canvas, 20 × 24½ in., signed at lower left: J. Alden Weir (Arizona, Phoenix Art Museum, Gift of the Friends of Art, 1964)*

6.7 J. Alden Weir, Upland Pasture, *about 1905, oil on canvas, 39⅞ × 50¼ in., signed at lower left: J. Alden Weir/Branchville (Washington, D.C., National Museum of American Art, Smithsonian Institution, Gift of William T. Evans, 1909).*

contrast to works by such early twentieth-century realists as John Sloan (1871–1951) and William Glackens (1870–1938), who offered a more down-to-earth view of urban life—closer and more sordid renditions of New York streets. As always, Weir, the archetypal American Impressionist, endows even a potentially ugly subject with elegance.

A similar approach is apparent in Weir's important landscape *Building a Dam, Shetucket* (about 1908, fig. 6.20), which depicts a dam built near his Windham home between 1907 and 1909.[2] Once again, as in *The Red Bridge* (about 1895, color plate 24) and *The Factory Village* (1897, color plate 30), man's intrusion into nature is made to appear gentle and, in its own way, lovely. The apparatus for constructing the dam—the cranes, the poles, the barges—are here barely noticeable among the tree trunks and foliage; they are used to establish a rectilinear grid on which Weir has placed pastel blue and green strokes, broken, but almost stiff in their application. This painting too resulted from careful preparation; *Building a Dam No. 2* (about 1908, present location unknown) was probably a study for the larger work. The silvery palette and renewed sense of design evident in *Building a Dam, Shetucket*, also appears in some of the river views Weir painted around 1910 near Norwich, Connecticut: *Norwich-on-the Thames* (about 1910, fig. 6.21) and *River Scene* (about 1910, Evanston, Illinois, The Daniel J. Terra Collection). In these two paintings, the effects of industry are introduced without

6.8 J. Alden Weir, Danbury Hills, *about 1905, oil on canvas, 23⅞ × 33⅞ in., signed at lower right: J. Alden Weir (Colorado, The Denver Art Museum, Gift of the Daughters of Charles F. Hendrie in Memory of Their Father, 1928).*

6.9 J. Alden Weir, The High Pasture, *about 1905, oil on canvas, 24 × 33½ in., inscribed at lower left: To my friend Benson [?]/[illegible line]/J. Alden Weir [illegible date] (Washington, D.C., The Phillips Collection).*

6.10 J. Alden Weir, Afternoon by the Pond, *about 1908–1909, oil on canvas, 25¹/₁₆ × 30 in., signed at lower left: J. Alden Weir (Washington, D.C., The Phillips Collection).*

destroying the serenity of the landscape. *The Spreading Oak* (1910, fig. 6.22), although a pure landscape in which reminders of man's presence are minimal, also relates to *Building a Dam, Shetucket:* it too is large in scale; it is painted in the same cool palette; and it displays the same concern for structure achieved through a framework of tree trunks and branches.

In the years from 1910 to 1919, the final decade of his career, Weir's health worsened and his ambition diminished, but he continued to produce landscapes that reveal his sensitive and personal response to nature. His compositions become less deliberately structured; his brushwork is looser and less delicately applied; and his palette is reduced mostly to soft pastel shades of blue and green. In paintings like *Fording the Stream* (1910–19, New Jersey, The Newark Museum), *The Old Laurel Bush* (1910–19, fig. 6.23), and *At the Turn of the Road* (1910–19, fig. 6.24), Weir's broken brushwork creates an overall pattern of lustrous color that dissolves the contours even of such solid forms as buildings, bridges, and tree trunks. The sites are so generalized in appearance that even when a picture represents a familiar locale, as does *The Fishing Party* (about 1915, fig. 6.25), a view of the pond on the artist's Branchville farm, the place is difficult to recognize. The charming scenes, suffused in light, seem to

6.11 J. Alden Weir, The Border of the Farm, *about 1909, oil on canvas, 50 × 39½ in., signed at lower right: J. Alden Weir (Virginia, The Chrysler Museum at Norfolk, Gift of Walter P. Chrysler, Jr.).*

6.12 J. Alden Weir, Early Morning, *about 1906, oil on canvas, 20½ × 25½ in., signed at lower left: J. Alden Weir (Washington, D.C., Hirshhorn Museum and Sculpture Garden, Smithsonian Institution).*

6.13 J. Alden Weir, Pan and the Wolf, *about 1907, oil on canvas, 34 × 24 in., signed at lower left: J. Alden Weir (Washington, D.C., The Phillips Collection).*

represent an idyllic world set apart from the realities of modern life. During these late years, Weir, hoping to regain his health, went to Nassau to rest. He was restored to his earlier srength for a brief time, and turned again to his work. *The Wharves, Nassau* (1913, fig. 6.26) is the best painting he did there; in it he not only captures the brilliance of the Caribbean light but he also works with renewed assurance, applying his glistening colors to the strongly designed framework provided by the wooden dock with its bustling inhabitants.

Weir never stopped painting figures, but after the turn of the century his work in this genre did not display the vitality retained in so many of his landscapes. To Weir and to many of his contemporaries, the contemplative woman remained a popular subject even while many of the real women around them began to move into the work force and to demand the rights and recognition enjoyed by their male peers. During the early years of the new century, several of Weir's friends were still representing elegant, tranquil women: Robert Reid showed them posed before brightly colored screens; Childe Hassam, in his window series, depicted them standing in front of thinly curtained windows, bathed in cool light;

6.14 J. Alden Weir, The Haunt of the Woodcock, *sometimes called* Driving the Cows Home, *about 1906, oil on canvas, 35 × 25 in., signed at lower left: J. Alden Weir (Amherst, Massachusetts, Mead Art Museum).*

6.15 J. Alden Weir, Moonlight, *about 1907, oil on canvas, 24 × 20 in., signed at lower left: J. Alden Weir (Washington, D.C., National Gallery of Art, Gift of Chester Dale, 1954).*

6.16 J. Alden Weir, Lantern Light, *about 1907–10, oil on canvas, 28¼ × 23 in., signed at upper left: J. Alden Weir (private collection).*

6.17 J. Alden Weir, Foggy Morning, *about 1907–10, oil on canvas, 50⅞ × 39⅜ in., unsigned (private collection).*

6.18 *J. Alden Weir,* The Bridge, Nocturne (Nocturne: Queensboro Bridge), *about 1910, oil on canvas mounted on wood, 29 × 39½ in., signed at lower left: J. Alden Weir (Washington, D.C., Hirshhorn Museum and Sculpture Garden, Smithsonian Institution).*

6.19 *J. Alden Weir,* The Plaza: Nocturne, *1911, oil on canvas mounted on wood, 29 × 39½ in., signed at lower left: J. Alden Weir (Washington, D.C., Hirshhorn Museum and Sculpture Garden, Smithsonian Institution).*

6.20 J. Alden Weir, Building a Dam, Shetucket, *about 1908, oil on canvas, 31¼ × 40¼ in., signed at lower right: J. Alden Weir. (Ohio, The Cleveland Museum of Art, Purchase from the J.H. Wade Fund, 1921).*

Frank Benson posed them, elaborately costumed, in gaily patterned interiors. The best of Weir's late figure pieces evince this decorative intent by depicting anonymous studio models whose costumes, poses, and accessories were selected to create an impression of genteel elegance. In *Caro Seated on a Chest* (about 1905, fig. 6.27), Weir's eldest daughter, and one of his favorite models, sits on a carved chest in front of boldly striped wallpaper; the chest that supports her and the framed pictures behind her add to the rectilinear design of the composition. *Peacock Feathers* (1909, fig. 6.28) is more restrained; only the few soft feathers held by the model embellish the sensitive portrait. Weir's palette in these figure paintings is somewhat subdued—the dresses are often white, toned down by the addition of gray or beige; the decorative elements, a soft pink or rose color; the backdrops, neutral and low-keyed colors. The paint, particularly that used to represent the figures, is applied thickly and then striated with the wooden end of the brush, a process that Weir often repeats, creating multiple layers of pigment. The technique is one that he had used occasionally during the 1890s in paintings such as *In the Days of Pinafores* (about 1893/94, color plate 26); around 1905, it became an exaggerated device in his work.

Most of Weir's studio paintings are austere: they usually focus on a single, half-length figure that is shown close up against a flat background, with relatively few accessories or props, and wearing a tasteful and sometimes out-of-fashion gown. Weir relies on his portrayal of facial expressions, poses, and gestures to express a mood or attitude. *A Gentlewoman* (1906,

6.21 J. Alden Weir, Norwich-on-the-Thames, *about 1910, oil on canvas, 23⅝ × 33 in., signed at lower left: J. Alden Weir (private collection).*

6.22 J. Alden Weir, The Spreading Oak, *1910, oil on canvas, 39 × 50 in., unsigned (Oregon, Portland Art Museum, Gift of Col. C. E. S. Wood in memory of his wife, Nanny Moale Wood, 1943).*

6.23 J. Alden Weir, The Old Laurel Bush, *1910–19, oil on canvas, 24 × 20 in., unsigned (New York, Coe Kerr Gallery).*

fig. 6.29) and *An American Girl* (about 1912, fig. 6.30) are typical: in the former, by the model's downcast eyes and folded hands he suggests thoughtful absorption; in the latter, he conveys determination and confidence by her direct gaze and her pose, her right hand purposefully placed on her hip. In a few of Weir's figure paintings his models engage in ladylike activities—making lace in *The Lace Maker* (1915, fig. 6.31) or strumming on a musical instrument in *The Lute Player* (about 1910–13, fig. 6.32)—but often they are simply sitting idle, as in *Portrait* (about 1913, fig. 6.33). Weir's figure paintings rarely reflect the realities of modern-day life that were then being explored by Robert Henri and his followers; rather, his women are detached from the mundane and convey a more universal ideal. *Knitting for Soldiers* (1918, fig. 6.34), which Weir painted in patriotic response to America's war effort, was viewed by his contemporaries as a general statement on American womanhood. Duncan Phillips, who purchased the picture from Weir in 1918, wrote to him: "You may never have thought of the picture as 'Knitting for Soldiers.' You may have thought only of the particular knitter, her sweetness and refinement. . . . Yet to me it is a splendid war-picture, very timely, very universal."[3]

Unlike the informal works Weir had done during the late 1880s, his portraits of the early twentieth century seem contrived in composition. Typical are the paintings he did of his

6.24 J. Alden Weir, At the Turn of the Road, *1910–19, oil on canvas, 20 × 24 in., signed at lower left: J. Alden Weir (Canajoharie, New York, Canajoharie Library and Art Gallery).*

friends Albert Pinkham Ryder (1902/1903, fig. 6.35) and Childe Hassam (1902/1903, fig. 6.36) to commemorate their long-overdue election as associate members of the National Academy of Design. These are identifiable portraits—Ryder's unkempt beard and Hassam's flushed face were well-known features of the men—yet Weir has placed both sitters in highly formalized poses: their rigidly held bodies are shown frontally and parallel to the picture plane; and, except for Ryder's hand and the handkerchief in Hassam's breast pocket, each composition is carefully balanced, each half a mirror image of the other. In the portrait of Ryder, Weir has captured the eccentric artist's otherworldly quality: his gaze is unfocused; his setting, a simple green background, does not suggest a specific time or place; and his ill-fitting coat and vest seem less than contemporary. On learning that Weir was painting Ryder, their mutual friend C. E. S. Wood called the subject "that sweetminded philosopher Bishop Ryder," an appropriate description of the personality projected by the portrait.[4]

Weir turned to still-life painting only infrequently after 1900. Some of the still lifes may have been done as commissions from collectors who admired his earlier work in the genre and encouraged him to return to it. *Pink Peonies* (1902, private collection) combines flowers with

6.25 J. Alden Weir, The Fishing Party, *about 1915, oil on canvas, 28 × 23 in., unsigned (Washington, D.C., The Phillips Collection).*

6.26 J. Alden Weir, The Wharves, Nassau, *1913, oil on canvas, 32½ × 36⅜ in., unsigned (private collection).*

6.27 *J. Alden Weir,* Caro Seated on a Chest, *about 1905, oil on canvas,*
72 × 40 in., unsigned (private collection).

6.29 *J. Alden Weir,* A Gentlewoman, *1906, oil on can-*
vas, 30 × 25 in., signed at upper left: J. Alden Weir
(Washington, D.C., National Museum of American Art,
Smithsonian Institution, Gift of William T. Evans, 1909).

6.28 *J. Alden Weir,* Peacock Feathers, *1909, oil on canvas, 25 × 30 in., signed at lower left: J. Alden Weir (New York, Ira Spanierman, Inc.).*

6.30 *J. Alden Weir,* An American Girl, *about 1912, oil on canvas, 26 × 28¼ in. (Illinois, The Art Institute of Chicago, Gift of William T. Cresmer, 1951).*

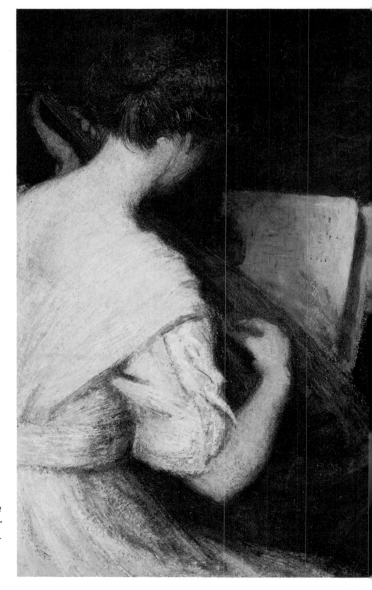

6.31 *J. Alden Weir*, The Lace Maker, *1915, oil on canvas, 30 × 25 in., signed at upper right: J. Alden Weir (New York, Hirschl & Adler Galleries).*

6.32 *J. Alden Weir*, The Lute Player, *about 1910–13, oil on canvas, 33½ × 23 in., signed at upper left: J. Alden Weir (Illinois, The Art Institute of Chicago, Walter H. Schulze Memorial Collection, 1924).*

6.33 *J. Alden Weir,* Portrait, *about 1913, oil on canvas, 39 × 31¼ in., signed at upper left: J. Alden Weir (Syracuse, New York, Everson Museum of Art).*

6.34 *J. Alden Weir,* Knitting for Soldiers, *1918, oil on canvas, 35 × 30 in., signed at upper right: J. Alden Weir (Washington, D.C., The Phillips Collection).*

6.35 J. Alden Weir, Albert Pinkham Ryder, *1902/1903, oil on canvas, 24¹/₈ × 20 in., unsigned (New York, National Academy of Design).*

6.36 J. Alden Weir, Childe Hassam, *1902/1903, oil on canvas, 24 × 20 in., inscribed on reverse: Childe Hassam/by J. Alden/ Weir/1903 (New York, National Academy of Design).*

6.37 J. Alden Weir, Still-Life, *probably 1900–1905, oil on canvas, 24½ × 36 in., signed at upper right: J. Alden Weir (Indiana, Indianapolis Museum of Art, James E. Roberts Fund, 1926).*

an exotic object—an oriental statue—in a composition not unlike those he had painted twenty years before. *Still-Life* (probably 1900–1905, fig. 6.37), which Weir reluctantly painted for a Portland patron, is a grandiose arrangement of pewter and porcelain, fruit and vegetables, in which the artist goes back to such French realists as Antoine Vollon for inspiration. Most of Weir's still lifes were large floral pieces—loose, casually arranged bouquets of open blossoms. *Still-Life: Flowers* (about 1905, fig. 6.38) shows a glass vase filled with white peonies and placed on a tabletop: some of the flowers have wilted and droop lifelessly; a number of petals have already fallen. In the flowers and leaves, Weir uses bold brushwork—the petals made with a palette knife and the leaves with long strokes of pigment—but the support and background are painted in a more restrained manner. *The Basket of Laurel* (1903, fig. 6.39) is set outdoors: a wicker basket has been placed at the base of a tree on the edge of a path. Weir used this opportunity to create a decorative pattern of textures: the uneven bark of the tree, the woven surface of the basket, the small rounded flowers and curving leaves of the bouquet. The effect of this patterning is intensified by Weir's restricted spatial recession; the horizon line is eliminated, and the landscape rises to the upper edge of the canvas.

During the final decade of his life, Weir spent much of his flagging energy on art organizations, often taxing his strength to help others. He had given informal assistance earlier to his less financially successful colleagues—John H. Twachtman, Albert P. Ryder, and Theodore Robinson, among them—but he now devoted his efforts to art institutions. Many of his activities were concerned with the National Academy of Design, where he

6.38 J. Alden Weir, Still-Life: Flowers, *about 1905, oil on canvas, 23¼ × 28¼ in., signed at upper right: J. Alden Weir (private collection).*

served on the Council, its governing body, from 1907 until 1914 (except for the 1910/11 season). Ironically, it was during that period that he was elected president of the Association of American Painters and Sculptors, which in 1913 presented the landmark International Exhibition of Modern Art, better known as the Armory Show. The radical group undoubtedly selected Weir not only because he occasionally expressed tolerance for modern art but also because they knew that his reputation would lend some respectability to their endeavors. As soon as Weir learned that the new organization was opposed to the principles of the National Academy, he resigned, claiming that the Academy was already "doing everything in its power for the promotion of art in this country."[5] Weir, who had helped organize the Society of American Artists' revolt against the Academy in the late 1870s and then had left the Society for The Ten American Painters twenty years later, was now willing to defend the establishment against a youthful challenge with which he could not sympathize. Despite his loyalty to the Academy and the principles it espoused, Weir still kept an open mind, even during his later years. In 1915, shortly after he was elected president of the National Academy of Design, he said he found some of the young modernists "really interesting. They're getting back to nature, that's what they are doing—breaking through traditions that

6.39 J. Alden Weir, The Basket of Laurel, *1903, oil on canvas, 34 × 24¼ in., signed at upper left: J. Alden Weir (private collection).*

are dead."[6] After two years in office Weir resigned as president of the Academy, but only because of ill health; even after his resignation he maintained close ties with the Academy and its members. The resolution passed by the Academy after his death, in 1919, is a testament to the place he had achieved not only within that institution but also within his generation:

> The members of the National Academy of Design have lost a friend and comrade, a man admired as a painter, respected as a citizen and loved by a world of friends whose hearts warm with thoughts of him; one whose mind was attuned to the highest ideals of Americanism and who was always in the vanguard of those who stood solidly for Art for Art's sake and he remained there until he laid aside his brush. "On Earth he lived. He did not merely stay."[7]

Notes

Symbols Used in Notes

BYU	Weir Family Papers, Brigham Young University, Provo, Utah
CMW	Carrie Mansfield Weir, JAW's sister
CWB	Cora Weir Burlingham
DeWP	Rev. DeWolf Perry, Princeton, Massachusetts
EBW	Ella Baker Weir, JAW's second wife
ENSAD/AN	Archives de l'École Nationale Supérieure des Arts Décoratifs, Archives Nationales, Paris
ENSBA/AN	Archives de l'École Nationale Supérieure des Beaux-Arts, Archives Nationales, Paris
E-S	Caroline P. Ely and Ann Ely Smith
JAW	J. Alden Weir
JFW	John Ferguson Weir, JAW's half brother
NAD	National Academy of Design, New York
RWW	Robert Walter Weir, JAW's father
SMBW	Susan Martha Bayard Weir, JAW's mother
SML/YU	John Ferguson Weir Papers, Sterling Memorial Library, Yale University, New Haven, Connecticut

See Short Title List for additional abbreviations.

In the italic picture captions, measurements are given in inches, height preceding width. In the signatures, upper and lower case lettering corresponds to that of the signature; script signatures are given in Roman type.

Introduction

1. Gerdts 1980, p. 75.
2. Ibid., p. 71.

Chapter 1

1. For information on Robert Walter Weir (hereafter cited as RWW), see Artists' Bibliography.

2. No major study has been done on John Ferguson Weir (hereafter cited as JFW), and the bibliography on him is surprisingly sparse (see Artists' Bibliography). The artist's daughter Edith Dean Weir Perry and her son the Reverend DeWolf Perry have presented a large collection of his manuscript papers to the Sterling Memorial Library at Yale University, which remains the major repository of information on the artist. I am grateful indeed to the Reverend Mr. Perry for permitting me to examine some JFW papers still in his possession, and for sharing his recollections about the artist.

3. Edidin, "Catalogue: Entries," in *An American Perspective: Nineteenth-Century Art from the Collection of Jo Ann & Julian Ganz, Jr.* (Washington, D.C.: National Gallery of Art, 1981), pp. 169–170. For an extensive list of the contents of RWW's studio, see Ortgies 1891.

4. JFW, "The Tenth Street Studio," box 9, folder 54, JFW Papers, Sterling Memorial Library, Yale University, New Haven, Connecticut (hereafter cited as SML/YU).

5. Julian Alden Weir (hereafter cited as JAW) to Mr. and Mrs. RWW, September 5, 1876, Caroline P. Ely and Ann Ely Smith (hereafter cited as E-S).

6. Doreen Bolger, "The Education of the American Artist," in *In This Academy: The Pennsylvania Academy of the Fine Arts, 1805–1976* (Philadelphia: Pennsylvania Academy of the Fine Arts, 1976), pp. 62–64.

7. Dunlap 1918, pp. 182, 190.

8. [Moss], "Catalogue," in *Robert Weir: Artist and Teacher of West Point* (West Point, New York: Cadet Fine Arts Forum of the United States Corps of Cadets, 1976), p. 27; S. J. Freedberg, *Painting of the High Renaissance in Rome and Florence*, 2 vols. (Cambridge: Harvard University Press, 1961), 1, pp. 569–570; 2, p. 692. For an authoritative discussion of Giulio's frescoes, see: Frederick Hartt, *Giulio Romano* (2 vols. Yale University Press, 1958, reprint ed., 2 vols. in 1, New York: Hacker Art Books, 1981), pp. 42–51, no. 3; fig. 78.

9. Dunlap 1918, p. 190.

10. Ibid., p. 191.

11. Ibid.

12. These lists appear in JFW, Sketchbook, which encompasses dates from 1858 to 1862 and bears the label of an Albany bookseller and stationer. One list (hereafter referred to as List A) includes twenty-four items; the other (List B), twenty-six. In addition to these two youthful lists of his paintings, JFW prepared a more comprehensive one later in his career, "List of Pictures painted by Jno. F. Weir," ms. coll. Rev. DeWolf Perry, Princeton, Massachusetts.

13. JFW, Sketchbook, List A.

14. Ibid.

15. Dunlap 1918, p. 190.

16. JAW to his mother, Susan Martha Bayard Weir (hereafter cited as SMBW), November 4, 1873 (E-S).

17. JAW to Mr. and Mrs. JFW, January 25, 1869 (E-S). For an illustration of RWW's *Self-Portrait* see: *Catalogue of American Portraits in The New-York Historical Society*, 2 vols. (New Haven, Connecticut: Yale University Press, 1974), 2, pp. 878–879.

18. For photographs of these early Weir works, see: Young "Records" 1, pp. 1, 3 (E-S).

19. JFW, "List of Pictures." *View of the Highlands of the Hudson* is included as "Hudson Highland W. P.—Summer Afternoon 20 × 34 Robt. L. Stuart—N.Y. Jan. 1863 250." For the complete history of this painting, see: Richard J. Koke and others, *American Landscape and Genre Paintings in The New-York Historical Society*, 3 vols. (Boston: G. K. Hall & Co., 1982), 3, pp. 252–253.

20. Jacob Kent Ahrens, "Robert Walter Weir (1803–1889)," Ph.D. diss., University of Delaware, 1972, pp. 31–32; 150–170; plates 7–1 and 7–2.

21. JFW to Mary French (later Mrs. JFW), April 12, 1862, box 5, folder 133; and JFW, Account Book [1858/71], November 21, 1859, box 1, folder 1, JFW Papers (SML/YU). The "Humbolt" referred to was Baron Friedrich von Humboldt (1769–1859), German naturalist, writer, and statesman whose philosophy exerted a powerful force on JFW's contemporaries, among them Frederic Church. John remained friendly with several Hudson River landscape painters, particularly Sanford R. Gifford and Jervis McEntee, but he later revised his opinion about the merits of the Hudson River School (JFW, "American Landscape Painters," *The New Englander Magazine* 32 [January 1873], pp. 140–151).

22. JAW to JFW, July 24, 1869 (E-S).

23. JFW, "Reminiscences of West Point," box 9, folder 52 (SML/YU).

24. JFW, Sketchbook.

25. Charles Larned, "F. Historical Sketch of Department of Drawing," in *The Centennial of the United States Military Academy at West Point, New York: 1802–1902*, 2 vols. (Washington, D.C.: Government Printing Office, 1904), 1, pp. 294–295. I am grateful to Michael Moss for bringing this article to my attention.

26. JAW to RWW, n.d. [1874] (E-S); RWW to JAW, n.d. and August 8, 1875, box 3, folder 18, Weir Family Papers, Brigham Young University, Provo, Utah (hereafter cited as BYU).

27. See figs. 3.1 and 3.2, Chapter 3.

28. Doreen B[olger] Burke, *J. Alden Weir and the National Academy of Design* (New York: National Academy of Design, 1981), p. 11.

29. JFW to Mrs. JFW, n.d. [about 1865/66], box 5, folder 133 (SML/YU).

30. Henry T. Tuckerman, *Book of the Artists: American Artist Life* (New York: G. P. Putnam & Son, 1867), p. 488.

31. JFW to Mrs. JFW, n.d. [about 1862], box 5, folder 133 (SML/YU).

32. *Sunny Moments*, long known as *The Artist's Studio*, is retitled here. "Sunny Moments—Studio interior. figures. 12 × 15" was listed as no. 47 in JFW, "List of Pictures." The picture was sold on December 30, 1864, in Artists' Fund Society of New York, *Catalogue of the Fifth Annual Exhibition*, no. 44, listed as *Sunny Moments*. The Yale painting corresponds exactly to that picture in specified size, date, and subject. Further, a review of the exhibition describes the picture, noting that "Half of its composition is monopolized by a quaint old piece of furniture, which has been most carefully and beautifully painted; while a woman, occupying a prominent place, is degraded to a secondary position" (*New York Times*, November 24, 1864, p. 5). I am grateful to Elisabeth Quackenbush for locating this review for me.

33. JFW to Mrs. Truman Seymour, February 12, [1869], box 4, folder 110 (SML/YU).

34. Weir 1957, pp. 46–47; JFW, Account Book [1858–1871], August 27 and 31; September 1–9; November 19, 20, and 22; 1864, box 1, folder 1 (SML/YU).

35. Young 1960, p. 13.

36. Weir 1957, p. 69.

37. Annette Blaugrund, "The Tenth Street Studio Building: A Roster, 1857–1895," *American Art Journal* 14 (Spring 1982), p. 71. Blaugrund incorrectly dates JAW's residence at the Tenth Street Studio Building to 1873–74. JAW was in Minnesota during the winter of 1872/73 and left for Europe in the fall of 1873, and so could have worked at the studio only in the summer of 1873.

38. JFW, Account Book, June 23, 1860; October 7, 1861; December 20, 1866; January 23, February 13, 17, and 18, and April 15, 1869; box 1, folder 1 (SML/YU).

39. JAW to JFW, n.d. (E-S). This letter is addressed "Studio B., 51 W. 10th St., N.Y. City."

40. Copybook, 1869–70, J. Alden Weir Comparative File, Yale University Art Gallery, New Haven, Connecticut.

41. JFW, Diary, January 6, 1869; December 22, 1868; and January 4, 1869; box 11, folder 5 (SML/YU); JFW to Mrs. Bradford Alden, n.d. [1873] (E-S).

42. JAW to JFW, June 11, 1874, Cora Weir Burlingham, New York (hereafter cited as CWB); JFW to JAW, February 25 and July 22, 1875 (CWB).

43. JFW to JAW, February 25, 1875; JAW to RWW, September 10, 1875; JFW to JAW, April 17, 1875; JAW to JFW, July 5, 1875 (CWB).

44. JAW to SMBW, April 14, 1876 (E-S).

45. National Academy of Design (hereafter cited as NAD), Council Minutes, January 3, 1870, Archives, NAD. Lemuel Wilmarth in his role as instructor at the National Academy of Design between 1870 and 1889 has been yet been studied. For additional information on Wilmarth, see Artists' Bibliography.

46. NAD Minutes, January 3, 1870, which include "Report of the Special Committee in Schools, Appointed by Resolution, at the Stated Meeting of the Academicians of the N.A.D. Nov. 10, 1869."

47. Ibid., January 13, 1873. The membership of the painting class is listed as "The Painting School" in "National Academy of Design, Register of Members of the Life School," following Session 1872/73.

48. NAD Minutes, November 7, 1870; March 20 and October 9, 1871. Unfortunately, the minutes and the student registers only give the students' date of admission; their attendance and departure cannot be documented. Dorothy Weir Young (1960, p. 13) stated that JAW may have begun his studies at the National Academy of Design as early as 1867–68. Unless her assertion was based on documents now lost, her information was unfounded.

49. "National Academy of Design, Register of Students, the Antique School," Session of 1870/71, Archives, NAD.

50. Ibid., Session of 1871/72.

51. Ibid. Little is known about Dabb, who was a student in the antique class at the NAD beginning on March 29, 1869, and which he probably continued to attend until the spring of 1872 (ibid., Sessions of 1868/69, 1869/70, 1871/72, Archives, NAD). His name appears twice in the life-class lists, in 1870/71 (although it has been crossed out) and 1871/72 ("National Academy of Design, Register of Members of the Life School," 1870/71, 1871/72, Archives, NAD). Dabb seems to have disappeared after exhibiting two landscapes at the NAD in 1873, at which time he gave his address as Elizabethport, New Jersey.

52. "National Academy of Design, Register of Members of the Life School, 1870–1871," Archives, NAD.

53. Page 1872.

54. JAW to RWW, December 17, 1871 (E-S).

55. NAD Minutes, January 23 and February 6, 1871. For further information on Brevoort, see: Artists' Bibliography.

56. Page 1872. Hawkins is also listed as anatomy lecturer in "National Academy of Design, Register of Students, the Antique School," Session of 1871/72, Archives, NAD. For information on Hawkins, see: Artists' Bibliography.

57. Page 1872.

58. For information on Rimmer's teaching activities at the NAD, see: NAD Minutes, November 28, December 5 and 19, 1870, March 6, 1871. For information on Rimmer, see: Artists' Bibliography.

59. Page 1872.

60. William Page, "The Art of the Use of Color in Imitation in Painting," *Broadway Journal* 1 (February 8–March 29, 1845), pp. 86–88; 114–115; 131–133; 150–151; 166–167; 201–202. For a discussion of Page's art theories, see: Joshua C. Taylor, *William Page: The American Titian* (Chicago: University of Chicago Press, 1957), pp. 73–84; 218–245.

Chapter 2

1. The standard source on the development of French academic training up to 1863 is Boime 1971. Subsequent developments are discussed in Boime 1977. For information on American students, see: H. Barbara Weinberg, "Nineteenth-Century American Painters at the École des Beaux-Arts," *American Art Journal* 13 (Autumn 1981), pp. 66–84. Dr. Weinberg's ideas on the effect of French training on American artists before 1900, on which she is preparing a comprehensive book, were presented in the class "American Painting, 1860–1900: The Impact of Foreign Travel and Training" at The City University of New York in the fall of 1981. Her analysis of the subject was instrumental in shaping my views on this aspect of Weir's development.

2. These statues were the two assigned in the École drawing class on May 25 and July 13, 1875, so one can assume that Weir executed the drawings after them at that time. (*Procès-verbaux originaux des jugements des concours des sections de peinture et de sculpture*, May 25 and July 13, 1875, AJ⁵² 78, Archives de l'École Nationale Supérieure des Beaux-Arts, Archives Nationales, Paris, hereafter cited as ENSBA/AN.)

3. Ibid., October 27, 1874; July 23 and August 24, 1875; March 20, 1877; AJ⁵² 77 and 78; *"Dossiers individuels des élèves, série antérieure au 31 décembre 1893"*; AJ⁵² 273 (ENSBA/AN). During his four years abroad, Weir became increasingly impatient with the rigors of the *concours*. In the summer of 1875 he wrote to his mother: "I regret exceedingly having stayed in Paris to make the concours this year, as the only time that one can work with comfort out doors I passed in the hot city" (JAW to SMBW, October 3, 1875 [CWB]). In 1876, the one additional year in which Weir would have been expected to take the *concours*, he did not, but that could have been by his own choice; he was hard at work on a portrait for the Salon (JAW to SMBW, February 27, 1876 [E-S]). The situation is further complicated in that Weir's name is inscribed twice in the *Registre matricule des élèves de la section de peinture*, as no. 4093 on October 27, 1874, and as no. 4298 on March 20, 1877 (AJ⁵² 236, ENSBA/AN). Matriculants were usually entered in the register and assigned a number only once. There is no reason for Weir's name to appear twice, although the second date is that of his final *jugement des concours* (AJ⁵² 78, ENSBA/AN).

4. "Art Notes," Paris, *The American Register*, January 23, 1875, p. 6.

5. The identities of the models, the duration of their poses, and their payment for the years 1873–75 can be found in the school's accounts (*"Dépenses,"* 1873–75, F²¹ 640 [ENSBA/AN]).

6. The *Prix de la Tête d'Expression* was established by Count Caylus in 1760. Until 1814 the exercise was executed in black pencil or pastel; thereafter it was painted (Boime 1971, pp. 194 [n. 82], 195 [n. 98]; figs. 21 and 22 [examples of this exercise by Victor-François-Eloi Biennourry and Paul-Joseph Janin]).

7. *"Concours et fondations: sections de peinture et de sculpture: Concours Caylus (peinture et sculpture),"* 1873–77, AJ⁵² 67 (ENSBA/AN). Relatively few École students actually participated in the *concours Caylus*, and it is not known whether Weir was among them.

8. *"Concours trimestriel de composition sur esquisse à un ou deux degrés, section de peinture,"* May 24, 1875; November 15, 1875; July 9, 1877; January 19, 1874; November 16, 1874; January 17, 1876; January 13, 1877; AJ⁵² 65 (ENSBA/NA).

9. Gerald M. Ackerman, "Catalogue and Commentaries on the Paintings," in *Jean-Léon Gérôme 1824–1904* (Dayton, Ohio: Dayton Art Institute, 1972), pp. 62–63.

10. Translated from Adolphe Yvon, *"Assassinat de Jules César," "Concours trimestriel de composition sur esquisse à un ou deux degrés, section de peinture,"* January 11, 1875, AJ⁵² 63 (ENSBA/AN). The first

section of the assignment was possibly included to set the scene. The last section, shifting to the past tense and underlined, was probably what the students were expected to sketch.

11. JAW to JFW, September 1, 1873 (E-S).

12. JAW to SMBW, October 1, 1873 (E-S). Weir formally enrolled in Gérôme's studio on October 21, 1873 ("*Registre d'inscription des élèves dans les ateliers de peinture, sculpture, architecture et gravure*," 1873–75, AJ⁵² 246 (ENSBA/AN).

13. Council of the National Academy of Design, Minutes, October 31, 1870, Archives, NAD. I am grateful to Abigail Booth Gerdts of the Academy for checking its library records for this book, which must have been extremely popular with art students everywhere during the late 1860s and early 1870s. See Charles Bargue, *Cours de Dessin, par C.B., avec le concours de J.-L. Gérôme*, 3 vols. (Paris: Goupil, 1868–70).

14. This list was compiled by comparing the enrollment records of the National Academy of Design and the École des Beaux-Arts (Register of Students, the Antique School, Sessions of 1870/71 and 1871/72, and Life School, 1871 (NAD); Weinberg 1981, pp.73, 81; "*Registre d'inscription des élèves dans les ateliers de peinture, sculpture, architecture et gravure*," 1873–75, AJ⁵² 246, and 1874–77, AJ⁵² 248 (ENSBA/AN).

15. JAW to RWW, November 10, 1873 (E-S).

16. See Artists' Bibliography. I am grateful to Gerald M. Ackerman, who has generously shared with me two chapters from his as yet unpublished book, *Gérôme, catalogue raisonné de ses oeuvres*. These chapters, "Theory and Practice" and "Gérôme at the École des Beaux-Arts," were most helpful.

17. Ackerman 1982, ms. pp. 401–402.

18. The two statements were published with the reminiscences of other American pupils of Gérôme. ("Open Letters: American Artists on Gérôme," *Century Magazine* 37 [February 1889], pp. 634–636; and "The Genius of J. L. Gérôme," *New York Herald*, magazine section, January 31, 1904, p. 8.)

19. JAW to RWW, October 19, 1873 (E-S).

20. JAW to JFW, November 7, 1876 (E-S).

21. Young 1960, p. 130.

22. JAW to JFW, January 11, 1874 (E-S).

23. JAW to JFW, March 11, 1875 (CWB).

24. Quoted in Boime 1974, p. 10.

25. Boime 1977, pp. 4, 12–13, 29.

26. The drawing is not signed or inscribed as to date or place, but in its style and composition it closely resembles other Weir drawings known to have been done at the École. It is also drawn on a sheet of paper with the French watermark "MICHALLET."

27. Charles Moreau-Vauthier, *La vie d'artiste, les arts*, no. 26, *Gérôme, peintre et sculpteur* (Paris, 1906), pp. 176–177, translated and quoted in Ackerman 1982, ms. p. 401. (A discussion of Gérôme's working method is given on pp. 408–413.)

28. Ackerman 1982, ms. p. 404. George de Forest Brush, who studied with Gérôme at the same time as Weir, wrote of the master's attitude: "He pleads constantly with his pupils to understand that although absolute fidelity to nature must be ever in mind, yet if they do not at last make imitation serve expression they will end up as they began—only children" ("Open Letters," *Century Magazine* 37 [February 1889], p. 635).

29. JAW to JFW, August 15, 1874 (CWB).

30. JAW to RWW, August 30, 1874; JAW to RWW, September 21, 1874 (CWB). For discussions of Weir's working practice in the painting *Harvesters of Brittany* see: JAW to "Cad" (his sister Carrie Mansfield Weir, hereafter cited as CMW), August 3, 1874; JAW to RWW, August 8, 1874; JAW to JFW, August 15, 1874; JAW to CMW, August 17, 1874; JAW to SMBW, August 26, 1874; JAW to RWW, August 30, 1874; JAW to SMBW, September 15, 1874; JAW to RWW, September 21, 1874 (CWB).

31. JAW to JFW, July 13, 1876 (E-S).

32. See: Gerald M. Ackerman and Gilles Cugnier, *Gérôme: Jean-Léon Gérôme 1824–1904: peintre, sculpteur et graveur: ses oeuvres conservées dans les collections françaises publiques et privées* (Vesoul, France: Musée de Vesoul, 1981), pp. 138–139, for illustrations of these landscapes.

33. JAW to Mr. and Mrs. RWW, October 9, 1876 (E-S).

34. JAW to Mr. and Mrs. RWW, September 16, 1876 (E-S).

35. Ibid.

36. Young "Records," 1, p. 39 (E-S).

37. See Artists' Bibliography.

38. JAW to RWW, March 30, 1874, and JAW to SMBW, April 21 and May 13, 1874 (CWB).

39. Young 1960, pp. 27–28.

40. JAW to RWW, December 7, 1873 (E-S).

41. See Artists' Bibliography. Jacquesson was a student at the École from 1858 until at least 1869. There he won medals and honorable mentions, most notably second place in the 1865 Prix de Rome. Between 1858 and 1871 he received commissions from the state for making copies after works by Prudhon, Flandrin, Cabanel, and Van Dyck. Brigitte Labat-Poussin, Conservator, Archives Nationales, Paris, kindly supplied information as to Jacquesson's copies and their locations.

42. JAW to JFW, January 11, 1874 (E-S).

43. *Fourth Annual Exhibition of the Yale School of Fine Arts* (1873), no. 61; JFW to John H. Niemeyer, June 8, 1900, and list of subscribers, June 8, 1900, box 4, folder 95 (SML/YU).

44. Boime 1974, p. 10.

45. JAW to JFW, January 19, 1874 (E-S).

46. See Artists' Bibliography.

47. JAW to JFW, January 11, 1874 (E-S).

48. JAW to SMBW, December 1, 1874 (CWB).

49. See Artists' Bibliography.

50. JAW to RWW, April 10, 1875 (CWB).

51. JAW to SMBW, April 20, 1875 (CWB).

52. Anne M. Wagner, "Learning to Sculpt in the Nineteenth Century," *The Romantics to Rodin*, ed. Peter Fusco and H. W. Janson (Los Angeles: Los Angeles County Museum of Art; New York: George Braziller, 1980), pp. 10–11.

53. Augustus Saint-Gaudens, *The Reminiscences of Augustus Saint-Gaudens*, ed. Homer Saint-Gaudens, 2 vols. (New York: The Century Co., 1913), 1, p. 69.

54. [Signature illegible], Le Ministre de l'Instruction publique, des Cultes et des Beaux-Arts, to Monsieur le Directeur de l'École de dessin et mathématiques, March 13, 1874, "*Élèves étrangers admis à l'École*," AJ⁵³ 143, *Archives de l'École Nationale Supérieure des Arts Décoratifs*, Archives Nationales, Paris (hereafter cited as ENSAD/AN). Twenty-one Americans were listed among the foreign students having gained admission to the Petite École for the 1873/74 academic year. It is difficult to evaluate whether the size of this group was extraordinary. The records for the admission of foreign students in the period 1870–73 do not seem to have survived. In 1875 and 1876 around the same number of foreign students were admitted as in 1874, but there were far fewer Americans. Although Weir's name does not appear on any subsequent lists, he must have continued to attend the Petite École during the 1874/75 academic year, for in his letters home he mentions taking the *concours* there (JAW to SMBW, October 19, 1874 [CWB]).

55. Relatively little is known about Faure, who worked as a painter and lithographer. He exhibited portraits regularly at the Salon during the 1840s and only occasionally thereafter. He served as an instructor at the Petite École from 1843 until 1878. Following his death, there were estate sales of his collections of old-master paintings and prints (see Artists' Bibliography). Aimé Millet is a better-known figure and was recognized as a successful sculptor during the period, although he did not exhibit every year at the Salon (see Artists' Bibliography).

56. "*Conseil des Professeurs, Procès-verbaux*," March 10, 1874, AJ⁵³ 5 (ENSAD/AN).

57. Ibid., March 14, 1874.

58. JAW to JFW, January 11, 1874; JAW to RWW, January 11, 1874 (E-S).

59. By 1879 students of each discipline were required to work in other fields; in 1883 the *cours simultané des trois arts* became a formal part of the École's curriculum (Boime 1977, p. 14).

60. "*Enseignement. Programmes des grandes concours*," April 10, 1874, AJ⁵³ 148 (ENSAD/AN).

61. JAW to RWW, February 23, 1874 (CWB).

62. JAW to SMBW, December 21, 1873 (E-S) and January 27, 1874 (CWB).

63. JAW to SMBW, November 4, 1873 (E-S); JAW to RWW, January 13, 1874; JAW to RWW, February 23, 1874; and JAW to SMBW, March 10 and March 24, 1874 (CWB).

64. JAW to SMBW, January 27, 1874 (E-S).

65. JAW to RWW, March 30, 1874 (CWB).

66. See Artists' Bibliography.

67. JAW to RWW, August 30, 1874 (CWB).

68. JAW to SMBW, March 14, 1875 (CWB). Weir's contributions to the Paris Salon are difficult to trace because of the ever-changing spellings of his name. In March 1874, he decided to sign his name J. Alden Weir in honor of his patroness, Mrs. Bradford Alden. In 1876, as Julian Alden-Weir, he exhibited no. 11, *Portrait de Mlle. E. A.* (present location unknown), and no. 12, *Tête de jeune fille, étude* (probably *Jeune femme* [1875, fig. 2.30]). In 1881, as Julian-Alden Weir, he exhibited no. 2110, *Portrait de M. Olin L. Warner* (1879/80, fig. 3.41) and no. 2111, *Jeune fille* (present location unknown); in 1882, as Alden Weiz, no. 2678, *Portrait de M. Delano* (1880, Hyde Park, New York, Home of Franklin D. Roosevelt, National Park Service), and no. 2679, *Un pot de fleurs* (possibly *Les petites roses* [1880, 3.52]); and in 1883, as Alden Weir, no. 2428, *Portrait de mon père* (1878, fig. 3.1), and no. 2429, *Flora; portrait* (1882, color plate 5).

69. JAW to SMBW, April 20, 1875 (CWB).

70. JAW to JFW, April 27, 1875 (CWB). Later, Weir cut the portrait down to just the head and submitted it to Gérôme for the end-of-the-year exhibition at the École (JAW to SMBW, July, 19, 1875 [CWB]).

71. JAW to SMBW, May 30, 1875 (CWB).

72. See: Artists' Bibliography.

73. The naturalist movement has recently received some scholarly attention. See Gabriel P. Weisberg, *The Realist Tradition: French Painting and Drawing: 1830–1900* (Cleveland: The Cleveland Museum of Art in cooperation with Indiana University Press, 1981), and Artists' Bibliography (Dagnan-Bouveret).

74. See: Artists' Bibliography.

75. Weir 1896, pp. 227, 229; JAW to RWW, April 25, 1875 (CWB).

76. JAW to JFW, April 27, 1875 (CWB).

77. "Jules Bastien-Lepage," *The Studio* 13 (January 31, 1885), pp. 146–147; 229–230; Young 1960, pp. 86–87.

78. JAW to SMBW, June 22, 1875 (CWB). The typescript reads "Frenchman," but the context suggests that Weir meant "Frenchmen."

79. JAW to SMBW, October 15, 1875 (CWB).

80. JAW to SMBW, October 20, 1875 (CWB).

81. JAW to JFW, September 10, 1875 (CWB). For information on JAW's work on this picture, see: JAW to SMBW, October 15 and 20, November 1, 1875 (CWB); July 5, 1875 (E-S).

82. JAW to JFW, September 10, 1875 (CWB).

83. JAW to SMBW, June 18, 1876 (E-S).

84. JAW to JFW, after July 23, 1875 (CWB).

85. For information on this picture see: JAW to SMBW, November 29, 1875 (CWB); January 16, February 12, March 13 and 21, 1876 (E-S); JAW to JFW, December 19, 1875; February 7, 1876 (E-S).

86. For information on JAW's work on this picture see: JAW to SMBW, November 29 and December 26, 1875 (CWB); January 16, 1876 (E-S); JAW to JFW, December 19, 1875 (E-S).

87. JAW to Mr. and Mrs. RWW, February 19, 1877, quoted in Young 1960, p. 120.

88. JAW to Mr. and Mrs. RWW, December 20, 1876 (E-S).

89. JAW to Mr. and Mrs. RWW, March 6, 1877, quoted in Young 1960, p. 120.

90. JAW to JFW, March 12, 1877, quoted in Young 1960, p. 121.

91. JAW to Mr. and Mrs. RWW, April 6, 1877, quoted in Young 1960, p. 122.

92. JAW to Mr. and Mrs. RWW, April 15, 1877, quoted in Young, 1960, p. 123.

93. JAW to Mr. and Mrs. RWW, August 22, 1877, quoted in Young 1960, p. 133.

94. Ibid.

95. Weir's opinion of Taine undoubtedly fluctuated while he was a student at the École des Beaux-Arts. He attended Taine's lectures, but wrote to his father: "You would like to hear [how] 'Taine' is thought of here. His works are much esteemed but considered as readings [for] leisure hours; his lectures are attended by men of letters and those of curiosity, but seldom by artists. . . . His lectures are not practical . . . still there is a certain poetry of expression in his writings that makes them always works valuable to an artist for leisure hours" (JAW to RWW, February 25, 1875 [CWB]). Later, he expressed a desire to purchase copies of Taine's works (JAW to RWW, November 22, 1875 [E-S]). He may have owned a copy of Taine's *Philosophy of Art in the Netherlands*, trans. John Durand (New York: Leypold & Holt, 1871), which was listed as being in the Weir–Young Library (Helmut Ripperger, comp., "Short Title Check List of Books in the House and Studio of the Late Mahonri Young, Ridgefield, Connecticut" [ca. 1960], Weir Family Papers, BYU). However, since this list includes books which belonged to Weir's daughter Dorothy and to her sculptor husband, Mahonri Young, it is impossible to determine which books were the artist's.

96. The contents of the Musée des Copies during Weir's stay in Paris are listed in a series of contemporary articles: "Le Musée des Copies: son catalogue," *La Chronique des Arts* (January 3, February 3 and 14, 1874), pp. 1–2, 51–52, 62.

97. For a perceptive discussion of the copy and its evolution in nineteenth-century French academic practice, see Boime 1971, pp. 124–125.

98. Slive 1974, pp. 11–12, no. 17.

99. JAW to JFW, December 19, 1874; JAW, Diary, January 8, 1875 (CWB). *Malle Babbe* is no longer attributed to Hals (Slive 1974, p. 140, no. D 34).

100. Slive 1974, p. 38, no. 62.

101. For a complete discussion of the revival of interest in Hals see: Frances Suzman Jowell, *Thoré-Bürger and the Art of the Past* (New York: Garland Publishing, 1977), pp. 284–314; and "Thoré-Bürger and the Revival of Frans Hals," *Art Bulletin* 56 (March 1974), pp. 101–117.

102. JAW to RWW, June 3, 1874 (CWB).

103. Chu 1974, pp. 6, 37, mentions Gérôme's visit to the Rijksmuseum in 1874, but discounts Hals's influence on the development of Gérôme's style.

104. JAW to JFW, December 19, 1874 (CWB).

105. JAW to SMBW, February 15, 1875 (CWB).

106. For a discussion of these important collections, see Chu 1974, pp. 4–5.

107. JAW to JFW, March 1, 1875 (CWB).

108. JAW to RWW, December 28, 1874 (CWB). Immediately before relating this anecdote, Weir mentioned "two fine heads by Van der Helst and one Frans Hals." Only one work by Frans Hals would have been in the Koninklijk muzeum van schoone kunsten in Antwerp when Weir visited there in 1874, *Fisherboy*, about 1630 (Slive 1974, p. 44, no. 72). *Stephanus Geraerdts* (ibid., pp. 97–98, no. 188) was not acquired until 1886. Thus, if Weir was copying Hals, which seems likely, he was certainly copying *Fisherboy*.

109. Slive 1974, pp. 47–48, no. 79.

110. Chu 1974, pp. 16–17; Jan Biatostocki, "Rembrandt and Posterity," *Nederlands Kunsthistorisch Jaarboek* (Netherlands Yearbook for History of Art) (1972), pp. 131–155.

111. John Ferguson Weir, "Article III—Taine's Philosophy of Art in the Netherlands," *The New Englander* 30 (January 1871), p. 54. Weir may even have owned this book (see note 95).

112. See Ortgies 1891: for books, no. 21; for facsimile reproductions, no. 359; for prints after Rembrandt's work, nos. 628–653, 655–656, 658; and for a drawing of *Woman with a Tray*, supposedly an original from which Bartolozzi engraved a plate, no. 991. Robert Walter Weir also owned a copy after a Rembrandt in Florence (JAW to JFW, October 2, 1873 [E-S]; and JAW to RWW, October 24, 1875 [CWB]).

113. *Catalogue of the Museum and Gallery of Art of the New-York Historical Society* (New York: New-York Historical Society, 1873), p. 37, nos. 328, 329, 330, 331.

114. JAW to Mrs. Bradford Alden, December 14, 1873 (E-S).

115. JAW to SMBW, March 1, 1874 (CWB).

116. Bonvin's *Le Cochon* (Reims, Musée Saint-Denis) and Vollon's *The Pig* (Mr. and Mrs. Joseph M. Tanenbaum) were both exhibited in the Salon of 1875 (Gabriel P. Weisberg, *Bonvin: la vie et l'oeuvre* [Paris: Editions Geoffroy-Dechaume, 1979], pp. 111, 190–191; and Louise d'Argencourt and Douglas Druick, eds., *The Other Nineteenth Century: Paintings and Sculpture in the Collection of Mr. and Mrs. Joseph M. Tanenbaum* [Ottawa: The National Gallery of Canada, National Museums of Canada, 1978], pp. 194–195).

117. JAW to SMBW, June 22, 1875 (CWB).

118. Gérôme to Adolph Rosenberg, September 7, 1899, quoted in Ackerman 1982, p. 408.

119. JAW to SMBW, February 15, 1875; JAW to RWW, February 24, 1875 (CWB).

120. JAW to SMBW, February 15, 1875 (CWB).

121. Robert Walter Weir owned many reproductive engravings after Rubens's paintings (Ortgies 1891, nos. 706–723); he owned books about Van Dyck and a lithograph and engravings after his work; he also made a copy after a portrait of Charles I by Van Dyck (ibid., nos. 20–24, 124, 192, 793–797, 866).

122. JAW to JFW, October 2, 1873 (E-S).

123. JAW to RWW, October 24, 1873 (E-S).

124. JAW to JFW, October 2, 1873 (E-S).

125. Weir was understandably fascinated by this particular painting acquired by the National Gallery in 1871, for it was the subject of an article by Alfred Michiels: "Le Chapeau de Paille Par Rubens," *Gazette des Beaux-Arts* series 2, 9 (January 1874), pp. 25–28. The pose and sometimes the costume worn by Susanna Fourment Lunden was adopted in portraits by Édouard Manet; by Weir's mentor, Gérôme; and by Weir's friend Abbott H. Thayer (Charles Sterling and Margaretta M. Salinger, *French Paintings: A Catalogue of the Collection of The Metropolitan Museum of Art*, 3 vols. [New York: The Metropolitan Museum of Art, 1967], 3, pp. 25–26; Gerald M. Ackerman and Gilles Cugnier, *Gérôme: Jean-Léon Gérôme 1824–1904: peintre, sculpteur et graveur: ses oeuvres conservées dans les collections françaises publiques et privées* [Vesoul, France: Musée de Vesoul, 1981]), frontispiece and p. 106; Doreen Bolger Burke, *American Paintings in the Metropolitan Museum of Art: Volume III: A Catalogue of Works by Artists Born Between 1846 and 1864*, ed. Kathleen Luhrs [New York: The Metropolitan Museum of Art in association with Princeton University Press, 1980, pp. 98–100]).

126. JAW to RWW, February 24, 1875 (CWB).

127. Ibid.

128. JAW to Mr. and Mrs. RWW, August 27, 1876 (E-S).

129. Ibid.

130. The artist would have known of Velázquez even as a boy in America. Robert Walter Weir owned engravings after Velázquez and had made copies after his portraits of Phillip IV and Innocent X (Ortgies 1891, nos. 801–803, 862, 895).

131. JAW to Mrs. Bradford Alden, December 14, 1873 (E-S).

132. JAW to SMBW, May 19, 1874 (CWB).

133. JAW to JFW, January 3, 1875 (CWB).

134. Lopez-Rey 1963, p. 141, no. 57.

135. JAW to Mr. and Mrs. RWW, August 27, 1876 (E-S).

136. JAW to Mr. and Mrs. RWW, October 29, 1876 (E-S).

137. See: Ortgies 1891, nos. 25, 102–104, 533, 593–622, for books about and engravings after Raphael; nos. 764–771, for engravings after Titian; and no. 901, for R. W. Weir's copy after Veronese's *Martyrdom of St. Agatha*. The elder Weir also showed his admiration for Titian in his picture *Titian in His Atelier* (present location unknown); ibid., no. 859.

138. H[ippolyte] Taine, *Lectures on Art*, trans. John Durand (New York: Henry Holt and Company, 1875), pp. 10, 17, 14.

139. JAW to SMBW, August 12, 1876 (E-S).

140. JAW to JFW, October 19, 1874 (CWB).

141. JAW to Mr. and Mrs. RWW, April 15, 1877, quoted in Young 1960, p. 123.

142. JAW to Mr. and Mrs. RWW, March 6, 1877, quoted in Young 1960, p. 120.

143. JAW to SMBW, May 6, 1876 (E-S).

144. JAW to SMBW, July 5, 1876 (E-S).

145. JAW to SMBW, May 27, 1876, (E-S).

146. Young 1960, p. 125.

147. JAW to JFW, May 12, 1877, quoted in Young 1960, p. 126.

148. Ibid.

149. JAW to Mr. and Mrs. RWW, May 1, 1877, quoted in Young 1960, p. 124.

Chapter 3

1. Wyatt Eaton to JAW, June 5, 1877 (E-S).

2. See Society of American Artists, *Seventh Annual Exhibition* (May 26–June 21, 1884), copy annotated by Kenyon Cox, New York Public Library. I am indebted to Jennifer Martin Bienenstock, a graduate student in the Ph.D. Program in Art History, The City University of New York, who is preparing her dissertation, "The Founding and Early Years of the Society of American Artists," and has generously shared her information with me.

3. Mary Cassatt to JAW, March 10, [1878] (E-S).

4. "Collections, Competitions, and Sales," *New-York Daily Tribune*, May 8, 1881, p. 2.

5. Weir exhibited two works, both entitled *Study for a Portrait* (nos. 88 and 92), in the 1878 exhibition of the Society; one of these was the study for his portrait of his father. Of the approximately 120 paintings in the exhibition, 5 were either called "study" or designated as a study for a head or portrait (Kurtz Gallery, New York, *Catalogue of the First Exhibition: Society of American Artists* [1878], nos. 82, 88, 90, 92, 111). At the Academy, which exhibited a total of about 720 paintings, about 35 were listed as sketches or as studies, although most of them appear to have been still-life paintings, with only about 9 designated as studies of figures or heads (NAD, *Catalogue of the Fifty-Third Annual Exhibition of the National Academy of Design, 1878* [1878], nos. 86, 111, 123, 248 [*A Study* by JAW], 293, 336, 341, 427, 620). The studies thus represented a slightly larger proportion of the Society's exhibition than of the Academy's.

6. For information on the Tile Club and its activities, see: Mahonri Sharp Young, "The Tile Club Revisited," *American Art Journal* 2 (Fall 1970), pp. 81–91.

7. "Among the Painters," *New-York Daily Tribune*, January 23, 1881, p. 5.

8. Ibid.

9. "Fine Arts," *New York Herald*, October 8, 1883, p. 8.

10. "Art News and Comments," *New-York Daily Tribune*, March 11, 1883, p. 2.

11. Minutes, March 19, 1894, American Water Color Society, New York.

12. "The Art Schools," *Art Interchange* 1 (October 16, 1878), p. 23.

13. Young 1960, p. 141.

14. "American Art News," *Art Interchange* 4 (January 21, 1880), p. 19.

15. "Notes and News," *Art Interchange* 11 (August 2, 1883), p. 34; "Art Association Notes," *Art Age* 2 (May 1885), p. 154.

16. Slive 1974, p. 9, no. 13; p. 22, no. 33.

17. Ibid., pp. 25–26, no. 42; pp. 105–106, no. 206; and pp. 96–97, no. 186. It is not known which of these portraits Weir had seen (if any), but *Frans Post*, included in two exhibitions at London's Royal Academy in 1873 and 1882 and auctioned in London on April 6, 1876, is the most likely one (ibid., pp. 105–106, no. 206).

18. Ibid., p. 99, no. 190.

19. JAW to RWW, February 28, 1875 (CWB).

20. For further information on the division of this picture, see: John I. H. Baur, "J. Alden Weir's Partition of 'In the Park,'" *Brooklyn Museum Quarterly* 25 (October 1938), pp. 125–129.

21. Slive 1974, pp. 3–4, no. 5.

22. Ibid., pp. 13–14, no. 20.

23. Ibid., p. 13, no. 19; and Department of Paintings of the Rijksmuseum, Pieter van Thiel, Director, *All the Paintings in the Rijksmuseum, Amsterdam* (Amsterdam: Rijksmuseum and Maarssen: Gary Schwartz, 1976), pp. 346, 257.

24. Jowell 1977, p. 305.

25. The poem was enclosed in a letter from JAW to RWW, January 8, 1875 (CWB).

26. See: Lionello Venturi, *History of Art Criticism*, trans. Charles Marriott (New York: E. P. Dutton & Co., 1936), pp. 228–230.

27. Lopez-Rey 1963, pp. 163–164, no. 124; and p. 158, no. 105. .

28. JAW to RWW, August 3, 1878, quoted in Young "Records," 1, p. 55 (E-S).

29. For descriptions of these paintings, see: JAW to RWW, August 3, 1878, and JAW to unspecified correspondent (probably RWW), August 3, 1878, quoted in Young "Records," 1, p. 56 (E-S).

30. See fig. 5.1, Chapter 5.

31. See fig. 3.77.

32. JAW to RWW, April 24, 1876 and July 19, 1880 (E-S).

33. John H. Twachtman to JAW, January 2, 1885 (Ira Spanierman, Inc., New York).

34. Weir 1896, pp. 231–232.

35. "Bastien-Lepage: The French Artist About to Visit the United States," *New York Herald*, September 9, 1883, p. 170. For more information on Bastien-Lepage's proposed visit, see: "Arts and Letters," *Art Folio* 1 (December 1883), p. 119; "Art News and Comments," *New-York Daily Tribune*, January 13, 1884, p. 4.

36. "Jules Bastien-Lepage," *The Studio: A Journal for the Fine Arts* n.s. 13 (January 31, 1885), pp. 145–151; and JAW, A. Saint-Gaudens, and F. D. Millet, *Monument to Bastien-Lepage* (1887), broadside (E-S).

37. For information on Robert Wylie, see Chapter 2, pp. 67 (ill.), 68 and Artists' Bibliography.

38. "Fifty Seventh Academy," *Art Interchange* 8 (March 30, 1882), p. 74.

39. Weisberg 1981, pp. 123–124. I am grateful to Jennifer Bienenstock for bringing this painting to my attention.

40. "Fine Arts: Society of American Artists," *New-York Daily Tribune*, April 1, 1980, p. 7. The placement of the partly draped figure in *The Good Samaritan* could also be compared to Manet's *Dead Toreador* (1863, Washington, D.C., National Gallery of Art). See Rouart and Wildenstein 1975, 1, pp. 80–81, no. 72. For a comparison of Manet's and Gérôme's treatments of figures of this type, see Gerald M. Ackerman, "Gérôme and Manet," *Gazette des Beaux-Arts* series 6, 70 (September 1967), pp. 163–176.

41. I am grateful to Jennifer Bienenstock for bringing this trend to my attention.

42. Young "Records," 1, p. 62 (E-S). For information on Newman, see: Marchal E. Landgren, *Robert Loftin Newman 1827–1912* (published for The National Collection of Fine Arts by the Smithsonian Institution Press, 1974).

43. "Society of American Artists," *New-York Daily Tribune*, April 3, 1881, p. 7.

44. JAW to JFW, May 24, 1881, quoted in Young, "Records," 2, p. 94 (E-S).

45. Ichabod T. Williams to JAW, May 14, 1884, ibid.

46. Weir copied from the writings of Sir Joshua as early as 1869/70 (see Copybook, 1869/70, J. Alden Weir Comparative File, Yale University Art Gallery). He often commented on Sir Joshua while he was in Europe studying; see: JAW to JFW, [1873]; JAW, Diary, September 23–27, 1873; JAW to Mr. and Mrs. RWW, September 23, 1873; JAW to RWW, September 26, 1873; JAW to RWW, September 27, 1873; JAW to JFW, October 2, 1873 (E-S).

47. Boime 1971, pp. 16–18.

48. For a discussion of these American developments, see: Weinberg 1980, pp. 160–165.

49. Robert Fernier, *La vie et l'oeuvre de Courbet*, 2 vols. (Paris: Fondation Wildenstein; Lausanne: La Bibliothèque des Arts, 1977), 1, pp. 122–123, no. 202; Rouart and Wildenstein 1975, 1, pp. 50–51, no. 31; pp. 60–61, no. 49. For information on the Bastien-Lepage portraits, see: William Steven Feldman, "The Life and Work of Jules Bastien-Lepage (1848–1884)," Ph.D. diss., New York University, 1973.

50. JAW to RWW, April 24, 1876 (E-S).

51. Rouart and Wildenstein 1975, 1, pp. 54–55, no. 37 and pp. 112–113, no. 115.

52. Ibid., pp. 86–87, no. 79. For information on the history of this and the other Manet paintings

purchased by Weir, see: Frances Weitzenhoffer, "First Manet Paintings to Enter an American Museum," *Gazette des Beaux-Arts* series 6, 98 (March 1981), pp. 125–129; Young 1960, pp. 145–146; "Art Gossip," *New York Sun*, December 10, 1911, p. 4.

53. Rouart and Wildenstein 1975, 1, pp. 62–63, no. 51.

54. Ibid., pp. 210–211, no. 260; pp. 224–225, no. 280.

55. *Les Gitanos* (ibid., pp. 56–57, no. 41) was divided into the following canvases: *Bohémien* (ibid., pp. 56–57, no. 42) and *Le Buveur d'eau* (ibid., pp. 56–57, no. 43).

56. Ibid., pp. 56–57, no. 43; pp. 122–123, no. 129.

57. Ibid., pp. 60–61, no. 50.

58. See Chapter 2, pp. 45–46.

59. *Sections de peinture et sculpture Concours Caylus*, AJ⁵² 67, 1876 (ENSBA/AN).

60. Doreen Bolger Burke, *American Paintings in the Metropolitan Museum of Art: Volume III: A Catalogue of Works by Artists Born Between 1846 and 1864*, ed. Kathleen Luhrs (New York: The Metropolitan Museum of Art in association with Princeton University Press, 1980), pp. 138–139.

61. Because the pieces were reassembled and mounted on a second piece of paper, the drawing can still be examined today.

62. George Gurney, "Olin Levi Warner (1844–1896): A Catalogue Raisonné of His Sculpture and Graphic Works," 3 vols. (Ph.D. diss., University of Delaware, 1978), 2, pp. 437–446.

63. Young "Records," 2, p. 107.

64. The major sources of Weir as a still-life painter are: Arthur Edwin Bye, *Pots and Pans or Studies in Still-Life Painting* (Princeton, New Jersey: Princeton University Press, 1921), pp. 200–202; Gerdts and Burke 1971, pp. 210–211; William H. Gerdts, *Painters of the Humble Truth: Masterpieces of American Still-Life 1801–1939* (Columbia, Missouri: Philbrook Art Center with University of Missouri Press, 1981), pp. 219–221.

65. This is presumably the painting that Dorothy Weir Young described in her published list, although her description does not quite fit the picture: "Flowers: Tall jar and a small vase, both filled with tulips and other flowers on the right, and a bowl full of flowers placed on two books on the left. Tall Chinese blue and white vase, brass lantern, pewter plate, and some flowers on a table. In the background is the wheel of a spinning wheel" (Dorothy Weir, "List of Paintings," in Appreciation 1921, p. 129).

66. Dorothy Weir Young dates this copy to 1881, when Weir made a number of copies in the National Gallery, London (Young "Records," 6, p. 79). However, it could well have been done on an earlier trip, perhaps that in 1877. Unfortunately, the volume of the copyist register for this period at the National Gallery has been lost.

67. According to Nicki Thiras of the Addison Gallery (conversation with the author April 1982), this picture is neither signed nor dated. When it was included in Weir's memorial show at the Metropolitan Museum of Art in 1924, however, it was catalogued as being "signed and dated: *J. Alden Weir 80(?)*" (Metropolitan 1924, p. 2, no. 10). Judged on stylistic grounds, this date would appear to be correct.

68. Dorothy Weir Young's notes indicate that the former was identified in an annotated catalogue of the exhibition, which called its "madonna fascinating" (Young "Records," 6, p. 32a). She gives the catalogue's location as the library, M. Knoedler & Co., but the catalogue is now lost. The second still life is mentioned in a review that notes its subject as "a bronze of the well known St. John relief" ("Fine Arts: Seventh Annual Exhibition of the Society of American Artists," *New York Herald*, May 25, 1884, p. 6).

69. See: J. Cavallucci and Émile Molinier, *Les Della Robbia: leur vie et leur oeuvre* (Paris: Libraire de l'art, J. Rouam, Imprimeur-Éditeur, 1884), ill. p. 105; Françoise de la Moureyre-Gavoty, *Institut de France, Paris, Musée Jacquemart-André, Sculpture Italienne* (Paris: Édition des Musées Nationaux, 1975), p. 35.

70. Sir Joshua Reynolds, *Discourses on Art*, ed. Robert R. Wark (New Haven, Connecticut: published for the Paul Mellon Centre for Studies in British Art [London] by Yale University Press, 1975), p. 52.

71. Ingvar Bergström, *Dutch Still-Life Painting in the Seventeenth Century* (New York: Thomas Yoseloff, 1956), pp. 204–208; Arnauld Brejon de Lavergnée, Jacques Foucart, and Nicole Reynaud, *Catalogue sommaire illustré des peintures du Musée du Louvre: 1: École flamande et hollandaise* (Paris: Éditions de la Réunion des Musées Nationaux, 1979), pp. 36, 60, 80, 115, 127.

72. See Elizabeth Hardouin-Fugier and Étienne Grafe, *Fleurs de Lyon 1807–1917* (Lyons, Musée des Beaux-Arts, 1982), pp. 43, 47, 154–157, 303–318, 324–328.

73. David Freedberg, "The Origins and Rise of the Flemish Madonnas in Flower Garlands: Decoration and Devotion," in *Münchner Jahrbuch der Bildenden Kunst* 32 (1981), pp. 115–150.

74. For a summary of Daniel Cottier's career, see: W. E. H., "Daniel Cottier 1838–1891," in Galleries Durand-Ruel, Paris, *Catalogue of Ancient and Modern Pictures: Important Works of the French, English and Dutch Schools* (1892), pp. ix–xiii.

75. For illustrations of Cottier interiors and furnishings, see: Clarence Cook, *The House Beautiful: Essays on Beds and Tables, Stools and Candlesticks* (New York: Scribner, Armstrong and Co., 1878).

76. Young 1960, p. 155.

77. Young "Records," 6, p. 418 (E-S).

78. Ibid., p. 61.

79. "Art News and Comments," *New-York Daily Tribune*, March 18, 1883, p. 5.

80. For an illustration, see: Sotheby Parke Bernet, Inc., New York, *Important Impressionist and Modern Paintings and Sculptures* (sale catalogue, October 19, 1977), no. 25a. The picture was in the collection of Henry Gibson of Philadelphia, and was bequeathed in 1896 to the Pennsylvania Academy of the Fine Arts. A second Fantin, *Roses*, was at that time in the collection of A. E. Borie of Philadelphia (Earl Shinn [Edward Strahan], *Art Treasures of America*, 3 vols. [Philadelphia: George Barrie, 1880], 2, p. 162).

81. This undated still life is no. 59 in Ortgies 1889 (Young "Records," 2, p. 149 [E-S]).

82. The photograph is mounted on cardboard and inscribed: "To J. Alden Weir/ [butterfly symbol]/ Whistler."

83. For information on the Chardin revival see: John W. McCoubrey, "The Revival of Chardin in French Still-Life Painting, 1850–1870," *Art Bulletin* 46 (March 1964), pp. 39–53; and Gabriel P. Weisberg with William S. Talbot, *Chardin and the Still-life Tradition in France* (Cleveland, Ohio: The Cleveland Museum of Art, 1979).

84. Gerdts and Burke 1971, pp. 200–204; Emil Carlsen, "On Still-Life Painting," *Palette and Bench* 1 (October 1908), pp. 6–8.

85. Compare this picture to *The Copper Water Urn* (Paris, Musée du Louvre), ill. Rosenberg 1970, pp. 184–186.

86. It was no. 23 in the show (see Rouart and Wildenstein 1975, 1, p. 132, no. 140).

87. Young 1960, p. 143.

88. "Movements of Artists," *Art Interchange* 8 (June 22, 1982), p. 143.

89. See: Artists' Bibliography.

90. John Douglass Hale, "The Life and Creative Development of John H. Twachtman," 2 vols., Ph.D. diss., Ohio State University, 1957, 1, p. 63.

91. Council of the NAD, Minutes, May 13, 1885, Annual Meeting (NAD).

92. Ibid., March 22, 1886.

93. Ibid., January 10, 1887.

Chapter 4

1. "The New Water-Colors," *New York Times*, January 31, 1880, p. 5.

2. In 1882, nine new members were elected from a list of twenty-six nominees, one of whom was Weir (Minutes, March 15, 1882, American Water Color Society, microfilm N68-8, Archives of American Art, Smithsonian Institution, Washington, D.C.; "The American Water Color Society," *The Art Interchange* 9 [November 23, 1882], p. 117). The following year two members were elected from a list that included eleven other candidates, Weir among them (Minutes, March 21, 1883, American Water Color Society; "General Home Notes and News," *New York Herald*, March 25, 1883, p. 25). He was finally elected at the seventeenth annual meeting of the Society on March 19, 1884 (Minutes, March 19, 1884, American Water Color Society).

3. "Art Notes, "*New York Times*, December 2, 1883, p. 5; "Boston Art Items," *Art Interchange* 15 (January 31, 1884), p. 29.

4. *Port Jefferson* appeared as no. 118 in NAD's *Illustrated Catalogue: Fifteenth Annual Exhibition of the American Water Color Society* (1882).

5. Richard J. Boyle, *John Twachtman* (New York: Watson-Guptill Publications, 1979), pp. 26–27, color illustration of *New York Harbor* (about 1879, Ohio, Cincinnati Art Museum).

6. Rouart and Wildenstein, 2, pp. 102–108, nos. 243–257. See also p. 36, color illustration of no. 256, *Les Péniches*, 1874.

7. "Nineteenth Water Color," *Art Age* 3 (February 1886), p. 119.

8. For information on La Farge's watercolor still lifes, see: Kathleen A. Foster, "The Still-Life Paintings of John La Farge," *American Art Journal* 11 (Summer 1979), pp. 4–37.

9. NAD, *Illustrated Catalogue: Seventeenth Annual Exhibition of the American Water Color Society* (1884), no. 338, illustrated as frontispiece.

10. Marie Berhaut, *Caillebotte: sa vie et son oeuvre: catalogue raisonné des peintures et pastels* (Paris: La Bibliothèque des Arts), pp. 51 (color illustration); 86–87, no. 28.

11. For information on Abbey's watercolors, see: Michael Quick and Kathleen A. Foster, "Watercolors and Pastels," in *Edwin Austin Abbey (1852–1911)* (New Haven, Connecticut: Yale University Art Gallery, 1973), pp. 61–65.

12. Weir exhibited three works with the Society of Painters in Pastel in 1888. No catalogues exist for the 1889 or 1890 exhibitions, but some idea of Weir's contribution can be determined from reviews of the exhibition. For information on the Weir-Twachtman sale, see Ortgies 1889.

13. Dianne H. Pilgrim, "The Revival of Pastels in Nineteenth-Century America: The Society of Painters in Pastel," *American Art Journal* 10 (November 1978), pp. 43–62.

14. "Fine Arts," *New York Herald*, October 8, 1883, p. 8.

15. "The Painters in Pastel," *New York Sun*, May 17, 1890, p. 6.

16. Young, MacDonald, Spencer, and Miles 1980, text, pp. 17–20, no. 38; plates, 28.

17. For information on Weir's etchings, see: Pach 1911; Weitenkampf 1912; Frank Weitenkampf, "Weir's Excursions into Print-Land," *Arts and Decoration* 12 (January 1920), pp. 208–209; Margery Austin Ryerson, "J. Alden Weir's Etchings," *Art in America* 8 (August 1920), pp. 243–248; Elisabeth Luther Cary, "The Etched Work of J. Alden Weir," *Scribner's Magazine* 68 (October 1920), pp. 507–512; Zimmerman 1923; Zimmerman October 1923; Dorothy Weir Young, "Etchings by J. Alden Weir," 2 vols. of labeled photographs [1920s–1940s] (E-S); Ely 1927; Baskett 1966; Nelson 1967; Flint 1972; Frances Weitzenhoffer, "Estampes impressionnistes de peintres américains," *Nouvelles de l'estampe* 28 (July–August 1976), pp. 7–15; Getscher 1977; David Wilson, "The 'Unknown' American Whose Etchings Portray the Isle of Man," *Manx Life* (March/April 1981), p. 19.

18. Mrs. Ely, who was herself an etcher, found some fifty plates in her father's studio and printed them in limited editions of twenty-five each. It seems that the plates were those included in a 1927 exhibition at Frederick Keppel & Co. (see Ely 1927).

19. Quoted in Young 1960, p. 180, where the source is given as Pach 1911. While Pach does discuss some of the same issues, the quotation does not appear in his article.

20. Ely 1927, unpaged, says that Weir began etching in 1887 and ceased in 1894 "and never took it up again"; Nelson 1967, unpaged, notes that Weir's etching "was restricted to the years 1885–1893"; Flint 1972, p. 5, says 1887–93.

21. See Ortgies 1891 for catalogue of Robert's collection.

22. Dunlap 1918, p. 184; Weitenkampf 1912, p. 3.

23. Weitenkampf 1912, p. 7. Weir attended other exhibitions at Derby's (see JAW to JFW, n.d. [E-S]).

24. JAW to JFW, April 27, 1875 (CWB).

25. Weitenkampf 1912, pp. 1, 9–12.

26. For information on these exhibitions, see: catalogues of the New York Etching Club exhibitions, held at the NAD (1882–1893); *Official Catalogue of Exhibits: World's Columbian Exposition* (Chicago: W.B. Conkey Company, 1893), p. 36; American Art Galleries, New York, *Paintings Pastels and Etchings by J. Alden Weir and John H. Twachtman* (1893); "A Group of Impressionists," *New York Sun*, May 5, 1893, p. 6; "Some Dazzling Pictures," *New York Times*, May 4, 1893, p. 6; "Work by Weir and Simons," ibid., February 19, 1895, p. 5.

27. Only the one copy of this print is known (etching, image size 12¾ × 14¾ in., signed in the plate at lower left: *J.A.W. sc;* and at lower right: *Robt W. Weir/Pinx.*). In 1882 Robert Weir prepared a document which read: "I hereby give J. Alden Weir permission to have photographed heliotyped or otherwise reproduced & copyrighted my picture of Santa Claus with the additional permission of buying said picture for the sum of five hundred dollars ($500)." (October 27, 1882, witnessed by Charles G. Weir [BYU].)

28. Zimmerman 1923, no. 70. The impression of this print at the Library of Congress is inscribed: *"copy of a Vandyke etching by J. Alden Weir 1888"* (see Nelson 1967, pl. 74, for illustration).

29. Zimmerman 1923, no. 64.

30. Ibid., no. 33.

31. Ibid., no. 96, *Dogs on the Hearth No. 1.*

32. Ibid., no. 97, *Dogs on the Hearth No. 2.*

33. Ibid., no. 46.

34. Ibid., no. 21. In addition to those already discussed, drawings exist for other prints. Drawings in the collection of Brigham Young University: *Eternal Rest* (Flint 1972, pp. 26–32); *Reflections No. 1* (Zimmerman 1923, no. 27); *On the Porch* (ibid., no. 57); *Devotion, Purity, and Sincerity* (ibid., no. 40); *Portrait of Theodore Robinson* (ibid., no. 67); *Large Head in Profile* (ibid., no. 30); and *Dutch Schnapps* (ibid., no. 99). Drawings in private collections: *Portrait of Miss Hoe* (ibid., no. 19); *The Welsh Doll* (ibid., no. 47); *On the Porch* (ibid., no. 57); *Washington Arch No. 2* (ibid., no. 75); *Reading Out of Doors* (ibid., no. 17); and *Woman with a Muff* (Flint 1972, fig. 19).

35. Zimmerman 1923, no. 101.

36. Ibid., no. 104.

37. Weitenkampf 1912, p. 9; NAD, *Catalogue of the New York Etching Club Exhibition* (1882).

38. Baskett 1966, p. 32; Getscher 1977, p. 167.

39. Quoted in Young 1960, p. 180, where the source is given as Pach 1911.

40. Zimmerman 1923, no. 84.

41. Ibid., no. 85.

42. JAW to Mr. and Mrs. RWW, August 25, 1877, quoted in Young 1960, p. 133.

43. Young, MacDonald, Spencer, and Miles 1980, text, p. li.

44. Zimmerman 1923, no. 83.

45. Ibid., no. 13.

46. Ibid., no. 14.

47. Getscher 1977, p. 161.

48. Zimmerman 1923, no. 48.

49. Allen Staley, "Introduction," in *The Stamp of Whistler* (Oberlin, Ohio: Allen Memorial Art Museum, Oberlin College, 1977), p. 7.

50. Zimmerman 1923, no. 80.

51. Ibid., no. 77.

52. Getscher 1977, p. 161.

53. Zimmerman 1923, no. 113.

54. Ibid., no. 65.

55. Ibid., no. 67.

56. Ibid., no. 72; "Arcturus," *Scribner's Magazne* 13 (May 1893), p. 603.

57. Frank Weitenkampf, "Weir's Excursions into Print-Land," *Arts and Decoration* 12 (January 1920), p. 208.

58. Zimmerman 1923, no. 2.

59. Ibid., no. 3.

60. Ibid., no. 1. Janet Sumner of The National Arts Club informed the author in a telephone conversation in December 1982 that the collection was published not as a book but as a series of loose prints.

61. Ibid., no. 19.

62. Frances Weitzenhoffer, "Estampes impressionnistes de peintres americains," *Nouvelles de l'estampe* no. 28 (July–August 1976), p. 15.

63. See color plate 24.

Chapter 5

1. Weir's impressionist phase has received attention in several recent treatments of this movement in America: Donelson F. Hoopes, *The American Impressionists* (New York: Watson-Guptill Publications, 1972); Moussa M. Domit, *American Impressionist Painting* (Washington, D.C.: National Gallery of Art, 1973); Richard J. Boyle, *American Impressionism* (Boston: New York Graphic Society, 1974); Gerdts 1980; Harold Spencer, Susan G. Larkin, and Jeffrey W. Anderson, *Connecticut and American Impressionism* (Storrs: William Benton Museum of Art, University of Connecticut, Storrs, 1980); Barbara Novak, Donald R. McClelland, and Susan Hobbs, *Impressionnistes Américains* (Washington, D.C.: Smithsonian Institution Traveling Exhibition Service [SITES], 1982).

2. JAW to Mr. and Mrs. RWW, April 15, 1877, quoted in Young 1960, p. 123.

3. JAW to RWW, April 24, 1876 (E-S).

4. See Gerald Ackerman, "Gérôme and Manet," *Gazette des Beaux-Arts* series 6, 70 (September 1967), pp. 163–176.

5. Geneviève Lacambre, "Carolus Duran," in *The Second Empire: 1852–1870: Art in France under Napoleon III* (Philadelphia: Philadelphia Museum of Art, 1978), pp. 265–266; Weisberg 1981, pp. 279–280; Maureen C. O'Brien, "John Singer Sargent (1852–1925): Portrait of Ernest-Ange Duez," in *The American Painting Collection of the Montclair Art Museum: Research Supplement I* (Montclair, New Jersey: Montclair Art Museum, 1979), pp. 11–16.

6. See Chapter 3, pp. 114–115. Weir acquired the Manets for Erwin Davis, a New York collector. The Degas was presumably also bought for Davis. I am grateful to Madeleine Fidell-Beaufort for bringing Weir's purchase of the Degas to my attention. The work was entitled *Danseuses* (ex coll.: Faure) and was bought for 8000 francs from Durand-Ruel on June 27, 1881. In 1883, Davis lent it to the benefit exhibition for the Bartholdi Pedestal Fund. It is the *Danseurs* (1880–85) now at the Hill-Stead Museum in Farmington, Connecticut. See P.A. Lemoisne, *Degas et son oeuvre*, 4 vols. (Paris, 1946–49), 2, no. 617 (ill. p. 351), and Frances Weitzenhoffer, "First Manet Paintings to Enter an American Museum," *Gazette des Beaux-Arts*, series 6, 98 (March 1981), p. 129.

7. See: James L. Yarnell, "John H. Twachtman's 'Icebound,'" *Bulletin of the Art Institute of Chicago* 71 (January–February 1977), pp. 2–5; James Lomax and Richard Ormond, "Impressionism," in *John Singer Sargent and the Edwardian Age* (Leeds and London: Leeds Art Gallery and National Portrait Gallery), pp. 37–52; Sona Johnston, *Theodore Robinson, 1852–1896* (Baltimore: Baltimore,

Museum of Art, 1973), pp. xx–xxi; Robinson diary, December 15, 1892, and passim.

8. "The Academy of Design," *Art Amateur* 24 (January 1891), p. 30.

9. "Art Gossip," *Art Interchange* 26 (May 9, 1891), p. 146.

10. I am grateful to Frances Weitzenhoffer and Madeleine Fidell-Beaufort, who both brought to my attention this purchase of September 10, 1889.

11. Blakeslee Galleries, *Catalogue of Recent Paintings by J. Alden Weir* (January 21–February 7, 1891).

12. JAW to JFW, n.d. [1891], quoted Young 1960, p. 178.

13. "Paintings by Mr. J. Alden Weir," *Art Amateur* 24 (February 1891), p. 56.

14. JAW to JFW, August 23, 1891, quoted in Young "Records," 3, p. 198b (E-S).

15. There is evidence that he did do some additional work on these pictures. The current state of several differs from that in photographs (E-S) believed to have been taken late that summer. Dorothy Weir Young notes that a large group of paintings were all photographed at the same time, presumably at the end of the summer when Weir wrote to his brother John (see n. 14). She speculates that these are among the paintings Weir referred to in that letter (Young "Records," 3, p. 198b).

16. Young 1960, p. 180. The concluding sentence from this letter is a paraphrase of a quotation from Thomas à Kempis, "Man proposes, but God disposes" (*Imitation of Christ* [about 1420], Book I, Chapter 10).

17. See Artists' Bibliography. Weir undoubtedly knew of Cassatt's work. While he was a student in Paris, Mrs. Bradford Alden, his patroness, who was distantly related to the artist, had encouraged him to meet her. Later, he had urged Cassatt to send works to the 1878 exhibition of the Society of American Artists (see pp. 88–89). By 1894, he owned one of her color prints (Robinson diary, February 11, 1894). For information on Cassatt's *Family*, see: Adelyn Dohme Breeskin, *Mary Cassatt: A Catalogue Raisonné of the Oils, Pastels, Watercolors, and Drawings* (Washington, D.C.: Smithsonian Institution Press, 1970), p. 83, no. 145.

18. JAW to JFW, August 23, 1891, quoted in Young "Records," 3, p. 197.

19. Weir may have been familiar with works of the Post-Impressionists. Some of Georges Seurat's paintings were included in the 1886 exhibition in New York organized by Durand-Ruel (see NAD, *Special Exhibition: Works in Oil and Pastel of the Impressionists of Paris* [1886], no. 112, *Island Grande Jatte;* no. 133, *12 Studies;* no. 170, *Bathing*).

20. For information on this decorative project, see: JAW, letters to Ella Baker Weir (hereafter cited as EBW), summer 1892 (E-S); F. D. Millet, "The Decoration of the Exposition," *Scribner's Magazine* 12 (December 1892), pp. 692–709; "Decorations at the World's Fair: A Talk with Mr. Carroll Beckwith," *Art Amateur* 28 (December 1892), p. 4; W. Lewis Fraser, "Decorative Painting at the World's Fair," *Century* n.s. 24 (May 1893), pp. 14–21; *Art Interchange* 31 (September 1893), p. 80; F. D. Millet, "The Decoration of the Exposition," in *Some Artists at the Fair* (New York: Charles Scribner's Sons, 1893), pp. 7, 27–28; Pauline King, *American Mural Painting: A Study of the Important Decorations by Distinguished Artists of the United States* (Boston, Massachusetts, 1902), pp. 62–92; Edwin H. Blashfield, "A Painter's Reminiscence of a World's Fair," *New York Times Magazine*, March 18, 1923, p. 13; Young 1960, pp. 181–183.

21. Many of the participating artists had been trained in schools that stressed the connection between between the fine and decorative arts. At the École des Beaux-Arts, students had been required to work in other disciplines by 1879; four years later the *cours simultané des trois arts* had become a part of the official curriculum (Boime 1977, p. 14). The Petite École, where Weir also studied in the 1870s, was a training ground primarily for decorative artists and artisans, but also for many painters and sculptors. French training of this kind prepared Weir and his contemporaries for the decorative work many of them undertook in their mature years.

22. "A Group of Impressionists," *New York Sun*, May 5, 1893, p. 6.

23. Ibid.

24. Ibid.

25. Young 1960, p. 178.

26. Weir's study of Japanese prints has been discussed in passing by several scholars. See: Linda Ferber, "Julian Alden Weir 1852–1919," in *From Realism to Symbolism: Whistler and His World* (New York: Trustees of Columbia University, 1970), pp. 136–137; Patricia C. F. Mandel, *Selection VII: American Paintings from the Museum's Collection, c. 1800–1930* (Providence: Rhode Island School of Design, Museum of Art, 1977), pp. 187–190; Mary Ellen Hayward, "The Influence of the Classical Oriental Tradition on American Painting," *Winterthur Portfolio* 14 (Summer 1979), p. 110.

27. The bibliography on *japonisme* is extensive. See: The Cleveland Museum of Art, *Japonisme* (Rutland, Vermont: Charles E. Tuttle Co., 1975).

28. Young 1960, p. 187.

29. "Work by Weir and Simons," *New York Times*, February 19, 1895, p. 5.

30. S. Bing to JAW, itemized invoice, 1894, Scrapbook I (E-S). Weir may have purchased his

Japanese prints and a complete run of *Le Japon Artistique* (Paris, 1888–1890), which Bing published, during the dealer's visit to America, believed to have been made early in 1894. For information on Bing, see: Gabriel P. Weisberg, "Samuel Bing: patron of art nouveau," *Connoisseur* 172 (October 1969), pp. 119–125 (December 1969), pp. 294–299; 173 (January 1970), pp. 61–68.

31. Dorothy Weir Young asserts that Weir began collecting Japanese prints "in the eighties when their vogue was just beginning in the United States" (Young 1960, p. 186), but this seems unlikely.

32. Heromichi Shugio is a relatively obscure figure whose profession was given as "Art Director" in a list of Tile Club members (J. B. Millet, Appreciation 1921, p. 78). His name appears first in the 1881/82 New York City Directory under a residential listing and thereafter regularly until 1891, when his residence is specified as Japan. He then disappears from the city directory, although he was certainly in New York in 1894, for he attended a dinner party at Weir's home (Robinson diary, April 8, 1894). His firm, The First Japanese Manufacturing and Trading Company, had branch offices in Paris, Vienna, and Tokyo, and was active in New York by 1881 and as late as 1903. I am grateful to Lauretta Dimmick, a graduate intern at The Metropolitan Museum of Art, who researched Shugio's activities for me. It is possible that he was the "Shugio Hiromichi" through whom Frank Lloyd Wright purchased some prints in Tokyo in 1916 (Julia Meech-Pekarik, "Frank Lloyd Wright and Japanese Prints," *Metropolitan Museum of Art Bulletin* 40, no. 2 [1982], p. 54).

33. Weir's collection of Japanese prints was presumably left to his widow. After Ella's death it was divided among his three daughters, Caroline, Cora, and Dorothy. Dorothy's prints are now at Brigham Young University; most of the remaining prints have been retained by the family. I am grateful to Julia Meech-Pekarik, Associate Curator, Far Eastern Department, The Metropolitan Museum of Art, and to Joan Mirviss, a volunteer in that department, for identifying prints in Weir's collection.

34. The mark is a small red oval, about 5/16 of an inch in diameter, enclosing a monogram in which *W* is the principal letter, the *J* suspended from its apex and the *A* formed by adding a horizontal line across its center; it seems to have been used only for his Japanese prints. It is not recorded in Frits Lugt, *Les Marques de collections de dessins and d'estampes* (Amsterdam, Vereenidge Drukkerijen, 1921), or in the supplement to that publication (La Haye: Martinus Nijnoff, 1956).

35. T. Hayashi to JAW, December 29, 1893; February 25, 1895; March 15, 1895; March 20, 1899; December 27, 1900; H. Shugio to JAW, May 15, 1894, Scrapbook I (E-S).

36. S. Bing, invoice, March 20, 1894; itemized invoice, 1894; Scrapbook I (E-S).

37. S. Bing to JAW, April 26, 1896; S. Bing, invoice, November 25, 1899; S. Bing to JAW, February 22, 1900, Scrapbook I (E-S).

38. Julia Meech-Pekarik, "Frank Lloyd Wright and Japanese Prints," *Metropolitan Museum of Art Bulletin* 40, no. 2 (1982), p. 52. Weir seems to have visited Chicago again to see the American paintings on view at the exposition; he could easily have visited the display of Japanese art as well (Robinson diary, November 10, 1893).

39. Robinson diary, October 31, 1893.

40. Ibid., November 30, 1893.

41. Ibid., January 6, 1894.

42. Ibid., February 16, 1894.

43. Ibid., March 20, 1894.

44. Ibid., January 30, 1895.

45. T. Hayashi to JAW, Scrapbook I (E-S).

46. Robinson diary, April 8, 1894.

47. Ibid., February 11, 1894.

48. For an illustration of *From the Holley House*, see: Harold Spencer, Susan G. Larkin, and Jeffrey W. Andersen, *Connecticut and American Impressionism* (Storrs: University of Connecticut, The William Benton Museum of Art, 1980), p. 18.

49. For an illustration, see: The Cleveland Museum of Art, *Japonisme* (Rutland, Vermont: Charles E. Tuttle Co., 1975), p. 74, no. 74. Weir's impression of this print is now in the collection of Brigham Young University.

50. For an illustration, see: Julia Meech-Pekarik, *Metropolitan Museum of Art Bulletin* 40, no. 2 (1982), p. 50.

51. *Baby Cora* was completed around the end of February 1894, when Robinson saw it in Weir's studio (Robinson diary, February 27, 1894).

52. By 1894 Weir had purchased her *Banjo Lesson* (about 1893, private collection) (Robinson diary, February 11, 1894); Adelyn Dohme Breeskin, *Mary Cassatt: A Catalogue Raisonné of the Graphic Work* (Washington, D.C.: Smithsonian Institution Press, 1979), p. 65, no. 156; ill., p. 150.

53. Young, MacDonald, Spencer, and Miles 1980, text, pp. 26–27, no. 50; plates, 34; Robinson diary, November 10, 1893.

54. *In the Dooryard* was not quite finished. Caro's raised hand is the one area that remains incomplete.

55. Young, MacDonald, Spencer, and Miles 1980, text, p. 13, no. 34; plates, 19.

56. For a discussion of John F. Weir's industrial subjects and a comment on J. Alden Weir's Willimantic scenes, see: Betsy Fahlman, "John F. Weir: Painters of Romantic and Industrial Icons," *Archives of American Art Journal* 20, no. 2 (1980), pp. 2–9.

57. The 1903 view is illustrated in Harold Spencer, Susan G. Larkin, and Jeffrey W. Anderson, *Connecticut and American Impressionism* (Storrs: William Benton Museum of Art, University of Connecticut, 1980), p. 80.

58. The view of Willimantic similar to the painting now at The Brooklyn Museum is *Willimantic Landscape*, oil on canvas, 21½ × 25⅝ in., signed at lower left: J Alden Weir (private collection).

59. Robinson diary, February 27, 1894.

60. Weir and Paul Remy, the Branchville farm's Alsatian caretaker, built "The Palace Car" around 1890, when Weir was making a special study of the landscape around his farm (see Young 1960, p. 173). The contraption, which later fell into disuse and was made into a playhouse for Weir's daughters, can be seen in his painting *The Palace Car* (after 1900, Provo, Utah, Brigham Young University). Weir was not the only artist of this period who built an outdoor studio of this sort: Emil Carlsen and Edwin Martin Taber (1863–1896), two painters of snow scenes, used similar vehicles.

61. JAW to Charles Erskine Scott Wood, August 5, 1898, quoted in Young "Records," 3A, p. 239b.

62. Charles Erskine Scott Wood to JAW, July 27, 1899, Charles Erskine Scott Wood Papers, Henry E. Huntington Library and Art Gallery, San Marino, California.

63. For information on The Ten American Painters, see: Gerdts 1980, pp. 77, 79; and Childe Hassam, "Reminiscences of Weir," in Appreciation 1921, pp. 67–69.

64. "Ten American Painters," *The Collector* 9 (April 15, 1899), p. 180.

Chapter 6

1. JAW to Charles Erskine Scott Wood, January 13, 1911, quoted in Young "Records," 4A, p. 409.

2. Harold Spencer, "Reflections on Impressionism, Its Genesis and American Phase," in *Connecticut and American Impressionism* (Storrs, University of Connecticut, William Benton Museum of Art, 1980), p. 61.

3. Duncan Phillips, letter to JAW, January 4, 1918, in Young "Records," 5, following p. 459.

4. Charles Erskine Scott Wood, letter to JAW, November 10, 1902, Charles Erskine Scott Wood Papers, Henry E. Huntington Library and Art Gallery, San Marino, California.

5. JAW, letter to the editor, *New York Times*, January 3, 1912, quoted in Young 1960, p. 238.

6. "Weir, Liberal, Talks of Art," *New York Evening Post*, May 1, 1915, in JAW Scrapbook III, p. 46 (E-S).

7. Minutes of the Council, NAD, December 16, 1919, Archives (NAD).

Short Titles

Ackerman 1982

Gerald M. Ackerman. *"Gérôme, catalogue raisonné de ses oeuvres."* Ms. in preparation [1982], to be published in 1984.

Appreciation 1921

J. B. Millet, ed. *Julian Alden Weir: An Appreciation of His Life and Works*. New York: The Century Club, 1921.

Baskett 1966

Mrs. Mary Welsh Baskett. "Prints." In *A Retrospective Exhibition: John Henry Twachtman*. Ohio: Cincinnati Art Museum, 1966.

Boime 1971

Albert Boime. *The Academy & French Painting in the Nineteenth Century*. London and New York: Phaidon, 1971.

Boime 1974

Albert Boime. "Curriculum Vitae: The Course of Life in the Nineteenth Century." In *Strictly Academic*. Binghamton: University Art Gallery, State University of New York, 1974.

Boime 1977

Albert Boime. "The Teaching Reforms of 1863 and the Origins of Modernism in France." *Art Quarterly* n.s. 1 (1977), pp. 1–39.

Chu 1974

Petra Ten Doesschate Chu. *French Realism and the Dutch Masters*. Utrecht: Haentjens Dekkert Gumbert, 1974.

Clement and Hutton 1879

Clara Erskine Clement and Laurence Hutton. *Artists of the Nineteenth Century and Their Works*. 2 vols. 1879; 1884. Reprint, 2 vols in 1. St. Louis: North Point, 1969.

Dunlap 1918

William Dunlap. *A History of the Rise and Progress of the Arts of Design in the United States*. Edited by Frank W. Bayley and Charles E. Goodspeed. 3 vols. Boston: C. E. Goodspeed & Co., 1918, 3.

Ely 1927

Caroline W. Ely. "Introduction" and "Notes." In *Catalogue of an Exhibition of Etchings by J. Alden Weir*. New York: Frederick Keppl & Co., 1927.

Flint 1972

Janet A. Flint. *J. Alden Weir, An American Printmaker*. Washington, D.C.: National Collection of Fine Arts, 1972.

Gerdts 1980

William H. Gerdts. *American Impressionism*. Seattle: Henry Art Gallery, University of Washington, 1980.

Gerdts and Burke 1971

William H. Gerdts and Russell Burke. *American Still-Life Painting*. New York: Praeger Publishers, 1971.

Getscher 1977

Robert H. Getscher. "Catalogue." In *The Stamp of Whistler*. Oberlin, Ohio: Allen Memorial Art Museum, Oberlin College, 1977.

Hale 1966

John Douglass Hale. "The Life and Creative Development of John H. Twachtman." 2 vols. Ph.D. dissertation, Ohio State University, 1957.

JFW, "List of Pictures"

John Ferguson Weir. "List of Pictures painted by Jno. F. Weir." Ms., n.d., Rev. DeWolf Perry, Princeton, Massachusetts.

JFW, Sketchbook

John Ferguson Weir. Sketchbook, 1858–1862, box 11, folder 9, John Ferguson Weir Papers, Sterling Memorial Library, New Haven, Connecticut.

Jowell 1977

Susan Suzman Jowell. *Thoré-Bürger and the Art of the Past*. Ph.D. dissertation, Harvard University, 1971. New York and London: Garland Publishing, 1977.

Lopez-Rey 1963

José Lopez-Rey. *Velázquez: A Catalogue Raisonné of His Oeuvre*. London: Faber and Faber, 1963.

Metropolitan 1924

Memorial Exhibition of the Works of J. Alden Weir. New York: The Metropolitan Museum of Art, 1924.

NAD Minutes

Council of the National Academy of Design, Minutes, Archives, The National Academy of Design, New York.

Nelson 1967

Jon Nelson. "Introduction to the Catalogue" and "Catalogue." In *The Etchings of J. Alden Weir*. Lincoln: University of Nebraska Art Galleries, 1967.

Ortgies 1889

Fifth Avenue Art Galleries, Ortgies & Co. *Catalogue of Paintings in Oil and Pastel by J. Alden Weir, N.A., . . . and John H. Twachtman* (sale catalogue, February 7, 1889).

Ortgies 1891

Fifth Avenue Art Galleries, Ortgies and Co. *Catalogue of Oil Paintings and Water Colors by Robert Walter Weir, N. A., and His Collection of Engravings, Etchings, Illustrated Books* (sale catalogue, February 19–21, 1891).

Pach 1911

Walter Pach. "Peintres-Graveurs Contemporains: M. J. Alden Weir." *Gazette des Beaux-Arts* series 6, 6 (September 1911), pp. 214–215.

Page 1872

[William Page]. "President's Address." Annual Meeting, Council of The National Academy of Design, Minutes, Archives, The National Academy of Design, New York.

Robinson diary

Theodore Robinson diaries, 1892–1896. Copy in Frick Art Reference Library, New York.

Rosenberg 1970

Pierre Rosenberg. *Chardin 1699–1779*. The Cleveland Museum of Art in cooperation with Indiana University Press, 1970.

Rouart and Wildenstein 1975

Denis Rouart and Daniel Wildenstein. *Édouard Manet: catalogue raisonné*. 2 vols. Lausanne and Paris: La Bibliothèque des Arts, 1975.

Slive 1974

Seymour Slive. *Frans Hals*. 3 vols. London: Phaidon, 1974, 3.

Weinberg 1981

H. Barbara Weinberg. "Nineteenth-Century American Painters at the École des Beaux-Arts." *American Art Journal* 13 (Autumn 1981), pp. 66–84.

Weir 1896

J. Alden Weir. "Jules Bastien-Lepage (1848–1884)." In *Modern French Masters*. Edited by John C. Van Dyke. New York: The Century Co., 1896, pp. 227–235.

Weir 1957

The Recollections of John Ferguson Weir: Director of the Yale School of the Fine Arts 1869–1913. Edited by Theodore Sizer. New York and New Haven: The New-York Historical Society and The Associates in Fine Arts at Yale University, 1957.

Weisberg 1981

Gabriel P. Weisberg. *The Realist Tradition: French Painting and Drawing: 1830–1900*. The Cleveland

Museum of Art in cooperation with Indiana University Press, 1981.

Young 1960

Dorothy Weir Young. *The Life & Letters of J. Alden Weir.* Edited by Lawrence W. Chisholm. New Haven: Yale University Press, 1960.

Young "Records"

Dorothy Weir Young. "Records of the Paintings of J. Alden Weir." Ms. 6 vols. [1920s–1940s] (E-S).

Young, MacDonald, Spencer, and Miles

Andrew McLaren Young; Margaret MacDonald; Robin Spencer; and Hamish Miles. *The Paintings of James Abbott McNeill Whistler.* 2 vols. New Haven: Yale University Press, 1980.

Zimmerman 1923

Agnes Zimmerman. *An Essay Towards a Catalogue Raisonné of the Etchings, Dry-Points and Lithographs of Julian Alden Weir.* New York: The Metropolitan Museum of Art *Papers:* Volume I; Part 2 (1923).

Zimmerman October 1923

Agnes Saumarez Zimmerman. "Julian Alden Weir—His Etchings." *Print Collector's Quarterly* 10 (October 1923), pp. 288–308.

Artists' Bibliography

Jules Bastien-Lepgage

"Jules Bastien-Lepage." *The Studio: Journal of the Fine Arts* n.s. 13 (January 31, 1885), pp. 145–151 (report of a lecture that JAW presented at the Art Students League on January 17, 1885).

Weir 1896, pp. 227–235.

William Steven Feldman. "The Life and Work of Jules Bastien-Lepage (1848–1884)." Ph.D. dissertation, New York University, 1973.

Kenneth McConkey. "The Bouguereau of the Naturalists: Bastien-Lepage and British Art." *Art History* 1 (September 1978), pp. 371–382.

William S. Feldman. "Jules Bastien-Lepage: A New Perspective." *National Gallery of Victoria Bulletin* 20 (1979), pp. 3–9.

Kenneth McConkey. " 'Pauvre Fauvette' of 'Petite Folle': A Study of Jules Bastien-Lepage's 'Pauvre Fauvette.' " *Arts Magazine* 55 (January 1981), pp. 140–143.

Gustave Boulanger

M. H. Spielmann. "Gustave Boulanger." *Magazine of Art* (1889), pp. 70–72.

Charles Bouvet. "Gustave Boulanger collaborateur de Charles Garnier à L'Opéra." *Gazette des Beaux-Arts* series 5, 12 (November 1925), pp. 301–311.

James Renwick Brevoort

Sutherland McColley and Carl J. Black, Jr. "Introduction." In *The Works of James Renwick Brevoort: 1832–1918: American Landscape Painter*. Yonkers, New York: The Hudson River Museum, 1972.

Charles-Emile-Auguste Durand (called Carolus-Duran)

Claude Vento. *Les Peintres de la Femme*. Paris: Librairie de la Société des gens de lettres, 1888, pp. 271–300.

C. H. Stranahan. *A History of French Painting from Its Earliest to Its Latest Practice*. New York: Charles Scribner's Sons, 1888, pp. 354–357.

Mrs. Arthur Bell [N. D'Anvers]. *Representative Painters of the XIXth Century*. London and New York, 1899, pp. 121–124.

Will H. Low. *A Chronicle of Friendships*. New York: Charles Scribner's Sons, 1908, pp. 12–25.

Genevièe Lacambre. In *The Second Empire 1852–1870: Art in France under Napleon III*. Philadelphia: Philadelphia Museum of Art, 1978, pp. 265–267.

Mary Cassatt

Adelyn Dohme Breeskin. *Mary Cassatt: A Catalogue Raisonné of the Oils, Pastels, Watercolors, and Drawings*. Washington, D. C.: Smithsonian Institution Press, 1970.

———. *Mary Cassatt: A Catalogue Raisonné of the Graphic Work*. Washington, D. C.: Smithsonian Institution Press, 1979.

Pascal-Adolphe-Jean Dagnan-Bouveret

Gabriel P. Weisberg. *The Realist Tradition: French Painting and Drawing: 1830–1900*. The Cleveland Museum of Art in cooperation with Indiana University Press, 1981.

———. "P. A. J. Dagnan-Bouveret, and the Illusion of Photographic Naturalism." *Arts Magazine* 56 (March 1982), pp. 100–105.

———. "P. A. J. Dagnan-Bouveret, Jules Bastien-Lepage, and the Naturalist Instinct." *Arts Magazine* 56 (April 1982), pp. 70–76.

Albert Edelfelt

Edelfelt correspondence, The Art Museum of the Ateneum, Helsinki, Finland.

Ur Albert Edelfelt Brev (Letters of Albert Edelfelt). Helsinki: Holgerschilkdts Förlag, 1917.

Bertel Hintze. *Albert Edelfelt*. Helsinki: Söderström & Co. Förlagsaktiebolag, n.d.

Benjamin Waterhouse Hawkins

Benjamin Waterhouse Hawkins. *Comparative Anatomy as Applied to the Purposes of the Artist*. Edited by George Wallis. London: Winsor & Newton, 1883.

Appleton's Cyclopaedia of American Biography. Edited by James Grant Wilson and John Fiske. New York: D. Appleton and Company, 1888, 3, p. 119.

National Cyclopaedia of American Biography. New York: James T. White & Co., 1911, 11, p. 169.

Jacquesson de la Chevreuse

"Jacquesson de la Chevreuse, Marie, Louis, François." *"Dossiers individuels des élèves, série antérieure au 31 décembre 1893,"* AJ[52] 263.

Clara Erskine Clement and Laurence Hutton. *Artists of the Nineteenth Century and Their Works*. 2 vols. 1879; 1884. Reprint (2 vols. in 1). St. Louis: North Point, 1969, 2, p. 6.

"Nécrologie." *La Chronique des Arts* (December 19, 1903), p. 339.

"Nouvelles." *La Chronique des Arts* (May 7, 1904), p. 154.

Henry C. White. *The Life and Art of Dwight William Tryon*. Boston and New York: Houghton Mifflin Company, 1930, pp. 37–42.

Helen D. Perkins. "Charles Noel Flagg, A.N.A., 1848–1916." *Connecticut Historical Society Bulletin* 40 (October 1975), pp. 98–99, 101–102.

Raimundo de Madrazo y Garreta

Untitled, unsigned article in *American Architect and Building News* 61 (September 10, 1898), p. 82.

Victor-Aimé Millet

Stanislas Lami. *Dictionnaire des sculpteurs de l'école française au dix-neuvième siècle*. 3 vols. 1919. Reprint. Nedeln, Liechtenstein: Kraus Reprint, 1970, 3, pp. 451–459.

William Rimmer

William Rimmer. *Art Anatomy*. Boston: Houghton, Mifflin and Company, 1884.

Truman H. Bartlett. *The Art Life of William Rimmer: Sculptor, Painter, and Physician*. 1890. Reprint. New York: Da Capo Press, 1970.

Jeffrey Weidman. "William Rimmer: Critical Catalogue Raisonné." 7 vols. Ph. D. dissertation, Indiana University, Bloomington, Indiana, 1981.

John Ferguson Weir

John Ferguson Weir Papers. Sterling Memorial Library, Yale University, New Haven, Connecticut.
———. Archives of American Art, Smithsonian Institution, Washington, D. C.
———. Rev. DeWolf Perry, Princeton, Massachusetts.
Henry T. Tuckerman. *Book of the Artists: American Artist Life*. New York: G. P. Putnam & Son, 1867, pp. 487–488.
Weir 1957.
Theodore Sizer, ed. "Memories of a Yale Professor." *The Yale University Library Gazette* 32 (January 1958), pp. 93–98.
Gerdts and Burke 1971, pp. 211, 255.
Betsy Fahlman. "John E. Weir: Painter of Romantic and Industrial Icons." *Archives of American Art Journal* 20, no. 2 (1980), pp. 2–9.
Linda Ayres. "The American Figure: Genre Paintings and Sculpture," and Stephen Edidin, "Catalogue Entries." In *An American Perspective: Nineteenth-Century Art from the Collection of Jo Ann & Julian Ganz, Jr*. Washington, D.C.: National Gallery of Art, 1981, pp. 58–59.

Robert Walter Weir

Weir Family Papers, Brigham Young University, Provo, Utah.
Henry T. Tuckerman. *Book of the Artists: American Artist Life*. New York: G. P. Putnam & Son, 1867, pp. 203–215.
Ortgies 1891.
Charles Larned. "**F**. Historical Sketch of Department of Drawing." In *The Centennial of the United States Military Academy at West Point, New York: 1802–1902*. 2 vols. Washington, D.C.: Government Printing Office, 1904, 1, pp. 294–295.
William Dunlap. *A History of the Rise and Progress of the Art of Design in the United States*. Edited by Frank W. Bayley and Charles E. Goodspeed. 3 vols. Boston: C. E. Goodspeed & Co., 1918, 3, pp. 176–193.
Jacob Kent Arens. "Robert Walter Weir (1803–1889)." Ph. D. dissertation, University of Delaware, 1972.
———. "Robert Weir's 'Embarkation of the Pilgrims." *Capitol Studies* 1 (Fall 1972), pp. 59–71.
———. "The Portraits of Robert Walter Weir." *American Art Journal* 6 (May 1974), pp. 4–17.
———. "The Religious Paintings of R. W. Weir." *Antiques* 103 (April 1973), pp. 744–749.
William H. Gerdts, "Robert Walter Weir: Artist and Teacher of West Point"; James T. Callow, "Robert W. Weir and the Sketch Club"; [Michael Moss], "Catalogue." In *Robert Weir: Artist and Teacher of West Point*. West Point, New York: Cadet Fine Arts Forum of the United States Corps of Cadets, 1976.
William Cullen Bryant II, "Robert Weir as a Teacher"; Captain Joseph Fox, "The Poetry of Robert W. Weir." In *Robert Walter Weir of West Point: Illustrator, Teacher and Poet*. West Point, New York: United States Military Academy, 1976.

Lemuel Wilmarth

"American Painters: Seymour Joseph Guy, N. A.–Lemuel Wilmarth, N. A." [New York] *Art Journal* 1 (September 1875), pp. 276–278.
Clara Erskine Clement and Laurence Hutton. *Artists of the Nineteenth Century and Their Works*. 2 vols. 1879; 1884. Reprint (2 vols in 1). St. Louis: North Point, 1969, 2, p. 355.
National Cyclopaedia of American Biography. New York: James T. White, 1898, 8, pp. 424–425.
American Art Annual 15 (1919), edited by Florence Levy, p. 284.
George C. Groce and David H. Wallace. *The New-York Historical Society's Dictionary of Artists in America 1564–1860*. New Haven, Connecticut: Yale University Press, 1957, p. 692.

Robert Wylie

Michael Quick. *American Expatriates of the Late Nineteenth Century*. Ohio: Dayton Art Institute, 1976, pp. 31–32, 144, 158.
David Sellin. *Americans in Brittany and Normandy: 1860–1910*. Arizona: Phoenix Art Museum, 1982.

J. Alden Weir Bibliography

No comprehensive bibliography of writings on J. Alden Weir has yet been published. This bibliography is selective. It has been assembled by consulting standard periodical indexes, published and unpublished library catalogues, and existing bibliographes on related artists and topics. Within catego-ries, the bibliography is arranged alphabetically: unless otherwise specified, unsigned material appears first, in order by title, followed by signed material, in order by author. In all categories, an asterick indicates an item that contains substantial information about the artist.

1. *Artist's Statements.* These contain writings by and interviews with the artist, arranged chronologically. For additional material, see Young 1960, passim.

*[J. Alden Weir], "Jules Bastien-Lepage." *The Studio: Journal of the Fine Arts* n. s. 13 (January 31, 1885), pp. 145–151 (report of a lecture that JAW presented at the Art Students league on January 17, 1885).

*J. Alden Weir. "Jules Bastien-Lepage." *Modern French Masters.* Edited by John C. Van Dyke. New York: The Century Co., 1896, pp. 227–235.

J. Alden Weir et al. "Open Letters: American Artists on Gérôme." *Century Magazine* 37 (February 1889), pp. 634–636.

————. "John H. Twachtman: an Estimation." *North American Review* 176 (April 1903), pp. 554–562.

————. "The Genius of J. L. Gérôme." *New York Herald*, magazine section, January 31, 1904, p. 8.

J. Alden Weir, interview with Maude Carrell. "This Year's Exhibit to Eclipse All." *Pittsburgh Dispatch* (April 1911), clipping in JAW Scrapbook III, p. 24.

"Weir, Liberal, Talks of Art." *New York Evening Post*, May 1, 1915, pp. 1, 3.

*J. Alden Weir. "Address to the National Academy of Design Banquet." (March 14, 1917), Archives, NAD.

*J. Alden Weir et al. "What is Art?" *Arts and Decoration* 7 (April 1917), pp. 316–317, 324, 327.

2. *Monographic Books and Pamphlets on J. Alden Weir.*

Edwin H. Blashfield. *A Commemorative Tribute to J. Alden Weir.* New York: The American Academy of Arts and Letters, 1922.

*Burke, Doreen B[olger]. *J. Alden Weir and the National Academy of Design.* New York: The National Academy of Design, 1981.

Ely, Caroline Weir. *11 East 12th Street New York.* Privately printed, 1969, unpaged pamphlet.

*Millet, J. B., ed. *Julian Alden Weir: An Appreciation of His Life and Works*. New York: The Century Association, 1921 (includes "List of Paintings" by Dorothy Weir). Reprint. New York: E. P. Dutton & Co., 1922, Phillips Publication No. 1.

*Young, Dorothy Weir. *The Life & Letters of J. Alden Weir*. Edited by Lawrence Chisholm. New Haven, Connecticut: Yale University Press, 1960.

3. *Books*

Barker, Virgil. *A Critical Introduction to American Painting*. New York: William Edwin Rudge for the Whitney Museum of American Art, 1931, pp. 38, 50–51.

Baur, John I. H. *Revolution and Tradition in Modern American Art*. Cambridge: Harvard University Press, 1958, p. 83.

Benjamin, S. G. W. *Art in America: A Critical and Historical Sketch*. New York: Harper & Brothers, 1880, pp. 200, 204, 207.

Bizardel, Yvon. *American Painters in Paris*. Translated by Richard Howard. New York: The MacMillan Company, 1960, p. 162.

Boime, Albert. *Thomas Couture and the Eclectic Vision*. New Haven: Yale University Press, 1980, pp. 577, 608–609, 658.

Boyle, Richard J. *American Impressionism*. Boston: New York Graphic Society, 1974, pp. 54, 57, 69, 73, 88, 127, 134, 143, 145, 147–150, 157–164, 228, 230–231.

Brown, Milton W. *American Painting: From the Armory Show to the Depression*. New Jersey: Princeton University Press, 1970, pp. 3, 47, 53–54, 81, 98.

———. *The Story of the Armory Show*. Boston: New York Graphic Society for the Joseph H. Hirshhorn Foundation, 1963, pp. 31–41; 298–299.

Bryant, Lorinda Munson. *American Pictures and Their Painters*. London and New York: John Lane, 1920, pp. 177–178; ills. opp. pp. 174 and 175.

Burroughs, Alan. *Limners and Likenesses: Three Centuries of American Painting*. Cambridge: Harvard University Press, 1936, pp. 177–179, 186, 206; fig. 150.

Bye, Arthur Edwin. *Pots and Pans: or Studies in Still-Life Painting*. New Jersey: Princeton University Press, 1921, pp. 200–201.

Caffin, Charles H. *The Story of American Painting*. New York: Frederick A. Stokes Company, 1907, pp. 163, 272, 275.

Clark, Eliot. *History of the National Academy of Design: 1825–1953*. New York: Columbia University Press, 1954, pp. 106, 128, 133–134, 169.

Cohen, George M. *A History of American Art*. New York: Dell Publishing Co., 1971, p. 153.

Cook, Clarence. *Art and Artists of Our Time*. 3 vols. New York: Selmar Hess, 1888, 3, pp. 260–261; ill. opp. p. 262.

*Ely, Caroline Weir. "Grandmother's Attics" and "My Fathers Friends." In *"Lest We Forget."* Privately printed, 1965, pp. 39–46; 47–57.

*Ely, Catherine Beach. "J. Alden Weir," in her *Modern Tendency in American Painting*. New York: Frederic Fairchild Sherman, 1925, pp. 27–35. (Reprints her essay "J. Alden Weir" in *Art in America* 12 [April 1924], pp. 112–121.)

Flexner, James Thomas. *That Wilder Image*. New York: Bonanza Books, 1962, p. 324.

Gerdts, William H. *The Great American Nude: A History in Art*. New York: Praeger Publishers, 1974, pp. 140, 143, 144.

*———. *Painters of the Humble Truth: Masterpieces of American Still Life 1801–1939*. Columbia: Philbrook Art Center with University of Missouri Press, 1981, pp. 219–221.

*Gerdts, William H., and Russell Burke. *American Still-Life Painting*. New York: Praeger Publishers, 1971, pp. 135, 193, 204, 210–211.

Green, Samuel N. *American Art: A Historical Survey*. New York: The Ronald Press, 1966, pp. 390, 391–392, 423.

Hartmann, Sadakichi. *A History of American Art*. 2 vols. Boston: L. C. Page & Co., 1902, 1, p. 249; 2, pp. 243, 245–248, 273.

Hoopes, Donelson F. *The American Impressionists*. New York: Watson Guptill Publications, 1972, pp. 82–83; 84–85.

Isham, Samuel. *The History of American Painting*. New York: The MacMillan Company. Rev. ed., 1915, pp. 364, 368, 388–389, 453, 544. 2nd rev. ed., 1936, edited by Royal Cortissoz, pp. 564, 566, 573, 587.

King, Pauline. *American Mural Painting*. Boston: Noyes, Platt & Company, 1902, pp. 62–92.

LaFollette, Suzanne. *Art in America*. New York & London: Harper & Brothers, 1929, pp. 122, 211–214; ill. opp. p. 214; pp. 232, 301, 313.

Landgren, Marchal E. *Years of Art: The Story of the Art Students League*. New York: Robert McBride & Company, 1940, pp. 42, 57, 63–64, 96.

Larkin, Oliver W. *Art and Life in America*. Rev. ed. New York: Holt, Rinehart and Winston, 1966, pp. 262, 265, 269, 272, 305–307, 314, 325, 335, 364.

Lynes, Russell. *The Art-Makers of Nineteenth-Century America*. New York: Atheneum Publishers, 1970, pp. 354, 406, 440, 472, 485.

*McSpadden, Joseph Walker. "Julian Alden Weir: the painter of the personal equation." In his *Famous Painters of America*. New York: Dodd, Mead & Company, 1916, pp. 377–393.

Mellquist, Jerome. *The Emergence of an American Art*. New York: Charles Scribner's Sons, 1942, pp. 71–72, 78, 115–116, 139.

Mendelowitz, Daniel M. *A History of American Art*. New York: Holt, Rinehart and Winston, 1971, pp. 307, 324.

Millet, Frank D. "The Decoration of the Exposition." In *Some Artists at the Fair*. New York: Charles Scribner's Sons, 1893, pp. 1–42.

Morgan, H. Wayne. *New Muses: Art in American Culture, 1865–1920*. Norman: University of Oklahoma Press, 1978, pp. 12, 50, 118–119, 134, 136.

*Morris, Harrison S. *Confessions in Arts*. New York: Sears Publishing Company, 1930, pp. 145–154.

Muther, Richard. *The History of Modern Painting*. 4 vols. London: J. M. Dent & Co.; New York: E. P. Dutton & Co., 1907, 4, p. 319.

Neuhaus, Eugen. *The History & Ideals of American Art*. California: Stanford University Press, 1931, p. 264; ill. p. 246.

Perlman, Bernard B. *The Immortal Eight: American Painting from Eakins to the Armory Show, 1870–1913*. Westport, Connecticut: North Light Publishers, 1979, pp. 104, 113–114, 123, 203.

Phillips, Duncan. *A Collection in the Making: A Survey of the Problems Involved in Collecting Pictures Together with Brief Estimates of the Painters in the Phillips Memorial Gallery*. New York: E. Weyhe; Washington, D.C.: Phillips Memorial Gallery, 1926, p. 40; pls. l-liii; p. 110.

Pierce, Patricia Jobe. *The Ten*. Concord, New Hampshire: Rumford Press, 1976, pp. 141–151.

Richardson, E. P. *A Short History of Painting in America*. New York: Thomas Y. Crowell Company, 1963, p. 209.

————. *Painting in America*. New York: Thomas Y. Crowell Company, 1966, pp. 276, 306.

Roof, Katharine Metcalf. *The Life and Art of William Merritt Chase*. New York: Charles Scribner's Sons, 1917, pp. 94–95, 307.

Saint-Gaudens, Homer. *The American Artist and His Times*. New York: Dodd, Mead & Company, 1941, pp. 158–160, 172, 197, 204, 260.

————, ed. *The Reminiscences of Augustus Saint-Gaudens*. 2 vols. New York: The Century Co., 1913, 1, p. 246; 2, p. 43.

*Sheldon, G[eorge] W[illiam]. *American Painters*. Rev. ed. New York: D. Appleton and Company, 1881, pp. 174, 191–193; ill. opp. p. 192.

*Smith, F. Hopkinson, and Earl Shinn [Edward Strahan]. *A Book of the Tile Club*. Boston: Houghton Mifflin and Company, 1886, ills. opp. p. 41; pp. 89, 101, 104.

Stebbins, Theodore E., Jr. *American Master Drawings and Watercolors*. New York: Harper & Row, 1976, pp. 227, 232, 236.

Van Rensselaer, M. G. *Book of the American Figure Painters*. Philadelphia: J. B. Lippincott Company, 1886, unpaged.

Walker, John. *Great American Paintings: From Smibert to Bellows: 1729–1924*. London: Oxford University Press, 1943, p. 17; pl. 85.

Weir, Irene. *Robert W. Weir*. New York: House of Field-Doubleday, 1947, pp. 132–137.

*Weir 1957.

Weitenkampf, F[rank]. *American Graphic Art*. New York: Henry Holt and Company, 1912, pp. 25, 105, 166, 199, 340–341.

Wilmerding, John. *American Art*. New York: Penguin Books, The Pelican History of Art, 1976, pp. 155–158, 166, 170; fig. 195.

Young, Mahonri Sharp. *The Realist Revolt in American Painting: The Eight*. New York: Watson-Guptill Publications, 1973, pp. 19, 75, 79–80, 106.

4. *Encyclopedias and Dictionaries*

Britannica Encyclopedia of American Art. Chicago: Encyclopedia Britannica Educational Corporation, 1973. Entry by D[avid] W. S[cott], pp. 589–590.

Dictionary of American Biography. Edited by Allen Johnson and Dumas Malone. New York: Charles Scribner's Sons, 1937, 19, pp. 609–611.

The National Cyclopaedia of American Biograpy. New York: James T. White & Co., 1932, 22, pp. 296–297.

5. *Exhibition Catalogues*

The exhibition catalogues are divided into three sections: (a) one- and two-man exhibitions; (b) general exhibitions; (c) major annuals represented by compilations (See chronology for additional listings). Within each section, exhibition catalogues are listed alphabetically by originating institution or gallery, with organizers and authors and their contributions annotated.

A. *One- and Two-Man Shows*

For additional information, see: 8. *Sale Catalogues*.

American Academy of Arts and Letters, New York. *J. Alden Weir: 1852–1919: Centennial Exhibition: Paintings, Drawings, and Etchings* (1952). Contains "J. Alden Weir—An Appreciation" by Mahonri M. Young.

American Art Association, New York. *Special Exhibition: Paintings, Pastels, and Etchings by J. Alden Weir and J. H. Twachtman* (1893).

Babcock Galleries, New York. *J. Alden Weir* (1942).

Blakeslee Galleries, New York. *Catalogue of Recent Paintings by J. Alden Weir* (1891).

Boussod, Valadon & Co., New York. *Paintings and Pastels by J. Alden Weir* (1897).

Buffalo Fine Arts Academy, New York. *A Collection of Paintings by J. Alden Weir* (1911).

Century Association, New York. *Memorial Exhibition of Paintings by the Late J. Alden Weir* (1920).

Cincinnati Art Museum, Ohio. *Special Exhibition of Paintings by Mr. J. Alden Weir* (1912).

Ferargil Galleries, New York. *Paintings by J. Alden Weir* (1920).

Frederick Keppel & Co., New York. *Catalogue of an Exhibition of Etchings by J. Alden Weir* (1927), with an introduction and notes by Caroline Weir Ely.

Richard K. Larcada, New York. *J. Alden Weir* (1966).

R. E. Lewis, Inc. *Rare Etchings by J. Alden Weir* (1980).

Macbeth Gallery, New York. *Figures and Landscapes By the Late J. Alden Weir* (1929).

The Metropolitan Museum of Art, New York. *Memorial Exhibition of the Works of J. Alden Weir* (1924). Contains an essay by William Coffin.

Montclair Art Museum, New Jersey. *J. Alden Weir* (1972). Catalogue by Fearn C. Thurlow.

Montross Gallery, New York. *Exhibition of Pictures by J. Alden Weir* (1907).

National Collection of Fine Arts (now the National Museum of American Art), Washington, D.C. *J. Alden Weir: American Impressionist 1852–1919* (1972). Catalogue by Janet A. Flint.

University of Nebraska Art Gallery, Lincoln. *The Etchings of J. Alden Weir* (1967). Contains "J. Alden Weir 1852–1919" by Robert Spence; "Introduction to the Catalogue" and "Catalogue" by Jon Nelson.

The Phillips Collection, Washington, D.C. *Paintings by Julian Alden Weir* (1972). Contains an essay by Mahonri Sharp Young.

Vose Galleries, Boston, Massachusetts. *Memorial Exhibition of Paintings by J. Alden Weir, P.N.A.* (1920).

H. Wunderlich & Co., New York. *Exhibition of Water Colors by Mr. J. Alden Weir, Catalogue* (1883).

————. *Catalogue: Drawings and Etchings by J. Alden Weir* (1895).

B. *General Catalogues*

These are arranged alphabetically by organizing institution.

*Allen Memorial Art Museum, Oberlin College, Ohio. *The Stamp of Whistler* (1977). Introduction by Allen Staley. Catalogue by Robert H. Getscher, see pp. 160–164.

The American Federation of the Arts, New York. Traveling exhibition, *A University Collects* (1969).

————. *The Heritage of American Art: Paintings from the Collection of The Metropolitan Museum of Art* (1975), pp. 168–169.

Art Museum of South Texas, Corpus Christi. *The Ten* (1977). Essay by Donelson Hoopes, pp. 4–6. Biography by Melinda M. Mayer, pp. 20–21; ill. pp. 45–47.

*Brooklyn Museum. *Leaders of American Impressionism: Mary Cassatt, Childe Hassam, John H. Twachtman, J. Alden Weir.* (1937). Reprint. New York: Arno Press, 1974, pp. 38–43; plates X–XII.

————. *Theodore Robinson 1852–1896* (1946).

*Carnegie Institute, Museum of Art, Pittsburgh. *Directions in American Painting 1875–1925: Works from the Collection of Dr. and Mrs. John J. McDonough* (1982). Catalogue by Oswaldo Rodriguez Roque, see pp. 90–91.

Cincinnati Art Museum, Ohio. *A Retrospective Exhibition: John Henry Twachtman* (1966). "Introduction" by Richard J. Boyle. "Prints" by Mary Welsh Baskett.

Department of Art History and Archaeology, Columbia University, New York, in cooperation with the Philadelphia Museum of Art. *From Realism to Symbolism: Whistler and His World* (1971). Contains essays by Allen Staley and Theodore Reff. Entry on Weir by Linda Ferber, pp. 136–137.

Corcoran Gallery of Art, Washington, D.C. *Commemorative Exhibition by Members of the National Academy of Design 1825–1925* (1925), pp. 35, 160.

The Grand Central Art Galleries, New York. *Tonalism: An American Experience* (1982). Contains "American Tonalism: An Artistic Overview" by William H. Gerdts, pp. 17–28.

*The Heckscher Museum, Huntington, New York. *A Private Eye: Fifty Nineteenth-Century American Paintings, Drawings, & Watercolors from the Stebbins Collection* (1977). Catalogue by Carol L. Troyen, see pp. 104–105.

*Henry Art Gallery, University of Washington, Seattle. *American Impressionism* (1980). Catalogue by William H. Gerdts, see pp. 70–75.

Lowe Art Museum, University of Miami, Coral Gables, Florida. *French Impressionists Influence American Artists* (1971). Essays by William I. Homer; Ira Glackens; Richard J. Boyle; Van Deren Coke, see pp. 60, 64.

Metropolitan Museum of Art, New York. *19th-Century America: Paintings and Sculpture* (1970). Introduction by John K. Howat. Texts by John K. Howat and Natalie Spassky, nos. 195–196.

*————. *American Impressionist and Realist Paintings and Drawings from the Collection of Mr. and Mrs. Raymond J. Horowitz.* New York: The Metropolitan Museum of Art, 1973. Catalogue by John K. Howat and Dianne H. Pilgrim, see pp. 73–75.

Museum of Art, Saint Petersburg, Florida. *"The New Vision": American Styles of 1876–1910* (1976). Catalogue by Marvin D. Schwartz.

National Academy of Design, New York. *American Drawings: Paul Magriel Collection* (1979), p. 9.

————. *A Century and a Half of American Art: Commemorating the 150th Anniversary of the Founding of the National Academy of Design* (1975), pp. 128–129.

National Collection of Fine Arts (now the National Museum of American Art), Washington, D.C. *Academy: The Academic Tradition in American Art.* Washington, D.C.: Smithsonian Institution Press, 1975. Essays by Lois Marie Fink and Joshua C. Taylor, see p. 208.

*National Gallery of Art, Washington, D.C. *American Impressionist Painting* (1973). Catalogue by Moussa M. Domit, see pp. 140–144.

University of New Mexico Art Gallery, Albuquerque. *Impressionism in America* (an exhibition presented by the Junior League of Albuquerque in collaboration with the University of New Mexico Art Gallery), 1965. Unsigned essay and entries, see pp. 57–68.

New Orleans Museum of Art, Louisiana. *A Panorama of American Painting: The John J. McDonough Collection* (1975). Catalogue by E. John Bullard, see pp. 54, 93.

The Parrish Art Museum, Southampton, New York. *William Merritt Chase in the Company of His Friends* (1979). Catalogue by Ronald G. Pisano, see pp. 10, 34, 66.

Pennsylvania Academy of the Fine Arts, Philadelphia. *In This Academy* (1976). "American Impressionism" by Richard J. Boyle, see pp. 140–144, 151, 155–156, 159, 200.

Vassar College Art Gallery, Poughkeepsie, New York. *Vassar College Art Gallery: Selections from the Permanent Collection* (1967), p. 53.

West Point Museum, Cadet Fine Arts Forum of the United States Corps of Cadets. *Robert Weir: Artist and Teacher of West Point* (1976), pp. 43, 85.

Whitney Museum of American Art, New York. *A Century of American Landscape Painting 1800 to 1900* (1938), p. 29.

———. *The Painter's America: Rural and Urban Life, 1810–1910.* New York: Praeger Publishers, 1974. Catalogue by Patricia Hills, see pp. 97, 106.

———. *Turn-of-the-Century America* (1977). Catalogue by Patricia Hills, see pp. 73, 75, 194.

*William Benton Museum of Art, University of Connecticut, Storrs. *Connecticut and American Impressionism* (1980). "Reflections on Impressionism, Its Genesis and American Phase" by Harold Spencer, pp. 30–81. "The Cos Cob Clapboard School" by Susan G. Larkin, pp. 82–113. "Biographies of the Artists: J. Alden Weir," pp. 177–178.

University of Wyoming, Art Museum, Laramie. *American Art from the Phillips Collection: A Selection of Paintings, 1900–1950* (1975). Introduction by Laughlin Phillips.

C. *Major Annuals*

Phoenix Art Museum, Arizona. *Americans in Brittany and Normandy: 1860–1910* (1982). Catalogue by David Sellin.

*Smithsonian Institution Traveling Exhibition Service (SITES). *Impressionnistes Américains* (1982). "L'Impressionnisme américain: sources et réflexions" by Barbara Novak. "Réflexions sur L'Impressionnisme américain" by Harold Spencer. "Biographies: J. Alden Weir" by Susan Hobbs, pp. 142–145.

Sterling and Francine Clark Art Institute, Williamstown, Massachusetts. *The Ten: Works on Paper* (1980). Catalogue by Christine Bartolo. "J. Alden Weir," pp. 33–35.

Marlor, Clark S. *A History of The Brooklyn Art Association with an Index of Exhibitions.* New York: James F. Carr, 1970, p. 372.

Naylor, Maria, ed. *The National Academy of Design Exhibition Record: 1861–1900.* 2 vols. New York: Kennedy Galleries, 1973, 2, pp. 1005–1006.

6. *Periodical Articles and Serials*

These have been limited to mongraphic articles and notices, reviews of one- or two-man shows, and articles placing Weir in context. Articles simply mentioning Weir or reviewing his paintings during his lifetime are too numerous for inclusion. Additional information can be found in the following periodicals and serials: *American Art Annual, American Art News, American Art Review, The Art Age, The Art Amateur, The Art Collector, The Art Interchange, The Art Journal, Brush and Pencil, International Studio,* and *Studio: A Journal of the Fine Arts.*

[Untitled]. *American Art News* 4 (December 23, 1905), p. 5.

"Accessions: A Painting by J. Alden Weir." *Bulletin of The Detroit Museum of Art* 11 (November and December 1916), pp. 17–18.

"Acquisitions." *Academy Notes* 3 (October 1907), p. 87.

"Alden Weir." *Outlook* 110 (May 19, 1915), p. 120.

"Americans at Vose's." *American Art News* 14 (February 26, 1916), pp. 1, 5.

"Arcturus." *Scribner's Magazine* 13 (May 1893), p. 603.

"Art Notes." *Art Interchange* 22 (February 16, 1889), p. 49.

"Art Notes." *Art Interchange* 26 (January 31, 1891), p. 34.

"The Christmas Tree." *Century* Magazine 59, n. s. 37 (December 1899), p. 224.

"Cleveland Museum acquires a fine Weir." *Art Digest* 2 (November 1, 1927), p. 13.

"Comment on the Arts." *The Arts* 2 (January 1922), pp. 230–231.

"A Connecticut Farm." Princeton University *Record of the Museum of Historic Art* 2 (Fall 1943), p. 13.

"The Cover." *Bulletin of the Art Institute of Chicago* 32 (April 1938), p. 58.

"Decorations at the World's Fair: A Talk with Mr. Carroll Beckwith." *Art Amateur* 28 (December 1892), p. 4.

"Etched Portrait of John F. Weir." *International Studio* 85 (September 1926), p. 49.

"Exhibitions." *Art Interchange* 38 (April 1897), p. 95.

"Exhibition of American Art." *Bulletin of the Art Institute of Chicago* 9 (December 1, 1915), pp. 109–110.

"In the Galleries." *American Art News* 4 (December 2, 1905), p. 6.

"In Memoriam. Julian Alden Weir." *Academy Notes* 15 (July–December 1920), p. 69.

"J. Alden Weir." *Art Bulletin* 6 (January 5, 1906), p. 1.

"J. Alden Weir Centennial." *Art Digest* 26 (February 1, 1952), pp. 16–17.

"J. Alden Weir, the New President of the National Academy of Design." *Outlook* 110 (May 19, 1915), p. 136.

"Julian Alden Weir." *Bulletin of the Rhode Island School of Design* 8 (January 1920), pp. 8–9.

"Julian Alden Weir." *Mentor* 8 (December 1920), pp. 22–23.

"Mr. J. Alden Weir's Exhibition." *Art Amateur* 32 (April 1895), pp. 133–134.

"The National Academy of Design." *Art Review* 1 (December 1887), pp. 84–87.

"Newly Appointed Members of the National Commission of Fine Arts." *Outlook* 114 (November 8, 1916), p. 549.

"News and Views." *The Collector* 8 (March 1, 1897), p. 131.

"Obituary: Julian Alden Weir." *American Art News* 18 (December 13, 1919), p. 4.

"Paintings by Mr. J. Alden Weir." *Art Amateur* 24 (February 1891), p. 56.

"Paintings and Pastels by J. H. Twachtman and J. Alden Weir." *The Studio: Journal of the Fine Arts* 4 (February 1889), pp. 43–45.

"The Passing Shows." *Art News* 41 (October 15, 1942), p. 27.

"The Phillips Memorial Art Gallery." *American Magazine of Art* 102 (February 1921), pp. 52–54.

"Recent Pictures by J. Alden Weir." *The Studio: A Journal of the Fine Arts* n.s. 6 (January 31, 1891), pp. 81–82.

"Second Annual Exhibition." *Academy Notes* 3 (August 1907), pp. 33–39.

"The Thirteenth Annual Exhibition of Selected Paintings by American Artists at the Albright Art Gallery." *Academy Notes* 14 (July–September, 1919), pp. 76–99.

"Three Special Exhibitions: II. J. Alden Weir." *The Collector* 1 (February 1, 1891), p. 78.

"Two painters." *Outlook* 123 (December 17, 1919), p. 494.

"Two paintings by J. Alden Weir." *Brooklyn Museum Quarterly* 13 (October 1926), pp. 124–125.

"Union Square, by J. Alden Weir." *International Studio* 84 (August 1926), p. 79.

"The Walter H. Schulze Memorial Gallery of Paintings." *Bulletin of The Art Institute of Chicago* 19 (January 1925), pp. 7–9.

"Weir." *Literary Digest* 63 (December 27, 1919), pp. 31–32.

"Weir Canvases Recreate Quiet of Past Era." *Art Digest* 17 (October 15, 1942), p. 9.

"The Weir and Twachtman Exhibition." *Art Amateur* 20 (March 1889), p. 75.

Allan, Sidney. "Masterpieces of American Portraiture." *Bulletin of Photography* 16 (June 9, 1915), pp. 722–723.

Baldinger, Wallace Spencer. "Formal Change in Recent American Painting." *Art Bulletin* 19 (December 1937), pp. 580–591.

Barrangon, L[ucy] L[ord]. "Portraits of President Seelye." *Smith College: Hillyer Art Gallery Bulletin* series 18, no. 8 (March 30, 1925), pp. 1–9.

*Baur, J. I. H. "J. Alden Weir's Partition of In the Park." *Brooklyn Museum Quarterly* 25 (October 1938), pp. 124–129.

B[enedikt], M[ichael]. "J. Alden Weir [Larcada]." *Art News* 65 (November 1966), p. 70.

Blaugrund, Annette. "The Tenth Street Studio Building: A Roster, 1857–1895." *American Art Journal* 14 (Spring 1982), pp. 64–71.

Boime, Albert. "Newman, Ryder, Couture, and Hero-Worship in Art History." *American Art Journal* 3 (Fall 1971), pp. 5–22.

Born, Wolfgang. "American Still Life Paintings From Naturalism to Impressionism." *Gazette des Beaux-Arts* series 6, 29 (May 1946), pp. 303–318.

*Brandegee, Robert B. "Living Artists No. 1: J. Alden Weir." *Art Review International* (May 1919), pp. 9–10.

Brumbaugh, Thomas B. "Albert Pinkham Ryder to John Gellatly: A Correspondence." *Gazette des Beaux Arts* series 6, 80 (December 1972), pp. 361–370.

*Butler, Howard Russell. "J. Alden Weir: President of the National Academy of Design." *Scribner's Magazine* 59 (January 1916), p. 129–132.

Cary, Elisabeth Luther. "Collecting American Etchings." *American Magazine of Art* 11 (May 1920), pp. 235–241.

*Clark, Eliot. "J. Alden Weir." *Art in America* 8 (August 1920), pp. 232–242.

Cortissoz, Royal. "Egotism in Contemporary Art." *Atlantic Monthly* 73 (May 1894), pp. 645–652.

*Cox, Kenyon. "The Art of J. Alden Weir." *Burlington Magazine* 15 (May 1909), pp. 131–132; plate 11.

*Du Bois, Guy Pène. "The Idyllic Optimism of J. Alden Weir." *Arts and Decoration* 2 (December 1911), pp. 55–57, 78.

De Kay, Charles [Henry Eckford]. "The Century's American Artists Series." *Century Magazine* 57, n.s. 35 (April 1899), pp. 851, 956–957.

Edgerton, Giles. "Pioneers in Modern American Art: A Group of Men Whose Influence Has Greatly Aided Its Development." *Craftsman* 14 (September 1908), pp. 597–606.

Eglington, Guy G. "Art and Other Things." *International Studio* 79 (May 1924), pp. 150–151.

Eldredge, Charles. "Connecticut Impressionists: The spirit of place." *Art in America* 62 (September–October 1974), pp. 84–90.

*Ely, Catherine Beach. "J. Alden Weir." *Art in America* 12 (April 1924), pp. 112–121.

F. "Boston Art Notes." *Art Interchange* 12 (January 31, 1884), p. 29.

Fahlman, Betsy. "John F. Weir: Painter of Romantic and Industrial Icons." *Archives of American Art Journal* 20, no. 2 (1980), pp. 2–9.

*Field, Hamilton Easter. "Julian Alden Weir: an optimist." *Arts and Decoration* 12 (January 1920), pp. 200, 202.

Fraser, W. Lewis. "Decorative Painting at the World's Fair." *Century* n.s. 24 (May 1893), pp. 14–21.

Gerdts, William H. "The bric-a-brac still life." *Antiques* 100 (November 1971), pp. 744–748.

———. "The Square Format and Photo-Modernism in American Painting." *Arts Magazine* 50 (June 1976), pp. 70–75.

H. E. "Painters of the Nineties." *Brooklyn Museum Quarterly* 19 (April 1932), pp. 52–55.

Hassam, Childe. "Twenty-five Years of American Painting." *Art News* 26 (April 14, 1928), pp. 22–38.

Hayward, Mary Ellen. "The Influence of the Classical Oriental Tradition on American Painting." *Winterthur Portfolio* 14 (Summer 1979), pp. 107–142.

Howard, W. Stanton, "A Portrait by J. Alden Weir." *Harper's Monthly Magazine* 114 (January 1907), pp. 286–287.

———. "Lizzie Lynch by J. Alden Weir." *Harper's Monthly Magazine* 127 (September 1913), pp. 536–537.

———. "Landscape: Pan and the Wolf." *Harper's Monthly Magazine* 131 (July 1915), pp. 246–247.

I., W. M., Jr. "An Exhibition of the Etched Work of Julian Alden Weir." *Bulletin of the Metropolitan Museum of Art* 16 (February 1921), pp. 26–28.

J., A. F. "Art in America." *Burlington Magazine* 11 (June 1907), pp. 199–200.

*King, Edward. "Straightforwardness versus Mysticism. With original illustrations by John [sic] Alden Weir." *Monthly Illustrator* 5 (July 1895), pp. 29–32.

Lyman, Lila Parrish. "The Tile Club and its members." *The American Collector* 14 (April 1945), pp. 10–11, 19.

McBride, Henry. "Alden Weir as of today." *Art News* 51 (March 1952), p. 49.

Mann, Virginia. "Connecticut Impressionism." *Arts Magazine* 55 (November 1980), pp. 166–167.

Mather, Frank Jewett. "The Expanding Arena." *Magazine of Art* 39 (November 1946), pp. 292–308.

M[illiken], W[illiam] M. "Building a Dam, Shetucket." *Bulletin of The Cleveland Museum of Art* 14 (October 1927), frontispiece and p. 131.

Millet, F. D. "The Decoration of the Exposition." *Scribner's Magazine* 12 (December 1892), pp. 692–709.

N., C. "J. Alden Weir." *Arts Magazine* 41 (November 1966), p. 63.

Novak, Barbara. "American Impressionism." *Portfolio* 4 (March–April 1982), pp. 68–81, 142.

O'Connor, J., Jr. "From our permanent collection: Ploughing for buckwheat." *Carnegie Magazine* 26 (November 1952), pp. 320–321.

P., W. D. "American Paintings." *John Herron Institute Bulletin* 19 (September 1932), pp. 38–43.

*Pach, Walter. "Peintres-Graveurs Contemporains: M. J. Alden Weir." *Gazette des Beaux-Arts* series 6, 6 (September 1911), pp. 214–215.

Phillips, Duncan. "American Old Masters." In *A Bulletin of the Phillips Collections Containing a Catalogue and Notes of Interpretations Relating to a Tri-Unit Exhibition of Painting and Sculpture February to May 1928. . . .*, pp. 28, 31–32.

*———. "J. Alden Weir." *American Magazine of Art* 8 (April 1917), pp. 213–220.

*———. "J. Alden Weir." *Art Bulletin* 2 (June 1920), pp. 189–212.

Pilgrim, Dianne H. "The Revival of Pastels in Nineteenth-Century America: The Society of Painters in Pastel." *American Art Journal* 10 (November 1978), pp. 43–62.

Price, F. Newlin. The Johnsons of Uniontown." *International Studio* 80 (December 1924), pp. 193–201.

———. "Phillips Memorial Gallery." *International Studio* 80 (October 1924), pp. 8–18.

———. "Weir, the great observer." *International Studio* 75 (April 1922), pp. 126–131.

Rand, Harry. "American Impressionism." *Arts Magazine* 50 (May 1976), p. 13.

*Ryerson, Margery Austen. "J. Alden Weir's Etchings." *Art in America* 8 (August 1920), pp. 243–248.

Saint-Gaudens, Homer. "Other Days, Other Paintings." *Carnegie Magazine* 8 (February 1935), pp. 259–270.

Sellin, David. "The First Pose: Howard Roberts, Thomas Eakins, and A Century of Philadelphia Nudes." *Bulletin: The Philadelphia Museum of Art* 70 (Spring 1975), pp. 1–56.

Sherman, Frederic Fairchild. "Some Likenesses of Albert Pinkham Ryder." *Art in America* 26 (January 1938), pp. 32–33, 35.

Talbot, William S. "American Landscape Paintings in the Cleveland Museum of Art." *Antiques* 104 (November 1973), pp. 906–917.

Van Vleck, Jane. "J. Alden Weir's Etchings." *Brooklyn Museum* 13 (July 1926), pp. 81–82.

W[atson], F[orbes]. "Exhibitions Coming and Going." *The Arts* 15 (February 1929), pp. 121, 127.

W[ehle], H[arry] B. "The Julian Alden Weir Exhibition." *Bulletin of The Metropolitan Museum of Art* 19 (March 1924), pp. 58–59.

Weinberg, H. Barbara. "American Impressionism in Cosmopolitan Context." *Arts Magazine* 55 (November 1980), pp. 160–165.

———. "Nineteenth-Century American Painters at the École des Beaux-Arts." *American Art Journal* 13 (Autumn 1981), pp. 66–84.

Weisberg, Gabriel P. "P. A. J. Dagnan-Bouveret, and the Illusion of Photographic Naturalism." *Arts Magazine* 56 (March 1982), pp. 100–105.

*———. "P. A. J. Dagnan-Bouveret, Jules Bastien-Lepage, and the Naturalist Instinct." *Arts Magazine* 56 (April 1982), pp. 70–76.

Weitenkampf, Frank. "Weir's Excursions Into Print-Land." *Arts and Decoration* 12 (January 1920), pp. 208–209.

Weitzenhoffer, Frances. "Estampes impressionistes de peintres américains." *Nouvelles de l'estampe* 28 (July–August 1979), pp. 7–15.

———. First Manet Paintings to Enter an American Museum. *Gazette des Beaux-Arts* series 6, 98 (March 1981), pp. 125–129.

Wilson, David. "The Unknown American Whose Etchings Portray the Isle of Man." *Manx Life* (March/April 1981), p. 19.

Young, Mahonri Sharp. "Impressionism in Connecticut." *Apollo* n.s. 112 (December 1980), pp. 418–419.

———. "The Tile Club Revisited." *American Art Journal* 2 (Fall 1970), pp. 81–91.

*Zimmerman, Agnes. "An Essay Towards A Catalogue Raisonné of the Etchings, Dry-points, and Lithographs of Julian Alden Weir." The Metropolitan Museum of Art *Papers:* Volume I; Part 2 (1923), pp. 1–50.

*———. "Julian Alden Weir—His Etchings." *Print Collector's Quarterly* 10 (October 1923), pp. 288–308.

7. *Collection Catalogues*

Addison Gallery of American Art: Handbook of Paintings, Sculpture, Prints and Drawings in the Permanent Collection. Andover, Massachusetts: Phillips Academy, 1939, pp. 60–61.

American Art in The Newark Museum: Paintings Drawings and Sculpture. New Jersey: The Newark Museum, 1981, p. 394.

The American Painting Collection of the Montclair Art Museum. New Jersey: Montclair Art Museum, 1977, p. 227.

**American Paintings in the Museum of Fine Arts, Boston.* 2 vols. Greenwich, Connecticut: New York Graphic Society, 1969, 1, pp. 280–281, no. 1014; 2, fig. 477.

The Brooklyn Museum American Paintings: A Complete Illustrated Listing of Works in the Museum's Collection. New York: The Brooklyn Museum, 1979, p. 122.

A Catalogue of American Paintings: Indianapolis Museum of Art. Bulletin of The Indianapolis Museum of Art 56 (Autumn 1970), p. 162.

Catalogue of Painting Collection: Museum of Art, Carnegie Institute, Pittsburgh. Pittsburgh: Museum of Art, Carnegie Institute, 1973, pp. 178–179.

Catalogue of the Paintings and the Art Treasures of The Players. New York: The Players, 1925, p. 9.

Catalogue of the Permanent Collection of American Art: The Butler Art Institute. Youngstown, Ohio: The Butler Art Institute, 1951, p. 12.

Catalogue of the Permanent Collection of the Canajoharie Library and Art Gallery. Canajoharie, New York: Canajoharie Library and Art Gallery, n.d., nos. 49–51.

Catalogue of Water Colors and Drawings: The Reading Public Museum and Art Gallery. Pennsylvania: The Reading Public Museum and Art Gallery, 1964, unpaged (alphabetical).

Complete List of European and American Paintings in the Permanent Collection of the John Herron Art Museum. Indiana: Art Association of Indianapolis, 1958, unpaged.

Complete List of American and European Drawings, Paintings and Watercolors in the Collection of the Lyman Allyn Museum. New London, Connecticut: Lyman Allyn Museum, 1966, p. 45.

National Gallery of Art: American Paintings and Sculpture: An Illustrated Catalogue. Washington, D.C.: National Gallery of Art, 1970, pp. 118–119.

Paintings in the Art Institute of Chicago: A Catalogue of the Picture Collection. Illinois: The Art Institute of Chicago, 1961, pp. 480–481.

Paintings in the Detroit Institute of Arts: Third Edition: A Check List of the Paintings Acquired Before May, 1970. Michigan: The Detroit Institute of Arts, 1970, p. 158.

Pennsylvania Academy of the Fine Arts, Philadelphia, Pennsylvania, Checklist, Paintings, Sculptures, Miniatures from the Permanent Collection. Philadelphia: Pennsylvania Academy of the Fine Arts, 1969, p. 66.

The Phillips Collection: A Museum of Modern Art and Its Sources: Catalogue. New York: Thames and Hudson, 1952, pp. 107–108; plates 78–79.

Smithsonian Institution: National Collection of Fine Arts: Preliminary Catalogue Listing of Paintings, Drawings and Sculpture. Washington, D.C.: National Collection of Fine Arts, 1963, p. 103.

Anderson, Dennis, R. *Three Hundred Years of American Art in The Chrysler Museum.* Virginia, Chrysler Museum of Norfolk, 1976, pp. 168–169.

Bénédite, Léonce. *The Luxembourg Museum: Its Paintings.* Paris: H. Laurens; London: T. Fisher Unwin, 1913, p. 59.

Bolton, Kenyon C., III; Peter C. Huenink; Earl A. Powell III. *American Art at Harvard.* Cambridge: Fogg Art Museum, Harvard University, 1972, unpaged. (Included in "An Abbreviated Inventory of American Art in the Collections of Harvard University.")

*Burke, Doreen Bolger. *American Paintings in the Metropolitan Museum of Art: Volume III: A Catalogue of Works of Artists Born between 1846 and 1864.* Edited by Kathleen Luhrs. New York: The Metropolitan Museum of Art in association with Princeton University Press, 1980, pp. 137–143.

*Chambers, Bruce W. *American Paintings in the High Museum of Art: A Bicentennial Catalogue.* Atlanta: The High Museum of Art, 1975, pp. 68–69.

*Hawkes, Elizabeth H. *American Painting and Sculpture.* Delaware: The Wilmington Society of Fine Arts, 1975, pp. 60–61.

de Lavergnée, Arnauld Brejon, and Dominique Thiébaut. *Catalogue sommaire illustré des peintures du musée du Louvre: Italie, Espagne, Allemagne, Grande-Bretagne et divers.* Paris: Ministère de la Culture, Éditions de la Réunion des musées nationaux, 1981, p. 72.

*Lerner, Abram, ed. *The Hirshhorn Museum and Sculpture Garden.* New York: Harry N. Abrams, 1974, pp. 757–758.

*Mandel, Patricia C. F. *Selection VII: American Paintings from the Museum's Collection, c. 1800–1930.* Providence: Museum of Art, Rhode Island School of Design, 1977, pp. 187–190.

*Phillips, Dorothy W. *A Catalogue of the Collection of American Paintings in the Corcoran Gallery of Art.* 2 vols. Washington, D.C.: The Corcoran Gallery of Art, 1973, 2, pp. 9–11.

*Pisano, Ronald G., and Carol Forman Tabler. *Catalogue of the Collection: Paintings and Sculpture.* Huntington, New York: The Heckscher Museum, 1979, pp. 78–79.

Ross, Barbara T. *American Drawings in The Art Museum, Princeton University.* New Jersey: Princeton University Press, 1976, p. 125.

*Stebbins, Theodore E., Jr., and Galina Gorokhoff. *A Checklist of American Paintings at Yale University.* New Haven: Yale University Art Gallery, 1982, pp. 166–167.

*Sweeney, J. Gray. *American Painting at The Tweed Museum of Art and Glensheen: The University of Minnesota, Duluth.* Duluth: The Tweed Museum of Art, 1982, pp. 78–79, 219–220.

8. *Sale Catalogues*

These have been limited to those of the artist's contemporaries and patrons.

American Art Galleries, New York. *Catalogue of the Private Art Collection of Thomas B. Clarke, New York* (February 15–18, 1899), p. 114.

———. *A Catalogue of the American Paintings Belonging to William T. Evans* (January 31, February 1 and 2, 1900), pp. 78–79; no. 163.

———. *The James S. Inglis Collection* (March 10, 1910), nos. 62, 101.

Fifth Avenue Art Galleries, Ortgies & Co. *Paintings in Oil and Pastel by J. Alden Weir, N. A., . . . and John H. Twachtman* (February 7, 1889), nos. 1, 3, 5, 7, 9, 11, 13, 15, 17, 19, 21, 23, 25, 27, 29, 31, 33, 35, 37, 39, 41, 43, 45, 47, 49, 51, 53, 55, 57, 59, 61, 63, 65, 67, 69, 71, 73, 75, 77, 79, 81, 83.

———. *Catalogue of Modern Paintings Belonging to Erwin Davis, Esq.* (March 19 and 20, 1889), nos. 32, 88.

9. *Newspapers*

Those listed provide important information on Weir and his work, particularly reviews of one- and two-man exhibitions. Additional articles can be found in the following newspapers that regularly contain such articles and reviews of general exhibitions, such as those of the National Academy of Design: *New York Times, New York Sun, New York Evening Post, New York World, New York Commercial Advertiser, New-York Daily Tribune, New York Herald.*

"American and Foreign Paintings." *New York Herald*, May 9, 1893, p. 10.

"American Galleries: Paintings by Monet, Besnard, Weir, and Twachtman Described." *New York Times*, May 4, 1893, p. 9.

"Around the Galleries." *New York Sun*, January 10, 1907, p. 8.

"Art Gossip." *New York Sun*, December 10, 1911, p. 4.

"Art News." *New York Evening Post*, February 27, 1897, p. 16.

"Art Notes." Paris, *The American Register*, January 23, 1875, p. 6.

"Art Notes." *New York Times*, December 2, 1883, p. 5.

"Artists Give Dinner To J. Alden Weir." *New York Times*, November 26, 1913, p. 5.

"Artists to Honor J. Alden Weir." *New York Tribune*, November 26, 1913, p. 4.

"The Chronicle of Arts." *New-York Daily Tribune*, February 24, 1895, p. 24.

"The Chronicle of the Arts: Exhibitions & Other Topics." *New-York Daily Tribune*, February 21, 1897, p. 3.

"Current Art Exhibitions." *New York Sun*, February 4, 1889, p. 4.

"A Group of Impressionists." *New York Sun*, May 5, 1893, p. 6.

"Impressions by J. Alden Weir."*New York Times*, January 24, 1891, p. 4.

"Notes of the Fine Arts: Drawings and Etchings by J. Alden Weir." *New York Sun*, February 17, 1895, p. 7.

"Paintings by Americans." *New York Times*, February 21, 1897, p. 5.

"Pictures by Messrs. Weir and Twachtman." *New-York Daily Tribune*, February 7, 1889, p. 7.

"Porcelains and Pictures." *New-York Daily Tribune*, May 4, 1893, p. 6.

"Some Dazzling Pictures: Two French & Two American Painters of Sunlight." *New York Times*, May 4, 1893, p. 9.

"A Spirited Picture Sale." *New York Times*, February 8, 1889, p. 5.

"The Week in the Fine Arts." *New York Times*, May 7, 1893, p. 16.

"The Weir-Twachtman Exhibition." *New York Evening Post*, February 6, 1889, p. 4.

"The Weir-Twachtman Paintings." *New York Times*, February 3, 1889, p. 13.

"Weir and Twachtman Pictures: The Collection Recently Exhibited Brings $7,413 at Auction." *New York Sun*, February 3, 1889, p. 3.

"Work by Weir and Simons." *New York Times*, February 19, 1895, p. 5.

Blashfield, E. H. "A Painter's Reminiscence of a World's Fair." *New York Times Magazine*, March 18, 1923, p. 13.

Cortissoz, Royal. "A Memorial Exhibition at The Metropolitan Museum." *New York Herald Tribune*, March 23, 1924, section 7–8, p. 16.

Kurtz, Charles M. "Paintings by J. Alden Weir." 1891, clipping in JAW Scrapbook I, pp. 18–19 (E-S.).

10. *Dissertations and Theses*

Feldman, William Steven. "The Life and Work of Jules Bastien-Lepage (1848–1884)." Ph. D. dissertation, New York University, 1973, pp. 22, 79–80.

Hale, John Douglass. "The Life and Creative Development of John H. Twachtman." 2 vols. Ph. D. dissertation, Ohio State University, 1957, 1, pp. 27–29, 44–48, 66–69, 81, 83, 88–91, 93–98.

Haley, Kenneth Coy. "The Ten American Painters: Definition and Reassessment." Ph. D. dissertation, State University of New York, Binghamton, 1975, pp. 110–117, 322–332.

11. *Manuscripts*

These are arranged alphabetically by private owner and then for public institutions by city of repository.

*Cora Weir Burlingham. J. Alden Weir Papers: typescripts of JAW letters, January 1869–November 1875; photographs of the artist and his family.

*Caroline P. Ely and Ann Ely Smith. J. Alden Weir Papers: typescripts of Weir letters, 1869–1878; typescripts and original letters from such artists as Charles Baude, Wyatt Eaton, Albert Edelfelt, Robert Hinckley, John H. Twachtman, as well as from members of the Weir Family; original draft of article on Jules Bastien-Lepage; photographs of the artist, his studio, family and friends; three scrapbooks of clippings (1891–1919) about the artist and his work; two notebooks of photographs of Weir's etchings; nine volumes of photographs of Weir's paintings, annotated with information on their provenance and exhibition record. Much of this material is also available on microfilm from the Archives of American Art.

Rev. DeWolf Perry. John Ferguson Weir Papers: family photographs and memorabilia; Truman Seymour Papers, sketchbooks made during Seymour's European travels with JAW.

Akron, Ohio. Akron Art Institute, Edwin C. Shaw collection: typescripts of articles on JAW; information on works in the Shaw collection.

Berkeley, California. University of California, Bancroft Library, Regional Oral History Office. Sara Bard Field, Poet and Suffragist: typescript of an interview.

*New Haven, Connecticut. Yale University, Sterling Memorial Library, John Ferguson Weir Papers: typescripts of letters from JAW to JFW (1875–1919); JFW's memoirs; JFW account book (1858–1871); diaries of European trip (1868–1869); JFW sketchbook, with lists of paintings.

New Haven, Connecticut. Yale University Art Gallery, J. Alden Weir Comparative File, copybook (1869/70).

*New York, Frick Art Reference Library. Copy of Theodore Robinson diaries, 1892–1896; and Frederic Fairchild Sherman, typescript, "J. Alden Weir," 1927.

*New York, National Academy of Design, Archives. JAW, "Address to the NAD Banquet" (March 14, 1917); James Carroll Beckwith diaries, 1871–1894 and 1896–1917; Council of the NAD, Minutes; "Register of Members of the Life School"; "Register of Students, the Antique School."

New York, The New-York Historical Society. James Carroll Beckwith diary, 1895; E.H. Blashfield Papers.

New York, Ira Spanierman, Inc. John H. Twachtman Papers: typescripts of letters to JAW (1880–1892).

New York, The Metropolitan Museum of Art. Photographs of paintings in the 1924 Memorial Show.

*Paris, Archives Nationales. Archives de l'École Supérieure des Beaux-Arts, AJ^{52} and F^{21}: AJ^{52} 63; Concours trimestriel de composition sur esquisse à un ou deux degrés, Section de peinture; AJ^{52} 65, Concours semestriel de composition sur esquisse peintre et figure peintre; AJ^{52} 67, Concours et fondations; AJ^{52} 77–78, Procès-verbaux des jugements des concours des sections de peintre et de sculpture; AJ^{52} 246, Registre d'inscription des élèves dans les ateliers de peintre, sculpture, architecture et gravure; AJ^{52} 273, Dossiers individuels des élèves: série antérieure au 31 décembre 1893; F^{21}640, dépenses. Archives de l'École Nationale Supérieure des Arts Decoratifs, AJ^{53}: AJ^{53} 5, Proces-verbaux des délibérations du Conseil des professeurs; AJ^{53} 143, Élèves étrangers admis à l'École.

Paris, Bibliothèque Nationale. Cabinet des Étampes, Lettres de Jules Bastien-Lepage à Charles Baude.

*Provo, Utah. Brigham Young University, Harold B. Lee Library, Weir Family Papers: correspondents include Charles Baude, J. Appleton Brown, Charles DuBois, Wyatt Eaton, Albert Edelfelt, F. Childe Hassam, Robert Hinckley, A. D. Peppercorn, Theodore Robinson, Albert P. Ryder, John S. Sargent, John H. Twachtman, Robert W. Weir, Joseph Wencker, and Henry Wolf. Drafts of articles and addresses and two scrapbooks of original drawings.

*San Marino, California. Henry E. Huntington Library and Art Gallery, Charles Erskine Scott Wood Papers: Charles Erskine Scott Wood's letters to JAW, 1898–1919; "C.E.S. Wood on J.A.W. 1st dictated to DWY & then gone over & enlarged by him" [about 1920].

Washington, D.C. Smithsonian Institution, Archives of American Art, American Water Color Society, Minutes; John Ferguson Weir Papers; J. Alden Weir Papers (see Old Lyme, Connecticut, above).

Washington, D.C. The Corcoran Gallery of Art, J. Alden Weir Letters, 1914–1919.

Chronology

1852

August 30   Born in West Point, New York, to Robert Walter Weir, drawing instructor at the United States Military Academy, and his second wife, Susan Martha Bayard Weir.

October 13   Baptized at Church of the Holy Innocents, with Bradford R. Alden, Julia Bayard, and his father as his sponsors.

Spent his youth in West Point, where his father supervised his study of art. Despite the relative isolation of his home, met many of the leading art and literary figures of the day who came to visit his father.

1864

His half brother John Ferguson Weir, also a painter, took a studio at the Tenth Street Studio Building in New York, and Julian occasionally visited and worked there during the late 1860s and early 1870s.

1866

First drawings and paintings dated to this year.

1868/69

Winter   Occupied John's studio during the latter's trip to Europe. Back at West Point, painted a portrait of his father, who had constructed a studio for him in a shed so that he could paint in comfort during the summer months.

1869

Summer   Still at West Point, now painting outdoors. Went to New York to continue his studies at America's leading art school, the National Academy of Design.

1870–1872

Winters spent at the National Academy of Design, with principal instruction by Lemuel Wilmarth and lectures by James Renwick Brevoort, William Rimmer, Benjamin Waterhouse Hawkins, and William Page.

1870

November 7   Admitted to antique class.

1871

March 20   Promoted to life class.

October 9   Readmitted to antique class.

1872/73

Visited his uncle William Bayard in Rochester, Minnesota, where he recuperated from an illness.

1873–1877

Continued his studies in Europe, financed by Mrs. Bradford Alden, the widow of one of his baptismal
  sponsors. Lived in Paris, where he was a student in Jean-Léon Gérôme's studio at the École des
  Beaux-Arts. Painted in the French countryside, mainly at Pont Aven and Cernay-la-Ville, and
  traveled in Belgium, Holland, England, and Spain.

1873

September 10   Sailed for Europe, stopping in England ten days later to visit London.

September 29   Arrived in Paris.

October 21   Entered the atelier of Jean-Léon Gérôme.

November   Suspended briefly from Gérôme's studio after participating in a fight, and sought instruction in the private studio of Louis-Marie-François Jacquesson de la Chevreuse.

Enrolled in the École Gratuite de Dessin (the Petite École), a school dedicated to training artisans and
  decorative sculptors. Drew from life and the antique and studied sculpture under Amédée Faure
  and Aimé Millet, continuing his work there in the evenings during the winters of 1873/74 and
  1874/75.

1874

February   Resumed studies with Gérôme, with whom a close pupil/teacher relationship developed.

April–May   Supplemented his studies at the École in the independent studio of Gustave Boulanger.

Summer   Painted in Brittany at Portrieux and at Pont Aven, where he met Robert Wylie. Began work
  on two major paintings, *Harvesters in Brittany* (1874, present location unknown) and *Interior—
  House in Brittany* (1875, fig. 2.14).

October 27   Became an official matriculant at the École des Beaux-Arts, where in addition to his daily
  studies he attended evening drawing classes conducted by Adolphe Yvon.

December 1874–January 1875

Traveled to Holland and Belgium to study the works of the old masters and was particularly impressed
  by the paintings of Frans Hals.

1875

Spring   Growing friendship with the French naturalist Jules Bastien-Lepage and the young artists in
  his circle.

One of his portraits accepted for exhibition at the Paris Salon under the name Julien Alden-Weir.

Exhibited at the National Academy of Design for the first time, showing *Interior—House in Brittany*
  (1875, fig. 2.14). (With few lapses, he would be a regular contributor to the Academy's annuals
  from 1877 until 1917.)

July 23   Won the highest award given in Gérôme's studio, a second-class medal, in the year-end
  competition at the École des Beaux-Arts.

August   Painted at Cernay-la-Ville, a village in Ile-de-France southwest of Paris.

August 24   Placed fifty-eighth in the *concours des places* at the École des Beaux-Arts.

September   With other friends, visited Bastien-Lepage in his hometown, Damvillers, in northeastern
  France.

1875/76

Winter Still studied at the École des Beaux-Arts, but did more independent work in his rooms, painting portraits of Miss Eba Anderson (present location unknown) and Victor Thorn (present location unknown).

1876

Spring Exhibited two works, his portrait of Miss Anderson and *Tête de jeune fille, étude* (probably fig. 2.30), at the Salon under the name Julian Alden-Weir.

July Again painted in Cernay-la-Ville, where he finished *The Oldest Inhabitant* (1875/76, fig. 2.31).

August–September Visited Spain with his fellow student Filadelfo Simi. Sketched Spanish scenery, buildings, and figures, and studied the paintings of Diego Velázquez. Began *At the Water Trough* (1876/77, fig. 2.20), his only major painting on this trip.

1877

March 20 Placed sixteenth in the *concours des places* at the École des Beaux-Arts.

April Visited the third group exhibition held by the Impressionists and was highly critical of their work.

August–September In London, called on James Abbott McNeill Whistler.

October Returned to New York.

Began his artistic career, a leader among the young painters then returning from Paris and Munich. Established himself as a painter of figure and still-life subjects. Traveled to Europe as many as eight times by 1882; exhibited at the Paris Salon in 1881, 1882, and 1883; and maintained close ties with European friends and Americans living abroad. An active participant in the many art organizations then being founded in New York, he was elected a member of the Society of American Artists and joined the newly established Tile Club, making excursions to rural locales with the goup and painting on ceramic tiles.

1878

Exhibited *Interior—House in Brittany* (1875, fig. 2.14) at the Universal Exposition in Paris.

March Participated in the first exhibition of the Society of American Artists. (Except in 1893, he contributed with them until 1897; then resigning from the Society, he exhibited thereafter only in 1901 and 1906.)

Summer Returned to Europe, visiting London and Paris and painting again at Cernay-la-Ville, where he began work on *Children Burying a Bird* (1878, color plate 1).

Autumn Began teaching at the Cooper Union. Later took on a private drawing class and a portrait class at the Art Students League, where he taught for two decades.

1880

Began to exhibit at the American Water Color Society.

Elected vice-president of the Society of American Artists.

Summer In Europe again, visited Bastien-Lepage in Damvillers and purchased his *Joan of Arc* (1879, fig. 3.24) for Erwin Davis, a New York collector.

1881

Summer Once more in Paris, purchased a painting by Edgar Degas and three paintings by Édouard Manet—one directly from the artist—for Davis. Painted at Dordrecht in Holland with his brother John and John H. Twachtman. In London, renewed his acquaintance with Whistler.

1882

Acquired a farm in Branchville, Connecticut, where he spent much of his time for the remainder of his career.

Elected president of the Society of American Artists.

Awarded a silver medal at the Paris Salon.

Probably joined the Society of Painters in Pastel, although did not participate in the group's first exhibition in 1884.

Listed as a member of the New York Etching Club.

1883

April 24   Married Anna Dwight Baker.

April–September   On his honeymoon in Europe, traveled to Paris, Stuttgart, Nuremberg, Munich, Tyrol, Venice, Dordrecht, and The Hague. Acting as agent for Henry Gurdon Marquand, visited London and purchased a painting by Rembrandt.

September   Returned to New York and took a small apartment at 31 West 10th Street. For the next six years, seems to have remained in America, dividing his time between New York and Connecticut, where he visited his farm at Branchville and his wife's family home at Windham.

December   Exhibited his watercolors along with those of Régis Gignoux at H. Wunderlich & Co., New York.

A new direction now evident in his work: portraits and still lifes became smaller and more informal in composition. Inspired by Manet and other French artists, began a series of domestic genre scenes depicting his wife and, later, their daughter.

1884

January   A one-man show of his watercolors held at Doll & Richards in Boston.
March 19   Elected a member of the American Water Color Society.
March 24   Birth of first child, Caroline Alden Weir.
December   Bastien-Lepage dies, profoundly affecting Weir.

1885

May 13   Elected an associate member of the National Academy of Design.

1886

A major exhibition of French Impressionist paintings and pastels organized by the Paris art dealer Durand-Ruel and shown in New York at both the American Art Association and the National Academy of Design introduced the American public to French Impressionism.

May 12   Elected a National Academician.

Autumn 1886   Purchased house at 11 East 12th Street, in New York, the Weir residence for the next twenty-two years. Now worked in a studio in his home.

1887

Beginning of the period of his greatest interest in printmaking. (During the next seven years, produced about 140 prints, mainly etchings and drypoints.)

February   Birth of a second child, Julian Alden Weir, Jr., who died of diptheria shortly after his first birthday.

Summer   John H. Twachtman rented a house near Weir's Branchville farm; the two artists worked closely together, Twachtman strongly influencing Weir's prints and pastels.

1888

Demonstrated a greater interest in secondary mediums, particularly pastels and etching. Began to paint landscape subjects, usually views of his Branchville farm, more often.

Exhibited with the Society of Painters in Pastel for the first time. (Participated in their final two shows in 1889 and 1890.)

Began to exhibit at the annuals of the New York Etching Club.

Idle Hours (1888, fig. 3.39), shown in the Fourth Annual Prize Fund Exhibition, awarded two-thousand-dollar prize, and presented to The Metropolitan Museum of Art by a group of wealthy donors.

1889

February Exhibition and sale of his work and Twachtman's at the Fifth Avenue Art Galleries.

May Death of his father, Robert W. Weir.

Summer Returned to Europe with his wife for the first time in six years. Spent three weeks on the Isle of Man, working on a series of etchings. Attended the Universal Exposition in Paris, where he won a silver medal for painting and a bronze medal for watercolors and drawings.

1890

June 18 Birth of second daughter, Dorothy.

1891

January–February His first major one-man show, an exhibition of twenty-three paintings at Blakeslee Galleries, New York. He was now perceived as an Impressionist by his contemporaries.

Summer Worked on an important group of landscapes and figures in outdoor settings, which demonstrated his growing commitment to Impressionism, the primary influence on his style for the remainder of his career.

Joined a circle of younger painters who were quickly embracing Impressionism. Broken brushwork, lighter colors, and more informal compositions characterized his work during the 1890s; landscape became his principal subject.

1892

January 29 Birth of third daughter, Cora.

February 8 Death of Anna Baker Weir. Grief-stricken, he generated few new easel paintings that year.

August–October Executed a mural for the Manufactures and Liberal Arts Building at the World's Columbian Exposition in Chicago.

1893

Began work on an important series of life-size figures posed outdoors, including *The Hunter* (1893, fig. 5.27), *An Autumn Stroll* (1894, color plate 27), and *In the Dooryard* (probably 1894/95, color plate 28).

Again visited Chicago, where he was exhibiting paintings and etchings at the World's Columbian Exposition.

Resumed membership in the New York Etching Club after a ten-year hiatus.

May His work and Twachtman's included in an exhibition at the American Art Association with work by Paul Albert Besnard and Claude Monet.

October 29 Married Ella Baker, his first wife's sister.

December His work and Twachtman's exhibited at the St. Botolph Club in Boston.

1894

Became increasingly interested in Japanese prints; paintings such as *Baby Cora* (1894, color plate 25) and *The Red Bridge* (about 1895, color plate 24) show their strong influence on his development. His compositions now featured cropping, asymmetry, and oblique angles; his figures were treated as flat silhouettes; and pattern assumed a new role in his work. From about 1894 to 1897, also painted a number of snow scenes.

1895

February–March Exhibition of his drawings and etchings at H. Wunderlich & Co., New York.

1896

January   Won first prize at the Boston Art Club for his painting *The Old Rock*, also called *The Truants* (1895, New York, William Doyle Galleries, Inc., 1983).

1897

February–March   Exhibition of his paintings and pastels at Boussod, Valadon & Co.

Summer   At Branchville, began to teach summer classes, which he continued until 1901.

December 20   Resigned from the Society of American Artists.

1898

His paintings, particularly such figure subjects as *The Donkey Ride* (1899/1900, color plate 31), began to show a renewed academicism, and he depicted studio models for the most part rather than his wife and daughters.

Spring   The memorial window he designed, honoring his first wife, installed in the Church of the Ascension, New York.

April   Founding member and contributor to first exhibition of The Ten American Painters. Continued to contribute to the group's annual exhibitions until it disbanded in 1919.

1899

An occupant of the Tenth Street Studio Building at 51 West Tenth Street, where he had painted in his brother's studio more than thirty years earlier.

January   Gave up teaching in New York to devote himself exclusively to painting.

1900

Exhibited three paintings at the Universal Exposition in Paris, where he won a bronze medal.

1901

Participated in the Pan-American Exposition in Buffalo, New York.

Traveled to Europe with his wife and children. In London, visited John Singer Sargent and James Abbott McNeill Whistler; in Paris, Jean-Léon Gérôme, his old teacher.

1904

Won a gold medal for paintings and a silver medal for engravings at the Universal Exposition in St. Louis.

1905–1907

Painted a series of nocturnal subjects, including *Moonlight* (about 1907, fig. 6.13).

1907.

Joined the Council of the National Academy of Design, on which he served until 1914.

January–February   One-man show of his paintings held at Montross Gallery in New York.

1908

Moved to an apartment at 471 Park Avenue in New York.

1908–10

Painted several large, highly structured landscapes, among them *Building a Dam, Shetucket* (about 1908, 6.20) and two views of New York at night (about 1910, fig. 6.18, and 1911, fig. 6.19).

1911

December Elected president of the Association of American Painters and Sculptors, which later organized the landmark International Exhibition of Modern Art, better known as the Armory Show. Resigned on January 3, 1912, when the group announced its opposition to the National Academy of Design.

1911–12

A retrospective exhibition of his work traveled to the St. Botolph Club in Boston, the Century Association in New York, the Carnegie Institute in Pittsburgh, the Buffalo Fine Arts Academy, and the Cincinnati Art Museum.

Began to suffer from severe heart trouble.

1912

Traveled to Nassau, in the Bahamas. His strength renewed, he did paintings around the Caribbean island.

1913

February Opening of the Armory Show, where he exhibited twenty-five works.

July–October Last trip to Europe. Painted a series of watercolor scenes along the Itchen River in England.

November The Salmagundi Club honored him at a dinner.

1914

February An exhibition of his recent paintings held at Montross Gallery, New York.

1915

Elected to the American Academy of Arts and Letters.

April 28 Elected president of the National Academy of Design, a post he held for nearly two years before resigning on March 29, 1917.

May Served as a member of the international jury for the Panama–Pacific Exposition in San Francisco. Exhibited works at the exposition, where he was awarded a medal.

1916

Received an honorary degree from Princeton University.

Appointed the "painter member" of the National Commission on Fine Arts.

1917

Received an honorary degree from Yale University.

1919

May With other broad-minded academicians joined a group of young artists to found the exhibition organization, American Painters, Sculptors, and Gravers.

Summer In Connecticut, where health deteriorating rapidly.

November Returned to New York.

December 8 Died in New York.

J. Alden Weir
An American Impressionist
Catalogue

NEW YORK, THE METROPOLITAN MUSEUM OF ART
October 14, 1983–January 8, 1984
THE LOS ANGELES COUNTY MUSEUM OF ART
February 9–May 6, 1984
THE DENVER ART MUSEUM
June 13, 1984–August 19, 1984

Carrie in the Studio at West Point, about 1868
Oil on canvas, 23¼ × 20¼ in.
Unsigned.
Private collection (fig. 1.12).

Interior—House in Brittany, 1875
Oil on canvas, 29¾ × 32⅝ in.
Signed, dated, and inscribed at lower left:
   J. Alden Weir/Paris 1875.
Private collection (fig. 2.14).

Study of a Male Nude Leaning on a Staff, 1876
Oil on canvas, 25½ × 31½ in.
Signed, dated, and inscribed at upper left:
   J. Alden Weir/Ecole des
   Beaux-Arts/1876/Atelier de M. Gerome,
   JAW/'76; at lower right:
   Deutschul/by/J.A.W.
New Haven, Connecticut, Yale University Art
   Gallery,
Gift of Julian Alden Weir, 1914.3 (fig. 2.1).

At the Water Trough, 1876/77
Oil on canvas, 17 × 14 in.
Signed at lower right: J. Alden Weir
   (underscored).
Washington, D.C., National Museum of
   American Art, Smithsonian Institution
   (fig. 2.20).

Still Life in the Studio, about 1877–80
Oil on canvas, 30 × 48¼ in.
Signed at lower left: Julian Weir.
New Haven, Connecticut, Yale University Art
   Gallery, Gift of John F. Weir, 1880
   (fig. 3.49).

Children Burying a Bird, 1878
Oil on canvas, 22⅛ × 18⅛ in.
Signed at lower left: J. ALDEN WEIR
Canvas stamp (in an oval):
   illegible/HARDY-ALAN/illegible TOILES
   COULEURS.
Mr. and Mrs. Henry C. White (color plate 1).

Robert Walter Weir, 1878
Oil on canvas, 46 × 36 in.
Signed at upper right: J. Alden Weir.
Private collection (fig. 3.1).

Laughing Boy, about 1879
Oil on canvas, 24 × 20⅛ in.
Unsigned.
Private collection (fig. 3.16).

Wyatt Eaton, about 1879
Oil on canvas, 31¼ × 18⅛ in.
Signed at upper left: *J. Alden Weir*.
Washington, D.C., National Museum of

300

American Art, Smithsonian Institution, Gift
of William T. Evans, 1915 (fig. 3.11).

The Flower Seller, about 1879
Oil on canvas, 40⅞ × 22⅝ in.
Signed at upper left: J. Alden Weir.
New York, The Brooklyn Museum, Gift of
George A. Hearn, 1911 (fig. 3.12).

Union Square, about 1879
Oil on canvas, 30 × 25 in.
Signed at lower right: J Alden Weir.
New York, The Brooklyn Museum, Museum
Collection Fund, 1926 (fig. 3.13).

Snowstorm in Mercer Street, 1881
Oil on wood, 23¾ × 15½ in.
Signed at lower left: J. Alden Weir.
Private collection (fig. 3.14).

Boy Polishing a Brass Jug, late 1870s–early 1880s
Oil on canvas, 25⅛ × 29⅞ in.
Unsigned.
Private collection (fig. 3.20).

Port Jefferson, 1881
Pencil, watercolor, and gouache on paper, 6¾
× 9¾ in. (sight).
Signed and dated at lower right:
 J. Alden Weir/1881.
Oregon, Portland Art Museum, Gift of
Mr. and Mrs. William M. Ladd (fig. 4.3).

Flowers, early 1880s
Watercolor and gouache on paper,
 14 × 20⅛ in.
Signed and dated at lower left: *J. Alden Weir.*
Private collection (color plate 12).

Still Life: Peonies, 1881
Oil on canvas, 34 × 27¼ in.
Signed and dated vertically at lower right:
 J. Alden Weir (underscored) 1881.
Private collection (fig. 3.50).

Flower Piece, 1882
Oil on canvas, 29⅝ × 21⅝ in.
Signed and dated at lower right: J. Alden Weir
1882.
Oregon, Portland Art Museum, Gift of
Henry L. Corbett, Elliott R. Corbett, and
Hamilton F. Corbett, in memory of their
mother, Helen Ladd Corbett, 1936
(fig. 3.53).

Flora (Carrie Mansfield Weir), 1882
Oil on canvas, 44 × 34 in.
Signed and dated at upper left:
 J/Alden/Weir/——/1882.
Provo, Utah, Brigham Young University
 (color plate 5).

Anna with a Greyhound, about 1882
Oil on wood, 49 × 37½ in.
Unsigned.
Private collection (color plate 6).

Silver Cup with Roses, 1882
Oil on canvas, 12 × 9 in.
Inscribed on the rim of the chalice (with
 trompe l'oeil shadows, as if etched): To
 Anna Dwight Baker from J. Alden Weir; and
 on the body of the cup: May 18th/1882 N.Y.
Thyssen-Bornemisza Collection, Lugano,
 Switzerland (color plate 11).

Anna on the Balcony of Duveneck's Studio, 1883
Oil on canvas, 77 × 47 in.
Unsigned.
Provo, Utah, Brigham Young University
 (3.33).

On the Avon, 1883
Pencil, watercolor, and gouache on paper,
 6½ × 9½ in. (sight).
Inscribed and dated at lower right: Stratford on
 Avon/May 26th/83.
Provo, Utah, Brigham Young University
 (fig. 4.6).

Roses, 1883–84
Oil on canvas, 35½ × 24¾ in.
Signed at upper right: J. Alden Weir.
Washington, D.C., The Phillips Collection
 (fig. 3.55).

Roses, 1884
Oil on wood, 8 × 10 in.
Unsigned.
Mark Carliner (fig. 3.57).

Against the Window, 1884
Oil on canvas, 36⅛ × 29½ in.
Signed at lower right: J. Alden Weir '84
Private collection (color plate 7).

*Roses with a Glass Goblet and a Cast of Giovanni
 Bologna's "Venus After the Bath,"* 1884
Pencil, watercolor, and gouache on paper,
 17⁷⁄₁₆ × 12⅛ in. (sight).
Signed at lower left: J. Alden Weir/84.
New York, jointly owned by The Metropolitan
 Museum of Art and Erving Wolf
 Foundation, 1978 (color plate 13).

Flowers on a Window Sill, 1884
Pencil, watercolor, and gouache on paper, 19¼
 × 13¼ in. (sight).
Signed and dated at lower left:
 J. Alden Weir/'84.
Private collection (color plate 14).

Anna Sewing, 1885
Pencil, watercolor, and gouache on paper,
  12 × 9 in. (sight).
Signed and dated at lower left:
  J. Alden Weir/1885.
Private collection (color plate 15).

Two Dogs, 1885
Watercolor and gouache on paper,
  12½ × 18⅜ in. (sight).
Signed and dated at lower left:
  J. Alden Weir/85.
Private collection (color plate 10).

The Black Lace Dress, 1885
Oil on canvas, 36 × 30 in.
Signed and dated at upper right:
  J. Alden Weir—1885.
Private collection (fig. 3.21).

A Reverie, 1886
Oil on canvas, 20 × 25⅞ in.
Unsigned.
Private collection (fig. 3.34).

Portrait of a Child, 1887
Oil on canvas, 49⅛ × 36 in.
Signed and dated at lower left:
  J. Alden Weir—1887
Private collection (color plate 3).

Lengthening Shadows, 1887
Oil on canvas, 20¾ × 25 in.
Signed at lower left: J. Alden Weir—1887.
Dr. and Mrs. Demosthenes Dasco (fig. 3.77).

Anna and Caro in the Twelfth Street House, 1887
Pencil, watercolor, and gouache on paper,
  17½ × 13¼ in. (sight).
Signed and dated at lower left:
  J. Alden Weir/1887.
Private collection (color plate 16).

In the Library, late 1880s
Pencil, watercolor, and gouache on paper,
  30¾ × 20½ in. (sight).
Unsigned.
Private collection (4.10).

Anna by Lamplight, late 1880s
Oil on canvas, 16⅛ × 20⅛ in.
Unsigned.
Private collection (fig. 3.38).

Roses, about 1882–90
Oil on canvas, 9½ × 14¾ in.
Signed at lower left: J. Alden Weir.
Mr. and Mrs. Raymond J. Horowitz (fig. 3.64).

Fruit, about 1888
Oil on canvas, 21⅛ × 17¹³⁄₁₆ in.
Unsigned.

New York, The Metropolitan Museum of Art,
  Gift of Robert E. Tod, by exchange
  (fig. 3.66).

Idle Hours, 1888
Oil on canvas, 51¼ × 71⅛ in.
Signed and dated at lower right:
  J. Alden Weir—1888.
New York, The Metropolitan Museum of Art,
  Gift of Several Gentlemen, 1888 (fig. 3.39).

Bas Meudon, No. 2, 1889
Etching, 3⅞ × 5⁵⁄₁₆ in. (plate).
Signed in the plate at lower right: J. A. W.
Private collection (fig. 4.34).

Castle Rushen—Isle of Man, 1889
Etching, 8¾ × 11⅞ in. (plate).
Signed in the plate at lower middle:
  J. Alden Weir (in reverse); inscribed in the
  plate at lower right: *Castle Russian/Isle of Man*.
Private collection (fig. 4.39).

The Blacksmith Shop, 1889?
Etching and drypoint, 10¾ × 7¹³⁄₁₆ in. (plate).
Signed in the plate at lower right:
  J. Alden Weir.
Private collection (fig. 4.35).

Man on a Quai, Paris, probably 1889
Pencil, watercolor, and gouache on paper,
  6⅜ × 9¼ in. (sight).
Signed at lower left: J. Alden Weir.
Private collection (fig. 4.15).

The Windowseat, 1889
Pastel and pencil on paper, 13¼ × 17½ in.
  (sight).
Signed and dated at lower right:
  J. Alden Weir/1889; and at upper right:
  J. Alden W——.
Private collection (color plate 21).

Vase of Roses, late 1880s
Pastel on paper, 16 × 14 in.
Signed at lower right: J. Alden Weir.
Mr. and Mrs. Ralph Spencer (fig. 4.27).

Olin Levi Warner, about 1889
Oil on canvas, 21¼ × 17 in.
Unsigned.
New York, National Academy of Design
  (color plate 9).

The Dutch Shoe, 1890
Oil on wood, 21 × 15 in.
Signed and dated at upper right:
  J. Alden Weir/1890.
Private collection (fig. 3.65).

Farmer with Oxen, about 1890
Pencil and watercolor on paper, 6⅞ × 11 in.
  (sight).
Unsigned.
Private collection (fig. 4.14).

The Lesson, about 1890
Etching, 6¹⁵⁄₁₆ × 4⅞ in. (plate).
Signed in the plate at lower right: J. A. W.
Private collection (fig. 4.28).

Portrait of Miss Hoe
Drypoint, 10 × 6⅛ in. (plate).
Unsigned.
Mr. and Mrs. Raymond J. Horowitz (fig. 4.42).

Anna Looking Down, about 1890
Oil on wood, 15¾ × 11¾ in.
Unsigned.
Private collection (fig. 3.44).

Early Spring at Branchville, 1888–90
Oil on canvas, 20¼ × 25¼ in.
Signed at lower left: J. Alden Weir.
Private collection (fig. 3.75).

Anna Dwight Weir Reading a Letter, about 1890
Pencil, watercolor, and gouache on paper,
  12½ × 9¼ in.
Unsigned.
New York, The Metropolitan Museum of Art,
Mr. and Mrs. Norman Schneider Gift, 1966
  (fig. 4.12).

The Letter, 1890
Pencil, watercolor, gouache, and chalk on
  paper, 30¼ × 20¼ in.
Signed and dated at lower left:
  J. Alden Weir—1890.
Private collection (color plate 17).

The Christmas Tree, 1890
Oil on canvas, 36 × 25¼ in.
Signed at upper left: J. Alden Weir.
Private collection (color plate 8).

The Orange Ribbon (The White Cravat), 1890
Oil on canvas, 33½ × 24 in.
Signed and dated at upper left:
  J Alden Weir—90.
Private collection (color plate 2).

In the Livingroom, about 1890
Oil on canvas, 25 × 20 in.
Unsigned.
Private collection (fig. 5.2).

The Farmer's Lawn, about 1890
Oil on canvas, 20¾ × 29. in.
Signed at lower right: J. Alden Weir.
Private collection (fig. 5.3).

Early Moonrise, 1891
Oil on canvas, 34¼ × 24⅝ in.
Signed at lower right: J Alden Weir—91.
Private collection (fig. 5.5)

Midday, 1891
Oil on canvas, 34 × 24½ in.
Signed and dated at lower right:
  J. Alden Weir '91.
Fall River, Trina, Inc. (fig. 5.7).

The Grey Trellis, 1891
Oil on canvas, 26 × 21½ in.
Signed and dated at lower left:
  J. Alden Weir—91.
Private collection (fig. 5.6).

Connecticut Fields
Pencil and pastel on gray paper,
  11⅛ × 16¾ in. (sight).
Unsigned.
Private collection (4.21).

The Edge of Webb Farm
Pencil and pastel on light gray paper,
  8 × 10⅝ in. (sight).
Unsigned.
Private collection (fig. 4.23).

The Ice House
Pencil and pastel on paper, 11¾ × 9 in. (sight).
Unsigned.
Private collection (color plate 19).

Branchville Pond
Pencil and pastel on paper, 8¹³⁄₁₆ × 9³⁄₁₆ in.
Unsigned.
Private collection (color plate 20).

The Tulip Tree, Branchville
Pencil, watercolor, and pastel on paper,
  13¼ × 9½ in. (sight).
Unsigned.
Private collection (color plate 22).

The Hunter, 1893
Oil on canvas, 70 × 40 in.
Unsigned.
Provo, Utah, Brigham Young University
  (fig. 5.27).

Willimantic Thread Factory, 1893
Oil on canvas, 24⅛ × 33½ in.
Signed and dated at lower left:
  J. Alden Weir—93.
New York, The Brooklyn Museum,
  John B. Woodward Memorial Fund
  (fig. 5.30).

*U.S. Thread Company Mills, Willimantic,
    Connecticut*, about 1893–97
Oil on canvas, 20 × 24 in.
Signed at lower left: J. Alden Weir.
Mr. and Mrs. Raymond J. Horowitz (fig. 5.21).

Obweebetuck, mid-1890s
Oil on canvas, 19½ × 23¼ in.
Unsigned.
Private collection (color plate 29).

Conanicut Island, about 1894
Pencil and pastel on paper, 7⅞ × 10¼ in.
    (sight).
Signed at lower middle: *J. Alden Weir*.
Private collection (fig. 4.22).

A Look Across the Fields, about 1894
Pencil, ink and brush on paper, 9⅝ × 14⅝ in.
Signed at lower right: *J. Alden Weir*.
Provo, Utah, Brigham Young University
    (fig. 5.19).

In the Hammock, about 1894
Ink wash on paper, 9½ × 9¾ in. (sight).
Signed at lower right: *J. Alden Weir*.
Private collection (fig. 5.15).

The Laundry, Branchville, about 1894
Oil on canvas, 30⅛ × 25¼ in.
Signed at lower right: J. Alden Weir.
Private collection (color plate 23).

In the Days of Pinafores, about 1893/94
Oil on canvas, 34¼ × 27⅛ in.
Signed at lower left: J. Alden Weir.
Private collection (color plate 26).

In the Shade of a Tree, 1894
Oil on canvas, 27 × 34 in.
Signed and dated at lower left:
    J. Alden Weir—1894.
Lincoln, Nebraska Art Association, Sheldon
    Memorial Art Gallery, University of
    Nebraska (fig. 5.24).

An Autumn Stroll, 1894
Oil on canvas, 70 × 40 in.
Unsigned.
Provo, Utah, Brigham Young University
    (color plate 27).

Baby Cora, 1894
Oil on canvas, 70 × 40 in.
Inscribed at upper right: BABY CORA; signed and
    dated at left middle: J. Alden Weir—1894;
    dated on the dog's collar: 1894.
Cora Weir Burlingham (color plate 25).

In the Dooryard, probably 1894/95
Oil on canvas, 80⅛ × 47⅛ in.
Unsigned.
Private collection (color plate 28)

The Ice Cutters, 1895
Oil on canvas, 20¼ × 24⅛ in.
Signed at lower right: J. Alden Weir '95.
Private collection.

The Red Bridge, about 1895
Oil on canvas, 24¼ × 33¾ in.
Signed at lower left: J. Alden Weir
New York, The Metropolitan Museum of Art,
    Gift of Mrs. John A. Rutherfurd, 1914
    (color plate 24).

Face Reflected in a Mirror, 1896
Oil on canvas, 24¼ × 13⅝ in.
Signed and dated at lower left:
    J. Alden Weir—1896.
Providence, Rhode Island, Rhode Island
    School of Design, Museum of Art,
    Jesse H. Metcalf Fund (fig. 5.29).

Girl Standing Beside a Tree, 1896
Pencil and pastel on paper, 14⅞ × 9⅜ in.
    (sight)
Signed and dated at lower right:
    J. Alden Weir '96.
Portland, Oregon, Arlington Club.

The Hunter, 1895–1905
Pencil, watercolor, and gouache on paper, 7⅜
    × 9¼ in. (sight).
Unsigned.
Private collection (fig. 4.17).

The Factory Village, 1897
Oil on canvas, 29 × 38 in.
Signed and dated at lower left:
    J. Alden Weir 1897.
New York, jointly owned by Cora Weir
    Burlingham and The Metropolitan Museum
    of Art (color plate 30).

Ploughing for Buckwheat, 1898
Oil on canvas, 48½ × 33¾ in.
Signed at lower left:
    J. Alden Weir—/Branchville—Conn.
Pittsburgh, Pennsylvania, Carnegie Institute,
    Museum of Art (fig. 5.34).

Cora Weir, 1898
Pencil on paper, 12⅞ × 8⅞ in. (sight).
Inscribed at upper left: CORA WEIR/1898; signed
    at lower right: J. ALDEN WEIR.
Private collection (fig. 5.36).

In the Sun, 1899
Oil on canvas, 34 × 26⅞ in.
Signed and dated at upper right:
    J. Alden Weir/'99.
Provo, Utah, Brigham Young University
    (color plate 32).

The Donkey Ride, 1899/1900
Oil on canvas, 49 × 38 in.
Unsigned.
Cora Weir Burlingham (color plate 31).

Rhododendrons, about 1900
Oil on canvas, 20 × 24 in.
Signed at lower left: J. Alden Weir.
Lucille and Walter Rubin.

Albert Pinkham Ryder, 1902/1903
Oil on canvas, 24⅛ × 20 in.
Unsigned.
New York, National Academy of Design
    (fig. 6.35).

The Basket of Laurel, 1903
Oil on canvas, 34 × 24¼ in.
Signed at upper left: J. Alden Weir.
Private collection (fig. 6.39).

Visiting Neighbors, about 1903
Oil on canvas, 24⅜ × 34¼ in.
Signed at lower right: J. Alden Weir.
Washington, D. C., The Phillips Collection
    (fig. 6.3).

A Day in June, about 1903
Oil on canvas, 23⅜ × 31¾ in.
Signed at lower left: J. Alden Weir.
Illinois, The Art Institute of Chicago,
    Walter H. Schulte Memorial Collection
    (fig. 6.2).

Danbury Hills, about 1905
Oil on canvas, 23⅞ × 33⅞ in.
Signed at lower right: J. Alden Weir.
Colorado, The Denver Art Museum, Gift of
    the Daughters of Charles F. Hendrie in
    Memory of Their Father, 1928 (fig. 6.8).

Upland Pasture, 1905
Oil on canvas, 39⅞ × 50¼ in.
Signed at lower left:
    J. Alden Weir/Branchville.
Washington, D.C., National Museum of
    American Art, Smithsonian Institution, Gift
    of William T. Evans, 1909 (fig. 6.7).

The Barns at Windham, about 1905
Oil on wood, 23⅛ × 33½ in.
Unsigned.
Private collection (fig. 6.5).

Caro Seated on a Chest, about 1905
Oil on canvas, 72 × 40 in.
Unsigned.
Private collection (fig. 6.27).

Building a Dam, Shetucket, about 1908
Oil on canvas. 31¼ × 40¼ in.
Signed at lower right: J. Alden Weir.
Ohio, The Cleveland Museum of Art, Purchase
    from the J. H. Wade Fund (fig. 6.20).

Norwich-on-the-Thames, about 1910
Oil on canvas, 23⅝ × 33 in.
Signed at lower left: J. Alden Weir.
Private collection (fig. 6.21).

The Spreading Oak, 1910
Oil on canvas, 39 × 50 in.
Unsigned.
Oregon, Portland Art Museum, Gift of
    Col. C. E. S. Wood in memory of his wife,
    Nanny Moale Wood, 1943 (fig. 6.22).

The Wharves, Nassau, 1913
Oil on canvas, 32½ × 36⅜ in.
Unsigned.
Private collection (fig. 6.26).

Photo Credits

Unless otherwise indicated, photographs are credited to the individuals, institutions, or firms owning the works that are reproduced. The sources for other photographs are: Brian Bates: 1.15, 2.2–2.6, 2.10, 2.18, 2.24, 2.33–2.34, 3.22, 3.33, 3.48, 3.71, 4.4–4.6, 4.18, 4.29–4.30, 4.32–4.33, 5.19, color plates 5, 27, 32; Bissell: 4.3; E. Irving Blomstrann: 3.67; Courtesy of Jeffrey R. Brown: 5.6; Richard Cheek: color plate 28; Christie, Manson & Woods International Inc.: 1.5, 4.1, 5.11; Geoffrey Clements: 1.4, 2.16–2.17, 2.32, 2.35–2.36, 2.38–2.39, 3.4, 3.10, 3.17, 3.34, 3.41, 3.43, 4.22, 4.27–4.28, 4.34–4.35, 4.37, 4.39–4.40, 6.35–6.36, color plates 2, 4, 6–10, 15–17, 19, 21–22, 25–26, 29–31; Courtesy of Coe Kerr Gallery: 6.23; Courtesy of Thomas Colville: color plate 1, 3.2; Documentation photographique de la Réunion des musées nationaux, Paris: 2.21, 3.25; Helga Photo Studio: 3.36, 3.54, 3.74, 4.42, 5.8, 6.31, 6.38; Courtesy of Hirschl & Adler Galleries: color plate 12; Courtesy of Kennedy Galleries: 3.77; Paulus Leeser: 1.12, 2.14–2.15, 2.37, 2.40, 3.14, 3.26–3.27, 3.30, 3.37–3.38, 3.47, 3.57, 3.65, 3.75, 4.9, 4.14–4.17, 4.19–4.21, 4.23, 5.2, 5.5, 5.9–5.10, 5.15, 5.31, 5.35–5.37, 5.41, 6.5, 6.16, 6.21, 6.27; Terrence McGinniss: 2.12, 3.5–3.6, 3.16, 3.20–3.21, 3.40, 3.44, 3.69, 4.8, 4.13, 5.13–5.14, 5.16–5.18, 5.20, 5.22–5.23, 5.25–5.26, 6.39, color plates 3, 14, 18, 20, 23; Peter A. Juley Collection, National Museum of American Art, Smithsonian Institution, Washington, D.C.: frontispiece, (no. J0073524), 2.8 (no. J0073373), 2.25 (no. J0073371), 5.12 (no. J0073492); Los Angeles County Museum of Art: 1.1–1.2; The Metropolitan Museum of Art, New York: 1.16–1.17, 2.30, 3.1, 3.3, 3.51, 3.56, 4.10, 4.24, 5.21, 5.27; National Museum of American Art: 3.70; Jim Peck: 3.50; George Walter Vincent Smith Art Gallery: 3.60; Courtesy of and copyright by Sotheby Parke Bernet, Inc.: 3.59, 3.61, 3.63, 5.3, 5.7, 5.32; Courtesy of Ira Spanierman, Inc.: 6.28, color plate 11; Herbert Vose: 3.19, 4.2, 4.26.

Index

Figures in heavy type indicate illustrations. Unless otherwise noted, the works of art are by J. Alden Weir